W9-AQV-727

Gladstone and Radicalism

Gladstone
and Radicalism

*The Reconstruction of
Liberal Policy in Britain
1885–94*

Michael Barker

University of Wales Fellow in History

BOOKS
10 East 53d St., New York 10022
(a division of Harper & Row Publishers, Inc.)

Published in the USA 1975 by
HARPER & ROW PUBLISHERS, INC.
BARNES & NOBLE IMPORT DIVISION

First published 1975 by
The Harvester Press, Hassocks
Copyright © Michael Barker 1975

ISBN 06-490303-6

Designed by Yvonne Dedman

Printed in Great Britain by
Western Printing Services Ltd, Bristol
Set in Linotype Granjon

To Jill

Contents

I The Radical Dilemma 1880–5   1

II The Radical Programme 1885–6   11

   1. *Gladstone and Radicalism*   11
   2. *Chamberlain's 'Unauthorized' Experiment*   24
   3. *The Radical Programme Superseded*   40

III The Liberal Party and Irish Home Rule   54

   1. *The Fate of the Irish Legislation of 1886*   54
   2. *Coercion*   75
   3. *Gladstone and the Class Struggle*   87
   4. *Bilateral Education and the ' "Disunion" of Hearts'*   96

IV The Anatomy of Caucus Politics   107

   1. *The Rise of the National Liberal Federation*   107
     Wales versus Scotland   117
   3. *Labour Representation*   128
   4. *London and the Eight Hours Controversy*   138
   5. *The Origins of the Newcastle Programme*   154

V The Polarities of Radicalism   165

   1. *The Parliamentary Ascendancy of Labouchere*   165
   2. *The Genesis of a New Liberalism*   175

vi Crisis and Recovery 1890–2   200
    1. *The Parnell Catastrophe*   200
    2. *The Rural Programme Rediscovered*   217
    3. *The Full 'Bill of Fare'*   233

vii Gladstonian Twilight   241

    Appendices   257
    A. *The 1885 Election and the effects of Redistribution (in
       England)*   257
    B. *Morley's Memorandum of 30 December 1890*   258
    C. *Gladstone's view of the Political Situation (July 1892)* 260

    Notes (and list of abbreviations)   262
    Unpublished Sources   297
    Index   299

Acknowledgements

The greater part of this work was completed at the University of Leicester between 1969 and 1973, and was aided by funds provided by the University's Research Board. A great personal debt is due to my friends and former colleagues in the History Department who in various ways helped to smooth the path towards publication.

Some of the material included in this book originally formed part of a University of Wales doctoral thesis, which has been greatly extended and amplified. I wish to thank Mr N. C. Masterman of the University College of Swansea for his constant kindness and help during the seven years of research which this book has entailed. Professor John Vincent of Bristol University has shown a great interest in the progress of my work, and I have benefited enormously from his counsel. Dr P. F. Clarke of University College London has also made some valuable suggestions.

I also wish to thank Earl Spencer, Viscount Harcourt, and Mrs Elizabeth Clay for allowing me to consult the papers which are in their possession. Sir William Gladstone, Mr W. B. Morrell, and the Passfield Trustees kindly gave me permission to quote from documents in public repositories.

Finally, I desire to express my gratitude to a long-suffering wife, not only for patiently reading and correcting innumerable drafts, but also for making so many sacrifices on my behalf.

University College of Swansea   MICHAEL BARKER
November 1973

The Radical Dilemma
1880-5

Polling in the general election of 1880 commenced on 31 March, and amongst the first returns broadcast to the nation was the news that in Birmingham the Liberal trio had secured re-election by a decisive margin. Early declarations in other English boroughs convinced Joseph Chamberlain, Birmingham's junior representative, that Gladstone and the Radicals had 'triumphed all along the line', thus inviting speculation concerning the future prospects of a fresh Liberal administration which would command a large majority. The two leading Radicals, Chamberlain and Sir Charles Dilke (member for Chelsea), remained keenly interested in the composition of the next cabinet, although neither had previously held ministerial office. Indeed the former was an M.P. of only four years' standing, and justified his claim to promotion on the grounds that he enjoyed the confidence of the advanced section throughout the country. Although Dilke was fully aware that he did not inspire such personal loyalty and enjoy such popular support, he had nevertheless been held in high regard in the House of Commons since his election in 1868, an advantage which Chamberlain did not share. However, Chamberlain's intense personal ambition was tempered by an acute sense of political realism. He was torn between an immediate avid desire to scale the Liberal heights at this opportune time, and misgivings lest he be isolated and powerless in a cabinet which did not sympathize with advanced ideas. To 'efface' himself by remaining on the backbenches would be unwise, but a passive acceptance of the rôle of 'radical minnow among Whig Tritons' might well tarnish his reputation.[1] At the earnest behest of Gladstone, Chamberlain eventually agreed to enter the cabinet as President of the Board of Trade, parting company with Dilke, who, to his chagrin, was offered no more than an under-secretaryship at the Foreign Office.

Chamberlain's acceptance of these terms was probably a mistake since it rendered impossible any action to 'organise a "pure Left" party in the House and the country, which should support the Government if they brought in Radical measures and oppose them everywhere if they did not.'[2] He evidently exaggerated his capacity to exert pressure upon timorous aristocrats, and altogether under-estimated the difficulties which confronted Radical leaders who were also members of a cabinet with a distinctly Whiggish complexion. Although the party was pledged to extend the county franchise, reform the structure of local government, and revise the land laws, these items of prospective legislation had not figured prominently during the elections. Interest had centred upon the alleged diplo-matic, military, and financial shortcomings of the outgoing ministry, and it is significant that Chamberlain himself did not suggest that 'a solid meal must be provided for the Liberal lions' until the sweep-ing nature of the electoral victory caused him to jettison more cautious plans.[3] Even Gladstone was moved temporarily to forget his preoccupation with the Balkans and he declared that a 'manageable' degree of land reform would be 'impossible to exclude from the first programme' of the new administration.[4] Yet despite these hopeful signs, the absence of a coherent and carefully framed domestic policy created a barren terrain which offered no shelter from an unbroken succession of Irish and Imperial storm-clouds. At its first meeting the cabinet rejected Chamberlain's conception of an appropriate programme, and, until Gladstone finally resolved to grapple with the franchise question, the legislative record of the government read like a catalogue of constant failure.[5] Local government bills for Ireland, the English counties, and London, were promised at the beginning of each session, yet of these only the abortive London government bill was actually submitted to parliamentary scrutiny. Relatively non-controversial bankruptcy and patents bills prepared by the Board of Trade required three turbulent sessions before reaching the statute book, whereas Chamberlain's most cherished infant – the merchant shipping bill – was unceremoniously smothered in order to ease the passage of franchise legislation.

Chamberlain resented deeply the marked absence of executive initiative and the lack of the determination to overcome obstacles which was essential if such calamities were to be avoided. Since his experience as mayor of Birmingham had been very different, he despaired of a premier who complained that 'the continually recur-ring demand for days on which to proceed with Bills is really a request to *manufacture time*', and who resorted to the expedient 'day to day to take that which presses most'.[6] Gladstone's reluctance to offer any positive lead to the cabinet stemmed primarily from his persistent desire to escape from office at the earliest opportunity, yet the unfortunate consequence of such prevarication (or self-deception) was a lack of constructive purpose. Exception was taken to an undignified recourse to 'count noses' and to the almost total absence of proper legislative planning. The main deficiency lay in Gladstone's aversion to cabinet meetings, particularly autumn cabinets which were devoted to legislative planning; but Dilke subsequently protested that Gladstone had allowed a secretive and unimaginative core of Whig magnates to resolve matters of the 'deepest moment' without reference to the opinions of Radical colleagues.[7] As a result of these irregularities, the government promised bills it had neither considered in detail nor adequately prepared. Even so vital a proposal as Dilke's revised county government bill was not fully drafted until 1884. Some measure of the desperation felt by Chamberlain and Dilke can be gauged by their insistence on the inclusion of this topic in the Queen's Speech of 1883, although they had given up all hope of being able to legislate effectively.[8] Hence, their notorious independence in the lobby, constant threats of resignation, premature disclosures to the press, and inflammatory speeches in the provinces, were not symptoms of factious and unstable temperaments, but were, in reality, frustrated acts to justify continued membership of a tired and discredited administration.

These unorthodox protests by Radical ministers against being placed in the unenviable position of 'continually accepting and supporting a policy which does not fully satisfy their sense of justice and which is often inconsistent with their previously declared opinions' ultimately proved to be counter-productive.[9] Almost imperceptibly a personal barrier between Chamberlain and his cabinet associates was erected; then became apparent a growing revulsion from the entire Birmingham-inspired political philosophy as well as from the character of its apostle and his disagreeable methods. On the other hand, this grave development was not compensated by any significant increase in affection or loyalty towards Chamberlain in the House of Commons. His failure to organize the parliamentary Radicals as a means of forcing an advanced programme down the throats of the Liberal establishment may be regarded as an extraordinary oversight. Herbert Gladstone, who dutifully suppressed his own left wing inclinations during these years of paternal embarrassment, exaggerated the true position when he claimed that approximately 70 members of the 1880–5 Parliament took 'orders for action or inaction ... directly or indirectly' from Chamberlain.[10] Dilke offered a more plausible explanation when he noted (in 1880) that backbenchers simply consulted Chamberlain and himself whenever they wished to influence government policy: 'I was the person approached in all Indian, Colonial, naval, and military questions, and Chamberlain in domestic ones.'[11] The Radical section clearly did not possess a coherent programme and informal whips, nor did Chamberlain summon his friends to regular meetings. Such a casual approach to the problem of co-ordination ensured that the mood of independence, which in 1880 had 'almost broken the spirit of the ministerial whips', was wantonly dissipated. During this first session the exuberant Radicals carried a local option resolution by 16 votes and forced the government to reconstruct the ground game bill. The high-water-mark of Radical success was reached in July with the defeat of ministerial plans to erect a statue in memory of the Prince Imperial of France (who had fallen on the battlefield during the Zulu War).[12]

However, Chamberlain was unable to capitalize upon these achievements because the cabinet had already adopted an unadventurous domestic programme, and was considering whether to commit an act of apostasy by implementing unpopular colonial and Irish policies. The government hesitated to dismantle the apparatus of Disraelian diplomacy, and at the beginning of 1881 announced its decision to reintroduce coercion in Ireland and to withhold immediate self-government from the Transvaal. Thus, Chamberlain and Dilke were obliged to defend a strategy which offended the moral scruples of many of their ardent supporters, especially those who favoured a pacific and strictly non-interventionist overseas policy and who jealously guarded civil liberties within the United Kingdom. Orthodox Radicals were disheartened by Chamberlain's insistence on upholding 'strongly patriotic and national opinions' in these two spheres, and consequently the resistance expected from the bewildered militants did not materialize. Only seven insurgents divided against the second reading of the coercion bill, whereas a mere 12 supported a motion of censure concerning the Transvaal. Nevertheless, the muted rebellion demonstrated that Radical cabinet ministers would find it increasingly difficult to maintain an obedient following in the country, let alone form a solid party in the House.[13]

The dangers which confronted Chamberlain can perhaps best be appreciated by tracing the rapid deterioration of the relationship between himself and his close associate John Morley. The breach only became irreparable in December 1885 when the former refused to endorse Gladstone's sudden public conversion to Irish Home Rule, and in a vigorous exchange of letters bluntly informed Morley that he had 'foreseen for a long time that we were drifting apart'.[14] In fact, the seeds of discord were sown when Morley entered the House of Commons in February 1883. Chamberlain was anxious to secure Morley's services as an intermediary between himself and backbench Radicals, a function which Dilke had performed until admission to the cabinet in December 1882 forced him to surrender all claims to independence. But instead of acting as the safety-valve for the relief of Chamberlain's troubled Radical conscience, Morley chose to voice opinions which his nominal leaders dared not countenance or express themselves. Shortly after his election for Newcastle, Morley refused to accept government reliance upon the operation of the Coercion Act, and signified his disapproval by voting with a handful of fellow Liberals in support of a land bill introduced by Parnell, the Nationalist leader.[15] Chamberlain complained that Morley was 'kittle-cattle to drive'. Twelve months later his confidence was shaken still further by Morley's alleged 'folly' and 'weakness' on the franchise question.[16] However, at this stage it is clear that Morley was perturbed less by the future of the franchise bill than by the dispatch of General Gordon to Egypt, and by the possibility of an annexation of the Soudan. The basic cause of friction was Morley's announcement that he could no longer tolerate the government's Egyptian escapades, a position which was reinforced by his vote in March 1884 in support of Henry Labouchere's motion of censure.

The years 1884–5 were critical ones in Morley's career. Inevitably he emerged as a rival claimant for Radical favour in the eyes of those who felt that Chamberlain ought to have resigned alongside John Bright, when British warships had bombarded Alexandria in 1882. Morley suspected that Chamberlain and Dilke were secretly foremost amongst the 'jingoes' in the cabinet who desired to pursue an imperialist policy in Egypt. This contention was borne out early in 1885 by their readiness to support a military initiative should the Whig leader, Lord Hartington, be called upon to form a ministry.[17] Hence Morley, who was intent on some 'hard swearing at the Jingoes', unexpectedly refused Chamberlain permission to vet the contents of a speech he planned to deliver at Glasgow in February,[18] and simultaneously placed upon the Commons' order paper a motion of censure concerning the expedition to Suakin. Superficially of course the censure motion was directed against Gladstone. But in reality Morley was arraigning a government which appeared to have forced its head to act against his better judgement. He wished to 'keep the Old Man in' because he thought that Gladstone and himself were the 'last of the Cobdenites'.[19] Thus, at a time when Morley was beginning to transfer his allegiance from Chamberlain to Gladstone, his former mentor had reason to believe that Morley was fast becoming a dangerously disruptive force in Radical politics. Morley did not expect more than 40 Liberals to support the censure motion, and was astounded to learn that over 70 members (exclusive of the Irish) were ready to follow him into the division lobby.[20] Resolute and courageous action on his part roused the Radicals from their prolonged slumber, and thrust Morley forward as the recognized spokesman for a significant section of backbench opinion. For a brief moment the Radicals recovered the sense of common purpose which they had possessed in 1880, and it seemed probable that the Egyptian crisis would act as a catalyst of Radical discontent, enabling them to destroy a faltering ministry. But the opportunity was lost because after years of humiliation and cruel disappointment the morale of Radical members was low. In the opinion of Labouchere, the 'so-called Radicals' were a 'contemptible set of weak humbugs [whose] aspirations do not go beyond wishing to remain in Parliament and if possible to be given a crumb or two'.[21]

This factor probably explains why Chamberlain was not tempted to exploit the growing tension between Radical and Whig by making positive efforts to secure the allegiance of the advanced section. Certain peril awaited those who paid heed to the persuasive Labouchere and resigned from the ministry in accordance with his wishes. Chamberlain and Dilke would then be 'driven to act with mere fanatics ... who are always ready to run on any fresh scent and whose support is but a hindrance'.[22] Moreover, the adoption of a coherent Radical programme automatically excluded 'crotchet-mongers' like Labouchere, Sir Wilfrid Lawson, and Samuel Storey, from full membership of the revitalized and unified party contemplated by Chamberlain. It was to be packed instead with 'loyal henchmen' from Birmingham such as Powell Williams, and with 'faithful Sanchos' cast in the image of Jesse Collings. Hence Chamberlain did not propose to choose his troops primarily from members of an unreformed House of Commons, but planned instead to muster the enfranchised masses with electrifying platform campaigns. These regiments of new voters would be drilled and provisioned by the National Liberal Federation, and eventually mobilized at a general election to secure the return of a large and disciplined corps of ardent Chamberlainite candidates.

By the winter of 1882–3 Chamberlain had become convinced that the country was 'ripe for a new departure in constructive Radicalism', and that should he be 'driven to fight' unimaginative moderates, the Radical wing would 'easily recruit an army'.[23] He sensed that the mood of the electorate had changed considerably since 1880; those who had originally been content to accept a modest reform programme were no longer satisfied with the limited social policies furnished by Chamberlain, a view shared by the author himself. In 1880 preoccupation with foreign affairs had distracted attention from worsening economic conditions within the United Kingdom. Optimists believed that the abandonment of a 'forward' overseas policy, accompanied by Gladstone's remarkable financial dexterity, would of itself revive trade. This illusion rapidly disappeared as the economic situation continued to deteriorate. Government possessed no ready answer to the problems faced by industry in its endeavours to compete with the technical superiority and material resources of Germany and the United States, or of agriculture, confronted by the large scale importation of cheap food from hitherto under-developed countries. The nature and extent of the depression which began in the 1870s destroyed the myth that natural economic laws, if untampered with, would ultimately restore prosperity. It also became painfully obvious that, despite decades of economic and technological advance, the wealth so created was not enjoyed by all. Unemployment coexisted with 'conspicuous consumption', irrefutable evidence that poverty and squalor had not been eliminated by the march of civilization or the increase in material comforts.

Awareness of this unpalatable reality was rudely awakened by the visit to Britain in October 1881 of the American land reformer, Henry George, and by the publication of a British edition of his book *Progress and Poverty*. Chamberlain feared that impressionable working-class electors might succumb to the lure of the Single Tax and so detach themselves from those who were portrayed as members of an inert and unsympathetic government. Indeed Morley reported London workmen as being spontaneously 'full of the ideas of Henry George', whereupon the miscellaneous prophets of land nationalization commenced an active campaign amongst constituency Liberal associations, under the auspices of the Land Reform Union.[24] Chamberlain reacted swiftly to this threat, attempting to discredit theories which he regarded as wild and extreme. He conceded that the 'enormous increase in general wealth had not been accompanied by [any] considerable decrease in Pauperism' (thus echoing George's view) and at once set to work on a popular alternative social programme.[25] Ultimately George failed to secure prolonged support from socialist bodies, and the true significance of *Progress and Poverty* lay in the acceptance of its diagnosis of social disorders by those who rejected its remedies as unworkable or confiscatory.

Conclusive evidence concerning the validity of George's premisses was not long in forthcoming. Morley suggested that those social improvements on behalf of the poor which had already been accomplished had suddenly 'opened people's eyes to the horror of what is left'.[26] The quest for accurate statistical data was inspired by Andrew Mearns, a Congregational minister in the East End of London, who published his findings in the autumn of 1883 as a pamphlet entitled *The Bitter Cry of Outcast London*. His grim revelations aroused immense public disquiet, and provoked an immediate response from leading Radicals. Chamberlain became convinced, as his personal experience in Birmingham had suggested, that the case for the adoption by local authorities of drastic powers to secure the well-being of their inhabitants was both conclusive and urgent. His contribution to the debate was embodied in an article entitled 'Labourers' and Artisans' Dwellings' in the December 1883 issue of the *Fortnightly Review*. Morley was so stirred by Mearns' enquiries that he requested the wife of Robert Spence Watson (a prominent Newcastle Liberal) to undertake a similar survey in his own constituency. The results dispelled his faith in the traditional formulae of individualistic Liberalism, compelling him to admit that there existed an 'Outcast Newcastle' as well as an Outcast London.[27] Dilke, with all the resources of the Local Government Board at his disposal, personally inspected the slums of London in November 1883. The evidence which he accumulated distressed him sufficiently to make public his most unsavoury findings, in a speech to his constituents on 11 December, and subsequently to establish the Royal Commission on the Housing of the Working Classes – over which he himself presided.[28] Though early legislation was not forthcoming, the work of Mearns and of other social investigators strongly influenced the contents and scope of the *Radical Programme*, a widely publicized handbook compiled on Chamberlain's directions which originally appeared as a series of articles in the *Fortnightly Review*. The important chapters on housing, the agricultural labourer, and education (published between October 1883 and January 1884) betray the same spirit of righteous indignation coupled with painstaking attention to detail evinced by the *Bitter Cry*.

These articles provided the text for the 'unauthorized' platform campaign which Chamberlain launched with three imaginative and controversial speeches in January 1885. In the previous month the House of Lords had grudgingly acquiesced in the final stages of the franchise bill, and under these fresh circumstances Chamberlain believed that it was both 'proper and expedient' to convey to the new voters 'some message of practical sympathy and goodwill'.[29] His underlying supposition was that the theoretical balance within the party between Radical and Whig had become an irritating myth; a timeworn façade which lacked substance and continued to exist for one reason alone – to curb the enthusiasm of the advanced section and curtail its tendency to identify with emerging left-wing political ideas. The virtual monopoly of cabinet places by hereditary custodians of moderate principles could, on strictly numerical grounds, no longer be justified, since the extension of the franchise had drastically reduced Whig influence in the constituencies. Thus, the pressing task which confronted the advocates of a Radical democracy was a total reconstruction of Liberal policy and personnel. The ossifying grip of Whig leadership had to be broken; the party needed to be purged of Whig traditions and heresies. Only then could the rejuvenated rump be transformed by Chamberlain into an instrument capable of fulfilling the aspirations of resolute social reformers.

The objective was conceived on a grand scale, yet the means by which Chamberlain sought to achieve it were no less ambitious. Two attractive alternatives were firmly lodged in his mind. He could either claim the liberty he had long sought by resigning forthwith, or retain his cabinet post in order to extract substantial concessions from the government. Should he adopt the first course, Chamberlain was confident that the extinction of the 'intolerant faction' could be ensured by running a Radical against a Whig candidate whenever the opportunity arose. On reflection, he decided to abandon this scheme because the discharge of ministerial duties had hitherto prevented him from attending to the necessary electoral organization.[30] It seemed preferable to exploit the weakest link in the Whig armour, namely, Hartington's evident reluctance to succeed Gladstone at once and be forced to treat with hostile ministers. Chamberlain was only prepared to serve under the Whig leader provided Commissions to investigate the Civil List and labour conditions were appointed.[31] The choice offered to Hartington was quite unambiguous. He could either accept a nominal premiership in a government committed to a distinctively Radical domestic policy, or he could dispense with Chamberlain's services altogether and rely instead upon support from the Conservative opposition. The latter course of action naturally entailed an immediate breakup of the party, and Chamberlain's persistent private and public ultimatums gave both Gladstone and Hartington ample grounds for presuming that complete destruction was in fact his 'farsighted' yet 'ominous' purpose.[32]

Chamberlain risked antagonizing Gladstone still further by remaining a defiant member of a visibly disintegrating ministry. His decision was possibly influenced by the accession to the cabinet in October 1884 of Sir George Trevelyan, and by an expectation (realized in the following spring) that he would shortly be joined by George Shaw-Lefevre and Lord Rosebery. However, the total failure to frame definite contingency plans for the creation of a Radical inner cabinet was an astonishing omission from Chamberlain's overall strategy. Since he refused to extend the dual alliance with Dilke to include the new recruits, their promotion did little to augment the strength of the Radical faction within the cabinet. Perhaps Rosebery's sensitivity and erratic career made a cordial relationship improbable, especially since the brilliance and immense popularity in Scotland of the younger man marked him out as a potential usurper of Chamberlain's Radical throne. By comparison Lefevre and Trevelyan were colourless and insignificant; Chamberlain quickly discerned that lowly ministers who had long coveted a cabinet post could not be trusted to uphold discordant views before they had fully tasted the fruits of high office. Trevelyan's unswerving fidelity to Gladstone during the cabinet wrangles on the Egyptian question betrayed a form of weakness which made Chamberlain doubt the wisdom of close collaboration.[33] Henceforth the latter adopted a posture of studied indifference towards Trevelyan and Lefevre, an attitude which seemed justified by their subsequent behaviour when the crisis concerning Irish policy reached its peak in May 1885. Out of misplaced loyalty to his former chief at Dublin Castle (Lord Spencer), Trevelyan did not rally immediately in support of Chamberlain's Irish Central Board scheme, and only cast in his lot with Chamberlain when Spencer proposed several unacceptable modifications to the expiring Coercion Act. Lefevre was equally determined to retain his individuality. He characteristically contemplated leaving the cabinet on the special issue of coercion, while Chamberlain and Dilke handed in their resignations on the separate subject of land purchase.[34]

This spate of resignations was rendered inoperative by the sudden collapse of the government in June. Chamberlain and Dilke secretly welcomed the calamity, since defeat on the budget bill obviated the danger of further clashes between the representatives of nonconformist Birmingham and cosmopolitan Chelsea, concerning the moral and fiscal implications of increased beer and spirit duties.[35] However, signs of disagreement amongst Radical cabinet ministers had become so pronounced during the preceding six months that the prospects of securing genuine unity in opposition were not auspicious. Fortunately, now that the restrictions imposed upon cabinet ministers had been lifted, the authority of the Radical 'shadow' cabinet could be strengthened by the inclusion of Morley. He had long been an integral member of a triumvirate from which both Trevelyan and Lefevre were rigidly excluded. But in spite of Morley's presence, the 'Cabal' which was scheduled to meet at 'fixed and short intervals' did not emerge as the powerhouse of the Radical party. On three consecutive Saturdays in July the Radical leaders assembled at Dilke's Housing Commission office, but the value of these conferences was limited since Rosebery was not issued with an invitation, and Trevelyan was absent from all except the first.[36] Moreover, the agenda was mainly confined to eve of recess problems concerning parliamentary tactics. For some inexplicable reason the possibility of formulating a co-ordinated electoral strategy was not raised; consequently members of the transitory 'Cabal' trod divergent paths as the general election approached.

II

The Radical Programme
1885-6

1. *Gladstone and Radicalism*

Throughout the course of an active ministerial career which spanned 60 years Gladstone never ceased to be an enigma, abused by opponents for apparent inconsistencies and incomprehensible even to admiring political friends. This consideration was extremely potent in the period between the conception of the Radical programme in 1883 and the general election of 1885 because Gladstone revealed extraordinary and paradoxical powers of leadership in a party experiencing seismic tremors. In the decade prior to his first retirement in 1875 Gladstone had possessed the essential qualities required in a Liberal chief. His debating prowess and exceptional talent as administrator and legislator were obvious recommendations; a strict Evangelical and mercantile background could be discounted since a youthful Gladstone had rapidly matured into a devout High Churchman and had acquired the impeccable status of a landed gentleman. However, he was not a mere *parvenu*, apeing the behaviour of upper-class society. Through his fortuitous marriage to Catherine Glynne, heiress to the substantial Hawarden estates in Flintshire, Gladstone could trace his descent from some of the most influential Whig notables. Lineal connections rather than innate ability – or the mere accumulation of wealth – contributed enormously to Gladstone's remarkable success in overcoming the handicap of a past stained by Liverpool Toryism. A party which paid lip service to ideas of liberal reform, but instinctively reflected aristocratic values and traditions, was dominated automatically by members of that exclusive caste.

These assets rapidly depreciated in value after 1880, and by 1885 had become a source of considerable embarrassment. Chamberlain struck a new chord in the councils of the party, whilst the strident voice of provincial middle-class nonconformity began to be heard through the medium of the National Liberal Federation. As the clamour increased in volume, many easy-going Whig families, who doubted Gladstone's capacity to withstand such pressures, began to sever their formal connection with the party of their ancestors. This slow outward drift had acquired the momentum of an avalanche even before Gladstone announced his conversion to Irish Home Rule. This placed Gladstone in a perilous and uncongenial situation when confronted simultaneously with the claims of brash manufacturers like Chamberlain. Unlike the majority of his aristocratic friends, he clung tenaciously to the hallowed principle of Whig leadership in a broad-bottomed party. Moreover, the churchman who had once longed to take Holy Orders and continued to cherish the fabrics of the Anglican Communion, steadfastly accepted the unwelcome fact that nonconformity now constituted the backbone of the party in the constituencies. Thus, Gladstone tacitly countenanced a movement which seemed intent on destroying denominational schools and threatened to sever the Established Church from the State. Finally, Gladstone discovered that he had become isolated from the Liberal intelligentsia – even from those who bore no class or religious prejudices. The orthodox sources of Liberal philosophy were Locke, Adam Smith, Bentham and John Stuart Mill; but Gladstone's gradual conversion to Liberalism was idiosyncratic and profoundly mysterious. His inspiration was derived not from modern authors (with the exception of Smith), but from the 'ancient' writings of Aristotle, St Augustine, Dante, and the eighteenth-century theologian, Bishop Butler. Minds steeped in medieval scholasticism were usually the prerogative of fossilized Tories, yet in the opinion of J. L. Hammond, 'if Gladstone had the divine melancholy of Cardinal Newman, deep in the Middle Ages, he had also the noble buoyancy of Charles James Fox, bred like himself on Homer and the Greeks'.[1] His intense learning revolved around the concept of the Universal Man and was dominated by an abiding sense of man's spiritual power and destiny. The wrongs which afflicted society stemmed from a deviation from the eternal principles which constituted the fabric of the 'ideal State'. Hence Liberalism, as Gladstone interpreted the doctrine, was the purest practical manifestation of that higher conservatism which had reached its apogee during the premiership of Sir Robert Peel.

It is scarcely surprising that such obscure and subtle reasoning perplexed Chamberlain, who was endowed with a less rarefied intellect. However, in spite of his mystification, Chamberlain was comforted by the knowledge that in both action and instinct Gladstone had proved himself a decided asset to the advanced section in the past and seemed likely to continue to be so in the future. In

Chamberlain's experience as a cabinet minister, Gladstone had usually aligned himself, on important matters of policy and principle, with the troublesome Radical minority, and not with his Whig intimates. When the twin issues of Irish local government and renewal of the expiring Coercion Act opened rifts in the cabinets of May 1885, Gladstone felt so strongly in favour of Chamberlain's Central Board scheme that he was actually prepared to resign if it was not adopted. Chamberlain justifiably reminded Dilke that 'on the greatest issue between us and the Whigs, Mr G. is on our side', and confidently predicted how this acquisition would 'immensely strengthen our position if we finally decide to press the matter'.[2]

Chamberlain was prepared to pin the hopes of Radicals in Gladstone at a time when the Duke of Argyll denounced the intellect of his old friend as a 'purely Destructive Force'.[3] Yet Lord Granville, who was on more intimate terms with Gladstone by this stage, was convinced that as long as he remained in politics Gladstone was 'a *Conservative* power which will not be replaced by Salisbury, Churchill, or some of the best Whigs'.[4] The curious combination of conservative instincts and Radical opinions, of caution balanced by enthusiasm, suggested that Gladstone was a victim of political schizophrenia. His readiness to espouse formidable schemes of reform was accompanied by a devotion to traditional formulae and an antiquarian's faith in the validity of historical precedent. Such radicalism was derived from conservative reasoning: loyalty to the aristocratic principle coexisted with a warm popular imagination. This mixture of incomprehensible and contradictory qualities made Gladstone a uniquely ambivalent leader, giving to his thought an unparalleled elasticity. There were no bounds to his ingenuity and no knowing the measures which he might eventually adopt.

In a well-known letter to Lord Acton, Gladstone deplored the inclination of the party towards 'construction', implying (as Granville subsequently learnt) that he was 'repelled' by Chamberlain's 'socialism'.[5] Yet stringent libertarians, austere economists, and Whig landlords, were fully conscious that Gladstone's second administration had taken considerable strides in 'constructive' legislation. One early success of the ministry was a Ground Game Act which transferred important rights from landlords to occupiers. The right of the Irish tenant to a fair rent fixed by a judicial tribunal was enshrined in the Land Act of 1881, clear proof that Gladstone did not hesitate to depart from orthodox principles and press forward vigorously with revolutionary projects once his limited plans were shown to be inadequate. He had wished originally to 'eschew the establishment of precedents which might hereafter be susceptible of a dangerous application outside that particular sphere'.[6] But closer investigation of the situation soon revealed that compensation for 'unexhausted improvements' could with propriety be transplanted from Ireland into England – where the relationship between land-lord and tenant was very different. Hence the Agricultural Holdings Act of 1883 constituted a further extension of State paternalism and interference with the sanctity of private contracts freely entered into. Clearly the gravity of the Irish land crisis had cast political economy to the winds. Gladstone faced a 'serious difficulty' in 1885 when confronted with ministerial plans to apply Irish remedies to the Scottish Highlands. His concern about the widespread adoption of 'exceptional expedients' was balanced by a strong conviction that the Crofters' title to demand legislation rested on the 'historical fact' that they had formerly enjoyed 'rights of which they have been surreptitiously deprived to the injury of the community'.[7] The tone of this statement unmistakably echoed Chamberlain's notorious utterances two weeks earlier on the subject of 'natural rights'.

Similar considerations applied in other spheres, for example in connection with Gladstone's embryonic plans to equalize the duties payable at death on real and personal property. The institution of a graduated tax upon landed estates would not only mulct large pro-prietors, thereby 'striking at the very heart of class-preference',[8] but also constituted a clear departure from established financial canons. However, measures designed to protect the vulnerable classes from exploitation by ruthless economic masters were by no means confined to the land. The Employers' Liability Act of 1880 (despite its imper-fections) was the first serious attempt to protect the industrial worker from the pernicious doctrine of 'common employment'. Moreover, Gladstone shared Chamberlain's passion for reforming the structure of local government in England and Scotland, betraying a degree of interest and involvement which has surely been underrated by historians. He showed keen interest in the complex question of metropolitan reorganization, and refused to be thwarted by Sir William Harcourt's vociferous protests concerning the erosion of Home Office control over the police force. Nor was Gladstone daunted by the resistance of those Whig magnates who suspected that their influence in Quarter Sessions was in jeopardy, since he insisted on placing the county and London government bills promin-ently on the agenda for 1884.[9] The class interests of the City Corporation were threatened by the proposal to deprive that prosper-ous body of its ancient privileges and endowments; wealthy vestries and Poor Law Boards deplored any equalization of rates to subsidize more needy authorities. Gladstone, who earnestly wished to 'purge' Liberalism of 'centralising tendencies', defended, in the name of local enfranchisement and local autonomy, what Radicals frankly demanded in the interests of social justice. Administrative devolution could scarcely be separated from its practical consequences, which entailed placing in the hands of a public body 'the business of the individual man'. Gladstone's emphasis on the virtues of decentralization, monetary efficiency, and the sovereignty of the ratepayer, was in essence whole-heartedly endorsed by Chamberlain, the principal exponent of a benign municipal socialism.[10] Consciously or otherwise, Gladstone had by 1885 become capable of countenancing a further extension of constructionist principles.

In fact Gladstone was considerably more distressed by the visible disintegration of the Liberal aristocracy, and his isolation from erstwhile colleagues like the Duke of Argyll, than he was alarmed by the prevalence of controversial theories. His response to the harsh realities of a severe economic depression reflected this conservative social outlook. Gladstone nurtured a 'very high duty to labour for the conservation of estates, and the permanence of the families in possession of them, as a principal source of our social strength, and as a large part of true conservatism'.[11] He firmly believed that the abandonment of restrictive covenants applying to entail and settlement for these 'moral and social' rather than 'political, or even economical, considerations' would relieve landowners of a grave and embarrassing burden. In his vision, a reform of the land laws would help to prop up the traditional patriarchs of the soil in circumstances where the financial means to support their proper social station eluded them. Gladstone considered that the sixth Duke of Newcastle (the son of an Eton friend) was 'one of the many victims of the law of entail', and accordingly he did not hesitate to subscribe a substantial cheque towards rescuing the Duke's encumbered estate.[12] It was characteristic of Gladstone that he was prompted by an essentially reactionary munificence to embrace a scheme of reform taken up by others for contrary reasons: for whereas Gladstone hoped to preserve the hereditary tradition, Chamberlain and the Radicals, tacitly or otherwise, expected a revision of the land laws to destroy the pre-eminence of both aristocracy and landlordism.

This dubious union of divergent philosophies recurred in the circumstances created by the rejection of the franchise bill by the House of Lords. When Dilke (the responsible minister) proposed to sweep away abuses such as the freehold qualification and university representation, and introduce universal male suffrage and equal electoral districts, he discovered that Gladstone was 'the strongest Conservative living upon the subject'.[13] Nevertheless, Gladstone, who alleged that it was tactically inopportune 'to do the work of our enemies by deck-boarding the ship',[14] reacted as strongly as did the Radicals to the mischievous act of sabotage against a measure

deliberately framed in moderate terms. He warned the Queen that,
were a dissolution forced upon him, steps would be taken to ensure
that it would centre upon 'organic change in the House of Lords'.[15]
Radicals exulted in the prospect of renewed combat, and the language
of Chamberlain and Morley was calculated to exacerbate the conflict.
But Gladstone shrank from a crisis; his forthright yet measured
language was designed to awaken the Peers to the folly of their
behaviour. He adopted the posture of defender of the hereditary
principle and custodian of aristocratic rights, a position he felt 'very
loath to abandon'. For this reason Gladstone unselfishly courted
personal unpopularity by endeavouring to restrain the ardour of his
most enthusiastic followers. Yet, in the final analysis, his democratic
sympathies were robust enough to overcome his initial prejudices.
Despite a reverence for the 'antiquities of our constitution', Gladstone could not accept the doctrine that 'the liberties of the people
ought to be sacrificed to an abuse of them'.[16]

The atmosphere of bitterness which contaminated the question of
an extended franchise was caused primarily by misgivings concerning the exact nature of the political climate which would materialize.
Radicals looked forward to an uninterrupted era of reform politics,
and even critics of the Act recognized that an intensification of social
demands would result from the new situation. It was totally unrealistic to have pressed for a wider electorate and then presume
that political requirements would remain unaltered – and quite
inconsistent therefore to brush aside the ideas broached by Chamberlain. Gladstone had compelled reluctant colleagues to take up the
franchise question, and with undiminished energy had pressed ahead
with an ambitious bill. He, not Chamberlain, had created the fresh
conditions, and it is idle to suppose that a statesman of cautious
temperament and unrivalled experience should suddenly recoil at
the appearance of doctrines which he had done so much indirectly
to foster. In Gladstone's opinion there was 'no crisis at all in view',
only 'a process of slow modification' which he did not believe would
bring about 'an acute or convulsive action'. Such serene composure
rested upon a touching and unshakeable faith in the 'sense of justice
which abides tenaciously in the masses'.[17] The 'upper ten thousand',
amongst whom were numbered those faint-hearted Whig aristocrats
who unwisely spurned their ancestral heritage, were consciously
guided by the narrow prejudices of class interest. In contrast, the
working classes successfully resisted such temptations, and so were
capable of emerging unscathed from a 'deep and searching moral
trial'.[18] Gladstone honoured the noble character of men who
eschewed selfish ambitions and fortunately remained uncorrupted by
the enervating charms of London society.

In 1885 Gladstone retained his faith in the people but had lost confidence in the aristocracy. At the height of the Eastern crisis (in 1877) he had complained of 'party lukewarmness on the aristocratic side',[19] a verdict shortly to be confirmed by the unyielding resistance of Whig cabinet ministers to necessary reforms. When Gladstone had selected his ministers in 1880, he had not been blind to the precarious existence of Whiggery and oblivious of the potential power of Radicalism. His mistake lay in the optimistic and naïve assumption that, through giving moderates a generous allocation of cabinet places, their dislike of progressive legislation might be overcome. When Hartington in particular failed to match these expectations, by dissenting to the policy of creating representative institutions in Ireland, Gladstone's attitude hardened. 'Rampant disorderliness' on the left wing was stoically accepted as a permanent hazard. Yet, despite extraordinary provocation from Chamberlain and Dilke, Gladstone still considered 'weak-kneed' Liberals to have caused him 'more trouble in the present Parliament than Radicals'.[20] His marked dissatisfaction with the state of inertia, even indifference, with which Hartington was identified guaranteed that were the party to break up he would not willingly be found in association with the Whig rump. As early as 1877 Gladstone had become convinced that 'the vital principle of the Liberal party ... is *action*, and that nothing but action will ever make it worthy of the name of a party'.[21] By 1885 the forces ready and eager for 'action' were amassed in the camp of Chamberlain.

In the last week of June 1885 such hypotheses concerning Gladstone's future behaviour would have been abruptly dismissed as idle speculation. Most observers assumed, when Gladstone surrendered the seals of office, that he had simultaneously relinquished the leadership of his party and had effectively terminated an illustrious career. Poor health throughout the winters of 1882–3 and 1884–5 constituted an obvious medical reason in favour of prolonged convalescence, but Gladstone confounded most political crystal-gazers by postponing his retirement. A remarkable recovery in health and spirits made him more amenable to pressure from both Hartington and Chamberlain on the grounds that his continued presence was indispensable to party unity. More dignified and cogent considerations naturally loomed uppermost in Gladstone's own mind. The chief arguments on behalf of withdrawal were nullified by the prospect of an imminent crisis in Ireland which duty forbade him to shirk. Nevertheless, until his return in September from a month-long cruise to Norway, Gladstone's future hung in the balance. Two weeks before the publication of the manifesto committing him to remain at his post, Gladstone was capable of informing the deputy leader that he still considered himself 'free to take a share or not in the coming political issues', and perversely added, 'I must weigh many things before finally surrendering this freedom.' Even Hartington was roused from his customary lethargy to admonish Gladstone how it was of the 'utmost importance' that a decision 'be formed and announced as soon as possible'.[22]

The paralysis which occurred within three months of a general election also placed Chamberlain in a strange predicament. Gladstone's hesitancy, combined with Hartington's notorious Waterfoot speech of 31 August, suddenly reanimated Chamberlain's schemes to displace the Whigs altogether rather than absorb them into a party controlled by Radicals. He at once reverted to a half-forgotten earlier project, which entailed putting up candidates in opposition to those who dared to attack him personally. However, at this late stage the 'unauthorized' campaign had already gathered momentum and could not be halted, election committees were difficult to improvise, and suitable candidates were in short supply. Although an unprecedented number of surplus Liberal candidates did materialize, Chamberlain's fifth columnists only operated against a few selected individuals. He rejoiced in the defeat at Bassetlaw of F. J. S. Foljambe (who had penned a 'most ferocious personal attack' in January), especially since no candidate prepared to 'trouble' the provocative Whig had actually been found.[23] The necessary corroboratory evidence of Chamberlain's complicity in double candidatures can be traced in only two seats, namely, G. J. Goschen's at Edinburgh and C. M. Norwood's in Hull. Such enterprise produced tangible dividends in the case of Norwood alone. Chamberlain's ill-concealed hatred stemmed primarily from Norwood's opposition to the abortive shipping bill of 1884. He was discontented merely with 'paying Mr Norwood out' verbally, so besides condemning the negligence of ship-owners in speeches at Hull, he also contrived the appearance of a Radical candidate.[24] N. B. Billany failed lamentably to gain much support, but he nevertheless contributed decisively to the main objective by capturing many votes from Norwood, thus enabling the Conservative candidate to emerge victorious.

The attempt to oust Goschen was a much more formidable proposition. Goschen was isolated within the party owing to his opposition to franchise reform. But his courageous repudiation throughout 1885 of Chamberlain's entire programme (when the bulk of the Whig leadership deemed it more prudent to remain silent) marked him out as spokesman for a significant segment of Liberal opinion. For this reason Chamberlain urged his friends to 'include a few hits' at Goschen in their speeches. Dilke was informed that 'we must make him our whipping boy and reply to Hartington and

Co. through him'.[25] Gladstone deplored this constant sniping at
Goschen, and sternly reminded Chamberlain that no one – however
eminent – was entitled to interfere between rival candidates.[26] At
Hawarden it was suspected that B. F. C. Costelloe had not appeared
spontaneously to contest Goschen's constituency, but had surreptitiously been encouraged by Chamberlain. The latter was scarcely in
a position to deny this damaging charge, since he had actually
established a close liaison with the chairman of Costelloe's election
committee.[27]

Sir Henry James deplored Chamberlain's strategy. The former
Attorney-General considered it to be 'cruel and fatal' and 'so want-
ing in Catholicity as to be apparently indefensible'.[28] But compromise
was a word rarely found in Chamberlain's political vocabulary. He
did not attempt to conceal his profound distaste for any return to
balanced ministries patterned on the 1880 model. In October
Chamberlain visited Hawarden and warned his host that should
Gladstone step aside at an early date the 'whole attitude' of the
Radicals 'would be changed'.[29] Chamberlain stated categorically
that Gladstone alone could count on his loyal (though possibly independent) support, whereas Hartington would be forced to accept
more stringent terms. Rather than acquiesce in a ministry headed
by Hartington, Chamberlain threatened to 'consolidate a
separate Radical party in the House and the country'. Gladstone insisted that he expunge a phrase which, if communicated to Hartington, would provoke an immediate and catastrophic split in the
party.[30]

So anxious was Chamberlain to avoid serving under a Whig
premier that he even suggested to Gladstone the notion of remaining
temporarily as purely titular leader.[31] In the circumstances, such
loyalty and devotion to an aged statesman appeared incongruous.
Reconstruction could evidently not take place while Gladstone clung
to public life, especially since the publication of the Midlothian
manifesto on 17 September had thrown a pall over the Radical programme. Gladstone seemed oblivious of the social forces released by
Chamberlain during his absence in Norway, and on his return was
impervious to strongly-worded personal appeals from Birmingham.
Preoccupation with the problem of Ireland exiled all other considerations from Gladstone's mind, to such an extent that he completely
over-looked Hartington's ill-judged hostility at Waterfoot to
Chamberlain's social programme (a challenge calculated to bring
the rival factions into open conflict) but fastened instead upon
Hartington's fleeting though disparaging references to Irish nationalism. Puzzled by this unexpected rebuke, Hartington rejoined that
although the speech had given 'considerable offence' to Radicals,

the passages to which Gladstone took exception had not 'hitherto met with much hostile comment'.[32]

In view of such defective vision, it is scarcely surprising that Gladstone declined to excite Radicals with clarion calls to the new democracy, but instead chose to issue a muted document of quite extraordinary imprecision. His practical programme was rigorously confined to four distinct proposals: representative local government, simplification of electoral registration, amendment of the land laws, and reform of parliamentary procedure. These useful though hardly original suggestions were designed as a supplement to the programme of his previous government, and therefore appealed exclusively to an almost extinct species of political animal. Even Hartington thought it a 'weak production', which, were the party not slavishly ready to 'take anything from him . . . would fall rather flat'.[33] Chamberlain's reaction was predictable; the manifesto was a 'slap in the face'.[34] Gladstone had been evasive upon the three propositions which Chamberlain regarded as indispensable, and important questions such as reform of the House of Lords and disestablishment had been consigned (so far as any meaning could be discerned) to the distant future. Chamberlain's special schemes found no place in Gladstone's programme; the latter did not venture beyond the limited outline which he had sketched for Hartington before his holiday. On the contrary, he had subsequently inserted a thinly veiled criticism of Chamberlain's objectives in education.[35]

Despite this rebuff, Chamberlain did not repudiate Gladstone's manifesto. He was tempted to go into outright opposition, but the impulse to 'smash' Gladstone rapidly gave way to a more realistic assessment of the situation and to subtler designs. An intensification of the vendetta against Hartington was skilfully coupled with equally strenuous efforts to court favour with Gladstone. In his 'ultimatum' speech at Lambeth on 24 September, Chamberlain announced that he would refuse to join any administration which *excluded* from its programme either free elementary education, or revision of the tax structure, or the means to enable local authorities to acquire land for allotments. Such displays of bravado were strictly reserved for the hustings. Two weeks later Gladstone was able to report that in private conversation Chamberlain spoke constantly of 'reducing to an absolute minimum his idea of necessary conditions'.[36] By October even the abrasive tone characteristic of Chamberlain's speeches had largely disappeared, and the vast array of controversial suggestions which had originally been thrown out for universal consumption was now confined to digestible portions.[37] These, in the interests of consistency, dignity, and personal influence, he was quite unable to discard.

It is not difficult to establish why Chamberlain considered the emasculation of his ambitious programme a sacrifice worth making to ensure Gladstone's continued leadership. He did not underrate the tremendous popularity and considerable residual powers of a venerable chief, and felt it necessary to take elementary precautions against the possibility that Gladstone might publicly dissociate himself from the Radicals by denouncing their programme as incompatible with the interests of party unity. In fact Chamberlain never seriously believed that Gladstone would act in this fashion, unless sorely provoked. Experience of the late government suggested to him that Gladstone was either 'squeezable or teachable', and would in due course 'probably give way to our views'.[38] Chamberlain anticipated that half measures would be discarded as totally inadequate once Gladstone actually took in hand the framing of urgent and complex legislation. The assumption that Gladstone would eventually be ready to swallow the main points of the 'unauthorized' programme was founded upon a 'brief hint' given in the previous May. Gladstone had then advised Chamberlain to see what effect 'the *new state of affairs* which will be presented after the dissolution' would have upon Hartington 'and on other minds' (including the author's) when they were forced 'to look at the matter *cominus* and not *eminus*, as actual, and not as hypothetical'.[39]

Gladstone clearly implied that he would not allow persistent Whig hesitancy to cloud his judgement and check his characteristically spontaneous reactions to changing political conditions. Early in September, when the manifesto was being composed, Gladstone was closeted with Whigs, and remained in complete ignorance of electoral currents. The delicate condition of his vocal chords prevented Gladstone from deriving moral inspiration and Radical fervour from direct contact with the masses. Hence Chamberlain did not doubt that Gladstone's 'quick popular instinct' would prevail when he took leave of scholastic pursuits at Hawarden and journeyed to Midlothian in November, meeting once more the 'true representatives of the public opinion of the county';[40] in other words, not drawing-room moderates but the turbulent masses who rejoiced in the Radical programme. Most important of all, Chamberlain perceived that a vital distinction ought to be drawn between the contents (and omissions) of the manifesto and the actual frame of Gladstone's mind. It was necessary to recall, before condemning the document out of hand, that the leader of a heterogeneous party could not 'definitely pronounce against the views of any section', and was 'almost bound to propose as his own policy the maximum which is accepted by all sections alike'.[41] There were indeed 'so many subjects' upon which it was difficult for Gladstone to 'speak or write with absolute plainness' that he had no choice other than to create for himself a great deal of room in which to manoeuvre.[42] His undistinguished and obscure manifesto amounted to a humiliating public confession that the party was divided by considerably more issues than it was united upon. There existed many matters on which he was compelled to 'hold back in opinion' because, as he explained to one candidate, 'You write to express your own sentiments, whereas the purpose of my paper is two-sided, and seeks to hold our left and right wings in track of one another for and through the Election.'[43]

Thus the document could not be construed as a total revelation of Gladstone's thoughts on leading questions. It was intended only as a 'footing' for the party at the elections – certainly not as a draft programme for an incoming Liberal government. Gladstone considered the latter proposition 'a thing far more free and open' since the extension of the franchise had given rise to vast imponderables, the mood of the electorate obviously being uncertain and incalculable.[44] He therefore took considerable pains to eschew any precise commitment to Chamberlain's programme, yet cautiously retained the freedom to adopt such parts of it as circumstances dictated. Hence, 'by a somewhat strained interpretation', Chamberlain found it possible to extract some crumbs of comfort from reading 'between the lines' of the manifesto. 'Extra powers to Local Authorities are hinted at, Revision of taxation in favour of the working classes is distinctly implied, and Free Schools are not finally disapproved.'[45]

Gladstone sensibly suspended judgement upon the Radical programme until the general election had been concluded and the true sentiments of the nation stood revealed. Chamberlain was confident that the constituencies favoured a thoroughgoing Radicalism, and anticipated that the next Gladstone government would promptly endorse his policies. He deduced that a lack of satisfactory evidence held Gladstone back, not a deep-rooted antipathy to Radicalism *per se*. 'The experience of the election will enlarge our knowledge', explained the latter, 'and it will show us, from Ireland *and elsewhere*, more clearly than we see them now, the proper conditions of a Liberal Government.'[46] It could reasonably be inferred that Gladstone's manifesto was capable of almost unlimited expansion in a Radical direction. Free education, disestablishment, reform of the upper chamber, together with the 'attributions and purposes' of local government bodies, were named as subjects not 'in a state to be brought into the programme for the Dissolution', but which might of necessity be included in a government programme. Chamberlain knew how 'loath' Gladstone was to employ 'any language which might be misinterpreted'.[47] Only a conclusive electoral verdict would satisfy Gladstone's private misgivings, remove his conditional opposition to advanced policies, and finally stir him belatedly into action. This circumspect attitude is clearly ascertainable in the case of Irish Home Rule, where an unambiguous national desire was easily determined. But the principle of conducting quasi-referenda had far wider application. Gladstone patiently awaited the judgement of electors upon sectional yet equally contentious issues like disestablishment, especially in Wales.[48] Chamberlain was therefore encouraged (and perhaps driven) to undertake a strenuous campaign so as to demonstrate that the desire for allotments and free schools was no less conclusive than the national aspirations of Wales and Ireland.

Hence the manifesto created a paradoxical situation. In tone and content the document offered little encouragement to Chamberlain, but the tactics upon which it was based worked overwhelmingly to the advantage of the Radical section. Gladstone emphasized that no one (except the author) was bound by the terms and limitations of the address, and went to extraordinary lengths to ensure that a personal statement was not mistaken for a definitive version of the Liberal programme. He did not consider it either 'usual or desirable' to try and lay down a common policy; this task was left entirely to the 'discretion of leaders'. Thus Gladstone modestly protested that his opinions carried only 'such degree of weight as anyone may think proper to give them'.[49] Such reserve naturally alarmed the retreating corps of Whig statesmen, who had struggled in vain to maintain their defensive positions. Gladstone's refusal to bind the entire party to an 'authorized' programme in effect allowed unlimited scope to those who were pressing ahead with distinctive policies. Many Whigs also foresaw that the return of sufficient Chamberlainite members would make an indelible impression upon Gladstone's yielding and resilient consciousness. Since Gladstone felt that it would be an act of 'gross presumption' to silence Chamberlain,[50] the Radicals were left perfectly free to extract unconditional pledges of support from Liberal candidates, thereby isolating those moderates who refused to submit to pressure. Much controversy was aroused by Chamberlain's labours (in conjunction with the constituency associations) to commit increasing numbers of candidates to the disestablishment policy propounded by the Liberation Society. Inevitably, several Whig churchmen voiced their disgust at Gladstone's connivance in this exploit, and, following the example set by the former Lord Chancellor (the Earl of Selborne), seized this opportunity to dissociate themselves from the Liberal campaign.[51] Conversely, Chamberlain triumphantly furnished Gladstone with evidence that a large majority of candidates in Scotland

and in London had been persuaded to endorse his ideas on the question of free education. By refusing to condemn or discourage such initiatives, Gladstone unwittingly ensured that the Radical programme was transformed from a 'friendly lead' to Liberal candidates into a 'great national policy [which] must be forced on at all hazards'.[52]

2. *Chamberlain's 'Unauthorized' Experiment*

It is difficult to assess how many successful Liberal candidates were so impressed by Chamberlain's dynamic personal crusade that they may properly be described as independent Radicals. Reliable statistics do not exist because the Parliament of 1886 was so short-lived; no specific test of allegiance arising before Irish Home Rule completely transformed the context of political debate. The retiring Chief Whip (Lord Richard Grosvenor) estimated that the Chamberlainites numbered a mere 101 persons out of a total complement of 333 Liberals.[53] Nevertheless, these hastily compiled figures ought not to be considered authoritative or impartial, especially since they do not appear to be verified by reference to an important contemporary summary of speeches and election addresses. It seems feasible to suggest that a minimum of 180 members, a majority of the parliamentary party, were committed to at least one of the measures which distinguished Chamberlain from the ordinary Whig or 'Gladstonian' Liberals.[54] In less than three years of unremitting endeavour, Chamberlain had succeeded in converting the bulk of the party to bold plans for reform in education and local government, and thus brought them forcibly into the arena of interparty controversy.

However, the dramatic sequence of events in December 1885 has tended to distort the true nature of Chamberlain's triumph, which, unfortunately, constituted a Pyrrhic victory. It is vital to recall that he had always assumed that the 'whole atmosphere' of the Commons would be transformed to Radical advantage, never considering the possibility that the Liberals might not be swept irresistibly back to power. Francis Schnadhorst and Dilke, who claimed to be fully acquainted with the electoral situation in the provinces and in the metropolis respectively, gave Chamberlain no grounds to question this incautious assumption.[55] They automatically considered the large towns to be an exclusively Radical preserve, and consequently were shocked and bemused by the results of the elections. Liberal candidates fared badly everywhere in the boroughs (which polled earliest), except in Birmingham. The results in London were particularly disastrous. Sweeping gains in the counties partially compensated for these unexpected reverses, enabling the party to emerge

– not with an overall majority – but with a bare half of seats available in the new House (see Appendix A).

Except in the case of London, poor borough representation could not be attributed to deficiencies in local organization. The impact of a disastrous legacy in the Soudan was universally discounted. According to Gladstone, the *'causae damni'* were 'Fair Trade + Parnell + Church + Chamberlain', in that order of importance.[56] Prior to the polls the party leaders had clearly underestimated the potency of the Fair Trade cry as the panacea for economic depression. In Lancashire, where the attraction of protectionist doctrine was unusually pronounced, the impact of the 'unauthorized' programme was correspondingly weak. Even Hartington experienced considerable difficulties in thwarting the appeal of his opponent, the Fair Trader Farrer Ecroyd.[57] Chamberlain of course realized that unemployment and industrial discontent would be exploited by the Conservatives, but had not expected this factor to be responsible for the loss of adherents from his special programme. It was not until his return to Birmingham in mid-October to contest his own seat that he became aware how thoroughly even his own city had succumbed to the lure of tariff reform. At the close of the 'unauthorized' campaign he discovered that all his remaining energy was required to dispel the protectionist illusion rather than to refute objections to various details of the Radical programme.[58] Nor did he anticipate that the long delayed 'vote Tory manifesto', issued by Parnell, would swing towards the Conservative party those urban seats (estimated at 25) where the expatriate Irish electorate was concentrated.

Hence Chamberlain deeply resented the suggestion that his advanced platform, by thoroughly alarming the moderate Liberals, was mainly responsible for the inconclusive verdict at the polls. He countered such criticism by alleging that a perfectly adequate and necessary programme had been hampered and attenuated at every point by the obstinacy and folly of his Whig associates.[59] But the attribution of defeat to the stultifying presence of the Whigs constituted an unwarranted and ungenerous attack upon a select minority who had, in fact, proved far from irreconcilable during the electoral campaign. For example, Lord Derby, one of the most unenterprising of the Whig leaders, became practically converted to Chamberlain's ideas in the space of three months.[60] Even Hartington, whose opening speech at Waterfoot he himself admitted was 'even clumsier than usual', emerged quite unexpectedly as an accommodating and conciliatory figure.[61] The most damaging criticism of all came not from Whigs but from a venerated Radical. John Bright protested in public against Chamberlain's 'new fangled propositions', and complained to Gladstone that such schemes as free education and land reform were injudicious, impracticable, and premature.[62]

The main shortcoming of the moderates was not ignorance and stubbornness but silence. Unlike Chamberlain, whose election campaign was the culmination of careful preparation spread over two years, the Whigs had not given any serious thought to the subject of electioneering. Nothing served to focus attention upon Radical policies more than the absence of either public dissent or alternative programmes. Goschen presented the only direct challenge, but he possessed no title to speak on behalf of official Liberalism. He warned Granville in August 1885 how 'really dangerous' it was 'to let the new gospel be preached as coming from an authoritative source accompanied by the silence of the other leaders of the party; a silence which will soon be interpreted to mean acquiescence'.[63] Though there was 'scarcely a day to be lost', Hartington had not hitherto attempted to stem the flood-tide of Radicalism. He soon discovered that this was a disagreeable task which others expected him to carry out single-handed. Gladstone, pleading his inability to conduct a speaking campaign, was a recluse at Hawarden, preoccupied with literary and theological as much as with political questions. Nor did aristocratic members of the late cabinet show much enthusiasm for electioneering. 'Where are the Whigs?' Hartington demanded in October. 'Also where are the Peers?' He contrasted the flood of Radical oratory with the conspicuous absence of any trickle of support for himself, and complained that the only peers who had ventured forth were supporters of the Radical programme. With unaccustomed sarcasm he wrote (referring to Rosebery), 'Are we to understand that the "coronetted Socialist" represents them?'[64] Granville's inadequate and evasive reply illustrates the unfortunate dilemma in which the peers found themselves. Hartington did not expect them to emulate Rosebery by 'stumping the country', but simply to indicate in public their support for his own policy. Even in this limited sphere, Granville doubted whether aristocratic exposure to public scrutiny would 'have much effect'.[65] Granville, Spencer, Kimberley, and Derby, did eventually make a fleeting appearance on the hustings, but they were a handful of indifferent orators; objects to be viewed with curiosity, and as such unable to compete with eloquent statesmen who undertook planned campaigns. It clearly did not matter to Chamberlain whether the peers spoke or not; 'if they did nobody would know and nobody would care'.[66]

If Chamberlain's programme did not contain the formula for victory in the towns, the responsibility rested in his own hands and could not properly be attributed to either Whig indifference or the 'wretched cowardice and feebleness' of the Radical section.[67] Many Radicals had sought the shelter of the 'umbrella' hoisted by Gladstone, and began to doubt the wisdom of pursuing their distinctive principles to a logical and disruptive conclusion. Thus, Chamberlain was able to maintain only a minimal degree of contact with Lefevre and Trevelyan, and rashly instructed Dilke to repudiate ostentatiously Rosebery's wayward suggestions for reforming the House of Lords. Dilke's 'authoritative pronouncement' on the subject in October dramatically underlined Rosebery's growing isolation from the Radical commoners.[68] Such a vendetta-stricken mentality as Chamberlain now betrayed, especially concerning Goschen, disconcerted his closest associates. The strange conduct of the oversensitive and truculent ex-minister during the elections revealed him in a fresh light as an exacting friend and a potentially dangerous and implacable foe. Personal friendship was to Chamberlain an 'innermost element in his own existence', and could not be divorced from political association. He was prepared to make considerable sacrifices to preserve amicable relationships, yet (as Morley darkly hinted) these concessions were 'bound up with expectations to match'.[69] All the elements for a violent explosion were present when Morley visited Rosebery at Mentmore in September in an unprompted effort to secure a reconciliation between the two extreme wings. He had already forfeited Chamberlain's confidence by remaining on good terms with unmentionable outcasts like Goschen and Derby, but this serious offence was aggravated considerably by Morley's refusal to endorse Chamberlain's 'ultimatum' speech. Morley, who chaired the Victoria Hall meeting, evidently did not intend to aid Chamberlain in his determined effort to break up the party. At the close of the elections he suggested that their 'Whig friends' could be dispatched at a 'more convenient season', stating categorically that he took the strongest exception to 'anything that looks like deliberate isolation on personal grounds from the rest of the party at a moment when there is no great *practical* issue . . . on which Radicals take a line of their own'.[70] Chamberlain reacted violently to this unwelcome advice. In a vigorous exchange of letters on the subject of Irish Home Rule, the 'thunders of excommunication' were rolled; the unhappy analogy of Fox and Burke was chosen; and Chamberlain insisted that they 'recognize the serious nature of these divergences, and not continue to cover them up with the ordinary expression of kindly personal feeling'.[71]

In view of such portentous events, Chamberlain had inadvertently committed a tactical error by raising so suddenly a wide range of controversial social and political issues. Practical unanimity in the Radical camp could not be achieved by creating the host of

difficulties which inevitably accompanied detailed explanations and
excessive frankness. Instead of encouraging the maximum degree of
party cohesion, Chamberlain succeeded only in dissipating Liberal
energies through fomenting bitterness and strife. Since he lacked
the whole-hearted co-operation of leading Radicals and was forced
to campaign virtually unassisted, Chamberlain's unique electioneering experiment could only give rise to intense personal disappointment in the event of failure. Few words of condolence were
forthcoming from those who had themselves fought on a Chamberlainite platform. One former junior minister, A. J. Mundella,
'frankly confessed' that any additions to Gladstone's programme
had been 'a decided hindrance'.[72] Another adherent, Reginald Brett,
pointedly reminded Chamberlain that the Radical programme would
not have been 'enthusiastically received in the towns' if individual
candidates had pressed it 'in *all its details*'.[73] Brett, and others who
suffered electoral defeat, were inclined to see hidden merits in
Gladstone's preference for a limited programme. One great advantage of the Midlothian manifesto was that it did not contain material
which might provoke unnecessarily the fears and prejudices of an
inert Conservative mass.

In contrast Chamberlain had stirred latent religious passions,
needlessly disturbing the hornets nest of clerical opinion by his
provocative references to education and disestablishment. He felt
that Liberalism had nothing to lose, though possibly much to gain,
by deliberately courting the hostility of the clerical party. The
Church of England evidently had failed to appreciate the services
rendered by those Whiggish members who in a previous era had
disestablished the Irish Church and had instituted a system of School
Boards. By 1885 the clergy had come to view with dread the insidious
transformation which was taking place within the Liberal party.
Cardinal Manning believed that the contagion of republicanism and
aggressive anti-clericalism which infected Catholic France had
crossed the Channel in the persons of Chamberlain, Dilke, and
Morley. He feared that English nonconformists and Radicals would
attempt to emulate France and would seize, as their initial objective,
on the confiscation of clerical property and the elimination of clerical
influence.[74]

Chamberlain did nothing to assuage such fears, failing even to
repudiate or modify the less than discreet references to education
and disestablishment which he had made prior to his entry into
Parliament, and which were now gathering dust in the pages of the
Fortnightly Review.[75] On the contrary, he rigorously ensured that
those hints of a possible compromise which had appeared in the
original version of the Radical programme were excised from the

articles when they were published in book form.[76] Chamberlain deliberately discarded the possibility of an agreed solution to the religious controversy because he chose to base his public campaign upon a narrow sectarian view which would appeal to the new electorate. There existed a clear dichotomy between his municipal programme, which inspired social reformers throughout the following decade, and his uncompromising denominational partisanship, which merely served to revive the sectarian strife endemic a decade earlier. In 1885 the National Liberal Federation seemed perilously near to emerging as the reincarnation of the National Education League; never in its short history had the Radical organization so flamboyantly reproduced Chamberlain's sectarian animosities. On the eve of the elections the N.L.F. adopted two motions on elementary education and disestablishment which held out no prospect of compromise with churchmen. The resolutions were moved by Jesse Collings and Dr Crosskey, Chamberlain's Birmingham associates in the defunct Education League: the articles in the *Radical Programme* upon which they were based were written (and rewritten) to Chamberlain's instructions by Francis Adams, the League's secretary, and by the former positivist, John Morley. Not without cause was Chamberlain often referred to as an English Gambetta – Morley presumably being cast in the rôle of Jules Ferry.

When Chamberlain decided to give prominence to the sectarian question he made a double miscalculation. He assumed that the lull in the denominational controversy constituted evidence that the political influence of the Church had atrophied, and was further mistaken in his belief that the extension of the franchise would provide a great impetus to militant nonconformity. The shattering experience of 1874 had not reduced Chamberlain's faith in the rallying power of urban nonconformity at general elections. Such confidence enabled him to view with equanimity the consolidation of Roman Catholic and Church of England opinion against his schemes.[77] Opposition from the Whig quarter could be expected, owing to the activities of Cardinal Manning and Lord Selborne, but the extent of the Conservative reaction should have given grounds for some concern. However, Chamberlain's most serious handicap stemmed from his failure to see any necessity to reconcile Radical churchmen to his policy, an oversight which obviously hampered the effectiveness of the party as an electoral unit. After the elections had been completed he continued to ignore this important section, and announced his intention to 'go for the Church' in earnest. Yet Dilke could not conceive how such a drastic step could be taken unless Chamberlain received '*some* Church support' for disestablishment.[78] The Liberal party was by no means an exclusively nonconformist pressure group; any attempt to reduce it to such was an invitation to commit political suicide.

For these reasons Gladstone deplored the suggestion that the Church stood in danger of immediate disestablishment. He considered that the question had been prematurely raised, and was one which had greatly damaged Liberal prospects in the English constituencies. In Midlothian he did not concern himself with disestablishment as an abstract principle, but with the political repercussions of allowing it to become a test question throughout Scotland. Since Chamberlain had not taken the precaution of confining his arguments to Scotland and Wales, Gladstone was anxious to prevent Conservatives from gaining an advantage by retaliatory measures which would make disestablishment a test question in England.[79] This difficult exercise required the virtual repudiation of Chamberlain's tactics by Gladstone, without his renouncing the expediency of disestablishment at the same time. In fact, Gladstone had long been reconciled to the principle involved. He had mused upon the 'almost insuperable difficulties' of a Scottish measure as long ago as 1874.[80] Such language alarmed Selborne who knew Gladstone well enough to realize that the contemplation of 'almost insuperable difficulties' was invariably the prelude to action. By 1877 Gladstone's contact with the party at constituency level had converted him to the belief that disestablishment was to be the 'great work' for the Liberal party once the crisis in the East had been resolved. He thought Scottish disestablishment a 'rather Lilliputian question', and contemptuously dismissed the outbursts of panic-stricken clerics as 'servile and superstitious'.[81] Hence, by 1885, Gladstone was secretly prepared to allow the constituencies of Scotland and Wales to galvanize him into action – it being a foregone conclusion that both countries would return a Liberal majority in favour of disestablishment. The only complication was the organic unity which existed between the Church in England and Wales.

It would be a mistake to suppose that Gladstone's rather ambiguous support for disestablishment was given for narrow party considerations. Some churchmen felt that disestablishment would liberate the Church from a bondage which restricted its vitality and weakened its appeal. One of these was Gladstone's eldest son, Stephen, the Rector of Hawarden, and this domestic influence probably inspired the father to adopt a sanguine tone in his election address.[82] Moreover, Gladstone avowed that his main care 'concentrates itself upon building up the Church to such a condition that she shall be prepared for all contingencies'. In placing himself at the head of an irresistible movement, Gladstone realized with perception that he would be able to protect the essential interests of the Church and thwart the destructive intentions of extreme Radicals.[83] But, above all, Gladstone was accustomed to view such controversial problems through a broader perspective. Though he genuinely revered the formularies of the Church of England, sectarian dogma concerned him less than the phenomena of religious indifference and of outright rejection of Biblical truth. The disturbing revelations of science made the Old Testament 'the battleground of belief', and to Gladstone the theologian this particular controversy was the 'one really absorbing subject'.[84] The continuation of denominational squabbles prevented the growth of an oecumenical movement which was necessary in order to defend Christianity itself.

Disestablishment alone was not sufficiently menacing to arouse intense feeling. It was difficult to be alarmed by a mere abstract proposition which both Gladstone and Chamberlain confirmed would not be dealt with by the forthcoming Parliament. However, the collatoral provision for disendowment was altogether different. In the absence of any alternative scheme, public attention centred upon a plan inspired by the Liberation Society and reproduced by Morley in chapter six of the *Radical Programme*. Gladstone predictably found utterly offensive proposals which paid no heed to the vital principles of 'equity and liberality'. He detested the Liberationist assumption that a disestablished Church would split asunder into its component liturgical elements. It appeared that the distasteful ambition of Radical nonconformity was not 'religious equality' but the complete destruction of the Anglican Communion. This was to be accomplished by simply refusing to acknowledge that the Church possessed a corporate existence. Instead of following the Irish precedent (by investing a board of Commissioners with plenary powers), Morley stated that only individuals would be entitled to receive compensation. Furthermore, the arbitrary designation of all churches founded prior to 1818 as 'ancient' and therefore 'national' property shocked Gladstone, who was prepared to 'fight to the death about the fabrics of the Church'.[85] It was surely lamentable for Morley to suggest that the use of such churches and cathedrals would not be confined to episcopalians but ought to be shared amongst different denominations, and to state that the buildings might even be appropriated for secular usage. Even Radical churchmen were repelled by an insensitive document which 'betrayed such a virulence against the Church . . . as to create general disgust. More than anything else in the book, it kindled hostility to the Radical cause, and so contributed to the defeat of the Unauthorized Programme.'[86] Gladstone was strongly tempted to reprimand Morley for concocting an 'outrageously unjust' scheme which had antagonized many 'among the best men'.[87] On only one occasion did he deem it prudent to recognize publicly the existence of the Radical handbook, and then it was to denounce the disendowment proposals as 'utterly impossible to be entertained either at the present or any other time'.[88]

The incorporation of the disendowment scheme into the Radical programme was a blunder of major importance. Chamberlain took great care to stress that his views on social reconstruction involved no manifold injustice; private landlords, unrepresentative corporations, and vested interests of every description, were promised equitable treatment and due compensation. But the provision for disendowment contained in the *Radical Programme* was tantamount to 'ransom', thus undermining his assurances that similar treatment would not be meted out to other forms of property. Unfortunately, the alienation of moderate Liberals and churchmen did not enhance Chamberlain's reputation amongst nonconformists. This latter group were already unequivocally committed to Gladstone and the Liberal party, and Chamberlain unnecessarily reduced the prospects of ultimate success by choosing to narrow the scope of his appeal. Chamberlain quickly discovered that a reversion to the methods employed by the National Education League did not stimulate enthusiasm for disendowment, especially since militant nonconformists disliked the outlines of his education policy.

Chamberlain grievously underestimated the conflicting passions which distorted and destroyed any plans for education reform when disendowment was part of the formula. He had always considered that the money to pay for free elementary education was to be obtained by appropriating the surplus revenues of the Church. This was not referred to specifically in the *Radical Programme*, but Chamberlain's real intentions became plain during the course of his Scottish campaign in September 1885. The National Liberal Federation of Scotland, an advanced Radical organization, was instituted in conjunction with his meeting at Glasgow, and immediately resolved – not only to make disestablishment a test question in Scotland – but also to finance free schools out of the funds made available by disendowment. Chamberlain's brisk disavowal of the former proposition as premature was totally nullified by his unqualified approval of the latter.[89] This damaging admission, infelicitously repeated by Collings at the Bradford congress of the N.L.F., gave credence to the suspicion that the spoliation of the Church and the confiscation of its revenues were the means – not to the advancement of education – but to the annihilation of the Voluntary ideal. Although Chamberlain protested that 'the schools might be freed tomorrow without in the slightest degree affecting the position of the denominational system', his arguments lacked conviction.[90] Fees were to be abolished only in Board schools, and by implication the alternative held out for voluntary schools was either to close or come under the surveillance of the State.

When Chamberlain had first broached the subject of free education in 1883, Dilke was lightly informed how he had 'fluttered the dovecotes tremendously'.[91] Yet Mundella, the minister responsible for education, had already borne the brunt of sectarian strife upon small matters (such as the siting of the new Welsh university college) and so appreciated that it was 'a much larger question than he seems to apprehend'.[92] However, Chamberlain was slow to respond to such warnings, and did not question his own ability to separate free education from considerations of denominational advantage until the autumn of 1885. In fact, when Gladstone stressed the 'religious difficulty' in his manifesto, Chamberlain was still capable of dismissing this legitimate objection as 'weak and irrelevant'.[93] He eventually saw the need to offer some concessions to the Voluntaryists, but these came too late to have any practical effect (other than to arouse the wrath of suspicious nonconformists).

The proposal to give an average grant of 2d per child to all schools where education was made free might have been a workable compromise had circumstances been less tense. But denominationalists resented any suggestion that double educational taxation was a sacrifice worth making while they remained financially inferior to the Board system – or were deprived of absolute control over their own schools. On the other hand, nonconformists were also averse to free education if it meant that voluntary schools would be compelled to shut down for lack of funds. Those who were unwilling to accept the financial responsibility for integrating displaced pupils into Board schools required 'judicious handling'. Mundella anxiously reminded Chamberlain that 'our Philistines are dead against *increased Rates*'.[94] However, Chamberlain could not now escape the consequences of his own impetuosity. When he sought to reassure his financial critics, in a public letter to Dr Plumptre (the Dean of Wells), by suggesting a grant-in-aid from the Exchequer instead of rate support, he only intensified the dissatisfaction which nonconformists had expressed at his explanations to the N.L.F. at Bradford.[95] By October it had become clear that Chamberlain did not intend to subject those voluntary schools where fees were paid by the State to any immediate form of public control. At Bradford the local M.P. (Alfred Illingworth) had successfully carried an amendment against Chamberlain which emphasized the unacceptability of this novel idea. Liberationists protested bitterly that 'there is not and cannot be unanimity among Radicals if *free* schools are to be rushed through without a scheme of popular control over sectarian schools going forward at the same time'.[96] The revolt of the nonconformists was complete. Schnadhorst, the secretary of the N.L.F., was himself an accurate barometer of nonconformist anxieties and prejudices, and even the *Birmingham Daily Post*, former mouthpiece of the National Education League, rejected a scheme which it considered to be unduly favourable to Voluntaryism. Chamberlain's worried colleagues submitted alarming reports of opposition from several influential Radicals, citing the names of Henry Richard and James Picton (M.P.s for Merthyr and Leicester) and Dr Rigg (chairman of the London Wesleyan Circuit) as prominent examples.[97] Mundella observed that Liberal associations in the metropolis preferred to '*stand aloof*' from those progressive members of the London School Board who propagated Chamberlain's extremely unpopular education policies. 'What is true of London', he predicted, 'is certainly true of Sheffield and many other large towns.'[98]

But Mundella's hasty judgement of the demoralized state of London politics proved to be less accurate than his fears for his native Sheffield. In the November elections most sitting advocates of free education retained their places on the London Board, one significant exception being their chief spokesman (Lyulph Stanley), whose vote plunged dramatically in the Marylebone district. However, in Sheffield Mundella was denounced '*right and left*' by the clerical party, resulting in a 'crushing defeat' for the progressive members of the School Board.[99] The 'drum ecclesiastic' was equally noisy during the parliamentary elections held later in the same month. Many Radicals suffered on account of their association with Chamberlain, Lefevre actually losing his seat at Reading owing to the hostility of the Church.[100] In London (where the influence of drink rivalled that of Dissent among labourers) Dilke discovered that even in middle-class constituencies the presence of a disciplined Church following could 'beat the non-cons out of the field'. When he learnt that the Conservatives in Chelsea were 'working Free Schools with the ratepayers as well as with the churchmen and Catholics', he was naturally tempted to repudiate the Radical programme.[101] In October Dilke had claimed that Chamberlain's schemes were virtually written into Gladstone's manifesto. But alarming canvassing returns subsequently forced him to water down his commitment to Chamberlain's programme. He denied that the funds for free education were to be found through disendowment, announcing that these ought now to be granted out of general taxation. When this concession failed to mollify suspicious clerics, he revealed a hitherto undetected enthusiasm for the Voluntary system as creating variety in education. Further protests from non-conformist constituents who disliked free education and 'implored' him to renounce disestablishment, finally convinced Dilke that his personal survival depended upon desperate measures. A week prior to the polls he stated categorically that subjects such as these, which were not contained in Gladstone's programme, could not possibly be dealt with in the next Parliament.[102] 'I'm now fighting the election entirely on City Guilds, and against protective duties,' Chamberlain was informed by the embarrassed apostate. 'These are the only two questions on which I find our views popular,' Dilke hastened to add. 'I fancy this applies to all west London.'[103]

The depressing results of the London elections were an 'awful disappointment' to Chamberlain. Advice to 'sit on the safety-valve till *after* the election' with respect to the schools question came too late to enable a fundamental revision of Radical tactics to be undertaken. Even in the face of adversity, Mundella continued to believe that this was 'the one article of the Radical programme that will secure the *largest adhesion*'.[104] However, as an 'urban cow', free education proved almost universally a failure. 'I put my money on free schools, but, judging by London, the electors do not care much about it,' was the epitaph Chamberlain sadly inscribed upon the tomb of metropolitan Liberalism.[105] He was totally nonplussed by the meagre dividends which his aggressive denominational partisanship had extracted from those provincial towns where nonconformists were most active and influential. 'We are dreadfully in want of an urban "Cow",' Chamberlain wrote during a post-mortem investigation. 'The boroughs do not care for our present programme and I confess I do not know what substitute to offer them.'[106]

Chamberlain's despondency was the more acute because his whole campaign was not, as is often thought, designed primarily to gain the rural vote, but had been deliberately geared to the interests of the urban constituencies. His real purpose had been to invigorate and strengthen the Radicalism of the cities which, on account of the Redistribution Act, seemed destined to provide the nucleus of a reorganized Radical party. A considerable increase in the representation of the larger towns now gave them a 'prerogative vote' (according to the *Radical Programme*), since the geographical 'area over which their political force will radiate will be more than proportionately extended'.[107] Hence, Chamberlain neither anticipated nor desired that the balance within the party would be shifted from the towns into the shires. An element of special pleading should be suspected in those like Labouchere who, with the benefit of hindsight, rhetorically enquired, 'Is not the cow working wonders for us?'[108] The catchphrase 'three acres and a cow' could not entirely explain the rural victory and was incompatible with Chamberlainite logic. The importance of the cry appears to have been exaggerated, particularly since it was usually utilized by opponents as a term of derision. Schnadhorst certainly believed that its influence had been 'unduly magnified by both sides', a curious statement in view of the fact that prior to the elections he had persuaded Chamberlain that the question which aroused most excitement 'especially in the rural districts . . . is that of the land'.[109]

However, it is impossible to gauge how much the Liberals owed their success to the gratitude of the emancipated classes towards Gladstone rather than to an expectation of beneficial legislation in the future. In any case, so much depended upon whether the down-trodden labourer had faith in the secrecy of the ballot that it was hazardous to anticipate with confidence how much impact the rural vote would make. The labourer himself could not pretend to be the decisive influence in a county constituency. Census returns showed that in 1881 only 16.6 per cent of the working population of England and Wales were engaged in agriculture. Perhaps four-fifths of these were actually labourers, and the numbers were inexorably diminish-ing in both relative and absolute terms. Victory in the agricultural constituencies depended less upon the support of the labourer than upon an ability to detach the tenant farmer from his traditional allegiance to the Conservative party. The revival of Liberal fortunes in the counties at the 1880 election could be attributed to success in this respect. Though the pro-Liberal Farmers' Alliance was mori-bund by 1885, the late Liberal government had endowed the farmer with material benefits, and Chamberlain was alive to the necessity of transforming these achievements into electoral assets. As early as 1881 he had suggested that the 'real business' of the Radicals was to 'outbid Chaplin and Co. with the Farmers'.[110] Yet evidence of such an intention to earn goodwill was oddly and conspicuously absent from the *Radical Programme*. Nevertheless, it would be incorrect to assume that Chamberlain ignored the interests of the farmer alto-gether. In his election speeches he referred to the extension of the Irish Land Act to England, proclaiming that tenant farmers urgently required 'a fair rent fixed by an impartial tribunal, with the right of free sale'.[111]

Chamberlain fully appreciated that this plea on behalf of the tenant aroused more opposition among Whig landowners than did the prospect of compulsory purchase to create allotments and small-holdings for labourers. Sir Henry James looked 'with almost horror' upon a suggestion which he considered amounted to 'absolute confiscation of private rights without any benefit to the com-munity'.[112] Whig proprietors rose in defence of their class against proposals which they found totally unacceptable. Yet such protests did not deter Chamberlain from continuing to address himself to the grievances of the farmer, even though his courageous perseverance reduced the chances of securing a favourable hearing for the allotments policy. It is important to recall that when Parliament met in January 1886, the Whigs did not first break with the Radicals on Collings' celebrated 'three acres and a cow' motion. The day before this amendment to the Address was put to the vote, a division had been taken upon a separate motion which sought to extend the principle of the Irish Land Act to England. This was moved by J. W. Barclay (Forfar) and was supported by the Radicals, but Hartington, Goschen, James, and 10 other Liberals repudiated the concept of tenant right by voting in the Conservative lobby.[113] When 18 Liberals, including those already mentioned, divided against Collings, an aversion to allotments did not rank high among their motives. In all probability Gladstone's views concerning Irish Home Rule influenced their behaviour, because the terms of the amendment cleverly disguised its real purpose – which was to express a want of confidence in the Conservative government's Irish policy.

Logic clearly impelled Chamberlain to lay the foundations of his new party upon what he imagined was the bedrock of urban Liberalism instead of upon the shifting sands of rural sentiment. He advised prospective candidates to seek out borough constituencies and to avoid rural ones.[114] Allotments appealed to a shrinking social class, the 'three F's' to a class which was politically unreliable; but the issue of religious and educational equality was designed to power the engine of urban nonconformity manufactured by the Redistribution Act. Yet these practical calculations were a symptom not the cause of the urban emphasis in Chamberlain's strategy. His personal experience and political outlook was entirely urban. The assurance with which he dealt with urban social problems (inspired by his success as mayor of Birmingham) contrasted with a remarkable ignorance of conditions in the countryside. Chamberlain first became acquainted with the abject circumstances of the rural poor during a visit to Wiltshire in the summer of 1885. By then his diagnosis of the rural problem, and suggested remedies, had already been written into the Radical programme. It was also significant that none of the Radical leaders sat for rural constituencies. Chamberlain was reliant upon information provided by Collings, who, despite his sincere concern for the labourers' welfare and his shadowy yeoman ancestry, had received a complete political education in Birmingham through carrying out the social projects with which Chamberlain was associated.[115]

Hence the rural programme was cast – not by agriculturalists for the benefit of labourers – but by urban Radicals in a form which would please urban electorates. Although Chamberlain was acquainted with Joseph Arch, there is no evidence to suggest that he thought of consulting the leader of the agricultural labourers at any stage of the land campaign. The sole organization used to disseminate knowledge of the *Radical Programme* was the N.L.F., a body to which few county divisional associations had sought affiliation. Chamberlain had only a superficial connection with the Allotments Extension Association, even though it had been founded by Collings at Birmingham in 1883 and acted as handmaiden to the Federation. Under the aegis of Arthur Arnold (M.P. for industrial Salford), the rival Free Land League espoused a more moderate land policy, yet concentrated its attention from the beginning upon London and the large towns. Even Collings attached the utmost importance to the task of converting the towns to land reform.[116]

It was not, therefore, incongruous for Chamberlain to have stressed the need for land reform to urban electors. Of the innumerable speeches which he made during his career as a Liberal, only one was delivered to an agricultural audience, and that (at Trowbridge) came at the end of the 'unauthorized' campaign. Perhaps the extensive press coverage which he received rendered this unnecessary; certainly rural electioneering was unsuited to the technique of the mass meeting. But in reality the main reason stemmed from the fact that the land crisis was as much an urban problem as a rural one. Chamberlain fervently believed (as he told a metropolitan audience) that land reform was 'of greater importance to the towns than it is to the country'. Radicals were convinced that economic stagnation and an unbalanced social structure in rural areas directly affected the well-being of urban society, depriving such manufacturing communities of an expanding market which 'far surpassed any that can possibly be expected from foreign countries and even from our own colonies'. More relevant to the immediate conditions of urban existence was Chamberlain's constant assertion that those wretched rural labourers who had been driven off the land crowded into towns 'to enter into competition with you, to lower the rate of wages, and to huddle population together until anything like decent and healthful dwellings becomes impossible'.[117]

This steady migration of population suggests that the most blatant examples of the 'rights of property' being misused occurred in respect of urban land, especially in London. 'Unearned increment', particularly the undeserved reward derived from the ownership of slums, was an abuse peculiar to the towns. Consequently, Radicals proposed to eliminate this scandal by enabling leaseholders to purchase the freehold to their property. In addition, local authorities would be empowered to expropriate slum landlords at a fair price in order to facilitate redevelopment schemes. Such a project had been completed in Birmingham, where the unfortunate inhabitants of centrally-located rookeries were ousted in cavalier fashion to make way for business premises, scant regard being paid to their future place of abode in an already congested city. Although Chamberlain had originally ignored such a fatal flaw in his policy, it would be misleading to infer that he remained insensitive to the appalling social consequences of redevelopment. During a conversation with Dilke in 1884, he revealed a strong desire to guarantee the supply of working-class houses. In his view there was no 'practical alternative' other than to compel developers to 'reserve such property permanently for the object, with State interference to secure fair rents'.[118] Not surprisingly Chamberlain kept these remarkable conclusions a close secret, and concentrated upon the more acceptable task of seeking means to reduce the excessive costs incurred by the ratepayers. Yet even if landlords were debarred from extorting exorbitant compensation, the funds for municipal enterprises were unlikely to be extracted in full from existing financial sources. Agricultural land values were declining inexorably, and the revenues which accrued from urban land taxation were static. Chamberlain's ambitious projects depended upon a capacity to tap additional sources of local revenue, and a convenient solution to the difficulty was found in the proposal to mulct the landowners themselves through the taxation of ground rents.

Slum clearance and the extinction of 'unearned increment' were inextricably linked in Radical terminology, and with them the interests of various classes in the towns. Tensions between employer and employee had arisen mainly as a result of a nationwide depression. Radicals hoped that a common hatred of the landowner, the traditional bugbear of the industrial community, would offset this potentially embarrassing situation and serve to reconcile disgruntled working-class electors to their Liberal industrial masters. According to Morley, monopoly capitalism was not 'half so great a curse as the monopoly of half of London by three or four Dukes'.[119] Few Liberal employers went so far as William Saunders (M.P. for Hull) who endorsed the confiscatory theories of Henry George as having 'business value for commercial men ... who were bound to profit by the extinction of property in land'.[120] But the capitalist who paid extortionate rents for the hire of business premises and the rack-rented inhabitants of slum dwellings shared the same opinions on the subject of urban landlordism. T. H. Green, the intellectual architect of a 'new Liberalism', argued that the real enemy of the working classes was not the capitalist but the landlord, because 'the capital gained by one is not taken from another, but one man cannot acquire more land without others having less'.[121] Andrew Provand (M.P. for Glasgow) subsequently differentiated between agricultural

and urban land ownership. The former could be compared with a
manufactured article, since the 'creative power' of cultivation
required the continual application of labour and capital, whereas
the latter possessed only an 'earning power', thus constituting a
direct tax upon industry.[122] In short, capitalist enterprise provided
employment and produced wealth: urban landlordism only hampered
commerce and extorted rent.

These distinctively urban proposals figured prominently in the
programme which Chamberlain announced at the beginning of
1885. An effective agitation in favour of rehousing schemes and
progressive land taxation had been aroused, but in the heat of the
electoral contest Chamberlain failed to impress this upon the public
consciousness or to continue stressing the relevance of agrarian
reform for the town workman. External pressures forced him to
adopt a defensive strategy throughout the autumn. His essential
interests could only be protected by developing an unnatural obsession with three proposals, none of which bore much resemblance to
the real needs of the towns. In the last resort Chamberlain was not
prepared to explore new bases of support, preferring to remain in
more familiar and congenial surroundings. All his political credit
was staked on the nonconformist desire for free schools. He had
apparently forgotten that three years earlier he and Morley had
planned to excite the town masses by denouncing urban landlordism.
Such was the degree of imbalance inherent in Chamberlain's outlook
that basic economic grievances were completely swamped by petty
sectarian jealousies. The task which confronted Chamberlain's successors in Liberal politics was to soothe the religious ulcer, restore
land to its proper urban context, and regain the confidence of the
rural community.

3. *The Radical Programme Superseded*

Chamberlain's presumption that a strong infusion of Radical members would compel the new Parliament to translate the Radical programme into legislation was rendered obsolete in December 1885 by
Gladstone's public conversion to Irish Home Rule. At one stage such
an abrupt change of strategy might have earned Chamberlain's
approval. Barely six months earlier he had demonstrated his faith in
the expediency of Irish self-government by pressing the cabinet to
establish a Central Board. Undeterred by the hostile reception
accorded to this scheme, Chamberlain resolved to 'put local government and the pacification of Ireland first in our programme'.[123]
Ireland monopolized Chamberlain's thoughts during the weeks
which elapsed after the fall of the Liberal government, and he

turned this freedom from official duties to good account. After preliminary consultations with Parnell, he made hasty arrangements to publish his proposals in the July issue of the *Fortnightly Review* and proceeded to incorporate the article entitled 'Local Government and Ireland' into the *Radical Programme*. In the meantime Chamberlain announced his willingness to suspend all electioneering activities while he and Dilke undertook a short fact-finding tour of Ireland. Unfortunately, Parnell and the Roman Catholic hierarchy disregarded Chamberlain's sincere and diligent efforts to reach a settlement because they suspected his true motives. When the Nationalist press contemptuously rejected his overtures, Chamberlain (whose political judgement was often impaired by such slights) reacted impetuously by losing all sympathy with the aspirations of the Irish. He no longer wished to extend the hand of friendship to a party which made seemingly exorbitant demands upon Radical allies while openly coquetting with the Conservative enemy. As Chamberlain's attitude hardened, the generous powers which he had been prepared to entrust to an Irish Central Board were gradually whittled away. By the autumn of 1885 he clearly contemplated nothing more drastic than a system of county councils identical to that which he intended to establish in England. After Chamberlain had crossed the Rubicon in his 'ultimatum' speech, Irish self-government ceased to exist as an issue worth pursuing for its own sake. Ireland now constituted a convenient lever which could be manipulated to exert pressure upon Gladstone, forcing him to accept the essentials of the 'unauthorized' programme. 'The Irish business is not the first just now,' Chamberlain wrote in October. 'We have our hands full with other things.'[124] Paramount amongst these competing matters was the reform of local government in Great Britain. Chamberlain assumed that this would be the first work of a Liberal ministry, and was anxious to crush any suggestion that the needs of Ireland, Scotland, and England were dissimilar. His reasons for preferring a single comprehensive measure to separate and distinct bills for each country were ingenious. Were he to succeed in sacrificing the interests of Ireland by coupling her name with that of England, Chamberlain perceived that he could then dictate the scope of all local government legislation. Powers to create allotments, fix fair rents, and rehouse slum dwellers, could not be withheld from English councils since these powers could scarcely be omitted from the Irish schedule by a Gladstone government which had previously incorporated such provisions in the Irish Land Act and the Irish Labourers' Act (of 1883).[125]

Unfortunately for Chamberlain, Gladstone did not view Parnell's devious conduct through Birmingham spectacles. Whereas

Chamberlain could not resist the temptation to chastise the impertinent Irishmen by denying them their right to Home Rule, Gladstone
rarely allowed the unpleasant characteristics displayed by some
prominent statesmen to colour his political judgement. Much of the
friction between the two Liberal leaders stemmed from the fact that
Gladstone never attached much importance to the arts of negotiation
and conciliation in Irish matters. 'I look at the question in itself'
was the resounding phrase which Gladstone chose to describe his
preference for maintaining an Olympian detachment,[126] a rôle which
Chamberlain could neither comprehend nor emulate. However, the
predictable clash of irreconcilable temperaments was delayed since
Chamberlain laboured under the illusion that the mounting pressure
of public opinion would compel an impetuous leader to reduce the
scope of his scheme until it resembled that which he himself favoured.
Consequently, Chamberlain agreed to join the cabinet of 1886 on
Gladstone's terms, and uncharacteristically suffered in silence the
indignity of seeing his tentative request for the office of Colonial
Secretary peremptorily brushed aside. He had sound reasons for
rejecting Gladstone's original offer of the Admiralty, a senior and
prestigious office, but one which was quite inappropriate (partly on
account of the lavish entertaining expected of the incumbent). Instead, Chamberlain accepted with alacrity the low-ranking cabinet
post of President of the Local Government Board. In this capacity
he possessed ample facilities to prepare his alternative scheme of
local government for the three Kingdoms. He was sure that the
cabinet enquiry into the question of Irish government would eventually shatter Gladstone's dreams, whereupon a strictly limited measure
would receive the undivided attention of a captive audience.

Chamberlain remained ignorant of the conclusions reached by the
Committee on Ireland until March, when the cabinet was presented
with a plan which fully endorsed Gladstone's original views. This
sudden disclosure momentarily took him aback, since he had accumulated evidence which suggested that the omens were auspicious
for a local government bill which incorporated the basic formulae of
the 'unauthorized' programme. The party was unequivocally
pledged to reform the local government structure at an early date.
A comprehensive scheme could gain general acceptance much more
easily now that the intractable Whigs (who had shunned Dilke's
modest proposals in 1883) had lost their official status. Moreover,
Gladstone seemed intent on early legislation because he had cryptic-
ally informed Chamberlain that the Local Government Board was
'an office of less rank, although with present prospects of much
greater political importance' than was the Admiralty.[127] The newly
appointed President regarded this as an instruction to prepare a local

government bill at once. He had no doubt that the inclusion of drastic powers of compulsory expropriation would meet with no opposition from colleagues who had recently adopted Collings' motion on 'three acres and a cow' in order to remove the Conservatives from office.

However, there existed some degree of confusion as to whether the government was in fact pledged to this particular item of the 'unauthorized' programme. Chamberlain and Dilke had actually drafted the Collings amendment in private, and the party leaders subsequently adopted it without discussion solely because it offered a means of escape from 'all their difficulties and differences'.[128] The real objective was to pre-empt the Irish motion which the Nationalists were certain to move, an initiative which would embarrass Gladstone and split the Liberal party prematurely. According to Sir Henry James, Gladstone 'thought nothing' of a vote which had 'turned upon a small matter of compulsion about which he cared but little'.[129] By this Gladstone probably meant that Radical ideas concerning the creation of allotments did not involve any fundamental and unacceptable principle. In Midlothian he had recently stated that the legislature possessed 'an undoubted title to expropriate every landlord if it were required for the public good', thus reiterating a remarkable proposition he had first made six years earlier.* Even a form of partial expropriation which discriminated between different classes was 'not unsound', and with a meticulous respect for precedent Gladstone further observed that the power contemplated by Chamberlain already reposed in existing local bodies.[130] Serious disputes could scarcely arise so long as Chamberlain kept his promise to attempt nothing more drastic than to make established procedures more effective by transferring them to more capable and willing authorities.

In practice, Gladstone would have preferred to 'try freedom first' by encouraging individual landlords to create allotments on their own initiative. 'But', he added, 'when it is considered how such a scheme must be tied up with safeguards, and how powerful are the natural checks, I hardly see . . . in this proposal *stuff* enough to cause a breach.' He was reluctant to create openings for reckless municipal extravagance, and could not 'see his way to a plan workable and equitable', experience having taught him to question whether Radical panaceas could yield the dramatic results which many fervently desired.[131] In this respect Gladstone's instincts were echoed by the depleted chorus of Whig landlords (including Granville, Kimberley,

---

* 27 November 1879. 'I freely own that compulsory expropriation is a thing which for an adequate public object is in itself admissible and so far sound in principle.' *Midlothian Speeches 1879*, 2nd ed. (Leicester, 1971) p. 102.

and Spencer) who experienced no difficulty in accepting Irish Land Purchase in 1886, but who had been 'startled and perturbed' hitherto by Chamberlain's 'hazy' and 'impracticable' allotments policy.[132] Nevertheless, Gladstone also recognized that prompt action was necessary to relieve the suffering endured by a large portion of the rural population. He lacked sympathy for outraged landlords who protested that Chamberlain wished to humble the aristocracy by engineering a social revolution in the countryside. The electors of Midlothian were even informed by Gladstone that he would be 'very glad indeed' if Chamberlain's ideas could be squeezed effectively into an 'efficient' legislative format.[133]

Gladstone's attitude towards the allotments scheme had become distinctly encouraging. When Parliament reassembled in January 1886, he utilized the opening day of the session to express his profound desire to alleviate the plight of the agricultural labourer. Yet it would be incorrect to assume that Gladstone's subsequent adoption of the Collings motion represented nothing more substantial than a public conversion to the policy of 'three acres and a cow'. In reality, the decision signified that a decisive shift of opinion within the party had taken place, and that the leader voluntarily accepted this as an established fact. An alert Duke of Argyll immediately pointed out to Gladstone that 'the parliamentary prominence which you give to a mere nostrum of the Radicals, distinctly outside your own programme, marks a decided patronage on your part of the Radical section as against the reasonable Liberals'.[134] Although the motion ostensibly camouflaged widening cracks concerning Irish policy, the party managers must have foreseen that the choice of subject matter could not possibly serve to muster a full complement of Liberals in the division lobby. At Gladstone's insistence support of the Collings motion was made mandatory upon all Liberal members. Anguished Whigs recognized that the 'sending out of a Whip in its favour was a fearful blow at the Moderate Party'.[135] The Chief Whip was so disenchanted with Gladstone's Irish policy that he made little effort to 'keep the men together',[136] a crucial factor which accounts for the unusually large number of Liberals who were absent unpaired (half of whom did vote eventually for the Home Rule bill). Grosvenor's slackness also eased the painful duty which awaited the followers of Hartington and Goschen. Those who were hostile to both the terms of the amendment and Gladstone's ulterior motives had no honourable alternative but to signify their withdrawal from the party by voting to keep the Conservatives in office.

Thus Chamberlain's endeavours to pledge candidates to the 'unauthorized' allotments policy produced unexpectedly rapid results. Neither he nor the 27 Radical members who had attended the annual meeting of the Allotments Association on 10 January could rationally have hoped to make such progress towards the 'practical application of the doctrines we have preached' before the month had ended. Shortly afterwards the council of the Free Land League, representing a further 62 Liberal members, had urged Gladstone to embark upon a scheme of land reform.[137] So effectively had these land reformers permeated the party that Gladstone deliberately chose to sacrifice the support of the moderate faction by selecting an amendment which was overtly designed to neutralize the suspicions of Radicals concerning his Irish intentions.

However, Chamberlain's rising expectations met with an almost instantaneous rebuff. Until his resignation in March, he laboured continually at the formidable task of constructing a bill to establish parish, district, and county councils. But this vital work excited little interest in the minds of other cabinet ministers, and in one telling sentence written for posterity Chamberlain revealed how deeply insulted he had felt at this apparent betrayal. 'No instructions whatever were given me as to details and as the Bill was never submitted to the Cabinet no judgement was ever pronounced on any of its intended provisions.'[138] Gladstone's failure to utilize the talents and energies of Chamberlain was referred to by Hammond as 'one of the greatest mistakes of his life'.[139] On the other hand, Gladstone surely had reason to suspect that Chamberlain wished to encourage dissension in the cabinet by producing a local government scheme as the alternative to his own proposals for Irish Home Rule. In retrospect Harcourt maintained that the 'presentation of a large plan of Local Government in Great Britain [had] constituted a leading feature in the programme of the Government'. He also claimed that nothing was accomplished solely because Chamberlain had, from the outset, been bent on destroying the ministry.[140]

Yet Chamberlain, too, had grounds for believing that in his anxiety to delay a fully comprehensive measure, Gladstone had betrayed a desire to settle the question of London government in isolation.[141] Gladstone's neglect of local government and his obsession with Home Rule gave Chamberlain a legitimate grievance. The attempt to reduce the salary of the Parliamentary Secretary to the Local Government Board by £300 was interpreted as a sign that Gladstone attached little importance to the work of the Board and did not appreciate the significance of Collings' special relationship with the agricultural labourers.[142] It was no consolation to Chamberlain to learn that a similar reduction in salary had already been inflicted upon Collings' counterpart at the Board of Trade. The insult to Henry Broadhurst (the first labour member ever to attain ministerial rank) would actually have been far more scandalous had he not been promptly transferred to the Home Office. Eventually, the place vacated by Broadhurst was filled by C. T. D. Acland, the son of an old friend from Gladstone's Oxford days, on conditions which were accepted without demur by his cabinet chief (Mundella).[143] Chamberlain and Collings reacted otherwise, and in the face of vigorous protests Gladstone was forced against his will to restore this salary to its original level.

Unfortunately, the solution to this unhappy episode did not eliminate the basic source of friction. Gladstone's impetuous recall of Henry Thring (the senior parliamentary draftsman) from duties with the committee on local government, in order to draw up the Home Rule bill, infuriated Chamberlain to a degree which Dilke was hardly able to placate.[144] Progress on the local government scheme virtually ceased at the beginning of March, and after the resignation of Chamberlain and Collings, Gladstone revealed no desire to complete the task. Samuel Whitbread, the influential but unambitious member for Bedford, was offered the vacant cabinet post on the understanding that 'labour would not be expected of him'.[145] Similar conditions were then imposed upon James Stansfeld, who returned to the post he had relinquished 12 years earlier despite his concurrence with Chamberlain that the party would 'suffer some loss' in the new county constituencies 'unless before another election you could do something to shew them that their interests had not been altogether postponed to the treatment of the Irish question'.[146] But the ageing Stansfeld, who had never forgiven Gladstone for reducing him to the ranks in 1880, lacked the qualities which made Chamberlain powerful, and could not pretend to have been hauled out of retirement to serve some great purpose. In any case, the preparation of local government legislation mattered less to him than the outcome of his private crusade to repeal the Contagious Diseases Acts. One odd symptom of the inferior status accorded to a weak stop-gap minister was Stansfeld's inability to thwart Gladstone's curiously persistent efforts to pare away the salary of the Parliamentary Secretary. Collings was replaced in April by William Borlase, member for Mid-Cornwall, a novice who was so gratified by Gladstone's solicitations that he willingly accepted parsimonious terms.[147] Five weeks elapsed before Stansfeld discovered the existence of this surreptitious arrangement – or could pluck up the courage to protest. He then wrote that 'the proposed reduction excites considerable feeling of dissatisfaction' within the Department, and complained that he himself had not even received an official statement of Gladstone's intentions.[148] Stansfeld requested a private meeting, but could not persuade Gladstone to yield on this trivial matter; still less was he capable of resisting a premier who insisted on giving absolute priority to Irish Home Rule, and then brazenly imposed upon the head of the Local Government Board his preference for registration reform over a local government measure.[149]

Many Radicals shared Stansfeld's distaste for Gladstone's dictatorial methods, and questioned the expediency of jettisoning every item of the government's domestic programme to meet the necessities of the Irish case. Indeed, an uncomfortably large and intrepid band of loyal Gladstonians claimed that Irish reform ought to be shelved temporarily to make way for other equally essential legislation. Such aggrieved politicians clung to the persuasive argument that if 'the voice of Ireland . . . constituted a demand which no statesman could ignore, was not the voice of the English electorate . . . prior in urgency to a claim never yet put before a single English constituency or swaying a single English vote?[150] Naturally the pleas of discontented members, who had no intention of turning Unionist, caused intense disquiet in the government, since it was imperative to keep the Home Rule ranks intact. In contrast, the cabinet could afford to ignore the protests of renegades like Chamberlain, although he obviously possessed the most unimpeachable title to feel affronted by the absence of any real initiative for social reform. His local government plan did not reach the cabinet room. The allotments bill (which Collings had introduced before the change of government) foundered during the second reading debate on 31 March, because Harcourt's brief words of commendation were not matched by the provision of necessary facilities in the official timetable.[151] Nor was any progress achieved on the subject of free education. In October Chamberlain had been promised a committee,[152] but the late Conservative government had established in the meantime the Cross Commission of enquiry into the working of the Education Acts, and this debarred Gladstone from fulfilling his pledge. Hence when H. P. Cobb (Rugby) enquired whether the Liberal government intended to implement the policy of free elementary education during the current session, he was informed by the Vice-President of the Council (Sir Lyon Playfair) that the matter could not be resolved until the report of the Royal Commission was printed.[153] This hackneyed statement of the government position was accepted by Chamberlain since it also precluded Voluntaryists from disturbing the *status quo*. Presumably, it was he who persuaded Collings to withdraw the free education motion which the latter had intended to move in the House.[154]

The sacrifice of much valuable domestic legislation to meet the exigencies of Irish Home Rule was perhaps inescapable, whatever the pious intentions and pledges of both the government and its supporters. 'It was quite certain', Morley later wrote in exculpation, 'that if the new plan were not at once propounded, no other public business would have much chance.'[155] Nevertheless, the validity of this contention was undermined by the success of one singularly controversial measure. The crofters' bill was a particularly significant exception to Morley's rule because it did not enjoy an easy passage through the Commons. The government came under heavy fire from those who wished to extend the scope of the bill until it virtually conformed to the recommendations made by the Napier Commission in 1883. This point was eventually conceded, but 10 Radicals still took the extreme step of dividing against the third reading, and received the support of 38 dissatisfied Irishmen and of 4 independent Crofters.[156] The government had embarked upon a most hazardous, time-consuming, and apparently thankless task instead of venturing forth with some of Chamberlain's attractive 'unauthorized' schemes. This choice can be explained partly by the appalling plight of the impoverished Highlanders. But it should also be noted that the presence in the House of an independent group, who were pledged to secure the redress of crofter grievances (yet remained tantalizingly neutral on the Home Rule question), rendered legislative action a tactical as well as a social necessity.

Gladstone fully appreciated the importance of shepherding the Crofter members into the correct lobby when the momentous division eventually took place; the support of four of the five Crofters could conceivably be sufficient to tilt the balance in favour of the Home Rule bill. Hence, at Gladstone's instigation, this tiny group received the prompt attention of the government and were blessed with every facility at its disposal. The Secretary of State for Scotland (Trevelyan) was given leave to insist on obtaining precedence for the crofters' bill over all other government business apart from necessary finance. According to Gladstone it was 'a case to make hay while the sun shines'.[157] However, Trevelyan alone was expected to perform this task, since in February and March Gladstone was immersed in the preparation of his Irish bills. Without the determined pilotage of Trevelyan, the crofters' bill could never have reached the comparative security of Committee shortly before everything was swept from the parliamentary stage to accommodate the government of Ireland bill. Gladstone drew upon his knowledge of Peel's practice when repealing the Corn Laws and demanded 'while we have this big Irish business ahead, that no other important issue of a disturbing character should be raised'.[158] Although he referred specifically to foreign affairs, the caveat applied equally to schemes of a 'disturbing character' favoured by Chamberlain. To proceed with too much controversial legislation would distract attention from Ireland and would impede the progress of the Home Rule plan. Mundella's railway rates bill had already soured the minds of several Liberal railway directors, and their protests soon began to divide the party at a time when unity alone could sustain the great Irish experiment. Above all, it was vital to allay the Queen's mistrust of Liberal legislation, 'as the day is near at hand', Gladstone foretold, 'when we shall want all our strength to be used in that quarter for the great purpose of the present juncture'.[159]

This 'great purpose' was to be achieved only in part by the establishment of a Parliament in Dublin. The administration was technically defeated upon the government of Ireland bill, but it is important to recall that many Liberal Unionists were actually less hostile to the concept of an Irish Parliament than to Gladstone's forthcoming land purchase bill. Though lost in the furore aroused by its more dramatic precursor (and quietly withdrawn after the defeat of the government of Ireland bill), Land Purchase constituted an integral and indispensable ingredient in the Home Rule settlement contemplated by the cabinet. Chamberlain and Trevelyan decided to resign office primarily for this reason. They feared that a tedious and protracted debate was bound to ensue upon so complex and incomprehensible a subject, an eventuality which would monopolize government time at the expense of the 'unauthorized' programme. When Chamberlain had originally broached the matter of a Central Board, the likelihood of serious inconvenience and delay had clearly been foreseen. He had tried to obviate this danger by insisting that any full settlement of the land question should be reserved to an Irish Board once established, instead of being completed beforehand at Westminster. More specifically, Chamberlain had intended the Irish alone to shoulder the crippling financial responsibility for land purchase, whereas Gladstone now proposed to buy out the Irish landlords by appropriating British credit to the order of £50 millions spread over three years. With a sinking heart, Chamberlain realized that such an 'enormous and unprecedented' liability would provide Gladstone with an excuse to channel government funds away from measures of domestic social reform.[160] He also knew that this 'tremendous obligation' would have the effect of postponing any revision of the tax structure, since Gladstone left his Chancellor of the Exchequer in no doubt that the necessities of the Irish emergency required all financial innovations to be severely resisted:

I am morally certain that it is only by exerting *to the uttermost* our financial strength (not mainly by expenditure but as credit) on behalf of Ireland, that we can hope to sustain the burden of an adequate Land measure ... It is the Government alone which, by keeping up its purchasing power, can maintain the balance of the [land] market. One main and indispensable basis of that power is surplus of income over charge; and this, as the country would ill-endure additional taxation for the purpose, involves moderation of expenditure.[161]

Gladstone attached the utmost importance to the task of restoring confidence in the stability of government credit – to avoid 'shocking the monied world, and acting on the Funds'. In accordance with established financial canons, he was determined to prove that the strength of government securities was not dependent upon his capacity to raise additional revenues, and, perforce, he ruthlessly abandoned his plans to implement a major revision of the tax structure.[162] Hitherto, Gladstone had intended to impose additional burdens upon large estates by means of death duties, and so enable a benevolent Liberal government to provide a 'free breakfast table' for the poor. At the beginning of the previous year Chamberlain had learnt that only a minor detail concerning the scope of a graduated income tax distinguished Gladstone's views from his own.[163] But he soon became converted to Gladstone's (and Harcourt's) predisposition 'to tax property as distinct from income'. This readjustment was made possible by Gladstone's approval of the crucial principle of graduation during the course of a conversation with Chamberlain in August 1885. Chamberlain could then report with satisfaction that even the cautious Gladstone 'was convinced of its fairness and favoured a graduated House Tax'.[164]

Yet all hope of reaching an objective which had bulked large in the 'unauthorized' programme was subsequently dashed by Gladstone's pursuit of an abstract fiscal notion. From the moment he assumed office in 1886, Harcourt began to slay the dragon of rising expenditure with a relish which greatly discomfited the chiefs of the two military departments. Hence the Chancellor of the Exchequer produced a disappointing and innocuous Budget which neither remitted the burden of indirect taxation upon the poor nor imposed new financial obligations upon the rich. Such ruthless economizing had the effect of stultifying Chamberlain's endeavours to coax the government into taking up any of those vital Radical projects which required the expenditure of public funds. Little sympathy could be expected from a Chancellor who completely forgot all prior declarations in favour of the 'unauthorized' programme, and secretly confessed that he was 'very much afraid of opening the Exchequer door without seeing any means of closing it'.[165] Chamberlain was quick to point out, during the debate on the Irish land purchase bill, that the money for purchase 'if forthcoming, was perhaps as much, if not more, needed in England, where State aid to the agricultural and artisan poor was as persistently denied as to the Scottish crofters, all of whom were as deserving of it as the people of Ireland'.[166] The extension of credit by issuing more consols was not strictly comparable with direct public expenditure. Nevertheless, Chamberlain had calculated that the cost of free elementary education to the Exchequer amounted to a mere £1.6 millions each year.[167] It was galling for him to discover that the sum required to provide for a disaffected Irish minority could have been applied far more profitably to abolish school fees in loyal (and Liberal) England for a period of at least 30 years.

In the highly-charged atmosphere of April–May 1886 Chamberlain desperately strove to rally support, and attempted to organize his small though influential core of supporters by appointing W. S. Caine (member for Bradford) as Radical Unionist whip. Unfortunately, this belated effort to consolidate a distinctive Chamberlainite party was handicapped by a personal catastrophe. At the beginning of May Dilke unexpectedly announced that he could no longer co-operate with Chamberlain since he had decided to support the Home Rule bill. The reality beneath their lengthy and celebrated alliance was stripped bare in a short but heated exchange of letters. The pretence of total political loyalty was dropped, Dilke contending that they had long regarded each other as rivals – an assertion which Chamberlain did not trouble to repudiate with genuine conviction.[168] However, the ferocity of Chamberlain's onslaught in 1886 upon his former associates materially reduced the appeal of the 'unauthorized' programme and temporarily checked the forward impetus of Radicalism. When an embittered Chamberlain learnt that he was being forced to suffer the ignominy of personal ostracism, as well as endure the capricious postponement of many cherished projects, naturally he preferred to view Gladstone as the real agent of strife. He soon convinced himself that Gladstone had wilfully sacrificed the interests of the party during the winter of 1885–6 in order to resolve the political difficulties and further the personal ambitions of a weary but haughty veteran. Chamberlain deduced that Gladstone had cunningly declined to court unpopularity by offering concessions to Hartington, yet had remained equally determined to guard his pre-eminence by not surrendering the initiative to the Radicals. Chamberlain therefore concluded that Gladstone could only have regained the premiership on his own terms by raising the Irish question 'in a form which would throw every other subject into the background, [and] relieve him of the difficulty of choosing between the Unauthorized and the Authorized programmes'.[169] In other words, Gladstone had consciously sought to bolster his waning prestige by diverting attention from popular Radical policies, thus neutralizing the influence exerted by an over-powerful lieutenant.

In view of Chamberlain's jaundiced remarks, it is clearly necessary to ascertain Gladstone's real motives during December 1885. At Hawarden it was presumed that Dilke's controversial speech at the Eleusis Club (in which he argued that the Conservatives ought not to be removed from office) had been inspired by a resentful Chamberlain. Gladstone had sound reason to suspect that this fresh Radical ploy amounted to a thinly disguised attempt to force him into immediate retirement. Yet it is by no means certain that Herbert Gladstone echoed his father's sentiments when he rashly sought to check Chamberlain's ambitions by flying the notorious Hawarden 'kite'. This clumsy manoeuvre only added to the confusion and uncertainty which surrounded Gladstone's increasing entanglement in the meshes of the Home Rule controversy, and so inevitably lent some substance to Chamberlain's theories. Gladstone had done everything in his power to circumscribe the limits of the 'un-authorized' programme during the election campaign, and he could not pretend to have shown much enthusiasm for several of its details. He had warned Chamberlain that Radical domestic policy would come to naught were the party shortly to be confronted with in-escapable demands from Parnell, and had then informed his con-stituents that the 'magnitude of the subject ... will sweep into the shade for the moment all those subjects of ordinary legislation on which I or others have addressed you'.[170] In the circumstances, Gladstone's bland assurance that his suggestion was not intended to be 'captious and a mantrap' was taken by Chamberlain to mean precisely that.[171] Even the unimaginative Granville could see how Gladstone's outspoken determination to remain in politics only if circumstances in Ireland required his presence, placed him 'on the edge of a razor' manipulated by Parnell.[172] Gladstone's innermost desire to enjoy an exciting political future virtually demanded a deterioration in Anglo–Irish relations, an association doubly un-fortunate since it was certain to be detrimental to the interests of both Gladstone and Ireland.

These various factors, if not negligible, are scarcely conclusive evidence of duplicity on the part of Gladstone. It is essential to recall that the majority of Radicals were quite prepared to accept Irish Home Rule as a short-term alternative to the 'unauthorized' pro-gramme. Gladstone must, equally, have considered the possibility that some extremists would regard the new policy merely as a heaven-sent opportunity to demolish the existing structure of the Liberal party. Labouchere, who hitherto had systematically poisoned

Chamberlain's mind against Gladstone, quickly forgot his spiteful utterances and began to hold out the tantalizing vision of a party rebuilt according to Chamberlain's own specifications:

> The Whigs would be cleared out... We might have grandiose revolutions – giving cows to agriculturalists, and free breakfast tables to artisans. We should be against Tories, Whigs and Lords... There never was such an opportunity to establish a Radical party, and to carry all before it . . . Ireland is but a pawn in the game.[173]

However, Chamberlain instantly rejected this cynical assessment of the situation. Although he could account for the dubious strategy of the Hawarden kite and resent its implications, he did not fully understand the deeper perspective of the Irish case and so could not possibly appreciate the impact which this made upon Gladstone's consciousness. The precise moment when Gladstone became converted to Home Rule cannot be pinpointed, but his forebodings that Ireland would thrust aside all considerations of domestic policy certainly pre-dated the construction of the Radical programme in 1883. The history of his second administration exposed this pertinent fact as self-evident. By 1885 the rise of the Irish Nationalist party, coupled with the breakdown of a bi-partisan approach to Irish questions, demonstrated that Ireland could no longer be governed on harsh and traditional lines or subordinated to the parochial interests of the English parties. It was no longer within the power of any statesman, not even an individual so eminent as Gladstone, to halt the 'onward march of a nation'. His talents could only be used to educate public opinion as the Irish crisis drew inexorably to a climax. Whether Irish demands were met or rejected, whether Home Rule was conceded or repression resorted to, both the facts of the past and events in the future offered conclusive proof that Radical programmes were destined to be crushed between the upper and nether millstones of conciliation and coercion.

III

The Liberal Party
and Irish Home Rule

1. *The Fate of the Irish Legislation of 1886*

When Gladstone introduced the ambitious Irish legislation of 1886 he probably miscalculated the strong feeling of silent unease and frustration which this precipitate action aroused amongst his followers. Radicals who unreservedly accepted the necessity for a bold and immediate departure in the system of Irish government were placed in a cruel and inescapable dilemma. They were torn between a sincere desire to consider the two bills in a favourable light and a bitter realization that such impartiality would result in fatal consequences for a sweeping programme of domestic reform. Loyal supporters of the government therefore felt justified in imposing the most stringent conditions upon Gladstone in return for the extraordinary degree of self-denial expected of them. Every clause was subjected to minute scrutiny, and important modifications were demanded wherever the legislative criteria adopted by the Radical section were infringed. The ill-conceived proposal to confer a second chamber upon Ireland attracted much criticism, especially since it would be responsible only to a privileged, propertied, and restricted electorate, and could exercise a veto against decisions reached by the popular assembly. Fortunately, this commonly-held objection did not strike a blow at the fundamental concept enshrined in the Home Rule bill of a separate Parliament sitting in Dublin. Yet the body of Radical opinion in the constituencies, which remained unaffected by the novelty of this essential principle, was agitated by the implications of a secondary provision which sought to lavish public money upon Irish landlords. This far more serious prejudice against the indiscriminate use of British funds for the endowment of an undeserving class with the capital value of excessive rents (which were exacted from an impoverished tenantry) found immediate public expression. When Shaw-Lefevre sought to re-enter Parliament at the first by-election to be held subsequent to the introduction of the two measures, he was returned on condition that he voted against the odious land bill.[1] After addressing an important public meeting at Newcastle on the very same day (21 April), Spencer himself was able to testify to the prevailing state of opinion. He candidly admitted that a partisan audience had responded frigidly to his painstaking defence of the land scheme, even though it warmly and unanimously approved of the Home Rule bill.[2]

Chamberlain's explanatory speech to his constituents (21 April) indicates clearly that the motive for his resignation from the government stemmed from an aversion to the terms of the land bill, and in this he was at one with the mass of Radical electors. However, his demand for considerable alterations in the Home Rule bill, which alone could guarantee his unconditional support, alienated most of his former adherents. The importance which Chamberlain attached to the future status of the Irish representatives at Westminster was not then appreciated by those who were personally unconcerned with the intricacies of Parliamentary procedure and were quite oblivious of constitutional niceties. Hence, regard for the preservation of abstract notions of Imperial integrity and unity was, for the present, largely confined to alert and far-sighted members of Parliament. Pressure upon the government on this point took the form of constant and direct negotiation between Chamberlain and Gladstone prior to the division on the second reading. Once the cabinet were agreed that it would be necessary in the interests of fiscal unity to exclude the arrangement of customs and excise from surveillance by the Irish Parliament, total exclusion of the Irish members became very difficult to defend. To cope with this new situation the cabinet acceded to Gladstone's recommendation that the chief objections could be met either by the readmission of Irish representatives whenever it was deemed essential to alter the scale of general taxation, or through the creation of a Standing Committee to deal with matters beyond the competence of the Irish Parliament.[3] Expedients such as these fell far short of Chamberlain's wishes. He insisted upon retaining the mode of representation enshrined in the Act of Union, but the cabinet found it impossible to contemplate this drastic solution. Even the optimistic and indefatigable emissary, Labouchere, conceded that exclusion was a 'fundamental principle' in any Home Rule settlement.[4] The die was cast not by Gladstone, who seemed disposed to consider alternative proposals, but by colleagues who stubbornly refused to consider any compromise which might satisfy Chamberlain's demands. However ardently Gladstone desired to reach an agreement with the dissentient Liberals, he could not afford to risk any further secessions from a weakened cabinet.

The defeat of the Home Rule bill relieved the government from yet another hazard, one which threatened to bring it into open conflict with the Nationalist party. Gladstone had unwisely drafted the financial clauses without consulting Parnell, and, had the bill survived its second reading, it might well have foundered in Committee since Parnell strongly disputed the quota of Imperial taxation that was allocated to Ireland.[5] Thus, defeat in the crucial division, coupled with the prompt decision to dissolve Parliament, preserved the government intact and staved off difficulties from the Irish quarter.

These advantages were offset by the circumstances under which the general election of July 1886 was fought. The fact that Gladstone's Irish policy constituted the central – perhaps even the single – bone of contention, not only served to consolidate the spirit of intractability in the party, but also brought to the forefront serious differences of opinion within the government which had hitherto been confined to the cabinet room. As soon as the decision to dissolve had been reached, Spencer anxiously sought assurances from the premier that no alteration in the existing relationship between the land bill and the main measure was being contemplated. Spencer clearly feared that, regardless of the pending electoral verdict, the perplexing and pressing issue of land purchase would continue to divide the party and preoccupy its leaders. This supposition proved to be completely accurate. For several years to come the land question hypnotized the party leaders incessantly and locked them in fratricidal strife; it also tended to divert attention from domestic issues, and so could be held responsible for the continued deferment of a comprehensive Radical programme. Yet, at the same time, it can be seen that the unabated hostility of Radicals to a land settlement, reinforced by Gladstone's increasing sensitivity to public opinion, ultimately made an ambitious Radical programme indispensable. Irish land purchase found no place in the programme which was eventually adopted. In the eyes of those who were exhausted by the futility of the land question, the Newcastle programme emerged as the brand new set of clothes with which to cloak the Irish skeleton in the Liberal cupboard.

This skeleton haunted Liberals from the moment Spencer warned Gladstone that he would be unable to 'put land altogether in the shade' during the electoral fray.[6] Spencer fervently believed that land purchase was a vital and inseparable part of the government's Irish policy, and was evidently under the impression that Gladstone was now inclined to show a disconcerting readiness to defer to Radical prejudices, in spite of the misgivings which they shared. Gladstone found himself placed in an impossible situation. Spencer echoed the sentiments of the Chief Secretary (Morley) and of the influential aristocratic element in the cabinet, and, moreover, his status as a former Viceroy expressed to perfection the complete transformation in Liberal attitudes towards Ireland. The formation of a Home Rule government would not have been possible without the support of Spencer, and his presence in the cabinet acted as a steadfast beacon of reassurance to nervous Liberals in the stormy waters which encompassed them. On the other hand, Gladstone was acutely conscious that the groundswell of Radical opinion, intensified by a persistent hankering for more congenial reforms, was rising decisively against the land bill. Electoral considerations made Gladstone indisposed to allow a defence of the land bill to form a substantial part of his campaign oratory. In spite of an avowal of 'great confidence in the real strength of the argument for it', he was patently anxious to find an excuse to drop a policy which had become an electoral encumbrance. He maintained that a measure specifically designed to conciliate the landlords of Ireland and their counterparts in Britain had been treated with contempt, the concession merely being exploited as a convenient instrument with which to damage Home Rule. Such conduct rendered the whole position 'most cloudy and equivocal' and had consigned the land policy to the 'shade'. 'The bulk of the Home Rule subject, swollen by stiff contest,' Gladstone concluded, 'will make the method of *pari passu* handling (I think) impossible.'[7] Thenceforth it became obvious that Gladstone's prime objective was to convince hesitant electors that should they accept his Irish policy they would be committing themselves to nothing more than the principle of a legislative body in Dublin for the management of exclusively Irish affairs. 'Both our Bills are for the moment dead,' he roundly declared in Midlothian. 'Only one survival I think is certain, and that is the survival of the principle and policy of self-government for Ireland.'[8] In subsequent speeches at Manchester and Liverpool (25 and 28 June) Gladstone stressed that the problems of Ulster, the projected two orders, and the Irish members at Westminster, were matters of detail and hence of secondary importance. But land purchase was not accredited even with subsidiary value. Under the new formula the Home Rule bill remained open only to adjustment, whereas the very existence of the land bill was jeopardized. The value Gladstone attached to purchase as an integral part of his policy can be gauged by the readiness with which he conceded that the future of the project depended solely on the verdict of constituencies which were known already to be hostile. Even Spencer was forced to retreat from his entrenched position. At Bristol (23 June) he found it expedient to admit that the government was no longer bound by any obligation to proceed simultaneously with both bills. This momentary lapse enabled Gladstone to capitalize upon the catastrophic result of the elections by entreating Spencer to abandon a hopeless cause and defer to the judgement of the country. Spencer did not whole-heartedly subscribe to Gladstone's interpretation of public opinion, but eventually he was prevailed upon to concede that he would be satisfied 'as long as the Land question is settled before, after, or concurrently with Home Government for Ireland'.[9] This surrender enabled Gladstone, in his next public statement, to acknowledge explicitly, and without fear of contradiction, that 'the sentence which has gone forth for the severance of the two measures is irresistible, and that the twinship which has been for the time disastrous to the hopes of Ireland, exists no longer'.[10]

Contrary to expectations, this formal recantation did not resolve any of the difficulties which pervaded the question of Irish land purchase. The quiescence of electors who had performed their duty with a vengeance was, in reality, the signal for the outbreak of a prolonged series of heated disputes among ministers who had peremptorily been reduced to the status of private members. Leaders who were now no longer bound in honour to defend the policy of the cabinet were obliged to attend to the hopeless task of piecing together the incomplete fragments of a shattered land scheme in anticipation of an early return to office. The dramatic upheaval of 1886 has tended to obliterate the remarkable fact that for the Gladstonian party the end of the electoral contest opened up as many fissures as it sealed. D. A. Hamer rightly stresses that even after 1886 Gladstone's Irish policy was 'in constant danger of losing its coherence through the examination and discussion of detail', a conclusion which appears to qualify Hamer's main contention that Home Rule was generally conceived and manipulated as the 'substitute for system' which alone could restore discipline and purpose to Liberal politics.[11]

The surreptitious emergence of two heretical doctrines on the land policy alone rendered it highly unlikely that Ireland could ever command the exalted position indicated by Hamer. In the prevailing climate of uncertainty, statesmen who were sensitive to the political barometer not only doubted the wisdom of persevering with the employment of British credit, but also asked themselves whether it would actually prove necessary for Parliament to pass a Land Act at all. The possibilities of adopting a policy which would enable Parliament to wash its hands of land purchase and leave the question to the Dublin legislature and Irish resources were sufficient to divide the Liberal leaders into two hostile camps. It did not take Spencer and Morley long to discover that for quite separate reasons their tenacious faith in the future of the land bill was resisted strongly by the formidable combination of Gladstone and Harcourt. In his capacity as a Whig aristocrat, Spencer was influenced primarily by considerations of class interest. Although his language was cloaked in the apparel of public obligations due to the Irish landlords on account of earlier legislation, his ulterior motive was to avoid leaving a small and privileged class – however undeserving it might be – to the tender mercies of Michael Davitt and the Land League. Morley, too, appreciated this danger. But in the eyes of Spencer the land bill was the redeeming feature of the new policy, whereas Morley viewed it simply as the surety for a measure of Home Rule which would be substantial and not illusory. The latter did not believe that any effective form of devolution was possible unless Irishmen could rely upon British credit. The capacity of an untested Irish executive to raise its own funds was problematical, and in any case would be a poor and expensive substitute for the strength and security of consols. Ireland could ill-afford so heavy a financial burden at the commencement of her experiment in self-government.

The somewhat paradoxical co-operation between Spencer and Morley can also be attributed to the aversion each felt at being cast in the rôle of courtier of public favour. Neither the remote patrician who completely lacked oratorical prowess, nor the highly-strung plebeian who was inhibited by a refined intellect, deigned to pay heed to fickle currents of popular opinion. In contrast Harcourt and Gladstone were robust and inveterate political weathercocks. The former was equipped with a keen parliamentary eye for party advantage, whereas the latter was invested with the obligation as leader to 'maintain unaltered, in this great Irish crisis, my relation to the average of the party'.[12] Thus Harcourt deferred to the accumulating anti-landlord feeling in the party, and was at variance with Spencer concerning the duties incumbent upon the British government and the rights of the Irish landlords. Gladstone, on the other hand, clashed with Morley because he believed that unless popular dislike of the land bill was mollified, the Liberals would not obtain a majority at the next election, and hence there could be no Home Rule bill – effective or otherwise.

This incipient conflict suggests that reasons unconnected with a pious desire to heal the schism between Gladstonian and dissentient Liberals had prompted the cabinet to resign in July rather than face the new Parliament in August. A consideration which had preyed upon the minds of ministers was the fear that should they decide to continue in office they might then find themselves placed in the embarrassing predicament of being unable to agree upon an Irish policy.[13] Such dire forebodings speedily received ample justification.

Once Gladstone had departed for Bavaria in August, an impatient Harcourt could no longer be restrained from voicing his dislike of the land bill to attentive audiences in the Commons' tea room. During the closing stages of the debate on the Address he even ventured to repudiate in the chamber itself the very notion of purchase, and stoutly defended his high-handed behaviour by alleging that 'you never can or will have Home Rule *with* a Land Bill. You may perhaps have it without. The Land Bill did, and always will, kill the Home Rule measure.'[14] Those who objected to such contemptuous language reacted so feebly and cautiously that protest served only to emphasize the inherent weakness of their position. Morley and Spencer dared not retaliate in kind because they knew that in spite of the gulf that yawned between themselves and Harcourt, an 'unmistakable disclosure of divided opinion' would destroy the coherence and morale of a party already shaken by electoral disaster.[15] Nevertheless, experience of this preliminary skirmish plunged the Gladstonian leaders into gloom as they watched with trepidation the movement in favour of reunification coming rapidly to a head. In these fresh circumstances it was extremely difficult to withstand a general desire to re-examine the Home Rule policy, and consequently the leaders were faced with the prospect of a further bout of exacerbating internal feuds.

Chamberlain entered the Round Table Conference armed with the draft of a land purchase bill. This version pleased Harcourt because it did not 'to any considerable extent pledge British credit or require the raising of large sums of money',[16] but no more was heard of Chamberlain's plan once the reunion talks had broken down. However, Chamberlain's initiative did leave an immediate and indelible mark upon Gladstone. At the beginning of 1887 Gladstone despaired of being able to reconcile his desire for land purchase with the strong prejudices of his supporters. 'Individually, I do not at this moment see my way as to the construction of a new *Land Purchase Bill*,' he confessed. 'I do not know how to construct any Bill so good as our Bill *on its financial side*.'[17] This state of deadlock was miraculously broken three weeks later when Gladstone perused Chamberlain's memorandum and at last discovered the elusive formula for securing a complete reversal of Liberal land policy:

Chamberlain's plan for Irish Land appears to be in the highest degree comprehensive ... I feel indebted to him ... for the manner in which he has opened the very large question. Is it possible to frame a good scheme of Land Purchase *without any use whatever of Imperial Credit?* I confess to having received from his paper new lights upon this vital portion of the subject; and am almost prepared to answer in the affirmative the question I have just put.[18]

Gladstone reserved a final judgement until he had sought the counsel of financial 'experts', but characteristically became so excited by his unexpected discovery that he spurned the advice proffered by Treasury officials who (like Edward Hamilton) could not conceive how such a solution as Gladstone now contemplated was 'within the bounds even of his ingenuity'.[19] Consequently, although the use of British funds was for practical purposes formally banished from the Liberal creed at a dinner held in Gladstone's honour on 17 March, no clear alternative proposal was ever committed to paper for detailed investigation. This deliberate oversight naturally did not meet with the approval of Morley and Spencer. They were alarmed by the depth of the chasm which had opened up between themselves and Gladstone, especially since the change in official policy enabled Harcourt to hasten this geological process by publicly deriding the recently abandoned doctrine.[20] Through no conscious effort on his part Chamberlain had succeeded in driving a wedge between his former associates. His ideas had certainly been instrumental in securing a change of policy, but it would be incorrect to assume that Gladstone was influenced by a genuine desire to seek an accommodation with him. Though Chamberlain might have regarded the alteration as a concession to himself, Gladstone argued that it was 'in reality a concession to the verdict of the country at the Elections which went generally and violently against the use of Imperial Credit, so much so that it received I think a mortal stab'.[21]

At this critical juncture attention began to shift to other equally controversial aspects of Irish policy. But with respect to the central issue of land purchase the respite was only momentary, the passage of time proving to have no healing properties. The sores were again inflamed in the autumn of 1888 when an alternative measure was submitted to parliamentary scrutiny by the government. The Chief Secretary (Arthur Balfour) proposed to extend the operation of the Ashbourne Act of 1885 by providing a further £5 millions of public credit to enable the Irish tenants to acquire the freehold of their holdings. Few Liberals could tolerate such spasmodic and insufficient treatment of a complex problem. However, Morley was distressed by the possibility that certain unscrupulous colleagues (who now included Trevelyan) would be tempted to appease truculent back-bench Radicals by coupling their denunciation of the government plan with explicit declarations against the use of British credit – or indeed against land legislation in any shape or form. On more than one occasion Morley imagined that he was being hounded by leaders

who refused to defend an unpopular policy, and after reading
Spencer's Glasgow speech of 26 October he even thought that his
closest ally had joined the ranks of those who rode in hot pursuit.
Morley's tormentors wisely allowed the enraged victim to escape
when they realized that he might carry out his threat 'either to
proclaim my strong dissent – or to retire from the field'.[22] The
frontbench carefully avoided the delicate issue of financial support
by agreeing to concentrate upon the argument that remission of
accumulated arrears ought to take precedence over every other kind
of remedial legislation. However, treaties concluded at Westminster
did not extend to the constituencies, and Harcourt could not be
deterred from undertaking a forced march to Morley's Newcastle
citadel solely in order to denounce the expediency of land purchase.[23]

In 1890 the government introduced a more ambitious bill, pledging
a further £33 millions of British funds. Morley was aware that the
size of the sum made it yet more difficult to muzzle Harcourt, and
he entreated that intrepid warrior not to 'shut the door to purchase'
altogether. But to judge from letters penned furiously to *The Times*
and from Harcourt's equally combative speech in the House, this
plea fell on deaf ears. Harcourt was convinced that 'our people will
not have it at any price', and needed no further incentive to resist
the government measure with unabated intensity when it was re-
introduced in a November session.[24] Fortunately, an irreparable
breach between Gladstone and Harcourt on one side, and Spencer
and Morley on the other, could be avoided, since Liberal objections
hinged on factors apart from the large scale use of British credit.
The most important of these was the total absence from Balfour's
plan of any provision for local control over a most cumbersome
method of collecting capital repayments. The Conservatives did not
contemplate the establishment of either a representative network of
local authorities on the pattern recently introduced in England and
Scotland, or a central Irish land agency as contained in the original
Liberal bill. Such a serious omission made the British government
the immediate landlord of a host of individual tenants scattered
throughout Ireland, and inevitably created a situation fraught with
danger. Morley, in particular, considered that an Irish agency provided security without which the massive British investment was
placed at great financial risk. Since Gladstone had deliberately sought
to avoid this contingency in 1886, Morley felt able to provide assurances that both he and Spencer could join their colleagues in resisting
the government proposal with a clear conscience.[25]

Morley proceeded to denounce the lavish use of British funds as
strongly as did either Gladstone or Harcourt. But it was a strange
interpretation of harmony that enabled him to keep in tune with

Gladstone, who considered the pledging of public money to be a flagrant violation of the electoral judgement, or with Harcourt, who fulminated against any endowment of landlordism. Nevertheless, although the bill was constantly – if not consistently – opposed until its passage into law, one vital fact did not escape the notice of the reluctant bedfellows on the opposition frontbench. Whatever the shortcomings of the government measure, its very existence helped to relieve of considerable difficulties those who were committed one way or the other on the subject of purchase in the event of a Liberal return to office. An incomplete land settlement would assuredly obstruct the passage of a second Home Rule bill (as it had the first) and so would delay the implementation of a Radical programme. By 1890 the temptation to shelve the question of Irish land had become very great, even though some of the younger Liberals led by R. B. Haldane protested that a policy which was in itself commendable ought not to be sacrificed merely to placate disgruntled Radicals. Sir Edward Grey joined Haldane in a public demonstration of dissent from the stratagem of sabotaging otherwise appropriate Conservative legislation. He justly accused his own leaders of attempting to obtain all the benefits of a Conservative land bill (in so far as it paved the way for Home Rule), and yet trying simultaneously to appropriate all the credit for having resisted unpopular legislation.[26] The two malcontents threatened party unity by voting in support of the bills of 1888 and 1890–1, but no other Liberals joined this tiny 'cave'. Any possibility of further disruption rapidly receded when it became apparent that the final instalment of Conservative land legislation had effectively dispatched that troublesome issue from the parliamentary arena.

This convenient method of escape from one major difficulty did not set the Liberal leaders free to concentrate upon the more agreeable task of constructing a domestic programme, because great confusion still surrounded the details of their Home Rule policy. They had hitherto been quite unable to solve the puzzle of Irish representation at Westminster, and no conceivable action on the part of the government could lighten a dead weight which constituted the most unmanageable package in the Liberal burden. The formula of 1886 had been exclusion subject to certain contingencies. But immediately after the general election Gladstone informed Harcourt that in no circumstances would he permit his preconceived notions or personal feelings to stand between Ireland and a genuine settlement, or between faithful Gladstonians and the reunification of the party.[27] Harcourt interpreted this statement literally, and at the Round Table Conference was speedily converted to Chamberlain's heretical view on the expediency of retention in full.[28] Such waywardness brought Harcourt into conflict with Morley, who was suspicious of Chamberlain's motives and strongly believed that any deviation from the original proposal would be manufactured into an excuse for 'putting Ireland off with the mischief of a sham Parliament'.[29] Gladstone now found it necessary to intervene before an unseemly quarrel broke out between his two principal lieutenants. His tender concern for Morley's troubled conscience was nicely balanced against the weight of Harcourt's incessant cajolery, but external considerations eventually forced Gladstone to support Harcourt's claim that public overtures to the Liberal Unionists ought to be made. Gladstone appreciated fully the possibility that if he stubbornly refrained from any conciliatory gesture towards the dissentients, he and his following might then be branded – not as helpless and unwilling participants in the dispute – but as the very instruments of faction.

The first practical step towards a revision of the authorized Home Rule text was taken when Gladstone suggested at Swansea (during a tour of South Wales in June 1887) that the provisional retention of Irish members could become an acceptable alternative to total exclusion. Morley was 'well satisfied' with this compromise since Gladstone had been careful to defer a conclusive judgement to a more propitious and appropriate occasion. Nevertheless, he still believed that there was 'something childish in this hurry about details, when we have not yet got the constituencies to accept the principle', and sensed that concessions really amounted to a public admission that the laboriously prepared bill of 1886 was imperfect.[30] Undue readiness to consider alternative models raised a host of fresh hazards. It became very difficult to refuse to elaborate further and avoid any precise commitments; it was quite impossible to curb public curiosity and confine popular debate to manageable proportions; and, above all, the bleak prospect of heightened internal tensions and divisions became more likely. Morley was extremely anxious to convince Gladstone that such considerations made it unwise to quench the insatiable thirst of electors with further revelations of definitive policies, and argued that it would be absolutely necessary to 'steer clear of details about Home Rule'. A speedy decision became essential when Gladstone announced that he intended to speak on Home Rule at an important meeting of the N.L.F. on 19 October. Morley visited Hawarden a few days beforehand, and, emboldened by Harcourt's active concurrence, begged his leader to tell the expectant delegates 'no more about modification'.[31] This evidently produced the desired effect since Gladstone eschewed details at Nottingham and categorically refused to bind the party to any particular framework. But the handwork of Swansea could not be undone; in Morley's words the new formula 'opened just as many new difficulties as it closed old ones'.[32]

Foremost among these new difficulties was the stimulus given to the doctrine of federalism, or 'Home Rule all round'. Considerations of equity and consistency appeared to demand that retention of the Irish members should be accompanied by the concession of local parliaments to other constituent parts of the United Kingdom. Support for the federal principle was generally confined to Scotland and Wales, nations which had grown restive as a result of their inferior numerical status at Westminster. Few Englishmen genuinely sympathized with this expression of national aspirations, and even among Liberal leaders the usual reaction was negative and derisory. Morley's credentials as a Home Ruler were impeccable, yet he could with perfect sincerity repudiate the concept of a subordinate Scottish Parliament. In his view Ireland was an altogether exceptional case, and certainly ought not to be treated as a prototype for the whole of the United Kingdom. He, Harcourt, and Spencer, were not prepared to have their minds 'reconstructed' on a federal basis. The general response of English Liberals was accurately reflected in Morley's public speeches and private correspondence, where he emphasized that he remained 'dead against breaking up the old British Parliament as it was before the Irish Union'.[33]

Scottish representatives were harassed by their constituents on the issue and therefore reacted quite differently. A Scottish Home Rule Association had been formed shortly after the introduction of the first Home Rule bill, and included on the executive committee were several Gladstonian M.P.s. At the close of 1886 Sir Henry Campbell-Bannerman confidently dismissed the movement as an 'inactive volcano'.[34] But the apparently extinct volcano soon erupted with great force. In October 1887 the Scottish Liberal Association adopted a Scottish Home Rule resolution during its annual conference at Castle Douglas.[35] This victory was consolidated in Parliament by the eloquence and persistence of Dr G. B. Clark (Caithness). By 1889 he had succeeded in securing the votes of a substantial minority of backbench Scottish Liberals on behalf of the first of his annual motions on the subject of a national Parliament.[36] However, all hope of further progress ended in frustration because in Edward Marjoribanks (the Scottish whip) Clark found a powerful and relentless critic. The patent lack of unanimity among Scottish Liberals placed Campbell-Bannerman and others who were sympathetic to federalism in an invidious dilemma.[37] Bold initiatives might succeed in shepherding energetic Scottish patriots (who were not all Gladstonians) into the Liberal fold, but would surely arouse the wrath of distant English colleagues. How to suppress a heresy which derived its strength from the steady and spontaneous assertion of national feeling was a question which Morley and Harcourt prudently declined to answer.

In so far as Gladstone (in his capacity as member for Midlothian) addressed himself to this burning topic, his meaning was obscure and ambiguous. At first he did not think that Scotsmen would 'largely bite at such a bait as a cut and dried plan of Home Rule. My correspondence, which is large, in no way leads me to expect it.'[38] However, his attitude soon changed when favoured correspondents began to argue that Liberal Unionism in Scotland could be destroyed if only he would utter some guarded words of encouragement to Scottish Home Rulers.[39] But although Gladstone successfully overcame any lingering scruples against having a federal solution thrust upon him, he still dared not countenance the movement openly. In April 1889 he refused to vote in favour of Clark's 'abstract' Scottish Home Rule motion, and at the instigation of Marjoribanks he subsequently declined a request to receive a delegation on the subject.[40] Hence, no unequivocal statement was ever extracted from Gladstone, in spite of the pressure which from 1889 began to be exerted by English members who sat for Scottish constituencies. H. H. Asquith threw the entire party into disarray by publicly challenging the leaders to announce their Home Rule plan, perhaps wishing to convince the electors of East Fife that even a London barrister could embrace the cult of Scottish patriotism.[41] Hugh Childers was another English refugee (from Pontefract) who betrayed an anxiety to pacify mutinous Edinburgh constituents, the source of conflict in this case being the member's continued failure to support Scottish disestablishment. As befitting a retired senior minister, Childers made his views known to Gladstone only through the medium of private correspondence, and so created less havoc.[42] But although their tactics were at variance, Childers and Asquith shared a common objective, *viz.* to persuade Gladstone to ratify the federalist demand.

The most effective agent of this strategy was Rosebery. It was natural that the supreme champion of Scottish rights should express sympathy for a movement which stressed national claims, especially since the principle of local autonomy was so obviously assimilable with the greater cause with which Rosebery was closely identified. In the eyes of Ronald Munro-Ferguson, his private secretary and factotum on the Imperial Federation League, the creation of subordinate national assemblies was 'an Imperial and not just a local matter'.[43] The liberation of the Westminster Parliament from purely domestic concerns was regarded as the first stage in the quest for Imperial Federation. Hence, throughout 1889, Rosebery exerted tremendous pressure upon Gladstone in an attempt to secure a revision of the Home Rule bill.[44] These federalist utterances inevitably provoked the hostility of English colleagues. Harcourt promptly condemned Rosebery's flirtation with Scottish Home Rule as 'a practical repudiation of the Gladstonian gospel', and hastened to reach a 'definite understanding' with Morley concerning the grounds upon which the two men would be able to 'put our foot down'.[45] Thus Gladstone was suddenly faced with urgent demands for a conference on the Home Rule policy in order to place on record the authorized edition of 1889. Unfortunately, Rosebery was confident that any revision would be worked out upon federal principles, whereas Harcourt and Morley were determined to confront Rosebery – and Gladstone – with an ultimatum couched in contradictory language.

Gladstone did not find it difficult to resist Rosebery's rather extravagant pleas for either the appointment of a formal committee to re-examine the bill of 1886, or the publication of a new version as a definitive document. The one claim was peremptorily dismissed as 'a devolution of my own responsibility', and the other was neatly countered by the statement that 'final decisions' on Home Rule policy could only be made 'in the light of *contemporary* public opinion'.[46] This convincing reply was not sufficient to protect Gladstone's status as the sole arbiter of Home Rule policy. Restive and refractory colleagues persisted in their demands for consultations, and in these menacing circumstances Gladstone deemed it prudent to relax so authoritarian a concept of sovereignty. Informal discussions could safely be encouraged once he had ascertained that no one except the 'arch-priest of plans' (Rosebery) seemed to favour the summary publication of any material changes of policy which might emerge from the enquiry.

The first conference since the 1886 election wholly devoted to an evaluation of the Home Rule policy was held at Hawarden in October 1889. Gladstone's original purpose had been to clarify for the benefit of colleagues Parnell's reaction to the idea of revision, and to consider whether a fresh agreement with the Nationalists could be reached. However, when autumn came the ostensible reason for summoning a special meeting was no longer relevant. Gladstone had written to Parnell in August inviting him to visit Hawarden at an early date, but the inscrutable Irishman had characteristically failed to reply, and a personal exchange of views did not in fact take place until the middle of December.[47] Nevertheless, Parnell's perverse behaviour did not destroy the utility of the Hawarden conference, since his inexplicable silence came to be regarded by Gladstone as far less embarrassing and inconvenient than the volubility of those who clamoured for further information. Such damaging public criticism culminated in an article penned by a malevolent back-bencher, L. Atherley-Jones,[48] and his stinging commentary on the demoralizing consequences of reticence probably emboldened Gladstone to grasp the painful nettle of federalism.

When the conference opened, Gladstone announced that he now favoured a limitation of Irish voting rights, though not an equivalent reduction in the number of representatives at Westminster.[49] The quartet of Granville, Harcourt, Morley, and the Marquess of Ripon, listened to this statement with apprehension, fully realizing that a decision to admit Irish members on none but imperial topics would cause rejoicing in the Scottish Home Rule camp at a most critical juncture. In November the Scottish Liberal Association was scheduled to discuss a prominent resolution on this very subject, and unless firm resistance was now offered, Rosebery would surely exploit his position as president of the Association by committing his country-men to a federal solution.[50] Rosebery might even have avoided subsequent recriminations by carrying the Scottish case for federation at Hawarden, but he was a conspicuous absentee, probably remaining aloof because his plea for detailed revision had been rejected. Consequently, Gladstone alone was required to submit to an inquisition mounted by unsympathetic English colleagues. A few hours of interrogation sufficed to purge him of federalist sins, and he soon confessed a preference for 'limitation not of voting but of numbers'.[51] This unstable compromise ultimately gave satisfaction to neither faction, though when Rosebery received Gladstone's explanatory letter he thought that he had scored a splendid victory. He mis-interpreted Gladstone's complete change of mind as meaning that representation was to be reduced for all purposes, and strangely failed to notice that in his absence the progress of federalist logic had been decisively checked.[52]

This fascination for the mathematics of Irish representation was a perilous act of self-indulgence. No firm decision could possibly be reached until the moment for legislative action arrived, an elemen-tary truth which appeared to escape some leading politicians when the situation was reviewed in the aftermath of the Hawarden conference. A short chapter of accidents soon revealed how com-pletely they had failed to solve the one really vital and perplexing question – the extent to which representatives of one nation were entitled to meddle in the domestic affairs of another. The process of enlightenment commenced with a violent outburst from Harcourt, the most pugnacious champion of retention in full. He was infuriated by the discovery that his colleagues had cunningly waited until he had left Hawarden before entering into a compact to reduce Irish representation at Westminster. As the injured party, Harcourt was perfectly justified in proceeding to expose with brutal force the existence of utterly confused motives and conflicting counsels among his deceivers. He expounded at great length the view that it would be impossible to conceive of a device more inconsistent or open to ridicule than that which had been concocted at Hawarden.[53] Such torrents of eloquence and remorseless logic contrasted starkly with Morley's feeble defence of an irrational and electorally ruinous contrivance. The latter feared that unless the influence exerted by Irish members over non-Irish legislation was curtailed, Parliament would be sorely tempted to intervene reciprocally in specifically Irish affairs.[54] This debate took a most unusual form, both sides struggling to capture the soul of Spencer (who had not been present at Hawarden). But although Harcourt quickly emerged victorious, his celebrations were abruptly forestalled by Gladstone, who added to the turmoil by resuscitating the notion that reversion to a policy of total exclusion ought not to be discounted as a fourth possibility.[55]

Harcourt retained sufficient presence of mind to realize that for the time being it might be wiser to tolerate these incompatible personal preferences rather than risk pressing the controversy to a fatal conclusion. He could even view the proliferation of discordant ideas with grim satisfaction, since further evidence of disunity only strengthened his case for the exercise of the utmost reserve and patience. He had arrived at Hawarden determined to impress upon his fellow guests the advisability of not settling troublesome details – even in private – until after they had formed a Home Rule government. In the present disorganized state of party leadership, Harcourt could plausibly argue that 'it would be the height of folly to embark on treacherous ground on which the enemy desires to engage us'.[56] But no heady dose of Malwood rhetoric was, in fact, required to convince Harcourt's colleagues that it would be madness to disclose additional information to the public. All were whole-heartedly agreed that the watchword of the moment was silence upon disputed points. Indeed, as soon as the conference ended Gladstone and Harcourt departed (for Southport and Caernarvon respectively) in order to put this necessary but unedifying doctrine into practice. However, no one took the precaution of forewarning Spencer of this development, and in an injudicious speech at Stockton on the following day (24 October) he completely wrecked a carefully contrived strategy. Harcourt's equanimity dissolved in an instant when he learnt of Spencer's transgression. He fired off a battery of letters in defence of the Hawarden formula, and met no deafening salvoes in return. 'On the subject of reticence, I agree with you to the *nth*,'

Gladstone replied. 'For myself I shall claim and hold to a rollicking liberty of choice.'[57]

Accusing fingers were pointed at the hapless orator who had only wished to demonstrate that though the party already possessed a practical policy, the principle of Home Rule could be carried out in several ways. Unfortunately, such a taxing dialectical exercise was quite beyond Spencer's capabilities. Hence he had panicked, becoming 'rather *churned*' when he had trodden on the 'thinnest of ice, close to questions on which we colleagues might differ'.[58] Spencer lamely attempted to explain away a speech in which he had argued the absurdity of discussing details until the electorate was fully converted to the principle, and then had foolishly proceeded to flounder among the various illogical modes of tackling the problem of Irish representation. Only a leader so lacking in political sagacity could have fallen headlong into the rather obvious trap of being 'nettled' in public 'at the constant jibes of our opponents as to our having no policy'. All the perils foreseen by Harcourt were borne out by this indiscretion, the speech being immediately 'pulled to pieces by opponents who rejoice to get a new thing to worry'. This chastening experience enabled Spencer to draw the appropriate conclusion. 'I shall not repeat the experiment,' Gladstone was assured. 'What I did proves how right you ... have been to refuse going into details.'[59]

With a hushed amen the incident was closed so far as the Liberal hierarchy was concerned. Henceforth a conspiracy of silence was rigidly observed. For just twelve months Gladstone was liberated from the shackles of Home Rule clauses; fortune smiled upon the party, and the flowing by-election tide promised at no distant date to surge onwards to ultimate victory. Gladstone's remarkable effrontery during a much publicized Midlothian campaign in 1890 bore eloquent testimony to the success of the new strategy. On 27 October he boldly asserted that there existed no valid reason why he should reveal any solution to the problem of Irish representation until after his return to office – and then only when the government was ready with a fresh bill. According to his calculations, nearly four years might elapse before the country need be offered the fullest information.

However, this era of deceptive tranquillity could not last indefinitely. In fact, the storm broke within a month of Gladstone's complacent speech, when Parnell emerged discredited but impenitent from the drama of the divorce court. The fanaticism and pride of one man transformed the adverse verdict into a source of acute anxiety for the Liberal party. Indeed, Gladstone might never have been drawn into the struggle which ensued within the Nationalist ranks had not Parnell cunningly sought to divert attention from a consideration of his personal fitness for leadership to that of Liberal good faith. At the end of November 1890 Parnell revealed his true intentions by publishing a lengthy manifesto which gave *inter alia* a highly idiosyncratic version of his conversation with Gladstone in the previous year. Two serious charges were levelled at the Liberal leader. Firstly, Parnell alleged that Gladstone intended neither to allow the Irish legislature to solve the agrarian difficulty, nor to force an unpopular land bill upon a reluctant party at Westminster. Secondly, he claimed that Gladstone and his colleagues had already decided unanimously to reduce Irish representation to a meagre 32. Only one conclusion could be drawn from this juxtaposition of evidence: 'it would be the height of madness for any Irish leader to imitate Grattan's example and consent to disband the army which had cleared the way to victory'.[60]

In spite – or because of – these pointed allegations, the Liberal leaders showed no disposition to deviate from their agreed strategy by divulging Home Rule details or by entering into specific pledges. During a hectic winter of innumerable intrigues, they expressed a profound aversion to listening to any overtures which sprang from a tainted and untrustworthy source, or (in Harcourt's pithy phraseology) to 'buying off this Gaul of Eltham with pledges'.[61] On three separate occasions the Irish emerged from the turmoil of Committee Room Fifteen to plead for assurances on the nature of a Home Rule settlement. But the Liberal leaders refused to negotiate until the Irish had settled the question of the chairmanship, and resolved it, Liberals darkly implied, in a sense adverse to Parnell's interests. Yet, even after this exacting precondition had been met, Gladstone did not relish making concessions to those Nationalists who at great personal sacrifice had striven hard to preserve the alliance between the two parties; giving definite pledges to proven Irish friends continued to be as distasteful a practice as attempting to appease the sworn Parnellite foe. Only when they found themselves in dire straits did the ungracious Liberals seek refuge in actual promises. Morley was quick to appreciate how completely the credit and credibility of the anti-Parnellite faction depended upon their ability to extract formal undertakings. Unless these were offered, influential non-combatants like John Dillon and William O'Brien would be alienated irretrievably, thus enabling a resourceful Parnell to become 'practically master of a demoralized party'.[62]

The 'guarantees' published in February 1891 bore only a tenuous relation to the controversies provoked by Parnell's manifesto. Scant attention was paid to the demands of a deposed leader who for purely selfish ends ruthlessly exploited long standing divisions within the Liberal party. Nationalists who genuinely wished to protect the interests of their country merely sought Gladstone's word that an alien police force would be disarmed and eventually disbanded, and that a final settlement of the land question would somehow be reached. On both these points they received full satisfaction. But an innocuous document which conspicuously avoided any reference to the troublesome issues of British credit and future Irish representation excited little interest outside Ireland. Gladstone subsequently discouraged prying minds by resolutely declining to 'alter a comma'. He shared Harcourt's view that the 'most serious mischief' arising from Parnell's vindictive disclosures was not the insinuation that the Liberal party intended to play Ireland false, but the 'very injurious effect' which such allegations would undoubtedly have upon Liberal opinion in Britain.[63] Parnell had deliberately revived several apprehensions which had previously lain dormant. These included the bogy of British subsidies to Irish landlords, the threatened erosion of Imperial sovereignty, and the temptation facing Irishmen to meddle in affairs at Westminster to which they no longer possessed a legitimate title. He also added weight to the more damaging charge that Gladstone had wilfully concealed unpalatable intentions from an electorate to which he outwardly exhibited such marked deference.

Unionist spokesmen promptly seized the weapons gratuitously provided by Parnell to turn the flank of their opponents. In the halcyon days of 1890 Liberals had found it easy to meet criticism with the glib statement that the moment for Home Rule revelations was inopportune. But this useful strategy could not be continued once an estranged Parnell had split the Nationalist party into warring factions. Nothing could prevent the 28 Parnellites from launching fresh diatribes against Gladstone whenever these appeared to serve the destructive cause which their frenzied chief had espoused. The subtle change which occurred in the outlook of the anti-Parnellite majority was, however, a far more serious proposition. Those 50 Irishmen who loyally adhered to the Liberal alliance kept an anxious eye upon their own constituencies, which stood in considerable danger of being infected with Parnell's reckless spirit. The instinct of self-preservation rendered them 'less able, if not less ready' to co-operate wholeheartedly with Gladstone by judiciously ignoring contentious issues.[64] Thomas Sexton gave notice of their aggressive intentions in February 1892 when he moved a Home Rule amendment to the Address, thus providing an opening for the Parnellite leader (John Redmond) to taunt the dumbfounded Liberals for having failed to produce their own scheme.[65]

Such strictures seemed all the more poignant on account of the proximity of a general election. Both Nationalists and Unionists accredited sinister motives to a party which constantly refused to take the nation into its confidence upon such a cardinal article of faith. This unprecedented situation tempted Lord Salisbury to propound a doctrine as devoid of constitutional propriety as it was effective in practice. In a speech at Birmingham on 24 November 1891 the Conservative premier maintained that the Liberals could claim no real mandate for a Home Rule bill unless they laid definite and detailed proposals before the country prior to the elections. Should the constituencies be denied this privilege, it would then be incumbent upon the upper chamber to reject out of hand any Irish bill which was submitted for ratification.

These portentous developments could not be ignored with impunity. Morley soon realized that only a frank and comprehensive declaration of intent could possibly save the Home Rule policy from harassment by Irishmen in the Commons, and from destruction by Unionists in the Lords.[66] In July 1891 he journeyed to Gladstone's holiday retreat at Lowestoft to press this view upon his leader. But, on arrival, he learnt that Gladstone had already reached the same conclusion. Threats to retard the progress of the Home Rule bill had not gone unnoticed by the frail and ageing statesman, and Gladstone now betrayed an anxiety to hold animated discussions upon a hitherto taboo subject with anyone who was prepared to listen. During the course of such conversations, Morley, Harcourt, and Spencer discovered that Gladstone had secretly invented a formula which, if divulged at once, might satisfy both Radical and Nationalist critics of existing policy. The new arrangement was deceptively simple. Gladstone proposed to keep the full complement of Irishmen at Westminster for a period of two years after the passage of the Home Rule bill. A separate land bill would follow, the government not resorting to British credit if they could devise an alternative form of financial security with the Irish. However, if the Irish members continued to be intractable once the two-year interval had expired, they were to be left to settle the question in Dublin, and their representation at Westminster would then be permanently reduced.[67] Morley held reservations concerning the practicality of this ingenious solution. He had received little 'daylight' on the 'fatal crux' of Irish representation, and disliked a land policy which would subject the loyalty of a disgruntled party to further strains. Parnell's behaviour since the split had so completely transformed Morley's attitude towards Irish land purchase that he now protested that it would be 'a frightful damper to our friends to find themselves struggling once more with the Serbonian bog of the Land Question'.[68]

The qualms of one individual did not constitute an insuperable

barrier to progress. But with a sinking heart Gladstone knew that
Morley's unfavourable reaction presaged disaster at the hands of
'a certain big friend of ours'. Harcourt's fervent belief that the
announcement of Irish plans would be 'the end of all things' had
not abated since 1889. Consequently, he was most disconcerted to
find his leader 'full of the *details* of the *Home Rule* Bill'.[69] When
Harcourt had recovered from the shock he wrote in a provocative
tone, 'Mr G. seems anxious for a *palaver*, which is to decide nothing'.[70] This ill-concealed relish for the prospect of renewed combat
caused consternation among those who were summoned to a special
meeting at Althorp in December 1891. The eternal Irish question
was not the only item on the Althorp agenda, but it proved, as
always, to be the most contentious. During the autumn Morley had
been busy drafting a series of Home Rule resolutions which he hoped
to move early in the next session. Harcourt predictably quashed this
notion, and with Spencer's support then reverted to his familiar
crotchet (the retention in full of Irish members) before Gladstone
adroitly diverted attention to less abrasive matters.[71] Thus the meeting adjourned without any constructive decisions having been
reached.

Gladstone made one final attempt to convince his colleagues that
further disclosures were necessary. On the eve of the dissolution he
submitted a memorandum on the subject to Spencer and Morley,
but both spurned his advice. Spencer perceived that a sudden
explanatory statement at so late a stage would be tantamount to
admitting that 'the Public has some right to more information than
they have hitherto received'.[72] Morley showed rather more concern
for their privileges as private members, believing that only responsible ministers could be expected to produce a Home Rule plan. In
his opening speech to his constituents Morley alleged that until such
an eventuality arose 'a narrow precision in every detail was alien to
the whole genius of our constitution'.[73] Gladstone was dismayed by
these rebuffs. He did not wish to invite scorn and ridicule by keeping
his lips sealed throughout the election campaign, and so composed
a manifesto in which he promised categorically to reveal the outlines
of the Home Rule scheme during one of his Midlothian speeches.
Before publication, however, he had succeeded in eliciting unexpectedly 'reasonable and satisfactory' views from an anti-Parnellite
deputation on the sensitive issue of further particulars.[74] Their
laudable moderation enabled Gladstone to modify his intentions by
denying the nation the benefit of becoming acquainted with the
exact format of the Home Rule bill. When Gladstone did fulfil his
engagement (30 June), he spoke with extreme brevity of his desire to
settle the land question at Westminster. He also avoided pledges

concerning the retention of Irish members on the grounds that the voters had not yet expressed 'any marked preference for any particular form of detail'.[75] Hence, with the life of a six-year Parliament finally extinguished, electors discovered that there was little upon which to feast their eyes other than the mouldering corpses of the bills of 1886.

This series of purely negative decisions engendered much political embarrassment. The tortuous history of the Liberal party since 1886 clearly indicated that if an opportune moment for detailed disclosures had ever existed it belonged not to the present but to the distant past. Every attempt to satisfy those who sought to amend the original Irish plan threw the party into hopeless confusion, and often brought the leaders into conflict with the Nationalists. Harmony amongst these various interests could not be achieved, though the illusion of progress towards this goal was only exploded when Parnell insidiously showed that the Irish could not be appeased without simultaneously damaging Liberal electoral fortunes. Hence Irish Home Rule remained in 1891–2 what it had always been, the most potent divisive force within the Liberal party. By comparison, the Radical ideas which had threatened to disrupt party unity in 1885 now appeared to be almost innocuous. Indeed, the evasion and ambiguity which from 1889 characterized so much of Gladstone's constructive Irish policy rendered a fresh emphasis upon hitherto neglected Radical grievances absolutely essential. In 1891 the leaders could still brood upon Ireland in the silent remoteness of the library at Althorp, but the multitudes assembled at Newcastle preferred to acclaim more popular material. Yet the effectiveness of the comprehensive Newcastle programme was decisively checked by the failure to reach an agreement at Althorp. The patent lack of cohesion upon a cardinal article in the Liberal catechism weakened the capacity of the party to inspire confidence in its supplementary programmes. Gladstone sacrificed many votes and seats in 1892 by concealing his Irish intentions, and unwittingly ensured that the Newcastle programme would founder upon the rock of a tenuous Parliamentary majority. Moreover, even an unpledged Gladstone could not escape the daunting duty of framing an acceptable Home Rule bill, which inexorably remained the first obligation of any Liberal government.

2. Coercion

The history of 1890–2 might have been very different had the Liberal party been compelled from a much earlier date to attend to domestic issues, instead of grappling continually with the particulars of Home Rule legislation. However, such a pronounced change in emphasis was not feasible prior to the breach with Parnell. Between 1886 and 1890 political debate had centred upon the Irish policy pursued at Westminster by the Conservative government, and upon its administrative performance in Ireland. Every other consideration was regarded as either irrelevant or of secondary importance by Liberal leaders who were deeply committed to an essentially pragmatic approach to Irish problems. They knew that the clamour for Home Rule details had been resisted – not through any discreet espousal of special Radical causes – but by keeping the 'nose' of the government firmly 'to the grindstone of Coercion'. Experience had also taught the leaders that the constitutional complexities of the Home Rule policy tended to cloud the primary issue, whereas the changes wrought by the enforcement of exceptional laws made a direct electoral impact. 'It is really on this battlefield that our success in the constituencies has been mainly achieved,' Harcourt asserted. 'I think the ordinary mind is a good deal more impressed by the *wrongs* than by the *rights* of Ireland.'[76]

This unpalatable truism created serious problems for Gladstone during the bleak winter of 1890–1. Many Liberals were convinced that Harcourt and men of his ilk wished to continue operating on '*negative and defensive* lines as against coercion' because it offered them an excuse to thwart a '*positive advance* in the direction of Home Rule'.[77] These suspicions were fully borne out by Harcourt's subsequent behaviour, even though the tactics of expediency turned out to be as vital in 1891 as they had seemed prudent hitherto. In his first public utterance after the divorce court verdict, Gladstone endorsed Harcourt's assessment of the situation. At Hastings (17 March) he claimed that the 'daily duty' of the parliamentary opposition was not, and had never been, to advocate Home Rule 'directly or perseveringly'. Their task had instead been simple and negative; to mirror the public outcry against coercion, and to 'mitigate and qualify it where we could not resist it'.[78] Gladstone realized that unless Liberal strategy continued to be based upon the twin pillars of exposing the iniquities of coercion and sustaining a popular crusade against its enforcement, the probable alternative would be a return to the utter confusion and demoralizing uncertainty which had prevailed towards the close of 1886.

In order to appreciate the basis of Gladstone's apprehensions it is necessary to consider the tortuous course negotiated by the Liberal party after its defeat at the general election of 1886. When Parliament was prorogued in the autumn of that year, the new Conservative government had not made any attempt to forestall the deterioration in the social condition of Ireland so clearly prognosticated by Parnell. Nor had Home Rulers been able to extract from ministers the outlines of an alternative policy to the one summarily rejected by the electorate. The party was also hampered by an inescapable obligation to explore the terrain leading to Liberal reunion, while striving simultaneously to preserve intact the 'union of hearts' with the Nationalists. In these circumstances the Liberal outlook for the winter campaign was grim. Fears loomed large lest a renewal of Irish turbulence should complete the disintegration of a party already decimated at the polls. Spencer, who was scheduled to address several meetings, anxiously sought the guidance of colleagues. Rosebery thought it wisest to cope with this thorny dilemma by cancelling all public engagements. He maintained that they ought 'to give the Tories a chance' and so 'avoid appearance of complicity with Irish agitation as connected with the crime which might spring up'. But Spencer discounted this advice, since he knew that there existed 'strong reasons' for speaking which were sufficient to overcome his personal distaste for the platform. 'We must keep on good terms with the Irish question and not show signs of eating our words, or backing down from our principles.'[79] The response elicited from this urgent appeal vividly illustrated the untenable nature of the Liberal position before illegality in Ireland had even commenced. Gladstone was more than usually enigmatic and uncommunicative, offering no means of escape from the impasse. Morley agreed with Spencer that 'we must keep our plan and policy firmly forward', but both he and Harcourt 'longed for a spell of quiet', and so deplored any propensity to 'rush through the land with the Fiery Cross.'[80] Unfortunately, they could not all follow the example set by Rosebery, who conveniently absconded on a world cruise.

The dangers of pursuing an active Irish policy, and the hazards of remaining silent, were both enhanced once the dread of disobedience to the law had materialized in the form of the Plan of Campaign. None of the Liberal leaders were prepared to countenance the existence of the Plan or dared justify the incendiary language of its promoters. However, this fact alone did not solve the real difficulty; 'the question rather is', Gladstone observed, 'how much disavowal'.[81] It was not easy to navigate a course which would be neither repugnant to British electors nor an affront to the Irish nation. Under these conditions it was 'very difficult to say anything definite', and no protests were entered against Harcourt's verdict that 'the most politic and dignified course is to keep quiet and to await events'.[82] Unionist strictures concerning the legitimacy of the Plan were evaded only by a resort to devious explanations, and these indicated how treacherous were the currents to be negotiated. Morley flatly refused to hazard any judgement on the legality of the Plan, on the grounds that this was the responsibility of the Irish judiciary and not the proper function of imperfectly informed laymen.[83] This attitude rendered the position of the former Viceroy peculiarly delicate and vulnerable. Spencer had already cancelled a meeting in Wales rather than run the risk of alienating moderate opinion by having his mild sympathy for the rent strike 'forcibly drawn' out.[84] Shortly afterwards the Plan was declared an illegal organization and a State prosecution was undertaken. But Spencer continued to procrastinate despite mounting pressure in the House of Lords. Eventually, he managed to excuse the behaviour of the Liberal frontbench with the specious plea that silence was mandatory now that the matter had become *sub judice*.[85]

In the meantime, however, two developments had helped to ease the gravity of the situation. Firstly, in a private interview with Morley, Parnell explained that he had been in no way responsible for organizing the Plan, and admitted that he personally disapproved of its form. He also promised to paper over the cracks in the Home Rule surface by taking immediate steps to curb the excesses of his prominent supporters.[86] Parnell's timely initiative enabled Gladstone and Morley to defend the logic of the Plan without being compelled also to extol the merits of the agitation itself. Thus, the Liberal leaders could place responsibility for the Plan firmly upon a government which had in the autumn rejected Parnell's conciliatory proposals, and upon landlords who had rashly spurned properly transmitted requests for reasonable abatements. Secondly, the 'season of comparative quietude', during which the Liberal party attempted 'to make bricks without straw', was drawing rapidly to a close. Even when at their most despondent, Liberals had never lost sight of the eventual avenue of escape. In November Morley had consoled a dispirited Harcourt with the thought that 'the first business next January, as it was last, will be *Coercion*. That blessed word will give a new shake to the kaleidoscope, and all the present talk will prove to be perfectly idle.'[87]

Confidence in the rectitude of their Home Rule policy was fully restored as soon as Liberals realized that Ireland was faced with an infinitely more menacing prospect than an unruly agrarian campaign. A new chapter in Liberal–Nationalist relations was opened when the reimposition of exceptional law was promised in the Queen's Speech of 1887. Irish fear of, and Liberal distaste for, repressive legislation did more to engender the celebrated 'union of hearts' than any commitment to establish a parliament on College Green. The instinctive revulsion felt by all true Liberals proved in some intangible way that perseverence with an intrinsically sound Irish policy in times of adversity did not eventually go unrewarded.

The rigours of coercion thrust upon a disorganized party the sense of vitality and cohesion which it was incapable of producing when left to its own resources. Furthermore, the undercurrent of unrest which seemed destined to divert attention from the active prosecution of the Home Rule policy was abruptly checked, and the emergence of new and controversial domestic programmes was postponed. In the highly-charged atmosphere prior to the downfall of Parnell, it was easier to sustain the argument that the government showed a callous indifference to the plight of the Irish peasantry, and ignored the wishes of their elected representatives, than to venture upon disputed terrain nearer home. So long as the political hybrid planted by the electorate produced such monstrous fruit as the criminal law amendment (Ireland) bill and the Members of Parliament (charges and allegations) bill, excursions into divisive domestic issues were quite unnecessary.

Balfour's coercion bill ground its way relentlessly through the Commons despite protracted and bitter opposition from the united Home Rule benches. Liberals detested a measure which not only eroded basic personal and political rights in one constituent part of the United Kingdom, but also openly transformed these attenuated liberties into a permanent instrument of government. They could now claim the status of custodian of popular freedom against the encroachments of an overpowerful executive. However, the majority of Liberal Unionist members refused to accept the validity of this historic Liberal contention, and continued to vote resolutely in support of repressive legislation. This act of apostasy brought Gladstone back to the centre of the political arena in order to issue a clarion call to his loyal supporters. He had not previously wished to destroy any prospect of securing reunion by speaking too freely, possibly because he had been afraid that excessive frankness would drive uncommitted Liberals into the Unionist fold. But every justification for discretion disappeared once Gladstone had finally convinced himself that the appeasement of Liberal Unionism was a consideration which ought to stand no longer between his conscience and the exposure of a tyrannical system of government. The voting behaviour of the Liberal Unionists proved beyond doubt that the government fortress was impregnable in the division lobbies, and suggested that the administration could only be brought down by sustained pressure from without. 'Now as in the Jingo time, our battle is to be fought in the country,' Gladstone announced. 'We are under no obligation to waste sense and breath upon an impenetrable majority.'[88]

This momentous decision was reached in the absence of any appreciable degree of public concern about the excesses of the coercion bill. A massive popular outcry did not materialize until the summer of 1887, when 31 counties were proclaimed by the Lord Lieutenant and the National League was brought within the purview of the Act. 'Events in Ireland slowly did more to bring opinion round than either solid thought or the best rhetoric,' Morley recalled. The suppression of public meetings and the trial of Nationalist leaders excited intense curiosity. For the first time electors could be regaled with tales 'as new and interesting as the narrative of an African explorer or a navigator in the Pacific' by the droves of Irish and Radical members who crossed and recrossed the Irish Sea.[89] This incessant flow of fresh indictments allowed the public conscience no respite. Whether the government was exposed to ridicule for prosecuting harmless newsboys instead of the editor and proprietor of the paper concerned, or held up to reprobation as an accessory to murder, the scope and variety of the material available guaranteed continued public interest.

During these turbulent years the attention of Liberals centred upon two aspects of the coercive regime: the alleged brutality and callous disregard for human life on the part of an armed constabulary, and the harsh treatment meted out to political prisoners (which apparently sought to eliminate agrarian crime by extinguishing the life of the prisoner). The 'massacre' at Mitchelstown and the death of John Mandeville were singled out for special analysis because these tragedies, though exceptional, accurately portrayed the seamier side of government policy. Gladstone was infuriated by Balfour's stubborn refusal to investigate conflicting reports of the shooting by policemen of several civilians at a public meeting at Mitchelstown in September 1887. Balfour's blatant partisanship, and the frustration of Liberal demands for an enquiry, demonstrated the irrelevance of the parliamentary opposition and exposed the futility of offering a constructive policy in the House. Ultimately the enfranchised nation could alone be held responsible for the direction of government policy. Hence, Gladstone saw as his supreme duty the need to transfer the party fray from a hostile Palace of Westminster to the more evenly-balanced electoral battlefield. He planned to enter into a partnership with the constituencies in order to enforce changes in the administration of Ireland. The annual convention of the N.L.F. at Nottingham in October afforded a unique opportunity for rallying the party to the new cause. Gladstone's text concentrated upon the poignant theme 'Remember Mitchelstown', and he set aside his habitual defensive armoury to 'speak plainly' on the actual operation of the Coercion Act:

I say that the law was broken by the agents of the law, and that it is idle to speak to the Irish people about obeying the law, if the very Government that so speaks ... has agents which break the law by advisedly and violently breaking the order of public meetings, and who are sustained in that illegal action.[90]

In subsequent speeches Gladstone inveighed against local officials, whether policemen, prison warders, or resident magistrates, as the demoralized agents of a debased Castle regime – but chiefly against Balfour as the source of all the mischief. His protests reached a new peak in 1888, when Balfour declined to express any regrets at the death of Mandeville. Such disdain was scandalous in view of the verdict recorded at the coroner's inquest, plus the highly suggestive fact that the prison doctor promptly committed suicide. Gladstone was so outraged by Balfour's studied indifference that he equated Conservative government with Czarist rule in Poland and with Naples under the Bourbon King Ferdinand, in terms which were reminiscent of his famous addresses to Lord Aberdeen 37 years earlier.[91]

These persistent and perhaps extravagant tirades against the government for setting a perfect example of illegal conduct in Ireland were welcomed by Gladstone's partisan audiences. Enthusiastic Radical delegates to the spectacular meetings of the N.L.F. were captivated by the fire of the old man's oratory. They were not disposed to criticize language which could be construed as incitement to insurrection, or willing to discourage the levelling of specific (and not altogether warrantable) charges against individual agents of Castle administration. But the effect of this conscious effort to 'Bulgarianize' upon disinterested persons when the speeches appeared in cold print on the morrow was calamitous. Atherley-Jones protested that it was ludicrous to compare Ireland with Bulgaria. 'To the sane Englishman Mitchelstown is not Batak; the Irish constabulary are not Bashi-Bazouks, nor Irish magistrates Turkish pashas.'[92]

As they listened to the original violent outburst at Nottingham (18 October 1887), Morley and Harcourt began to reproach themselves for having persuaded Gladstone to concentrate on denouncing Coercion. 'The capital tactic of the moment' was an unpredictable and acutely embarrassing weapon in the hands of a leader whose 'sense of proportion or degree is not his strong point.'[93] Morley complained that Gladstone

> did not seem to realise the delicacy of the ground he was treading upon; nor how shaky some of his evidence was ... A graver and deeper tone would have been more becoming ... Perhaps we may be able in a quiet way to show that we are not anarchists by any means. But it is not so simple.[94]

Harcourt agreed that many of Gladstone's statements betrayed an 'extraordinary rashness', and he could not understand why a seasoned campaigner should 'commit himself as he does as if he was an inexperienced boy of twenty'. Morley, Spencer, and himself surreptitiously combined forces so that they might encourage 'respectable people to emerge on our side'.[95] In a series of carefully co-ordinated speeches at the end of October, the trio bestowed a judicious leavening of praise upon the maligned Irish constabulary, thereby dissociating themselves from the more offensive of Gladstone's allegations.[96] Nevertheless, three isolated speeches could not undo the havoc wrought by one who showed no disposition to reduce the scale of his invective. In a Utopian vision Morley begged Spencer (who was about to visit Hawarden Castle) to 'be kind enough to lock up a certain G.O.M., and to bring the key away in your pocket'.[97] But once 'unmuzzled' Gladstone was not easy to confine.

Hence Gladstone's address to the N.L.F. at Birmingham in the following year was awaited with considerable trepidation. His apprehensive colleagues found no comfort in the sombre warnings which reached them from the pen of Farrer Herschell, Lord Chancellor in the late Liberal government. This august legal authority suggested that Gladstone's 'exaggerated language' and 'dangerous doctrines' on the subject of political prisoners had placed the party in an altogether 'false position'. Yet Gladstone himself was not impressed by the extreme caution manifested by those who claimed that 'the only safeguard for personal liberty is that obedience to the law should be enforced, because it is the law'.[98] He was in no mood to listen to Harcourt, Rosebery, or even his own son Herbert, and certainly had no intention of ignoring 'the more or less inaccurate and coloured reports of the Nationalists'.[99] When Harcourt reached Hawarden he learnt with dismay that James Stuart, zealous chairman of the (English) Home Rule Union, had arrived simultaneously '*hot foot* from Ireland with his pockets full of notices to quit, ejectments, etc., etc., each with a tale probably apocryphal attached to it'.[100] Stuart, who had provided the explosives for Gladstone's inflammatory Nottingham speech, felt no qualms about offending tender consciences in Britain. Thus Harcourt's advice to generalize as much as possible fell on deaf ears, and gave Morley reason to portend gloomily that 'a repetition of Nottingham will be a horrid disaster'.[101] At Birmingham (7 November) Gladstone made no attempt to reassure the hesitant and law-abiding voter, but repeated his old charges and buttressed these with new ones. In this dramatic fashion Gladstone cast aside colleagues who merely wished to launch a 'tremendous organized Peaceful agitation for Home Rule pure and simple',[102] and drew closer to more militant and less responsible elements within the party.

There was little chance of restraining Gladstone so long as he appeared 'as young as ever' when he went 'on the stump'. His infectious enthusiasm for the new crusade unquestionably invigorated him bodily and mentally at a point when the onset of old age might have been expected to follow its predictable course. A display of almost reckless courage, combined with an unerring popular instinct, suggests that in spite of his advanced years Gladstone was possibly closer to the public pulse than at any previous stage in his chequered career. He struck a responsive chord in the minds of many electors which he alone could pluck. Once the subject of Mitchelstown had been introduced into the political primer, he rejoiced 'to see with what an intense interest a vast assembly hailed the return to Ireland from extraneous matters'.[103] The secret of Gladstone's popularity with the Radicals and Nationalists rested upon his candid endorsement of the two main justifications for resorting to defiance of the law in Ireland. Firstly, he continually emphasized how easily the Conservatives could have avoided repression had they only accepted Parnell's tenants' relief bill in the summer of 1886. The government had actually brought the Coercion Act upon itself, because the summary rejection of a remedial measure had contributed substantially to agrarian distress, thus encouraging serious disturbances. Secondly, Gladstone was fully aware that the real purpose of the Coercion Act was not the suppression of crime, nor even the prohibition of meetings and the imprisonment of those who advocated or resorted to physical violence. Instead, Balfour's chief aim was to crush a deeply-rooted rural crusade for better conditions, by rigidly upholding and enforcing the ordinary law with respect to indebted tenants.[104]

The harsh mechanism of the eviction process genuinely horrified Gladstone and the host of Radical M.P.s who swarmed across the Irish countryside making eviction scenes their familiar haunt. No time was lost in regaling British audiences, especially at by-elections, with harrowing tales of impoverished and defenceless families being driven from their homes to face an Irish winter in the open, unwilling spectators to the 'tumbling' of their miserable cottages. The government was naturally accused of conniving at the clearances, since the lynch-pin of Balfour's Irish strategy was the defeat of the Plan of Campaign. Visible evidence of Castle complicity could eventually be produced in the form of lavish police protection for the evicting bailiffs. By 1890 Gladstone had begun to classify the constabulary as a mere rent collector for absentee landlords.[105] This outspoken condemnation of an unworthy class of landowners reaped considerable political dividends, because it helped to exonerate Gladstone from the odium which Radicals had heaped upon the authors of the land bill of 1886. But the Liberal frontbench was reluctant to express its approval of Gladstone's combative tone. Perhaps senior colleagues felt that Gladstone's excitable temperament had caused him to overlook the salient point that ejectments had commenced before the implementation of the Coercion Act. In fact, the most inhumane examples of wholesale clearances (on the estates of Lord Clanricarde at Woodford and Rowland Winn at Glenbeigh), had been completed before the parliamentary session of 1887 had even begun. However, had the sceptics also known that the government was supplying landlords with battering-rams paid for out of secret service funds, or that Balfour had surreptitiously created a special 'Syndicate' of weaker landlords to ensure that evictions only took place with his approval, the logic of Gladstone's posture would have been more obvious.

In the absence of such extraordinary information, Gladstone's personal campaign did not, paradoxically, receive official approval until attention had shifted from the operation of the Coercion Act in Ireland to proceedings in Parliament and the High Court. Three months after the delivery of Gladstone's controversial Birmingham speech a new surface was exposed to critical examination by vigilant Home Rulers. The sensational *dénouement* of February 1889 utterly transformed the tedious and laborious sessions of the notorious Parnell Commission. Liberals were stunned by the disclosure that upon the basis of letters forged by Richard Pigott but attributed to Parnell, the government in collusion with *The Times* had systematically and maliciously sought to discredit the Home Rule movement. The parliamentary circumstances in which the Special Commission was conceived, and the manner in which it was established, had been in themselves reprehensible. But when the Report was submitted to Parliament in February 1890, it produced (in Morley's words) 'a strong recoil against the flagrant violence, passion, and calumny, that had given it birth'.[106] Gladstone's reticent colleagues could now 'recoil' by endorsing their leader's views on the corrupt nature of Castle government. By 1890 Morley and Spencer had completely overcome their scruples that they might forfeit the confidence of the constabulary were a prospective Chief Secretary and Viceroy to condone or imitate Gladstone's rash language. After witnessing scenes of police brutality during the arrest of Dillon and O'Brien at Tipperary in September, Morley protested (without much success) against the callous behaviour of the authorities.[107] Even Spencer could occasionally forget his Whig prejudices and enthuse over Gladstone's combative speeches. 'I think

that he is right to hammer away even at Mitchelstown,' Granville
was informed. 'You cannot stick too much to a really good point.'[108]

Ironically, Gladstone's long standing contentions were accepted at
a stage when the frenzied onslaught upon the mechanics of coercion
was beginning to lose its momentum. As early as 1887 Herbert
Gladstone had reached the conclusion that it would be 'impossible
to keep the steam up in an agitation of this kind'. Bearing in mind
the precedent of a former Chief Secretary (W. E. Forster), he feared
that the malignity of his father's attacks would eventually provoke a
reaction in Balfour's favour.[109] Moreover, there was the obvious
danger that sooner or later the cabinet would be tempted to cut off
the flow of effective Home Rule propaganda at its source. The
government was indeed disposed to review the actual administration
of its Irish policy at Dublin Castle when confronted with a rising
scale of popular protest in Britain. Senior ministers believed that if
the Liberals were forced to rely upon stale news and monotonous
accusations, the country would soon tire of the exhausting Irish
question and restore Unionism to favour. By 1889 it was apparent
that a reaction of this character had commenced. After the deplorable
excesses of local bailiffs and 'emergency men' in 1886-7, Dublin
Castle began to encourage landlords to negotiate with the tenants,
and in cases where arbitration broke down the authorities took care
to supervise the conduct of evictions. Castle management was later
augmented through the creation of a landlords' Syndicate. Whenever
landlords of notoriety proceeded to evict against the advice of Castle
officials, police protection was ostentatiously withheld.

However, these fresh departmental instructions do not provide a
convincing explanation for the rapid fall in the number of evictions.
Other more durable and frequently overlooked factors deserve
consideration. In particular, the constructive programme of a
coercionist government provided many tenants with a greater degree
of protection from penury. The Land Act of 1887 reduced rents and
arrears; the relief works and railway construction programme of
1890 offered alternative sources of employment to displaced tenants;
and the lot of the poorest peasants in the south-west was alleviated
by the establishment of a Congested Districts Board under the terms
of the 1891 Land Act. In combination with a fortuitous recovery in
agricultural prices, this remedial legislation served to lessen the
intensity of the land war, and so curbed the influence of the Plan
and the power of the National League. By 1890-1 these conciliatory
measures had so successfully completed the work of pacification
which repression had begun, that several counties could be exempted
from the most stringent provisions of the Coercion Act. Although
the essentials of coercion remained inviolate, more discretion was

now employed in the manner of its enforcement. For example, the rigours of prison treatment were administered less robustly after the government had been shaken by the indignation aroused by the death of Mandeville. Balfour continued to deny that Crimes Act prisoners were entitled to special consideration, and presented a powerful *tu quoque* case against Spencer. But the rest of the cabinet did not wish to invite a recurrence of the Mandeville episode, and in 1889 resolved to treat political prisoners as first-class misdemeanants. The deference and consideration shown to Dillon and O'Brien upon their arrest indicated the extent to which the rules had been relaxed by 1891.

These important modifications in Irish policy were undoubtedly hastened by the unpleasant spectre of Richard Pigott. Conservative statesmen were chastened by the very real prospect of a total disintegration of Unionist principles, accompanied by the ignominious collapse of the government. They realized that such a calamity could best be avoided by pressing forward with the task of ameliorating the social and economic plight of the Irish peasantry. Yet the electorate was slow to appreciate this new sense of urgency, and at first failed to acknowledge the fact that Conservatives not only could improve conditions in Ireland, but had already succoured many of her inhabitants. Only gradually did it become clear that, far from destroying the moral fibre of the government, the revelations of the Parnell Commission had actually helped to consolidate the intellectual integrity of the Unionist philosophy. Ultimately, this reappraisal of Conservative aims and methods did not benefit the seemingly triumphant opposition. In their anxiety to celebrate the enormous popularity of a vindicated Parnell, and proclaim the imminent demise of Unionism, the euphoric Liberals lost their sense of proportion, and disregarded the alarming threat posed by the altered tactics of Dublin Castle. The unexpected turn of events in Ireland rendered the immediate construction of a Radical programme more than ever necessary. But the Liberal party was not disposed to forget the existence of the Coercion Act, and swallow the unpalatable truth that repression no longer constituted the mainstay of Unionist administration. Hence Pigott unwittingly interposed his dead body between a negative and faltering Irish strategy and the alternative Radical policies which alone could secure a decisive electoral victory. However, Liberal confidence in the political advantages of persevering with the attack on coercion rapidly evaporated when Parnell fell from grace. In his anxiety to remain on the battlefield of coercion, Harcourt protested that it had been a 'potent cry' in the past.[110] Indeed it had; but the government had learnt many lessons and had corrected many faults in the administration of Ireland while Liberals were busy paying homage to Parnell in England. At the close of 1890, therefore, the campaign against oppression in Ireland had become a broken reed. The Liberal party was now left with no alternative other than to focus its thoughts on those domestic issues which would make a more immediate electoral impact.

3. *Gladstone and the Class Struggle*

When Gladstone introduced his controversial Irish proposals into the cockpit of party politics, he shattered abruptly the unity of his own party and set in motion the complex series of negotiations which ultimately led to a dramatic realignment of existing political groups. The distant objective towards which Chamberlain had hitherto laboured so assiduously, yet unavailingly, was reached through the agency of one from whom such action was least expected. With one reluctant blow Gladstone finally severed the few remaining links between Whig families and their historic party allegiance. From 1886 onwards the counsels of Cavendishes and Grosvenors ceased to be heard at Liberal country houses; heirs to Whig titles, the Wolmers and Wodehouses, were no longer destined to appear effortlessly in future Liberal cabinets. Many powerful and distinguished politicians joined this imposing aristocratic retinue, including financiers like Goschen and Ferdinand de Rothschild, and men of learning and professional eminence such as Sir John Lubbock and Sir Henry James. However, following in the wake of the main body of avowed Hartingtonians was the incongruous spectacle of a defiant Chamberlain, accompanied by a mere handful of adherents from beyond the confines of his Birmingham *fief*. The personality cult fostered in the west Midlands demonstrated that Radical Unionism was a transitory and essentially a localized phenomenon. Elsewhere in Great Britain support for Chamberlain's distinctive brand of Unionism crumbled rapidly. Death removed Peter Rylands from Burnley early in 1887; coercion soon persuaded A. B. Winterbotham (Cirencester) to defect; and when Trevelyan and T. R. Buchanan resolved to 'find salvation', they promptly secured re-election as Gladstonian members for Scottish constituencies. Finally, W. S. Caine, Radical Unionist whip and ardent temperance reformer, returned to the Liberal ranks in 1890 on account of the licensing question – even though he sacrificed his seat at Barrow in the process.

These withdrawals suggest that the foundations of Chamberlain's position were highly unstable. On the one hand, severance from Gladstone deprived the Unionist movement of an established reservoir of votes, while on the other, the pressing need to placate Hartington and appease his new Conservative allies compelled

Chamberlain to discard the traditional cries of party warfare. For
these reasons Liberal Unionism seemed more suited to the refined
temperament of non-partisan 'armchair politicians' than it was
attractive to robust Liberals and pugnacious Radicals. 'I am only a
camp follower now', Dilke explained, 'but my place is not in the
camp of the Goschens.'[111] Those amongst Chamberlain's friends and
followers who had refused to coquet with their adversaries in the
past could not understand why their leader should now be prepared
to mortgage the future of Radical principles when it seemed more
appropriate to capitalize upon the exodus of the Whigs. It did not
require extraordinary powers of perception to appreciate that Home
Rule was bound to charge with excitement those Radical zealots who
genuinely believed in experiments in self-government and the extension of personal freedom. The departure of those who attached more
importance to abstract constitutional irregularities suddenly shifted
the centre of gravity within the party, thus ensuring the perpetual
ascendancy of the advanced element. Moreover, it soon became
evident that the scale of the electoral defeat in 1886 had actually
tilted the balance still further towards the Radicals. Only constituencies with entrenched Radical loyalties could effectively withstand a Conservative landslide, and these obviously tended to select
the most militant and advanced candidates. When Gladstone
proudly reviewed the 'small, though crack, army of 200 men'[112]
which had survived the disaster of July 1886, he knew that his
depleted forces owed their existence to the fortress which had
sheltered them. Their future clearly depended upon an ability to
forge a new range of weapons of domestic reform in the Radical
armoury.

In the meantime the Gladstonians were not disposed to allow the
mutineers to return. At the close of the elections Morley reported
that party workers throughout the country were obsessed with a
desire to wreak vengeance upon the Dissentient M.P.s at the next
general election.[113] An irate Labouchere spoke for a considerable
segment of opinion when he vouched 'never to lose an opportunity
of accentuating the differences between Whigs and Radicals'.[114]
Such pervasive feelings help to explain why the very notion of a
Round Table Conference evoked such bitter recriminations. These
stemmed partly from a deep distrust of Chamberlain, which
amounted to hatred of a fallen idol. But beyond this personal factor
lay a secret fear that the Liberal negotiators were busy constructing
a bridge which would enable Hartington and his retainers to return
unmolested.

The breakdown of the Conference in the spring of 1887 decisively
crushed all hope of formal reunion. The prospect of success was

perhaps unrealistic since the Unionist leaders were too firmly committed by their previous behaviour to retract with dignity their copious and unequivocal declarations against Home Rule. However, this consideration of personal honour did not apply to the host of Liberal electors who had voted against Gladstonian candidates in 1886, or had abstained from the polls; nor could it be employed to discipline the incalculable numbers who had supported Home Rule only with deep misgivings. The future outlook of this motley body of indeterminate opinion was largely settled by Gladstone's conduct of the Irish case after 1886. Although Gladstone continued to lament the loss of a leavening Whig presence, he could not deny that it had been by his hand that the fabric of the party had been rent in the first place. He admitted that the 'extreme wing' was rapidly gaining ground, but disclaimed all responsibility for inspiring this regrettable development. Instead, Gladstone blamed those who had resisted Home Rule for causing the advance of Radicalism. 'The amount will be measured by the duration and intensity of that resistance', he frequently alleged. 'The remedy or check is in passing Home Rule as quickly as possible.'[115] Yet in spite of these excuses, Gladstone himself ensured that the party could never be reconstituted upon its former basis when he decided to prosecute the Irish case with renewed vigour and determination, and chose also to espouse with enthusiasm the new Radical claims stimulated by the example of Ireland. A crusade of Bulgarian dimensions irretrievably alienated the hesitant and uncommitted voter, and this in turn facilitated Gladstone's compulsive gravitation towards those elements in the party whose ascendancy he so strongly deplored. For the first time he began to seek and value the advice of those who could not otherwise have penetrated the select social and political circles in which he had been accustomed to move. Gladstone acquired an insatiable thirst for any information which could be used to arraign the government, and so displayed a novel interest in the core of independent Radicals who possessed first-hand knowledge of conditions in Ireland. This fresh involvement rendered Gladstone more than usually unpredictable, but a wider range of contacts also endowed him with a lively appreciation of the exciting popular ideas coursing through the frame of the party.

Hence Gladstone did not lack encouragement to broaden the scope of the agitation, and in so doing bring home more forcibly to incredulous British electors the true nature of the injustices which prevailed in Ireland. He quickly perceived that the most effective way of creating a unity of interest between the two nations would be to introduce the concept of a class struggle into the campaign by boldly stressing the connection between the cause of Irish freedom and the rights of labour as a whole. Gladstone firmly believed that Ireland was an integral facet of the labour question, and both he and his colleagues, especially Morley, sought to expose this attractive surface whenever the opportunity arose.[116] Whether or not the Liberal leaders insidiously exploited the latent class-consciousness of the working man solely for purposes of narrow party advantage is, of course, a matter of conjecture. This dark thought certainly occurred to George Lansbury, a rare example of a bona fide Gladstonian labourer who could afford the expense of a visit to Ireland in order to inspect conditions for himself. He was struck immediately by the contrast between the readiness of many Liberals to offer State aid to Irish peasants and their refusal to regulate the wages and hours endured by British workers.[117] Another advanced London Radical, the journalist H. W. Massingham, complained that the working classes would remain indifferent to the plight of Ireland until Liberal leaders began to show 'for the East End docker the enthusiasm which they have rightly developed for the Connemara cottier'.[118] However, these valid criticisms do not contain the whole truth. Although the Liberal party did indeed consciously refrain from pursuing its Irish logic to the furthest limits, it is also evident that the deteriorating relationship between the government and organized labour on both sides of the Irish Sea rapidly compelled Gladstone to modify his own restricted social outlook.

In the initial stages of the Irish controversy Gladstone shunned a provocative campaign. As premier he had ventured openly to compare the good sense of the 'masses' with the obstinacy of the 'classes' in a manifesto of March 1886. But this experiment had alarmed timid spirits within the party, and Gladstone did not dare revert to this explosive theme until the autumn of the following year. News of the folly of the Irish constabulary at Mitchelstown coincided with the astonishing information that Metropolitan policemen were engaged in irregular activities in connection with political meetings held in Trafalgar Square. Gladstone was not slow to point out that coercion was a highly contagious disease, and he warned a deputation at Hawarden that the laws which oppressed Ireland could easily be applied to the whole of the United Kingdom. He subsequently declined to counsel resistance to the concept of law entertained by the Commissioner of Metropolitan Police, but, by drawing attention to the dangers faced by the British workmen, Gladstone indirectly fostered the demonstrations organized by Socialists on behalf of the London unemployed.[119] He was, therefore, denigrated as a seditious agitator by those who held him personally responsible for the disturbances on 'Bloody Sunday', 13 November 1887. Yet Gladstone ignored the torrents of abuse, and did not betray the

slightest trace of penitence for his behaviour. In an unusually revealing sentence he candidly admitted that 'if ever man had formed a
street revolution, I am the man'.[120] Personal vilification only served
to identify the Grand Old Man with the cause of the dispossessed
classes in England as well as with the oppressed in Ireland. 'Has it
never struck you', Granville curtly informed a rabid Duke of Argyll,
'that his hold on public opinion . . . is almost in exact proportion to
the violence of the abuse poured upon him?'[121]

Nor did it long escape Gladstone's notice that repressive and
illiberal practices in both Britain and Ireland had failed to curb civil
disorder. He attributed the reduction of outrages in Ireland – not to
the operation of the Coercion Act – but to the existence of the Plan
of Campaign. Gladstone did not accept the proposition that the
Plan was a strictly legal organization, but he was convinced that it
was an 'infinitely smaller evil' for Irishmen to rely on the machinery
of the Plan 'than to leave the people to perish' at the hands of
Dublin Castle. In his opinion combination was the 'only arm by
which a poor and destitute and feeble population are able to make
good their ground . . . against the domineering power of the State
and of the wealthy'.[122] Plan leaders who had successfully carried
out a bloodless revolution were viewed as pillars of moral rectitude
when compared to the violence perpetrated by Irish officialdom.
Gladstone commended their scrupulous insistence upon the need for
self-discipline, restraint, and a responsible and peaceable discharge of
common obligations. Similarly, he could see that the organization of
industrial labour in trade unions was the only practical and effective
antidote to the unruly behaviour displayed by the rioters in Trafalgar
Square. He roundly declared at Swansea in June 1887 that trade
unions had 'vindicated' the independence of the artisan, and 'upon
the whole have been productive of an enormous balance of good'.[123]
Illegal combinations of desperate Irish tenants cannot bear comparison with respectable British craft unions, but Gladstone's tacit
acceptance of boycotting and 'exclusive dealing' as a legitimate form
of trade union activity enabled him to sympathize with the phenomenon known as the 'new Unionism' – those massive combinations
of unskilled workers which sprang up in the late 1880s. Where
justice was on the side of those Irishmen who resorted to drastic
expedients in order to reduce exorbitant rents and guarantee the
security of their tenure, Gladstone could scarcely deny justice to
those English labourers who, in equally abject circumstances, used
similar methods to obtain reasonable wages and security of employment.

It is generally considered that Gladstone never really understood
the basic material needs of the working classes, and was certainly

not sympathetically disposed towards the growing militancy of the labour movement. However, this sweeping verdict has been questioned by one modern scholar who stresses that Gladstone 'knew the world of poverty as it was' since the range of his social activities was 'extensive and peculiar'. John Vincent admits that the record was 'curiously uncertain and various', but assumes that 'the G.O.M. became something of a diehard in his last years'.[124] This conclusion does not appear to be substantiated by an examination of Gladstone's reactions to the London dock strike of 1889, the most important battleground between the employers and the new unions. Shortly after the triumphant dockers had returned to work, he delivered a carefully prepared address at Hawarden in which he adopted the posture of an 'enlightened impartial observer'.

> In the common interests of humanity, this remarkable strike and the results of this strike, which have tended somewhat to strengthen the condition of labour in the face of capital, is the record of what we ought to regard as satisfactory, as a real social advance [that] tends to a fair principle of division of the fruits of industry.[125]

Gladstone began to show keen interest in the progress of the strike when he discovered that four-fifths of the work-force was composed of Irish immigrants – men who probably coupled their Roman Catholic faith with strong Home Rule convictions. Moreover, the renewal of his friendship with Cardinal Manning in 1886, after a painful lapse of several decades, supplied Gladstone with a fresh insight into the minds of poverty-stricken urban dwellers. The frail patron and spiritual guardian of the dockers subsequently drew Gladstone's attention to the fact that, beneath a militant exterior, the dockers' leaders were 'very reasonable, many of them Total Abstainers from all drink, and many of them sincerely religious. Further they have broken with the Socialist Theories', simply being intent on securing industrial and economic benefits.[126]

However, it would be dangerous to infer that Gladstone gave the matter his fleeting attention, remaining blissfully ignorant of the acute labour problems caused by the chaotic organization of the London docks. He had intervened on behalf of the coal whippers employed in the docks as far back as 1843, when he had carried a bill to establish a central employment office. According to his son, Gladstone continued to demonstrate his concern for the welfare of the coal whippers long after he had left the Board of Trade.[127] Hence, his guests at Hawarden in October 1889 ought not to have been 'shocked ... by some rather wild language on the Dock labourers question', presumably in defence of the 'sympathetic' strike.[128] His total identification with the cause of a restive working class did not 'commend itself' to the minds of Morley, Spencer, and Granville, which were trained to protect the individual from the tyranny of an uncouth majority.[129] But Gladstone was captivated by the nobility of the stevedores, lightermen, and other groups, who were 'not dependent upon one another in all cases', yet 'intended to make common cause' with the dockers in the interests of justice. He publicly congratulated the dockers for successfully copying the methods of combination used by Irish peasants. Shortly afterwards he emphasized that the exercise of the right of exclusive combination which in London was 'innocent and lawful, in Ireland would be penal and ... punished by imprisonment with hard labour'.[130] Gladstone implied that the dockers had only emulated the tactics of Plan of Campaign tenants on the Smith-Barry estates at Tipperary (who refused to pay rent to a landlord who had attempted to break the Plan in another county). This analogy clearly demonstrated that the freedom of association enjoyed by British workers was exceedingly fragile when it could be so ruthlessly denied to their Irish fellow citizens.

Gladstone supported the dockers chiefly because he could not trust the government to react impartially when confronted by the wave of strikes which swept across the country. The outbreaks of violence which accompanied the intervention of the constabulary in many of the labour disputes of this period seemed to bear out Gladstone's prediction that sooner or later those who were responsible for enforcing the law would be corrupted by the example set by their Irish counterparts. When policemen clashed with miners at a Durham colliery in 1891, the pacifist M.P. for Sunderland (Samuel Storey) accused Balfour of supplying Home Rulers with 'plentiful proof of how the evil seed which he has sown in Ireland has already taken root, and brought forth fruit in our own country of England'.[131] During the course of an earlier dispute between Will Thorne's Gasworkers Union and the London Gas Light and Coke Company, the government had indeed mobilized police and soldiers to intimidate the strikers in a manner which had become all too familiar in Ireland. Manning was incensed by the resort to military force on the part of a coercive and discredited regime. 'Are we under Martial Law?' he asked Gladstone. 'How long is this to go on in Ireland and in England? ... I remember Peterloo and Bristol and seem to be young again.'[132] The poignant historical analogy impressed one who shared these distant recollections, arousing Gladstone's deepest emotional instincts. He immediately responded to Manning's passionate appeal by publicly rebuking the government, the gas companies, and other recalcitrant employers. In Midlothian Gladstone boldly asserted that wherever there had been conflict (or what he characteristically referred to as 'competition') between capital and labour, 'where it has gone to sharp issues, where there have been strikes on one side and lock-outs on the other, I believe that in the main and as a general rule, the labouring man has been in the right'.[133]

Gladstone also noted with satisfaction that careful and considerate management on the part of his agent had successfully averted a coalminers' strike on the Hawarden estate.[134] Only a small portion of the credit for the existence of this harmonious relationship between masters and men can be attributed to Gladstone, since possession of the estate had been wholly transferred to his eldest son between 1875 and 1882. In fact, one of his last acts as sole owner had revealed him in a most unedifying light. A little known episode in June 1874 had indicated that in a private capacity Gladstone could combine the despotic traits of a feudal landowner with the rapacity of an early nineteenth-century industrial baron. When the miners of the Aston Hall colliery (one mile north of Hawarden) struck in protest against a 10 per cent reduction in wages, Gladstone, as a principal shareholder, had threatened to evict from their cottages all those who refused to comply with his request to return to work at once. This high-handed action had been defended by reference to classical Cobdenite doctrine, the Amalgamated Association of Miners having no right to inflict its wishes upon even a tiny group of four nonmembers. 'If one workman chooses to work for nothing, in the face of one thousand other men', Gladstone had postulated, 'he has as good a right to do so as the thousand men have to say what they will work for'.[135]

Nothing could contrast more starkly with this astonishing statement than Gladstone's attitude 15 years later. Instead of merely attempting to set a pious example of model conduct for other employers to follow if they chose, he welcomed the dramatic increase in the bargaining power of trade unions, and positively deplored the motives of those who wished to curb this power through fresh legislation. Gladstone's strong opposition to the insidious restrictions imposed by the courts on union activities constituted clear proof of his continuing good faith. In a number of controversial legal decisions the shortcomings of the trade union legislation of 1871-6 were exposed, especially in connection with the exact meaning of criminal intimidation.[136] Although the authority of union officials over their members was expressly protected by statute, their relationship with non-members during an industrial dispute was not defined, and the courts were obliged to seek guidance from the common law interpretation of conspiracy. This lack of precision was of crucial importance to the unions because employers could easily break strikes either by importing 'free' labour or by challenging in the courts the authority of a union to impose a 'closed shop'.

The worst fears of the unions were realized when Pete Curran of the Gasworkers Union was convicted of intimidation on account of his behaviour during the Plymouth dock strike of 1890. When the case of *Curran v. Treleaven* was heard at Plymouth Assizes, Judge Henry Bompas laid down the doctrine that although unions were entitled to protect the interests of their members, they could not resort to strike action to exclude non-unionists. Fortunately, the Court of Appeal overruled a judgement which in effect debarred unions from exercising their legal right to strike for higher wages and better conditions. But perhaps the most important consequence of this flagrant attempt to enforce the rights of property at the expense of organized labour lay in a different direction. The enormity of the offence caused many Liberals to reappraise the basic implications of a free market economy. A law which allowed a single powerful magnate to oppress his employees with impunity, but which utilized the doctrine of conspiracy to punish a few dock labourers who attempted to coerce a handful of their fellow workers came to be regarded as 'monstrous' and 'fundamentally unjust'. The growing belief that trade unions only resorted to what L. T. Hobhouse later referred to as 'coercion against coercion, differing possibly in form and method, but not in principle or in spirit' constituted an important landmark in the evolution of a 'new Liberalism'.[137] Gladstonians drew this vital distinction between the law and moral justice because they realized that the blatant discrimination in favour of employers closely resembled the preferential treatment extended to landlords in Ireland under the terms of the Coercion Act of 1887. Indeed, in a comparable trade union case at Newcastle, Judge Seymour explicitly imported this extreme definition of criminal conspiracy into the corpus of English law. Edmund Robertson, a barrister and M.P. for Dundee, raised this subject in Parliament in 1891 and 1892, protesting that the government wished 'to impose a bad law on England in order that they may have the benefit of it in Ireland'. He proposed to place the capricious law of conspiracy upon a definite statutory basis, and to compel the courts to accept the general principle that no action committed by a combination of persons should constitute a conspiracy unless the same act was criminal if committed by an individual. It is perfectly clear from Robertson's speech that his Liberal backers possessed a dual aim. They openly hoped to 'materially affect' the efficiency of the Coercion Act in Ireland by legalizing a 'closed shop' policy throughout the United Kingdom.[138] The propriety of this comparison between combinations in Ireland and Britain was sufficient to bring

the courts under heavy fire from Gladstone. After some careful
priming from Arnold Morley, he sprang to the defence of the
British pattern of 'exclusive dealing'.[139] At a conference in London
in December 1891 Gladstone explained why he wished to abolish
the special law:

> Under cover of this common law, whether owing to neglect or to
> prejudice, there have grown up proceedings which have flowed
> from the mere whim and personal notions or leanings of particular
> judges that have become in the aggregate extremely averse to the
> liberties of the people.[140]

Unequivocal declarations of this character were uttered at a time
when close identification with the demands of labour was a mixed
political blessing, thus revealing that the confidence of a new self-
conscious working class in Gladstone was founded upon the presence
of tangible virtues. Gladstone's keen interest in Irish problems
enabled him to respond with extraordinary warmth and understanding to critical changes in industrial practices and in the attitude of
labour leaders. His experience of the Plan of Campaign widened
his vision to such an extent that he could comfortably reconcile the
sober individualism of Henry Broadhurst and Thomas Burt with
the uncompromising militancy of John Burns and Ben Tillett. Many
of those who figured prominently in the counsels of the Labour
party in the twentieth century bore eloquent testimony to the 'uplift-
ing power' of Gladstone's 'matchless voice and superb vitality', and
confessed how 'the thrill of his splendid oratory' bound them to the
Liberal party in the old man's twilight years.[141] Frederick Rogers,
Arthur Henderson, Robert Smillie, and especially George Lansbury,
all acknowledged the debt which they owed to Gladstone. 'I can
hear his voice and see him now,' Lansbury wrote in the 1930s after
he had retired from the leadership of the Labour party.[142] These
enduring emotions suggest that the presence of Gladstone at the
head of the Liberal party constituted the principal obstacle to the
emergence of a coherent and independent labour movement.

4. *Bilateral Education and the ' "Disunion" of Hearts'*

The interdependence of the working-class movements of Britain and
Ireland is perhaps epitomized by the career of Michael Davitt, a
socialist activist and editor of an influential journal (the *Labour
World*) which he published for the benefit of British workmen. But
not until 1892 did the ex-Fenian convict and motive power behind
the Irish Land League secure a seat in a Parliament where momentous changes had occurred since 1886. Although the realignment of

parties in that year had vastly increased the pace of Radical politics, one equally important corollary to the wholesale defection of the Whigs is often overlooked. A complete transformation took place at Westminster when a gravely depleted Liberal army found reinforcements in the shape of an impressive battalion of more than 80 Irish votes.

No formal fusion of the two party organizations was implicit in the 'union of hearts', though it was evident that 'common action up to a certain degree would arise from the necessities of the position'.[143] Concerted action upon matters directly affecting Irish interests was clearly indispensable, but the implications of genuine co-operation were more far-reaching. Through her example Ireland brought to the forefront a wide range of new Radical objectives. For instance, crofter disturbances in the Scottish Highlands and tithe riots in rural Wales were deliberately modelled upon the 'no rent' manifesto and the Plan of Campaign. Gladstone also realized that the nationalist demands of Scotland and Wales had since 1886 been stimulated into 'a state of far more vigorous life than they would have been if our [Irish] proposal had been recognized ... as a Conservative proposal and allowed to pass ... without the fierce contest in which we are at present engaged'.[144] Hence, it was manifestly in the interests of the Nationalist party to ensure that upon such matters Liberals were kept up to the mark. When Dr Clark's Scottish Home Rule resolution came before the House in 1890, twice as many Irishmen as Scottish Liberals actually voted for the motion.[145] Similarly, Irish co-operation with the Liberal whips enabled the advocates of disestablishment to make significant strides in Parliament. Their laxity in attendance caused the Chief Whip (Arnold Morley) considerable anxiety,[146] but when the Nationalists did muster in full strength the results which could be achieved were remarkable. At John Morley's earnest request sixty Irishmen agreed to troop into the Liberal lobby at the close of a debate on Welsh disestablishment in February 1892. These included Parnellites and even a handful of Ulster Unionists, an unexpected bonus which helped to reduce an otherwise impenetrable government majority to a relatively precarious 47 votes.[147] Harcourt was very conscious of the value of this bloc of Irish votes since he, in effect, determined the tactics of the parliamentary party during Gladstone's prolonged absences. 'We cannot afford to diminish the number of the Irish votes,' he argued. 'Without it we shall never have a Liberal vote' (or parliamentary majority) once the Irish had obtained Home Rule.[148]

However, the façade of cordial co-operation between Liberals and Nationalists contained serious flaws. In the summer of 1889 both the strength and the weakness inherent in the 'union of hearts' were exposed in connection with the highly sensitive subject of furnishing the Prince of Wales with a supplementary grant of public money. The habitual agitators from below the gangway predictably seized upon a convenient excuse to vilify the composition of the Civil List itself. Far more serious was the embarrassing division on the Liberal frontbench between those who deferred to Gladstone's long standing reluctance to inconvenience the Crown and those ranged behind Harcourt and Morley to whom unconditional endowments were anathema. All but a handful of Radicals deserted their revered leader when he courageously undertook to support the government's generous financial offer to the Prince. Gladstone, astonishingly, seemed able to exercise more influence over the 'uncrowned king' of Ireland than over leading members of his own party. With what stoicism he could muster, Parnell stumbled in the wake of Gladstone, leading his obedient flock into the Unionist lobby as division followed division. No doubt Gladstone's private entreaties to dispel the widespread illusion that the Irish were by nature a disloyal race carried great weight with Parnell.[149] Two years earlier the Nationalists had foolishly given hostages to the enemies of Home Rule by voting solidly against the plan to hold a service at Westminster Abbey in honour of the Queen's golden jubilee. On that occasion T. P. O'Connor had carefully explained that a nation which was already confronted with a draconian coercion bill had little tangible cause for celebration. He had also protested that earlier in the same sitting many of his colleagues had fully demonstrated their loyalty to the Crown by declining to support a wrecking Radical amendment concerning the Duke of Connaught leave bill. However, the beneficial effect of this temperate statement had been destroyed by Arthur O'Connor and William Redmond, who had risen indiscreetly to contrast Irish poverty with royal wealth.[150] No attempt had then been made to rectify this unfortunate attitude, the Irish conspicuously remaining absent from the service of thanksgiving.

In the light of this precedent, the Irish obviously pursued a most uncongenial course in 1889, more distasteful even than their undertaking 12 months earlier to support the party of temperance upon the licensing clauses of the local government bill.[151] Moreover, it soon became glaringly apparent that the Nationalists had incurred the wrath of many zealous Liberal Home Rulers by choosing to swallow the bitter pill of Royal Grants. Such remarkable fortitude testifies to the reliability of the Irish vote and its total confidence in Gladstone's leadership. But Parnell's patience also suggests that the hand which gave added impetus to the Radical proclivities of the Liberal party was also capable of exercising some degree of selectivity concerning the kind of policy actually adopted. If the Nationalists were expected to make considerable personal sacrifices either in deference to Gladstone's wishes or in the interests of their Radical allies, they certainly possessed a perfect title to demand reciprocal concessions to meet the peculiar susceptibilities of Ireland.

The consideration which preyed most heavily upon the tortured mind of a Protestant Parnell was his duty as leader of a predominantly Roman Catholic nation in connection with the explosive issue of religious education. At the general election of 1885 the Irish party had posed with the Conservatives as staunch champions of the voluntary schools. Yet almost immediately afterwards the Nationalists performed a remarkable volte-face, agreeing to a secret truce with their Radical allies. This astonishing transition has strangely escaped the attention of historians, even though the operation of a veiled policy of reciprocity created serious problems for both parties. The mere existence of an entente concerning Home Rule did not in any way diminish Nationalist hostility to the Radical policy of submitting sectarian schools to secular control. A tense situation arose once it became plain that a disconcertingly large majority of enthusiastic Liberal Home Rulers fully supported Chamberlain's objectives in education, regardless of their mentor's inconvenient views on Irish policy. Co-operation between an essentially Catholic party and one composed mainly of nonconformists therefore posed seemingly insuperable difficulties. Gladstone feared that the Anglicized landowning gentleman who commanded the Irish would 'cut a somewhat Tory figure' when it suited his purpose.[152] Herschell also doubted the reliability of Parnell, alleging that the Nationalists 'could never be counted on, and on all questions which are Liberal touchstones, such as unsectarian education and protection they would vote against us to a certainty'.[153] But the Nationalists could not then afford to dispense with the services of their Liberal allies. It was obviously in the interests of both parties to ensure that potential sources of discord were kept in abeyance until the time arrived when Irishmen could safely settle controversial issues in Dublin. Friction could only be avoided by the exercise of caution and the utmost restraint. Fortunately, the defeated Liberals were in no position to redeem the uncompromising Radical pledges of 1885, and so remained quite content to allow the whole question to slumber. This consideration largely explains why the reactionary and provocative Report of the Cross Commission on Elementary Education was received in 1888 in an uncomfortable silence. Lyulph Stanley's vigorous minority report led directly to the foundation of the National Education Association, but this nonconformist protest organization never achieved the status which had been enjoyed by its notorious forerunner, the defunct Education League of Birmingham.

The thorny subject of State subventions to sectarian educational institutions was not broached in Parliament until 1889. However, impatient Radicals fully compensated for their previous inhibitions by clashing with the Nationalists on three separate occasions as the session drew to a close. The reason for this abrupt change in attitude is not difficult to establish. Parnell had inflicted a series of slights upon the Radicals and had wantonly betrayed one of their cherished causes by deserting the militants on the issue of Royal Grants. Harcourt reported that the backbenchers were now 'sulky' with the Irish and were no longer prepared to appease those who had signally failed to rally in their support.[154] When the Scottish local government bill entered Committee in July, P. Esslemont (Aberdeenshire) promptly proposed an amendment confining the benefits of free elementary education to Board schools. In the words of Campbell-Bannerman this would be tantamount to 'killing the denominational schools in Scotland'.[155] At his request the offending amendment was withdrawn. But Irish suspicions had been thoroughly aroused, and three days later (15 July) these were confirmed when a technical education bill, introduced by several Liberal backbenchers, was seen to contain clauses which conferred additional powers upon School Boards. The thoughts of Unionist churchmen were voiced by the Nationalist spokesman, B. C. Molloy, who contended that the promoters of the bill did not really wish to improve technical education but hoped to secure instead an unfair advantage for Board schools at the expense of the Voluntary system.[156] The inconsistencies of reciprocity finally came to a head when Parnell gave his cautious approval to Balfour's plan to establish a Roman Catholic university in Ireland. On the day prior to the prorogation, Radical members spoke disparagingly and openly of the 'extraordinary billings and cooings' between the government and the Irish benches.[157] By now Gladstone had become thoroughly alarmed. Although not without a sizeable share of personal responsibility for the breach, he privately reminded Parnell that the very mention of religious endowments in Ireland would be certain to sever the Nationalists from those nonconformists whom he avowed were the 'backbone' of the Liberal party.[158]

Fortunately, Balfour was unable to exploit the growing tension in the ranks of the opposition. He could not proceed with his offer since the conciliatory gesture had offended many bigoted Presbyterian Unionists, and, in any case, Parnell's defiance of Liberal opinion was soon neutralized by the emergence of divisions within the Nationalist party.[159] Justin McCarthy discounted the profusion of 'wild, alarmed discourse', and calmed Home Rulers on both sides of the Irish Sea with a reminder that a legislature in Dublin would be perfectly capable of enacting 'a far more satisfactory measure of university education ... than Mr Balfour could possibly carry through the Imperial Parliament'.[160] Most nonconformist Liberals possessed sufficient sense to realize that a self-governing Ireland could only be influenced by Irish requirements, but they also shared the view of a prominent minister, J. Guinness Rogers, who lamented that 'the impression of that unhappy episode will not easily be effaced'.[161]

Although the immediate pressures upon members were relieved by the close of the session, many constituents would not permit the quarrel to die a natural death. The party organizations were able to participate in the debate during the recess, and they expressed the sentiments of the nonconformist rank and file in no uncertain manner. At its annual meeting in December the N.L.F. unanimously adopted a resolution which condemned any endowment of a denominational college in Ireland as 'contrary to the spirit of past legislation, and opposed to the conscientious convictions of the great majority of the British people'. This terse statement echoed the verdict reached by the Scottish Liberal Association at Glasgow, where Balfour's scheme had already been emphatically dismissed as 'reactionary and injurious'.[162]

Under these circumstances it was evident that the 'union of hearts' would shortly collapse amidst bitter recriminations unless drastic surgery was undertaken. However, the initiative for this life-saving operation came from two wholly unexpected quarters – the Conservative premier and an illustrious English Catholic. On 26 November Lord Salisbury threw down the gauntlet to his adversaries, by informing delegates present at a conference of the National Union that the government intended to abolish fees in every public elementary school. Meanwhile Cardinal Manning had written to Morley requesting an interview on the 29th at which they could explore the possibilities of securing a reconciliation between the estranged Home Rule parties. Morley hastily communicated in the strictest secrecy with a fellow Radical M.P., Sydney Buxton (who had recently collaborated with the Cardinal during the London dock strike). The purpose of this desperate missive was to ascertain whether, in fact, any compromise was feasible, and Morley must have been heartily thankful to receive by return the germs of the necessary agreement which became public knowledge three months later.[163]

When Parliament met in February 1890, the Anglican educationalist, Arthur Acland, was quick to point out that in spite of Salisbury's declaration, the Queen's Speech contained no reference to free education. However, the independent Radicals and nonconformists showed no disposition to embarrass the Vice-President of the Council, Sir William Hart-Dyke. They were intent on a quite different object. Under the guise of attempting to elicit the views of the government, they were, in reality, challenging their own front-bench to announce the official Liberal policy. When Acland's motion had first appeared on the order paper, Morley took the precaution of conferring again with Manning, and possibly with some of the Irish members as well.[164] This private arrangement completely removed Mundella's justifiable fear that should the government utter words of encouragement to the Voluntaryists, Liberal leaders would be obliged to resist such *'impossible conditions . . . with the Irish against us'*.[165] In the early stages of a 'hot' debate Mundella could therefore broach with confidence the subject of the Buxton formula in order to test the reactions of expectant Radicals. Since no serious objections were forthcoming, Morley felt free to adopt this tentative proposition as the settled policy of the party:

> Our position, I think, is this – that when a school is intended for all it should be managed by the representatives of the whole community. Where, on the other hand, the school claims to be for the use of a section of the community, as, for example, the Catholics or the Jews, it may continue to receive public support as long as it is under the management of that sect.

Thomas Sexton rose in dramatic fashion as soon as Morley had resumed his seat, and cordially accepted this succinct statement on behalf of his Irish compatriots.[166] In the division immediately afterwards, he and 30 other Nationalists marched eagerly into the Liberal lobby.[167]

Morley and Mundella carefully refrained from offering any explanation as to why they had entered into this curious 'Concordat' with the Irish, or how they planned to secure general nonconformist acceptance of this compromise. For 18 months the Liberal front-bench succeeded in concealing its true intentions. Only during the debate on the free education bill in 1891 did the strict Wesleyan member for Wolverhampton (H. H. Fowler) admit, under pressure from Chamberlain, that his party frankly hoped to buttress the privileges enjoyed by Catholic institutions through active discrimination against Church of England schools.[168] However, most discerning observers had long been capable of unravelling the intricate thread of Liberal motivation. In the villages of England and Wales nonconformists were compelled to send their children to schools which were generally under Church of England management, and which habitually employed teachers who were active members of the Established Church. The injustice arising from this total absence of parental choice in single school districts constituted a powerful argument in favour of bringing all voluntary schools under the surveillance of elected School Boards. On the other hand, in areas where the population adhered exclusively to one denomination (as in Ireland), many Liberals were prepared to waive the right of popular control. It was, in any case, futile to challenge the authority of the parish priest in Irish villages, or to tamper with the management of convent schools, a lesson learnt in 1892 when Herbert Gardner (Saffron Walden) rashly suggested that public meetings ought to be held in every school, irrespective of the subject matter or the views of the school managers. Timothy Healy gently reminded his Liberal friends that such a proposition was a 'matter of some delicacy' for the Irish, but took care not to associate his remarks with Catholic schools elsewhere in the United Kingdom.[169] Outside Ireland Catholic schools were rarely found in villages and townships, and instead were concentrated in the great industrial centres to which the surplus population of Ireland migrated in search of employment. Liberal leaders were relieved and gratified to discover that Catholic schools alone could legitimately preserve their exclusive sectarian status without impinging in any way upon the religious freedom of children who adhered to other denominations.

Lyulph Stanley accepted the contention that the Roman Catholic Church neither pretended to be the national church in England, nor occupied a monopolistic position in the sphere of education. He therefore thought that Radical educationalists 'ought to be very considerate to those minorities who only plead for themselves, and who make corresponding financial efforts which may justify their petition for private management, coupled with a liberal measure of public support'.[170] However, many of his colleagues showed little sympathy towards a secret bargain with the Irish which was specifically designed to accord Catholic schools a special status in the community. The pages of the *Nonconformist* were filled with articles by prominent Radicals protesting that the slightest dilution of the twin principles of public control and non-denominational teaching conflicted with established Liberal policy and would inevitably strengthen the position of voluntary schools as a whole. At Stepney in March 1890 Morley courageously sought to dam the rising tide of Radical discontent by explaining that ideally the party ought to strive after the system which prevailed in Scotland, where voluntary schools were permitted to function in districts where every child was guaranteed access to a school under representative management. But in a constituency where nonconformists were (in London terms) relatively strong, these apologetic remarks were heard in stony silence. Only towards the close of the speech, when Morley lamely conceded that his suggestion had been received in the country 'with suspicion, with jealousy, and in some quarters with downright aversion', did the audience burst into applause.[171]

Once the initial hubbub had died down, Morley furtively began to explore methods of restoring to the Irish Catholics their improvised safety-valve of privileged treatment. He also feared that a group of equal standing with the nonconformists would soon grow impatient of any unnecessary delay in the granting of free education. Many impoverished agricultural labourers betrayed little interest in the democratic reorganization of the educational system, but strongly resented carping nonconformist politicians whose doctrinaire attitudes ensured that their precious school pence would continue to slip out of half-empty pockets. Hence the pragmatic 'Hodge', the Radical extremist, and the apprehensive Irish, all wondered whether the Liberal party would attempt to symmetrize this ill-proportioned triangle of competing claims. Harcourt suggested one possible answer when he wrote:

> I know the difficulties [of free education] especially for the Irish, but we cannot afford to drop it *vis à vis* of the English constituencies. But the *District Council* which is the corner-stone of rural political life ought to be prominently pushed forward. . . . This is just what we want for the county electoral programme.[172]

Harcourt was clearly implying that the agricultural labourer might forget his desire for free education if he was offered full compensation in a different field. Similar tactics could be extended to other affronted interest groups. The Radicals were indirectly being asked to barter their nonconformist scruples for attractive alternative policies. But before reactions to this tempting proposition could be assessed, Parnell wrecked the strategy by refusing to retire, after his exposure in November 1890. He proceeded to thrust the Irish along a collision course with the Liberals, thus impressing quite fresh considerations upon the minds of his former friends. The future of Home Rule now seemed to hinge upon the response of scandalized puritan M.P.s to the government's impending free education bill. On the eve of the critical debate (June 1891), Morley strove to avoid the bitter struggle with a divided Nationalist party which he knew the adulterous Parnell was planning to foment. In desperation, rather than hope, Gladstone was informed:

> I trust that when our course on Free Schools is settled, it will not be forgotten that our Irishmen will support the denominational schools strongly, and indeed they must. Parnell ... is looking forward, as I know, to this business as likely to create a coldness between them and us, and so helping his great aim of making us

lose the general election. From this point of view, it would seem to be desirable not to fight the Denominational question too pertinaciously, and to do as little as we can to delay the Bill. I should be sorry for my part to make the School question a very prominent matter at the next election, and the sooner we get it out of the way, the better for us.[173]

This wise counsel failed to reach the ears of the nonconformist-dominated N.L.F., which met on 15 June to consider the draft government bill. The general committee adopted a long and intemperate resolution, concluding with the statement that no settlement would be regarded as 'satisfactory or final unless . . . all schools supported by public money shall be subject to public representative control'.[174] No interest was shown in the Scottish version of a dual educational system. When Fowler attempted to implement such a compromise a fortnight later, the noted Congregationalist preacher Dr R. W. Dale scathingly dismissed this mark of the 'Concordat' as 'impotent and indefinite'.[175] In these circumstances the warring Irish would not rally behind Fowler, and his Instruction to Committee was defeated by the decisive margin of 101 votes. Only one Nationalist ventured to explain the reasoning behind their uncooperative conduct, and especially the presence of three Parnellites in the Unionist lobby. Colonel J. P. Nolan emphasized that the feud within the Irish ranks made 'little or no difference in this matter. . . . I have been expressly returned to vote upon most questions with the Liberal party, but I am equally pledged to support denominational education, and I cannot conceive any Irish member so pledged voting for this Instruction'.[176] Such intransigence at last converted even heavily-blinkered Radicals to Morley's view that the pursuit of complete popular control was a vain exercise. The Rochdale minister who, in 1896, trembled with indigation at the thought of Liberal M.P.s making 'promises in corners and ante-rooms to priests of more than one denomination' was an eccentric and solitary figure at the annual meetings of the N.L.F.[177] For all practical purposes the Liberal party had chosen, in 1891, to drop the schools question from the electoral programme rather than run the risk of alienating the Irish vote in Parliament and in British constituencies.

To no one was this news more welcome than Gladstone himself. In recent years his enigmatic Radical personality and performance had been marred by one gross deficiency, a tenacious faith in the virtues of the Voluntary system. Nevertheless, Gladstone dared not ride roughshod over his nonconformist supporters, and at an early stage seemed anxious to offer some concessions to their sectarian principles. He certainly did not believe by 1887 that in single school districts over-enthusiastic Voluntaryists were entitled to inflict their distinctive dogmas upon hapless nonconformist pupils merely because the law compelled them to subsidize Board schools elsewhere. This spurious claim was dismissed on the grounds that it corresponded exactly with nonconformist grievances against the Established Church. Gladstone proposed instead to resolve the burning conflict surrounding the issue of religious instruction by confining all teaching in voluntary schools to secular subjects during school hours. However, this suggestion shed little light upon the central problem. Nonconformists did not wish to amend the conscience clause of the 1870 Act, but were intent on bringing all schools in receipt of a government grant under direct popular control. On this vital latter point Gladstone was strongly 'disinclined to whatever places distinctive teaching at any real disadvantage', and Manning learnt that he remained 'very jealous of all attempts at cutting and carving religion by the State'.[178]

When the government's free education bill came before the House, Gladstone was confined to Hawarden by the illness and death of his eldest son. 'It is perhaps as well that I am out of the way,' he wrote with considerable relief. 'When people come to close quarters on that question, it may involve difficulty for me. For the present I let sleeping dogs lie'.[179] Gladstone knew that active nonconformists had hitherto refrained from criticizing his deep-rooted churchmanship only out of respect and affection for their veteran leader. But personal reverence had already been proved a thoroughly unconvincing motive for restraint. The Royal Grants affair had cruelly demonstrated that the militants were liable to disregard Gladstone's still lingering Tory and monarchist sentiments when it suited their own purposes. Yet it was also plain that the overriding importance of preserving a cordial relationship with the Irish did set a limit upon the ambitions of these assertive Radicals. Catholic nationalism therefore unwittingly provided Gladstone with an effective buffer between the dictates of his ecclesiastical conscience and the unwavering convictions of nonconformist Home Rulers. He now felt free to endorse Radical programmes without simultaneously dreading that through doing so he would also be compelled to gratify inconvenient nonconformist desires upon educational matters. This became relatively easy once Chamberlain, the author of the abrasive free schools policy of 1885, had left the party. Hence, by 1891, Gladstone could wholeheartedly perform a duty which he had been reluctant to undertake at previous general elections – namely, to bestow his unqualified blessing upon the Radical programme.

[IV]

The Anatomy of Caucus Politics

1. *The Rise of the National Liberal Federation*

In the spring and early summer of 1886 all eyes were focused upon the floor of the House of Commons, where Gladstone was engaged in an historic struggle on behalf of Irish Home Rule. However, a less widely-publicized but equally momentous conflict was also in progress inside an hotel overlooking New Palace Yard. An extraordinary meeting of the council of the National Liberal Federation had hastily been summoned to the Westminster Palace Hotel for the special purpose of considering the government's Irish policy. At this emotional conference on 5 May the President of the Federation, James Kitson of Leeds, took an unprecedented step. He declined to submit to the delegates the official resolution, which was designed to commit the organization to a Chamberlainite and Unionist policy, and supported instead an amendment proposed by John Ellis, M.P. for Rushcliffe and chairman of the powerful Organization subcommittee. This amendment was phrased in such a way as to pledge the Federation unconditionally to Gladstonian Home Rule. 'On Kitson asking for "in favour of the amendment" the whole room seemed to rise', Ellis exulted. '"Against",, a miserable straggling minority followed, and the cheering was terrific'.[1]

A week earlier the autonomous National Liberal Federation of Scotland had arrived at a similar conclusion, barely a score of delegates expressing dissent. But the verdict of Scotland failed to carry conviction because the meeting at Glasgow had not been thoroughly representative.[2] This charge could not be levied against its English counterpart. Hence Morley, who had actually been present at Glasgow, brushed aside this pioneering pronouncement and justly referred to Kitson's organization as being 'almost the single consolidating and steadying element in that hour of dispersion'.[3] The impact which provincial sentiment subsequently made upon London and its outlying suburbs certainly adds weight to this measured judgement. F. A. Channing (M.P. for East Northamptonshire) captured the London and Counties Liberal Union 'by storm' in similar fashion to Ellis, and even succeeded in 'overriding the strong feeling of many influential Liberals'.[4] Dilke was less fortunate when, on 18 May, he attempted to exert his influence in an opposite direction. He proved quite unable to exploit his position as President of the London Liberal and Radical Council, and could not prevent an unusually well-attended meeting of the Council from both denouncing Unionism and hissing the names of Hartington and Chamberlain.[5]

These demonstrations of personal affection and political loyalty made a deep impression upon Gladstone. He believed that the contrast between 'the action of what seems to be the nation' and the resistance which he had encountered within the parliamentary party was 'most remarkable'.[6] Enthusiasm for the Irish cause rekindled in Gladstone the lingering spirit of 1877. To the dismay of the official leaders of that era, he had acted with great daring after suffering a setback to his Balkan policy in Parliament. Working on the assumption that Disraeli's government could 'only be kept even decently straight by continuous effort and pressure from without', Gladstone had decided to attend the inaugural meeting of the N.L.F. and throw the weight of his authority behind its novel objectives. Chamberlain's ulterior designs in the 1870s had coincided with Gladstone's Balkan strategy. Consequently, when the latter had addressed the delegates at Birmingham on 31 May, he had been delighted to discover that nearly everyone present adhered to the 'high doctrine' of undiluted Gladstonianism on the Balkan question.[7]

Hence, almost a decade after he had shrewdly employed the nascent Federation to promote his Balkan policies, Gladstone instinctively returned once more to that body in order to enhance the prospects of the Home Rule bill. To the annoyance of Unionist Liberals, a division on the second reading was delayed until their local associations had regrouped to such an extent that they could at last exert pressure upon rebellious M.P.s. Francis Schnadhorst, secretary of the Federation, was suddenly ushered into the exalted company of those who decided high policy, on account of his unique and encyclopaedic knowledge of constituency politics. He, in fact, was the 'best electioneering authority' who persuaded Gladstone that further delay would be 'advantageous' to the Irish policy.[8] Schnadhorst's frequent conversations with Gladstone were reputed to have 'disgusted' the Chief Whip, since these impromptu councils of war made the task of converting the waverers much more difficult. Chamberlain felt that the disintegration of the party could have been avoided if only Schnadhorst had not retained a stubborn faith in Gladstone's capacity to carry the country with him.[9]

Gladstone possessed so much confidence in Schnadhorst's ability that he entrusted the very existence of the government to the care of his persuasive electioneering guidance. Immediately after the fateful division of 8 June he pressed upon the cabinet a memorandum compiled by Schnadhorst which urged a snap dissolution.[10] This hasty decision caused disaster at the polls. Gladstone soon began to question Schnadhorst's reputation for infallibility, when he realized that many by no means hopeless constituencies remained unequipped with Home Rule candidates. 'I never understood the policy of making the Dissolution so very early', he confessed after nominations had closed in July. 'But I did not set up my own opinion.'[11] The shortcomings of Schnadhorst were further exposed when a stream of injudicious telegrams started to pour out of the party offices in London. These were issued in Gladstone's name while the 'author' rested at Hawarden, but a largely innocent premier was held responsible for sending messages which seriously damaged the Liberal cause.[12]

Despite these gross blunders, Gladstone did not seek for an excuse to sever his connection with a thoroughly chastened Schnadhorst. He was perfectly aware that had it not been for the enthusiastic support of the caucus, the trouncing of Gladstonian candidates at the elections would have assumed the proportions of an utter rout. However, some comfort could be derived from the fact that the overzealous Federation was now equally hamstrung. Once Chamberlain and his Unionist confederates had been ejected *en bloc* from important offices within the organization, the remaining Federation leaders had no alternative but to merge their identity in Gladstone. Thus, the drama of 1886 inaugurated an enduring partnership between a grateful Gladstone and the purified Federation, a true 'union of hearts' in pursuit of a common Irish objective. The marriage was consummated by the allocation of favours in the dissolution honours list. A knighthood was conferred upon Walter Foster, chairman of the general committee, while the devoted Kitson received a still more generous token of Gladstone's appreciation. A baronetcy was promptly bestowed upon the Leeds industrialist when it became known that he had cheerfully sacrificed £5,000 of business income by concentrating so fully on onerous political duties.[13] These rewards for loyal service were reciprocated as soon as Salisbury took office, in the form of a clarion call on behalf of Home Rule issued by the Federation's Emergency Committee.

The growing harmony between the party leaders and the popular organization was symbolized in September 1886 by Schnadhorst's

decision to move at once from the 'utterly demoralized' atmosphere
of Birmingham and establish a headquarters in London.[14] The
Federation chose to occupy offices in Parliament Street adjacent to
those that housed the Liberal Central Association (the official instrument of the party leader which was controlled in person by the Chief
Whip). Schnadhorst simultaneously accepted an invitation to become
honorary secretary of the Central Association, coupling this rather
nebulous position with his Federation secretaryship. However, this
revolution in the organizational structure of the party was neither so
precipitate nor so unexpected as it appears at first sight. Although
the Home Rule crisis certainly provoked violent clashes within the
Federation, it is necessary to recall that the purge which followed
was merely the culmination of a series of fierce internal disputes
which had racked the Federation from its earliest days. Above all,
there exists sufficient evidence to suggest that the struggle to determine the Federation's Irish policy reflected a long standing desire
on the part of many provincial Liberals to free themselves from
personal domination by Chamberlain. Taken in conjunction, these
factors demonstrate the extent to which the Federation nourished a
secret hope of eventually being accepted by the parliamentary leadership as the authoritative source of constituency opinion.

Even prior to the foundation of the Federation, Chamberlain
could not suppress his irritation that it had been a 'great mistake' to
associate Manchester and Leeds with the venture. He considered
that their participation would 'seriously hamper' the freedom of
Birmingham to impose 'prompt and united action' upon the
affiliated associations.[15] This dictatorial outburst fully justified the
fears which Sheffield Liberals had entertained since the general
election of 1874, when Chamberlain had marched uninvited into the
city and split the party vote by contesting the seats of well-established
members. One of the inconvenienced M.P.s (Mundella) alleged that
there existed in Birmingham 'a narrowness, pettiness, and want of
generosity which disqualifies them for leadership'. Under these
circumstances Mundella had reason to suspect that 'appeals to the
associations will be made or neglected as Birmingham deems desirable, and Chamberlain moves Birmingham'.[16] These dark forebodings soon became established fact. The Federation was indeed
totally dominated by Chamberlain's Birmingham friends, and provincial opinion was being manipulated to serve his personal
ambitions. By 1882 the absence of even a pretence of prior consultation had reached the stage where Manchester contemplated leading
a secession in order to found a rival organization.[17] These tensions
burst out in October 1885 when the Federation council was in congress at Bradford. On the pressing question of free elementary

education, Alfred Illingworth voiced the sentiments of local non-conformists, and 'endeavoured by a mild amendment to the "cut and dried" scheme presented to the Conference to give a caution to Chamberlain and Jesse Collings'.[18] But Birmingham was by now intoxicated with power, and instantly crushed any deviation from its views. A few months later these same officials drew up a Home Rule resolution, which embodied the 'very soul of Chamberlain', without paying any regard to the opinions held by other associations. Such arbitrary behaviour was sufficient to fan the embers of resentment that rapidly gave rise to a conflagration of uncontrollable proportions. 'The imperiousness and perversity of the Birmingham school is now shewing itself,' wrote J. S. Mathers, President of the West Leeds association.[19] His patron Kitson was seething with indignation at the '*mauvais esprit*' of Birmingham, and despised their petulant inability to accept defeat.[20] He hastened to the Reform Club in Pall Mall where John Ellis was conferring with notables from Liverpool, Bradford, Sheffield, and elsewhere in the West Riding. Here, in the afternoon of 4 May, was cast the die which on the morrow led to the destruction of Chamberlain at the Westminster Palace Hotel.

While Birmingham nursed its bruises, Bright alleged that the revolt against Chamberlain had been inspired by the small-mindedness of those rivals who were 'affected with envy'.[21] But this common notion cannot survive close scrutiny. The Federation had already outgrown its initial dependence upon Birmingham, and could no longer tolerate being what Kitson later caustically referred to as a mere 'one man society'.[22] Yet great care was also taken to avoid any suggestion of jealous motives by ensuring that certain crucial links with Birmingham remained intact. Schnadhorst had shirked the responsibility of leading the insurgents against Chamberlain in the spring, but he was quickly forgiven and was wisely allowed to retain the key post of secretary. He was even permitted to fill the places vacated by his Birmingham colleagues with a fresh set of representatives from the same city, a manoeuvre which in later years caused the old cry of Birmingham hegemony to be revived.

When the Federation quitted Birmingham it gratefully left behind an antiquated set of political principles. Chamberlain had originally hoped that his machine would be 'detested by all Whigs and Whips'.[23] Its overt Radicalism was designed to exclude the former, while its distant geographical base precluded control by the latter. Chamberlain's twin ideals had therefore been quickly realized. The Chief Whip of the late 1870s (W. P. Adam) had not 'relished' the new organization, and had shared the unwillingness of Hartington to patronize an institution which the latter accused of representing one section only of a party which he endeavoured to lead as a whole.[24]

The theory and practice of rigid independence was consistently maintained until the early months of 1885. But as the general election drew nearer Chamberlain's iron resolution began to weaken, and was completely undermined by the discovery that Lord Richard Grosvenor intended to resign shortly from the post of Chief Whip. He now saw a golden opportunity of capturing the Central Association and using the patronage and vast funds at its disposal for the benefit of Radical candidates at the impending elections.[25]

In mid-July 1885 Chamberlain and Dilke, with the tacit support of Harcourt, held a series of private meetings with Gladstone and Grosvenor on the subject of party organization. Gladstone was urged to add more Radicals to the Whig-dominated executive committee of the L.C.A., to appoint Schnadhorst as joint secretary (with Wyllie, the incumbent) of the Association, and, finally, to nominate a Radical as Chief Whip when Grosvenor retired. A plan to install the Federation in Parliament Street was also considered.[26] These negotiations clearly blazed the trail which Kitson was to follow 12 months later. Indeed, Chamberlain's recommendations might even have been implemented before the close of 1885 had Grosvenor not been such an implacable foe of reconstruction. The brother of the Duke of Westminster resented Radical interference in operations which he haughtily considered to be a personal charge and above all an aristocratic preserve. Although Schnadhorst was duly nominated to the standing committee of the L.C.A. (which met daily until the elections ended), Grosvenor did not extend a welcoming hand to his new aide. In fact, he insulted the interlopers by ignoring Schnadhorst altogether and by refusing to open wide the L.C.A. treasure chest to left wing candidates like Jesse Collings. Chamberlain soon realized that 'Master Richard has made fools of us.' In an angry letter to Harcourt he alleged that Grosvenor had broken numerous promises and 'really means to do nothing at all for the Radicals and to keep all his benefits for the Whigs'.[27]

Such an explosive situation could not be allowed to continue indefinitely. Once the pressing need to present a united front during the elections had eased, Chamberlain sought to resolve the deadlock. He was no longer prepared to negotiate with a whip 'of Grosvenor's type', knowing that only the appointment of a professed Radical as Chief Whip could secure a permanent liaison between the Federation and the Central Association. The names which he and Dilke tentatively broached were those of Herbert Gladstone and W. S. Caine.[28] The final choice of a successor to Grosvenor rested with the leader alone, but by now Gladstone senior too had become aware of the gravity of the problem facing him. His nominee was Arnold Morley, son of a provincial dissenter and wealthy businessman whose public career had been devoted to philanthropic effort and the redress of nonconformist grievances. Samuel Morley epitomized the outlook of an earlier generation of eminent Radicals, the descendants of whom had gravitated towards the more aggressive and comprehensive Radicalism embodied in the N.L.F. Arnold Morley himself was described, perhaps unkindly, as 'a man of pleasure without a shred of real Nonconformity about him'.[29] It was true that he had not played an active rôle in the new political movement, but Gladstone's selection remained a highly significant one, because Arnold Morley's social background was totally alien to that of any of his predecessors. This factor alone guaranteed the concord which Chamberlain sought.

Arnold Morley remained at his post for nearly seven years. Shortly before his retirement in 1892 he reviewed with satisfaction the progress which had been accomplished. The Central Association had not collapsed into ruins as Grosvenor had predicted, but contrary to expectations had become 'more efficient and more in harmony with recent developments of Liberal thought' than it had ever been since its foundation in 1860. However, the Chief Whip could not escape the fact that the L.C.A. had been hard hit by the disruption of 1886. 'The condition of the Party both in regard to finance and voluntary assistance', he continued, had not only rendered his task 'extremely arduous', but had also 'impaired the efficiency of the strict Parliamentary duties attaching to the office.'[30] The dwindling band of Liberal peers, who constituted the traditional source of party funds, could no longer be relied upon to fill the campaign coffers. 'We have', Gladstone lamented, 'say one twelfth of the House of Lords, one twenty-fourth of the Squires, a small minority of the men of wealth, perhaps one acre in fifty of the Soil.'[31] This serious depletion meant that leaders in the House of Commons, who had their own election expenses to meet, soon began to hear the unprecedented sound of 'calls upon the purse'. Between August 1886 and September 1887 Gladstone voluntarily contributed £1200, adding a further £500 in 1892.[32] But these limited subsidies were quite insufficient to keep the L.C.A. solvent, especially since the wealthiest Liberal peer of all (Rosebery) failed to respond to Arnold Morley's supplications.[33] Ultimately, the party managers were driven to desperate and unethical expedients, such as the sale of honours to industrialists and the acceptance from a company promoter like Cecil Rhodes of large donations with strings attached. These practices may have been extremely dubious, but a party which had '9/10 or indeed 10/10 of the operations to carry on' could not be expected to refuse gifts when 'all our wealth except perhaps 1/10 has absconded'.[34]

In these straitened circumstances it was scarcely surprising that an inexperienced Chief Whip should have badly mismanaged the 1886 general election. The secretive and completely unrepresentative Central Association lost whatever influence it could bring to bear upon candidates and local committees once the supply of cash had run out. This irreparable deficiency ensured that in future a more active and important rôle would be assigned to the N.L.F. Enthusiasm for Home Rule would be called upon to replace the social mystique which had vanished, purely voluntary labours now being required to compensate for cancelled subscriptions. In stark contrast to the paralysis that afflicted the L.C.A., the Federation was proudly able to proclaim a massive accession of strength in 1886. More than 70 M.P.s who had not been connected with the Federation promptly signalled their adhesion; none of the 255 affiliated organizations withdrew, and within a month of the defeat of the Home Rule bill nearly 50 associations were admitted to membership.[35] After this dramatic breakthrough the pace of the advance quickened perceptibly. By 1890 the total stood at over 850, there even being affiliated associations throughout the barren terrain of the Home Counties. The Federation could justifiably claim that it 'practically embraced the whole sphere of Liberal organization and activity', especially since it now bore 'the burden of work and expense' which hitherto had been carried by the Central Association.[36]

However, the statistics compiled by Federation officials ought to be treated with some caution. Their desire to gain a psychological advantage over Chamberlain was so great that they tended to exaggerate the wholesome effect produced by their remaining loyal to Gladstone. The Federation did not, for instance, admit that in 1886 several associations had endorsed Unionist candidates without actually withdrawing from membership, notably in Birmingham itself. Nor did Schnadhorst ever explain why so many associations had simultaneously queued for admission. The simple truth was that those local organizations which he had reconstituted in preparation for the 1885 elections could not possibly be affiliated until the following year.[37] The extension of the rural franchise was bound to create a sudden bulge because very few county associations had previously sought affiliation. In fact the decisive impetus towards greater electoral efficiency came, not from the traumatic experience of 1886, but from the prosaic changes which had been wrought by the large scale redrawing of constituency boundaries. The creation of single member constituencies artificially inflated the number of applications for membership. For example, Leeds and Sheffield were no longer content with being represented as corporate entities, and in 1886 each of the 10 new divisional associations was admitted individually to Federation membership.

Despite these reservations, a revolution in the organization of

Liberalism did take place during the years 1886–7. There existed a pressing need to avoid future electoral calamities by undertaking an intensive campaign of political education. Thus, the speed which the party managers deemed essential demonstrates that they were fully aware of the importance of capitalizing upon the enthusiasm of the new crusaders by using them to instruct the host of voters who remained unconvinced by the arguments in favour of Home Rule. Many electors were completely ignorant of Gladstone's closely reasoned case, and could not therefore begin to appreciate the merits of adopting an enlightened attitude towards Ireland. Schnadhorst launched a number of enterprises in order to rectify this grave deficiency. In 1887 he co-operated with Arnold Morley to create the Liberal Publication Department, an institution best remembered for its patronage in the early 1890s of the influential weekly newspaper, *The Speaker*, and the monthly *Liberal Magazine*. The chairmanship was vested in the scholarly M.P. for Aberdeen (James Bryce), an Ulsterman who immediately edited a handbook on Home Rule and issued a wide range of pamphlets and leaflets for more popular consumption. Within a year 10,000 copies of the primer had been sold.[38] The select Eighty Club was next galvanized into action, publishing a fortnightly circular entitled *Current Notes*, which according to its prospectus gave 'precise information as to proceedings in Ireland'.[39] A list of 54 lecturers on the subject was also circulated throughout the country, and Gladstone soon received the glad tidings that these Eighty Club missionaries had converted many sceptics.[40] Finally, at the instigation of Schnadhorst and Sir Walter Foster, a series of conferences were held in various counties between November 1886 and December 1887. These were ambitiously designed to stimulate a wholly unprecedented form of popular organization, a network of well-drilled and articulate regional federations.

The most extensive changes occurred in the south-east, territory which the provincial N.L.F. had hitherto failed to penetrate. However, by the close of 1885 it had become evident that the ineffectual London and Counties Liberal Union and its partner, the nebulous London Liberal and Radical Council, no longer deserved to remain in the ascendant. Neither organization had sought to replace decrepit local oligarchies by efficient divisional associations, remaining blind to the serious dislocation caused by the recent redistribution of parliamentary seats. Since no truly popular associations existed anywhere (except in Chelsea), it was scarcely surprising that the poorly-equipped London Liberals should be routed at the polls.[41] The L.C.A. and the N.L.F. now combined forces to sweep away the institutional impediments to greater electoral efficiency. Schnadhorst was allowed to dissolve the L.C.L.U., and create a streamlined Home Counties Division of the N.L.F., while Arnold Morley concentrated upon the metropolis.[42] In February 1886 the Chief Whip established an Organizing Commission, under the chairmanship of W. S. Caine, for the purpose of rearranging the old-fashioned constituency associations upon a democratic divisional basis.[43] Unfortunately, as one member of the Commission (R. K. Causton) explained, another general election intervened before this lengthy task had been completed, thus preventing London Liberalism from redeeming itself in 1886.[44] Nevertheless, the onerous task was accomplished shortly afterwards. By January 1887 the ground was at last prepared for the inception of the powerful London Liberal and Radical Union.

To Schnadhorst's dismay, the English provinces were not destined to undergo so momentous a transformation. Towns which had already emancipated themselves from the thraldom of Whig control fiercely resisted any attempt to curtail their civic dignity. For example, the north-eastern federation which Morley had hoped to create in 1886 could not be founded owing to the prevalence of an intense rivalry between Newcastle and Sunderland.[45] Similar squabbles concerning the location of an area headquarters probably explain why regional federations for Lancashire and the Midlands were not established until the 1890s. Total catastrophe was avoided only because Scotland and Wales possessed a sense of national consciousness sufficiently strong to enable them to overcome their own geographical feuds. A deep rift between east and west had existed in Scotland since 1876, symbolized by the antagonism felt by Glasgow Radicalism towards a Whiggish Edinburgh. Although a truce had been concluded in 1881, hostilities soon recommenced when the Edinburgh-based Scottish Liberal Association was challenged by its brash young Glasgow competitor, the N.L.F. of Scotland. An enduring peace required the surrender of the Whig citadel, an event which took place once the Home Rule schism had left Edinburgh bereft of defenders. The necessary merger could now be implemented, with Glasgow imposing a distinctly Gladstonian programme upon its reluctant bedfellow in December 1886.[46]

This success coincided with the creation of a national organization in a country similarly afflicted with regional tensions. In Wales the rural north was so incurably suspicious of the more populous industrialized south that it became necessary to isolate them in separate federations; a decision which did not please the Mid-Walians who wished to truncate the Principality still further by establishing a third federation in Montgomeryshire. The correspondence of the county's M.P. (Stuart Rendel) provides a unique insight into the

parochial nature of a conflict which must have had far wider application.[47] Under Rendel's leadership Montgomeryshire Liberals were
soon engaged in a relentless triangular struggle to secure control of
the embryonic North Wales Federation, the other participants being
W. H. Tilston of Wrexham and the Rev. Thomas Gee of Denbigh.
Rendel resented the dictatorial and underhand methods employed
by Tilston, who fondly imagined that he was destined to play the
rôle of a Welsh Schnadhorst. He was still more afraid of the vitriolic
and autocratic spirit which animated Gee, the anti-tithe prophet who
edited *Y Faner*. Rendel was so anxious to preserve intact the political
status enjoyed by both the Liberal gentry and his fellow Welsh
parliamentarians that in November 1886 he invited Schnadhorst to
enter a nest swarming with intriguers. But a panic-stricken Rendel
suddenly remembered that Schnadhorst was 'no longer the great
independent organizer of Radical Caucuses [but] the servant of the
Treasury whip'. Hence he now abandoned Schnadhorst and
laboured to prevent the puzzled interloper from annexing North
Wales to the Parliament Street empire. When the county delegations
arrived at Rhyl on 14 December, it seemed probable that the meeting
would degenerate into a bear-garden. No greater tribute to Schnadhorst's dexterity as a wire-puller can be paid than to reveal how he
succeeded in taming the conference, calmly 'melting away all
objections ... and fears'. Gee's ruffled feelings were soothed by
inscribing upon the North Wales programme a strongly-worded
statement concerning agrarian tenures. Tilston received his reward
by being offered the post of secretary. But Schnadhorst's *pièce de
résistance* was to secure for an incredulous but highly flattered
Rendel the coveted Presidency of the new North Wales Federation.
Amidst mutual congratulations Schnadhorst was able to hasten to
Cardiff, where on 24 January 1887 he drew South Wales also within
the orbit of the N.L.F. He could now proceed peacefully with his
ingenious scheme to link both federations in a Welsh National
Council.

2. *Wales versus Scotland*

On the Saturday following the Rhyl conference Rendel arrived at
Parliament Street in an ugly mood. He was bent on extracting from
Schnadhorst a full confession of the true reasons behind the move to
affiliate Wales to the N.L.F., having first compiled a long list of
plausible objections. But during their conversation Schnadhorst
presented a case which brooked no argument. There existed no
officially-inspired plot to crush the independent spirit of Wales.
Instead his chief aim was to expand the organization, thus enabling

all Liberals to share in the benefits which would accrue to a large-scale enterprise. He tactfully reminded Rendel that particular localities like Wales and London had not hitherto achieved conspicuous success by relying on pride alone to sustain great causes.[48] In all probability Schnadhorst clarified his meaning by pointing out that England controlled 14 votes for every one wielded by Wales, and had shown little sign of being ready to cast them spontaneously in favour of minority movements. A still greater obstacle blocked the road to national self-determination. Unless the Welsh demand for disestablishment was quickly entrusted to Schnadhorst, their suit would surely be squeezed out of court by a combination of selfish Scotsmen and unsympathetic Liberal leaders.

As Schnadhorst spoke the events of the past year crowded into Rendel's troubled mind, convincing him that this sombre analysis of the situation was perfectly accurate. The general election of 1885 had wrought a decisive transformation in the social and political character of the Welsh members. Those who had previously been notorious for their torpor were replaced by men who would not tolerate any continuation of the languor which had long characterized the treatment of Welsh questions.[49] Unfortunately, the 30 M.P.s representing Wales and Monmouthshire soon discovered that the short-lived Home Rule ministry was powerless to rectify this unsatisfactory state of affairs. A Scottish contingent of double their number made a far greater impact upon a cabinet which contained no Welshmen but included a clan of five Scottish representatives – of whom three (Rosebery, Trevelyan, and Campbell-Bannerman) were known to favour Scottish disestablishment. This disparity in the relative strength of the two nations was reflected in the divisions on the disestablishment resolutions which L. L. Dillwyn (Swansea) and Dr Charles Cameron (Glasgow) moved in March 1886. Wales trailed Scotland by exactly 100 votes, a result largely explained by Harcourt's intervention in the Welsh debate. On Gladstone's instructions the Chancellor of the Exchequer stated categorically that the Church in Wales constituted an integral and inviolable part of the Church of England.[50] This gratuitous affront to the Welsh sense of nationality was aggravated by Gladstone's failure to introduce the intermediate education bill left over from his previous administration. Finally, Gladstone jarred a peculiarly sensitive nerve by appointing in June an inspector of mines for South Wales who could not speak Welsh. The group's chairman, Henry Richard of Merthyr, was now forced to inform Gladstone that 'there exists considerable soreness of feeling owing to what is thought to be persistent neglect of the interests and wishes of Wales by the Liberal Government'.[51]

Immediate counter-action was impossible on account of the

proximity of an emergency dissolution. But in the first weeks of the new Parliament the Welsh group (by now reduced, temporarily, to 27) congregated in a committee room to place their affairs upon a more methodical footing. William Rathbone and Arthur Williams were appointed joint secretaries, and an arrangement was made to meet on alternate Thursdays during the course of each session. The group then discussed the construction of a national programme, resulting in the creation of three subcommittees to prepare reports on disestablishment and disendowment, the land question, and secondary education.[52]

However, Rendel soon became disenchanted with this sober and unhurried approach to burning Welsh issues, fearing that the national cause might be prejudiced by the group's immersion in tedious academic exercises. The reports could not possibly be completed in time to influence the N.L.F., which was already framing policy resolutions in preparation for the annual meeting at Leeds in November 1886. Close inspection of the provisional agenda revealed an alarming departure from the Bradford charter of October 1885. In that year the Federation had 'urgently demanded' disestablishment throughout Great Britain, but the officers now proposed to replace this positive assertion with a muted and innocuous reference to 'religious equality'. Hence, on the eve of the congress Rendel threw caution to the winds, approaching the one Liberal statesman who was known to sympathize with Welsh and nonconformist grievances. He urged Morley to speak out at Leeds and prevent Welsh disestablishment from being phased out of the Federation programme. In reply Morley candidly acknowledged that Welsh disestablishment was 'a reform which cannot any longer be kept out of the active objects of the Liberal Party [and] must now form an indispensable article of Liberal policy'.[53] These two letters appeared in the press on the morning of the conference (3 November), giving great satisfaction to the many delegates who fretted at the novel restrictions being placed upon their Liberationist sentiments. They did not realize, however, that Morley had been the victim of a piece of sharp practice. In reality Rendel had hazarded the future of Wales by publishing confidential documents without first seeking permission. An understandably angry Morley described this procedure as being both 'inconvenient and mischievous'.[54]

Rendel must have had strong reasons for indulging in a flagrant attempt at political blackmail. These stemmed entirely from a covering letter of 30 October, in which Morley had hinted that it might be prudent to refrain from any public commitment in case he should 'rouse one single fresh antagonistic interest'. Rendel acutely perceived that it was really Gladstone whom Morley was desirous not to offend. He also knew that Morley was about to visit Hawarden, where Gladstone, Harcourt, and Spencer would surely issue their errant colleague with an express instruction to ignore the Welsh request.[55]

Subsequent events proved the validity of Rendel's contentions. Morley did indeed bow to the wishes of his superiors by remaining silent. It quickly transpired that Gladstone was perturbed by the '*superfoetation* of Radical ideas' which had emerged at Leeds. He informed Harcourt, with reference to Welsh disestablishment, that he was 'rather too old to put on a brand new suit of clothes'.[56] Harcourt and Spencer naturally sympathized with Gladstone's predicament since they too were reluctant to foment an agitation on behalf of Welsh disestablishment. This became apparent shortly afterwards when Schnadhorst asked each in turn to preside over the inaugural meeting of the North Wales Federation. The grandson of a former archbishop of York could not be expected to abandon overnight the inspiring ecclesiastical tradition which he had inherited. Harcourt had not hitherto shown much interest in either Wales or disestablishment and so promptly declined the invitation. Spencer initially succumbed to Schnadhorst's wishes. But this decision was injudicious because the Northamptonshire peer now betrayed in correspondence his complete ignorance of the real nature of Welsh politics. He was shocked by the news that Welsh militants advocated Irish remedies for the problem of land tenure, and became thoroughly alarmed when Schnadhorst and Morley advised him that it was pointless going to Wales unless he paraded in full disestablishment colours.[57] Spencer was obliged to manufacture an excuse in order to escape a confrontation with Welshmen who were intent on making disestablishment the paramount objective of Welsh Liberalism. Schnadhorst eventually secured the services of Mundella, a man who reputedly 'sniffed at the idea of *Welsh* Disestablishment'.[58] But Mundella was also a professed Liberationist, and could therefore create an embarrassing situation for the Liberal leadership. Gladstone only learnt the name of Spencer's replacement at the eleventh hour (from the newspapers). Fortunately, Hawarden straddled the route to Rhyl, thus enabling Gladstone to take the precaution of briefing his Sheffield colleague on the morning of the conference itself.[59]

This setback only encouraged Rendel to redouble his efforts to secure for Wales full official recognition of her national aspirations. Although the legitimate claims of Wales could not be disregarded in perpetuity, it was still necessary to convince the party leaders that the demand for Welsh disestablishment was irresistible, and that their patronage of the movement was essential. Now that the two Welsh Federations had joined the N.L.F., it became possible to

strive after this ideal without unduly inconveniencing the frontbench. Harcourt freely conceded that it was 'quite within the
competence of the Federation to raise the question and work it',
though he clearly did not anticipate that Schnadhorst's labours
would produce rapid results.[60] However, those Welshmen who
remained dissatisfied with the Leeds programme thought otherwise.
If Englishmen could be persuaded to accept resolutions on Welsh
disestablishment, it seemed likely that Welsh influence within the
N.L.F. would be extended proportionately. Hence Tom Ellis, M.P.
for Merioneth, infiltrated conferences which were supposed to ratify
the Leeds policy with a mischievous plan to extend its scope. He
achieved a notable victory at Runcorn in December 1886 by carrying
a rider which reproduced the substance of Morley's forthright letter
to Rendel. Schnadhorst simultaneously aided and abetted this process of conversion by exploiting his special relationship with the
frontbench concerning electioneering requirements. By 1887 the
location of public engagements, and even the substance of speeches
themselves, were being compiled on his directions. Harcourt jocu-
larly complained that he no longer enjoyed 'any independent
existence' but was 'a mere tool in Schnadhorst's hands'.[61] Thus,
when Spencer was detailed to attend the grand opening of the Welsh
National Council in October, he frankly admitted that 'I took my
orders from Mr Schnadhorst who knows what is wanted in various
localities, and what article to serve in particular places.'[62] Schnadhorst evidently guessed that timid politicians could only overcome
their hesitancy and confusion with respect to Welsh questions by
enforced personal contact with the patriots themselves. After listening to some impassioned speeches at Aberystwyth, Spencer became
convinced that the more headstrong delegates would constitute
'some real danger if we do not adopt Welsh Disestablishment as part
of our programme AFTER Ireland'. He continued in a vein which
must surely have perplexed Granville, who had been the recipient
of soul-searching letters barely twelve months earlier. 'I was so
impressed,' Spencer wrote, 'that I went further as to the Church
than I had decided to do before I got to Wales. I myself could have
gone even further than I did, but . . . I thought it right to wrap up
a little my step in advance of Mr Gladstone.'[63] The stage was
now set for Wales to command the attention of the N.L.F., which
was due to meet at Nottingham a fortnight later (19 October).
Rendel and his confederates arrived at the annual meeting brandish-
ing the National Council's impressive resolution, and were welcomed
with open arms. Consequently, the N.L.F. promptly inscribed the
Morley doctrine upon its official programme, and in so doing gave
Welsh disestablishment a 'tremendous lift'.[64]

A similar deputation from the Scottish Liberal Association slunk almost unnoticed away from the conference chamber. After Rendel had spoken, the crofter M.P. Angus Sutherland rose with the intention of placing Scottish disestablishment upon an equal footing. But Schnadhorst would not deny Wales her hour of glory, and was probably responsible for advising Kitson to inform the Scotsmen that the agenda could not suddenly be reconstructed to take account of their views.[65] This curt response explains why 'gallant little Wales' was beginning to draw ahead of her stronger northern rival in the disestablishment stakes. Scotland now paid the inevitable penalty for stubbornly remaining aloof from Schnadhorst and Kitson. The flaunted independence of the S.L.A. was a dubious privilege once it became clear that isolation from the N.L.F. served only to place control in flaccid hands, thereby weakening the influence of Scotland upon the direction of Liberal policy. Whigs like the ninth Earl of Elgin, chairman of the executive council, continually strove to 'keep unruly tendencies in check'. He characteristically brushed aside his Radical minions as 'opinionative men – fond of publicity [and] apt to insist on their rights as elected representatives'. With patrician scorn Elgin assured Rosebery that their 'vanity makes them desire to be consulted, and I have always found them extremely willing to listen'.[66] These were not the dynamic and democratic qualities which alone could draw attention to Scotland's requirements. Rosebery and his Westminster-orientated compatriots could safely disregard the S.L.A. and concentrate their attention upon the decisions reached by its assertive English counterpart.

The task which confronted Scottish Radicals was rendered more difficult by their failure to construct a convincing national programme. The exodus of the Liberal Unionists in 1886 had removed many leading defenders of the Established Church, leaving the formation of ecclesiastical policy in the charge of their jealous Presbyterian co-religionists (who had seceded from the Church of Scotland at the time of the great disruption).[67] However, this transformation proved to be illusory, since disestablishment still appealed only to a narrow sectarian interest. There could be no comparison with Wales because the Church of Scotland was justly viewed as an indigenous institution, being socially and linguistically in complete harmony with national traditions. The lack of a convenient focus for national loyalties therefore had a dire effect upon Scottish morale. The S.L.A. was paralysed by the growing independence of the labour movement and by a convulsive debate concerning the merits of Scottish Home Rule.

This unhappy situation enabled Wales to consolidate her advantage by intensifying the browbeating tactics which had been employed up to 1887. Recent triumphs emboldened the Welsh Liberals to dictate more specific terms to the parliamentary leaders. Two cognate factors inevitably brought matters to a head. Firstly, the prospect of Gladstone's return to office loomed larger as each year passed, quickening interest in the prospective legislative programme of the next government. Secondly, speculation upon this point was heightened by a pervasive mood of exasperation with Gladstone for being so equivocal on the subject of disestablishment. Zealous non-conformists were no longer prepared to tolerate statesmen who 'frigidly pronounce some words from a chair once for all on Disestablishment – and thenceforth chill all popular counsels'.[68] Gladstone invited criticism by remaining intent on preserving a strict balance between the conflicting claims of Scotland and Wales, an attitude which seemed to discriminate against the latter – where disestablishment was already 'a really burning question'. Schnadhorst accurately conveyed the feelings of the Principality when he protested that 'apart from a very small section of Liberationists, no one in England cares twopence about [Scottish disestablishment] as a question of practical politics. Indeed those oppressed with a sense of the urgency of Social problems are rather irritated at any prominence being given to it.'[69]

Gladstone finally exhausted Welsh patience on 14 May 1889, when he ostentatiously declined to support Dillwyn's Welsh disestablishment motion (the first since 1886). The rumblings of discontent continued throughout the summer, daunting even the valiant Harcourt. He required much 'sound cram' from Rendel before he could be prevailed upon to confront the 'choleric gentlemen' of the National Council at Caernarvon on 17 October. However, Harcourt created a sensation by expressing his 'clear conviction . . . that the time has come when the Church in Wales must cease to exist'.[70] Spencer hastily penned a letter of congratulation, pointing out that it was 'of immense moment that the Welsh Liberals should be kept in good humour with Liberal leaders'.[71] But the celebrations were premature. Although Gladstone had granted Harcourt permission to commit the party formally to Welsh disestablishment, the delegates at Caernarvon were so 'wrathly riled' with their leader that they passed a motion of censure upon him and instructed the hapless Rendel to transmit the unwelcome news to Hawarden.[72] 'Wales and Scotland are running a race one against the other and both are pressing me', Gladstone wrote on receipt of this communication. Yet the threat of an imminent Welsh revolt did not tempt him to reconsider his patently untenable position. Rosebery was firmly told that Gladstone did not himself 'think that any further declaration from me, or on behalf of the party, is expedient at this time'.[73]

Had Wales been content to accept Gladstone's decision as final, no further problems need have arisen. But in December representatives of the North Wales Federation wilfully disregarded Gladstone's wishes by descending in force upon Manchester, where the N.L.F. was holding its annual meeting. The Rev. William Tuckwell (the 'Radical Parson') complained that a party of Welshmen disturbed the officials at breakfast on the 3rd 'with a clamorous threat of secession unless [Welsh disestablishment] should be placed on the Federation programme. I recall Schnadhorst's anxious head-shake, and his strongly expressed conviction that the party must not commit itself; but he was converted or overruled, and the measure was there and then adopted'.[74] Schnadhorst knew that he was trapped between the Charybdis of Welsh fervour and the Scylla of Gladstone's disapproval. There was no escape from this predicament, since Ellis Griffith of Anglesey could exploit his position on the general purposes committee to obtain for the Welsh militants a more positive statement concerning Welsh disestablishment. On the afternoon of the 4th Ellis Griffith persuaded the delegates at Manchester to add to the 'omnibus' resolution an important rider which contained a pledge to seek the introduction of a Welsh disestablishment bill 'as soon as Irish Home Rule is attained'.[75]

Unfortunately for Schnadhorst the North Walians were not satisfied with this notable advance. '*We will not* submit to ... this treatment we are receiving at Mr Gladstone's hands,' Gee wrote in exasperation. 'We must bring this question to *a finish*.'[76] Consequently, the North Wales Federation assembled at Rhyl on 30 April 1890 and resolved upon a much more extreme course. The Welsh M.P.s were instructed to withhold support from a future Liberal government unless a Welsh disestablishment measure was introduced concurrently with, or immediately after, the production of the Irish Home Rule bill. This display of petulance and unprecedented presumption alarmed those Welsh M.P.s who differentiated between an abstract commitment to a principle and the imposition of precise legislative criteria. The general committee of the N.L.F. was equally anxious to counter this challenge to the parliamentary independence enjoyed by Liberal leaders, and promptly commissioned the select general purposes committee to negotiate with the less headstrong Welsh National Council. A delegation consisting mainly of Welsh M.P.s was received at the Westminster Palace Hotel on 17 July and a compromise was hammered out. Schnadhorst conceded two material points to the Welshmen. Firstly, he agreed to favour Welsh disestablishment with special treatment at the next meeting of the Federation's council. Ellis Griffith's Manchester rider would be incorporated into a separate resolution at Sheffield, and placed immediately after Home Rule on the agenda. Secondly, the Federation promised to ensure that a Liberal government would possess an undeniable mandate to legislate on Welsh disestablishment by pressing the leaders to include the issue in their electoral programme. In return the Welsh delegation was persuaded to accept the doctrine that the Federation could not possibly pledge any future government 'as to the precise order of procedure to be observed in their parliamentary action'.[77]

Rendel viewed these developments with dismay. He entirely disapproved of the Rhyl resolution, fearing that Wales would suffer for her intransigence by precipitating a vulgar scramble on the part of more powerful Radical sections to secure priority over the Principality. Moreover, he suspected that all English sympathy might be lost if Wales continued to lurch along a path which led to total independence. Such an eventuality would tempt Gladstone to drop Welsh disestablishment from the Liberal programme. 'This fear of holding relations with another set of Celts is a real danger,' Rendel wrote after a tense conversation with Gladstone, Morley, and Rosebery. 'No wise men will pledge their fortunes to such dangerous alliances.'[78] He therefore deplored the eagerness of the National Council to propagate the mischievous notion of a National League copied from the Irish model. But Rendel also appreciated the folly of encouraging the Welsh parliamentary party to adopt a passive rôle in its relations with the frontbench. The Scottish Liberal Members Committee was a standing reminder of how easily the spirit of nationality could be crushed. Scotland had acquired a reputation for harbouring ambitious English carpet-baggers and for producing an excessive proportion of official Liberals. These two groups completely dominated the infrequent meetings of the Committee, thus ensuring that national energies were channelled along orthodox lines.

In contrast, Wales produced only two occupants of the frontbench in 1886, Sir G. Osborne Morgan and Sir Edward Reed. These relatively obscure junior ministers could neither serve Gladstone effectively nor aid their expectant compatriots. Consequently, the independent Welshmen were racked by disagreements concerning the exact relationship which ought to exist between themselves and the Liberal party. A growing rift separated the followers of the old-fashioned Liberationist, Henry Richard, from the emerging 'Young Wales' faction inspired by the 'Parnell of Wales', Tom Ellis. Rendel was associated with neither bloc, being intent on combining in his own person the distinctive features of each. As a level-headed Englishman, naturally he proclaimed the futility of separatism, and needed only to stress his unswerving loyalty to

Gladstone (a personal friend) to secure the allegiance of the traditionalists. On the other hand, Rendel shared Ellis's belief that the Welsh members generally lacked 'energy and go'.[79] He also secretly resented Richard's timidity in the House of Commons with respect to Welsh disestablishment. In 1888 he had urged Richard to organize the balloting to obtain a favourable place on private members' nights. But the chairman had shrunk from commanding a jealous Dillwyn to deliver up his special charge. 'There has been a great deal of grumbling at the extent to which [balloting] is carried sometimes by the Irishmen,' Richard feebly explained. 'For all of us to do that may perhaps be rather a strong measure'.[80] Such irresolute leadership meant that Wales had been conspicuously unsuccessful since 1886 in securing time to debate issues in which she was interested. Quite apart from a deep silence on Welsh disestablishment, no opportunity could be found to debate the bills on intermediate education and local veto. Had Ellis not taken the initiative in June 1888 by raising the twin questions of land tenure and tithe, Wales, in three consecutive sessions, would have failed utterly to obtain a hearing for any of her distinctive needs.

Hence Rendel was uniquely qualified to take over the chairmanship when Richard died in August 1888. One of his first acts was to appease his many nationalist critics by reconstructing the machinery of the parliamentary party. In November the group agreed to dispense with joint secretaries and to elect instead two official whips. Arthur Williams agreed to make this transition, but his partner Rathbone was less amenable. The exile from Liverpool shared the aversion expressed by his Caernarvonshire colleague, J. Bryn Roberts, to a manoeuvre which threatened to set Wales further apart from English Liberalism. The nomination was then offered to Ellis, who declined – presumably because he suspected that, in practice, the change would be one of form alone. The post was eventually accepted by D. A. Thomas, a young Merthyr industrialist who had been an M.P. for barely eight months.[81] Both whips took their new duties extremely seriously. After consultations with Ellis, they summoned the Welsh members to a special meeting on the opening day of the 1889 session. At this gathering the Committee at last agreed to deploy their limited forces more effectively by implementing the Rendel policy of joint balloting.[82]

The new procedure bore immediate fruit. Not only did Dillwyn achieve success in the ballot for his Welsh disestablishment resolution, but Rendel also procured a day (15 May) for the second reading of his Welsh intermediate education bill. This full-dress debate helped to crystallize the position of Wales in the political spectrum. The semi-autonomous status of the Welsh Liberals furnished them with a considerable degree of flexibility in their parliamentary activities. Rendel recalled that Gladstone's unprompted intervention during the Intermediate Education debate had given the bill 'an extraordinary lift'. He also acknowledged his debt to Charles Bradlaugh, the notorious atheist who sat for Northampton. Bradlaugh was so conversant with the rules of the House that he unearthed a device which enabled Rendel to claim priority on all private members' nights.[83] Yet all these labours would have been wasted unless Rendel had also obtained the friendly services of W. H. Smith and Sir William Hart-Dyke, the ministers chiefly involved. Rendel succeeded in transforming a nakedly partisan cause into a truly national and disinterested demand by inviting the handful of Welsh Conservative M.P.s to participate in the venture. Hart-Dyke had previously refused to collaborate with Rendel. But when he discovered on 17 July that the Liberal Committee had temporarily been reconstructed upon a bi-partisan basis, he agreed to negotiate with the Welshmen.[84] Rendel was now promised official government assistance, a gesture which enabled the Conservatives to claim a large share of the credit for passing the bill. Rendel had shown that, so far as the educational interests of Wales were concerned, solid gains could in fact be achieved through a display of political non-alignment. Nevertheless, opportunities for collaborating with the Unionists in this fashion did not recur; Welshmen could not escape the reality of dependence on the good offices of English Liberals. Only a Liberal government could satisfy the Welsh hunger for national dignity, since disestablishment and the secularization of tithe in particular were clearly anathema to the Tory mind.

This pertinent fact was not easily digested by the vocal minority of Welsh members who wished to consolidate a separate nationalist party. Their abysmal failure to reach an agreement concerning the desirability of Alfred Thomas's national institutions bill might have induced caution had the Welshmen not included in their ranks a fiery young solicitor. The extreme Welsh Home Rulers were mesmerized by the eloquence and bellicose outlook of David Lloyd George, who had been elected for the Caernarvon Boroughs in April 1890. Lloyd George demonstrated from the beginning his contempt for 'Rendelism' and his readiness to dissent from the Liberal frontbench. He promptly joined Labouchere in the traditional charade of seeking to reduce the Estimates in order to draw attention to the absurdity of hereditary privilege.[85] In the following session (1891) he plunged in earnest into Welsh questions, harassing the government mercilessly in connection with the tithe and clergy discipline bills. These guerilla tactics were so successful that Goschen held him personally responsible for the failure of the ecclesiastical

part of the government programme.[86] But this accusation only
encouraged Lloyd George to carry obstruction one stage further in
1892. He ignored Gladstone's tender plea for moderation, and
announced his intention of dividing on every amendment when the
new clergy discipline bill returned from Committee to the floor of
the House. However, few of his compatriots found it expedient to
defy a highly indignant Gladstone. Only seven of the 51 Liberals
who voted against the crucial motion to curtail debate represented
Wales, and of these only Ellis and Samuel Evans persevered with
Lloyd George in the rebellion.[87] The Welsh party had not therefore
finally broken free from the tutelage of the Liberal whips. The
degree of independence which Lloyd George could achieve was
shown to be very limited; complete political separation stood exposed
as romantic chimera.

3. *Labour Representation*

'The petty cliques who have been accustomed to impose their
candidates upon the electors find that power is slipping away from
them,' Chamberlain declared at the first annual meeting of the
N.L.F. in January 1879. Yet even at this early stage he felt it necessary to caution the delegates 'to take care that we do not, as a result
of our operations, substitute one clique for another'.[88] Chamberlain
realized that the very perfection of an expanding organization would
tend to increase the distance between elected officials and the rank
and file. The N.L.F. stood in considerable danger of ceasing to
speak for those whom it claimed to represent, and of acting instead
on behalf of those who viewed its existence with suspicion.

Evidence to justify this prophecy was not long in forthcoming,
mainly because the sovereignty of the mass of individual Liberals
was a concept which soon began to crumble when confronted with
the stern economic realities of local politics. The democratic façade
of the Liberal 'hundreds' was preserved intact, but in most cases the
supremacy of the ordinary and uninfluential member was shortlived.
The powerful and democratic Leeds association, which had been a
founder member of the N.L.F., demonstrated how rapidly the
original ideal could be eroded. By 1883 the Leeds Liberals were
obliged to rely upon the generosity of about 20 subscribers, even for
the routine work undertaken between elections.[89] Another illustration
of inherent but concealed weakness can be seen in the financial
predicament endured by the Liberal 'four hundred' of Dorset after
the Unionist president Lord Stalbridge (Grosvenor) had been ousted
in January 1887. Despite this resounding victory over one of the
principal landowners in the county, Lord Wolverton alleged that

Gladstonian organization would 'collapse' were he also to retire. 'No one else will find the cash needed for organization and registration – it is at least £1,000 a year.'[90] Even the vigorous North Wales Federation could not survive without regular subsidies from Rendel and other M.P.s. It needed £400 annually in order to function effectively, but this paltry sum was constantly beyond the treasurer's reach. 'The Federation is a luxury', R. A. Jones wrote in exasperation. 'If the Welsh people do not pay for it, they must do without it.'[91]

The shrinking numbers of those who were willing to donate funds was accompanied by a pronounced reluctance on the part of many ordinary members to participate in the voluntary work upon which representative institutions depend. Once the initial burst of enthusiasm for a novel political instrument had lost its momentum, some relapse into indolence was inevitable. The growth of inertia in the Liberal party was politically dangerous because it widened the gulf between the actual practice of constituency government and the admirable principle of widespread participation upon which the local associations had been founded. This disparity was particularly noticeable in London. Here the principles of democracy had been carried to extremity. Yet within two years of the general reorganization of the metropolis, Sidney Webb of the Fabian Society was able to assert that scarcely a single constituency could muster sufficient volunteers to sit upon its general committee. The abolition of subscription tests and their replacement by the direct representation of one elector in every 25 (who were not necessarily *Liberal*) was wholly unrealistic and therefore doomed to failure. But apathy was more deeply rooted than this. Another Fabian socialist, George Bernard Shaw, 'coolly walked in' to a meeting of the St Pancras South association and demanded that he be elected to the executive committee, 'which was done on the spot by the astonished Association – ten strong or thereabouts'.[92] This audacious piece of Shavian hyperbole was uncomfortably close to the truth. A Parliament Street circular of 1891 drew attention to the unwelcome fact that 'for some time past London has been sinking into that condition of lethargy which is ruinous to the Liberal party'.[93] One of the signatories was convinced that apathy constituted 'our deadliest enemy' in the metropolis. Schnadhorst assured Gladstone that unless they were prepared to abandon London altogether, every Liberal of national standing had no option in 1892 but to throw himself into the turmoil of L.C.C. electioneering.[94]

When the N.L.F. decided in June 1890 to investigate the deterioration of party organization in the provinces, it became apparent that London was not the only derelict area. Harcourt felt that the

situation in the west country gave cause for considerable anxiety.
Eleven area agents were appointed for England in accordance with
his suggestions. They were responsible for the resuscitation of
moribund constituencies and for the supply of parliamentary candidates wherever these had failed to materialize.[95] These tasks were
charged with significance. One unmistakable indication of the
efficiency of a party organization – and the morale of its workers –
was the capacity to meet the challenge of a sudden general election.
The social standing and political outlook of the prospective candidate
was equally important. He was not only required to embrace the
views which prevailed in his constituency association, but he would
also participate (if elected) in the planning of national policy.

Most controversy arose in connection with the question of selecting a labour candidate as the Liberal nominee. A climate hostile to
the claims of ambitious manual labourers was engendered by the
indifference of most voters, and by the dependence of local associations upon the munificence of a few rich subscribers. 'The swamping
of the backward or Whig element in the caucuses by an influx of
Socialists or Radicals', Shaw wrote, 'is effectively checked by the
bankruptcy of the swamped caucus.'[96] The middle-class merchants
and industrialists who controlled many associations were slow to
endorse the political demands of labour. They reacted, in particular,
against any popular movement in favour of a labour candidate, even
in predominantly working-class districts. Only the miners possessed
the cohesion necessary to overcome the prejudices of employer-
dominated associations, though in the Rhondda William Abraham
('Mabon') was first required to undergo a trial of strength at the
polls. His success in 1885 was a rare occurrence. The stark fact
remained that the prevailing state of electoral law grievously handicapped impecunious candidates. The adoption of the caucus system
and the creation of single member constituencies in industrial areas
had not extinguished the attractions of wealth and rank. Social
considerations continued to impress electors, while the falling away
of subscribers after the Home Rule split increased the temptation to
adopt candidates who would not require subsidies. H. J. Wilson
discovered that private donations to his election campaign at Holm-
firth had dropped from £200 in 1885 to £43 in 1886, obliging him to
meet nine-tenths of his expenses out of his own pocket.[97] This
paucity of local funds must have been a common experience throughout the country. Undoubtedly, the most spectacular example of
near-insolvency was Midlothian. Gladstone was reluctantly informed
by the President of his constituency association that 'on looking over
the list of those who had subscribed most liberally before, I was
ashamed to find that nearly all had turned aside from us!' The

association had comfortably managed to reimburse Gladstone with the £1,100 expended in 1885, yet in the following July only one subscriber could be found who was willing to contribute towards the trifling sum of £191 incurred at uncontested elections in Midlothian *and* Leith.[98] It was not therefore surprising that well-connected aspirants, and those who were prepared to scatter largesse throughout a constituency, usually experienced little difficulty in finding seats. The correspondence which passed between Lord Edmond Fitzmaurice and Gladstone in 1892 illustrates the humiliation felt by an aristocrat of ministerial rank when this unwritten law was violated. Fitzmaurice regarded it as an egregious insult to be passed over by the Kirkcaldy Burghs committee in favour of J. H. Dalziel, a London journalist who was barely 24.[99]

During the decade which elapsed between the extension of the county franchise and Gladstone's final retirement, it became patently obvious that constituency parties had generally assumed a rigid and decidedly unfriendly posture towards labourers with pretensions to a seat in Parliament. Advocates of working-class representation slowly realized that Liberal 'hundreds' would not adopt a labour candidate except in places which were regarded as hopeless, or where a working man alone had any prospect of success. In due course labour spokesmen were compelled to sever their connection with Liberalism. In many cases the breach was made with reluctance. The quarrel did not usually revolve around the limitations of official policy; the leadership of the party was rarely disputed. The conflict centred instead upon the unrepresentative nature of the constituency Liberal association. 1888 was an important milestone along the stony road leading to total separation. In that year a vacancy arose at Mid-Lanark, but the miners' candidate was refused the Liberal nomination. The treatment meted out to Keir Hardie by the local caucus prompted him to found the Scottish Labour Party. Attercliffe (1894) and Newcastle (1895) were further signposts to the future, Ramsay MacDonald and Arthur Henderson being driven by their constituency associations into the arms of Hardie and the infant Independent Labour Party.

The Liberal managers in London were not blind to the potentially damaging consequences of such warranted defections. But the prevalence of several unfortunate preconceptions impaired a balanced appreciation of the gravity of the situation. These stemmed primarily from the extreme sensitivity of the associations concerning external interference with their domestic affairs. Federation officials were loath to arouse local pride because constituency autonomy was jealously guarded. In any case the Federation constitution specifically forbade any interference with the functions of affiliated organizations. This limitation was frequently invoked to justify a policy of inaction, and to evade the real issue of class prejudice. Schnadhorst claimed that 'beyond a certain point' it was impossible to exert pressure upon a local association. It should be noted, however, that similar arguments were employed in cases where no labour candidate was involved. Schnadhorst and his frontbench principals declared themselves powerless to influence the choice of the constituency party in connection with the candidature of W. S. Caine at Barrow in 1890. 'In the last resort', Caine was informed, 'the local association has to be recognized by those who are not on the spot.'[100]

This excuse failed to impress militant labour leaders, and alternative explanations were manufactured in order to justify a policy of continued sluggishness. Responsibility for the shortage of labour candidates was said to rest – not with the Federation, the Whips' office, nor even with the local oligarchies – but with the working classes themselves. Labour had denied itself the opportunity of making a decisive impact upon the party, owing, in some cases, to the brazen rejection of a candidate duly selected by the local executive, and in others by a degree of hesitation on the subject of whether a labour nomination was in fact desirable. Schnadhorst felt that prospective candidates like J. Havelock Wilson, the seamen's leader, were 'little good anywhere. Working men in the mass do not want them.'[101] The details of Wilson's rather chequered political career appear to absolve Schnadhorst from the charge of cupidity and arrogance. Wilson had stood (unprofitably) as an independent at Bristol in 1890, but he was quickly forgiven by the whips and placed at Deptford. Nevertheless, he ungraciously withdrew at the last minute in order to challenge an established Liberal candidate in Middlesbrough. R. B. Cunninghame-Graham, the socialist laird, also brought discredit upon the labour cause. Marjoribanks had taken great pains to find him a safe seat at Glasgow, only to see his nominee dislodged for exploiting the concession as a platform from which to attack the Liberal party. Even Gladstone was driven to protest against the proliferation of 'bogus' candidates.[102] It did not escape the notice of an infuriated Federation that several 'so-called labour candidates' like Ben Tillett had chosen to threaten the seats of such 'well-known and tried' Liberal members as Illingworth at Bradford. 'Nor can it be overlooked that in all these cases opposition is directed against Liberal members and in no single case against a Tory.'[103] Implicit in this rebuke was the allegation that the Conservatives were attempting to divide the Liberal and labour vote by promoting and subsidizing independent candidates. Hence Schnadhorst spoke of 'sinister influences' which he had 'reason to believe [were] at work behind many of them'.[104] Arnold Morley was positive that Wilson had been 'actively supported by a man from the Tory Central Office' at the Bristol by-election.[105] Whether or not such suspicions were justified is of little importance in the present context. The mere suggestion that labour candidates had followed the example set by H. M. Hyndman and the Social Democratic Federation in 1885, by being willing recipients of 'Tory gold', was sufficient to extinguish any inclination to accommodate those whose allegiance to labour was more conspicuous than was their devotion to Liberalism.

Consequently, no more than approximately 25 representatives of labour were selected by Liberal associations to contest the general election of 1892. Only 10 were successful, the same number as in 1886. The secretary of the Labour Electoral Association (T. R. Threlfall) protested that only 4 of the victorious 'Lib-Lab' candidates had 'either captured the caucus or out-generalled it'.[106] This factor applied with even greater force to those who suffered defeat. In 1891 the N.L.F. printed a list of 8 new candidates who had been formally adopted. But the 'substantial addition' faithfully promised by the Federation never materialized, and the express desire of the Metropolitan Radical Federation that the Liberals run 50 labour candidates remained unfulfilled.[107]

Without the largesse distributed by the L.C.A., it is doubtful whether even a handful of working-class candidates (including sitting members) could have gone to the poll. Labour representatives were often paid generous parliamentary allowances by their trade union, but election expenses were not usually met from this source. These were either provided by private subscription raised amongst wealthy Liberals, or the Chief Whip disbursed the requisite sum from a special and anonymous labour 'purse'. Donations to the L.C.A. were made without stipulation, except in so far as 'due controul (of course)' was exercised by the Chief Whip over the selection of intended beneficiaries.[108] For example, Arnold Morley readily agreed to furnish R. Cameron (a schoolmaster) with £250 when he learnt that two respected M.P.s, H. J. Wilson and Sir F. Mappin, were each prepared to contribute £100 towards the expense of a contest in Sheffield Central.[109] The number of 'wholly impecunious' but 'more or less suitable' working-class candidates who had been secretly 'settled' by the end of 1891 cannot have exceeded 20 (inclusive of sitting members). Hence the sum of £12,400 set aside for them by Arnold Morley virtually guaranteed that the constituencies involved would not be called upon to extend themselves financially.[110]

It is possible that a fraction of the accumulated fund may have been used for a different purpose, since Arnold Morley also defrayed the expenses incurred by the handful of working men who contested the L.C.C. elections in the spring of 1892.[111] However, the diffusion of patronage by the Whips' office had not been improvised hastily for the sole purpose of countering the threat posed by the advocates of an independent labour party. The policy of aiding suitable working-class candidates financially had been inaugurated by G. G. Glyn (Lord Wolverton) in 1868, and was continued by each of his successors. Nevertheless, the arrival of Schnadhorst in Parliament Street wrought a great change. Unlike many of his contemporaries, he knew that it was essential to rebuild the party upon a broader and more democratic basis. When he had been secretary of the Birmingham association, Schnadhorst had drawn up in 1879 a concordat between the Liberal caucus and the autonomous labour organization. The purpose of this agreement had been the selection of candidates to contest the pending city council elections.[112] The outcome proved to be entirely satisfactory, though attempts by less accomplished negotiators to repeat this novel experiment elsewhere did not always proceed so smoothly. Schnadhorst ignored these setbacks, and in 1890 instructed the commission of enquiry into local organization to ascertain whether untenanted constituencies were prepared to accept a labour candidate. Sidney Webb was then requested to compile a list of possible nominees. But at this point the prospect of any wholesale adoption of working men broke down. After a fruitless and heated interview with Schnadhorst in September 1891, Webb wrote: 'He really seems to have tried all *he* could to put them into seats. But, as I said at the end, the thing *was not done*; and however virtuous he may have been, the effect remains.'[113]

In the following week at Newcastle Gladstone maintained that a substantial increase in labour representation was 'not only desirable but in the highest degree urgent'.[114] But this exhortation failed to alleviate Webb's feeling of bitter disappointment. The plea that impoverished M.P.s possessed an 'irresistible' title to some form of State payment went unheeded by the delegates, and Gladstone's warm sympathy with the claims of labour served only to raise expectations which it was impossible to realize. Herbert Gladstone believed that labour leaders could not therefore 'fairly be blamed' for declaring themselves dissatisfied with mere expressions of goodwill. His father astonishingly shared the opinion that labour was perfectly justified in organizing on an independent basis in order to compel Liberals to translate official sympathy into positive action, an apparent indiscretion which aroused some consternation in Parliament Street.[115]

It soon became clear, however, that the party managers experienced more success in placing the labour independents who rejected the sovereignty of the caucus than was achieved with those loyalists

who preferred to work through the formal mechanism. Three independent candidates, Hardie, Wilson, and John Burns were elected
in 1892. To some extent each owed his success to the intercession of
the Whips' office. In the autumn of 1889 Marjoribanks had promised
Burns (the architect of the recent dockers' victory) a safe seat at
Battersea on condition that he withdrew from Dundee. Once this
had been safely accomplished, Marjoribanks turned towards the
newly formed Scottish Labour Party. With the approval of Hardie,
the negotiators agreed to install labour candidates in three Scottish
seats.[116] Schnadhorst had already promised Hardie a safe seat, and it
was only after these clandestine arrangements had been discovered
and repudiated by the constituency associations in question that
Hardie turned his attention to London. He decided to accept an
invitation to contest West Ham South as an independent, briskly
declining Schnadhorst's offers of financial aid. Despite his lofty
intentions, Hardie still owed his victory to the Liberal managers.
Schnadhorst intervened 'at the critical moment' (before nominations
had closed) and persuaded the faction-ridden West Ham association
to abandon their frantic search for a rival candidate.[117] He attempted
to render similar services at Middlesbrough, even though Wilson
had acted 'so treacherously and unfairly'.[118] On this occasion
Schnadhorst failed to secure the retirement of the official candidate,
but Wilson's unfortunate adversary seems to have received no
assistance from party headquarters.

Despite the good offices of Schnadhorst and the whips, there was
no possibility of the Liberal party being transformed into a party of
labour. Such an upheaval was never remotely considered by the
leadership, and it is probable that Trevelyan's vision of between 40
and 50 labour members constituted the limit of their ambitions.[119]
In pursuit of this goal the Gladstone family supplemented an abstract
desire for the better representation of working men by contributing
regularly to the labour purse. The head of the household had provided a lead in 1886 by donating £500.[120] Gladstone had written in
explanation:

> I think it extremely hard on the constituents of labouring men to
> be obliged, after bearing the charge of an election, to support them
> in actual Parliamentary service, while *pensions* provided for ex-
> holders of salaried (lay) offices are taken by men belonging to
> families of immense wealth.[121]

On the other hand, Gladstone continued to attach much importance to the participation of the leisured classes in Liberal politics,
never doubting that this was where leadership ultimately belonged.
He informed one custodian of the 'tradition and historic fame' of

the house of Russell that 'when the higher men recede the lower men will come in. I mean men of a lower stamp, not in their fortunes, but in themselves.'[122] Gladstone was implying that the humble as well as the highly-born had been elevated morally and spiritually above others in the Liberal party simply by their adherence to the concept of Irish Home Rule. Whig aristocrats stood to lose much in terms of social prestige and political advancement, whereas labour M.P.s sacrificed the opportunity of grappling with pressing industrial problems. This curious dichotomy in outlook pervaded the consciousness of Arnold Morley, who bore the responsibility for placing candidates. Working men were acceptable in moderate numbers, even though they could not strictly match the qualities of candidates endowed with the advantages of rank and education. On one revealing occasion the Chief Whip betrayed the values which he shared with Gladstone. H. J. Roby, the victor of the Eccles by-election of 1890, was hailed as a 'distinct gain' to the party – not because he had won the confidence of the working classes by campaigning on an advanced labour programme – but by virtue of being 'a senior Classic at Cambridge, and a successful merchant'.[123]

The social status of prospective candidates was therefore quite as important as questions of political philosophy in the eyes of the leadership. The overriding concern of the party managers was to retain in harness all who recognized some form of allegiance to Gladstone, however refractory they might be. Their task was to preserve some form of balance in the composition of the parliamentary party, but not to influence unduly the future shape of its programme. Even an open commitment to socialism did not prohibit a man from membership. The respectable middle-class theoreticians who belonged to the Fabian Society were quietly tolerated, and occasionally recommended (without success) to local associations as parliamentary candidates. Working-class socialists were perhaps less fortunate, though George Lansbury discovered that he did not lack influential benefactors. The financier Samuel Montagu, M.P. for Whitechapel, assured him that once in Parliament he would be free to 'preach all the Socialism you like: all I ask is support for the Liberal party, which is the best instrument even for your Socialism'.[124] Montagu's tone echoed that which prevailed in higher quarters. The official conception of what actually constituted an acceptable party programme was unusually elastic. When Burns sought a seat in Parliament, Marjoribanks merely insisted that 'he must come forward as the supporter of the Liberal programme, *plus of course such fads of his as he thinks indispensable*, before his candidature could fairly receive official recognition'.[125] Such generosity was truly remarkable, bearing in mind the fact that Burns was then formally committed to Marxist dogma. It reveals that the whips were unperturbed by the prospect of having extreme socialist doctrines aired from the Liberal benches – though the offer was probably made on condition that Burns resigned forthwith from the S.D.F. Quite different conditions were imposed upon Sam Woods, the miners' agent in Lancashire, before he could be accepted as candidate for the Ince division. He was required to submit a written guarantee that he would loyally support the actions of the parliamentary party. However, the restriction applied only to 'questions other than those specially affecting labour'. It was imposed – not because Woods held unwelcome opinions on certain social subjects – but solely because he (unlike Burns and other independents) had hitherto been 'anxious to remain unpledged on the Irish question'.[126] Provided labour leaders were reliable on this single supreme issue, they remained at liberty to persevere in their efforts to reshape the party in a socialist mould.

In theory, no one could cavil at the imposition of such reasonable terms. But the reality was very different. The whips no doubt imagined that they possessed sufficient authority at Westminster to overawe the wilder elements. They also confidently anticipated that the existing Lib-Lab parliamentary group would absorb the newcomers, and reconcile extremists to the view that it was essential to float in the mainstream of Radical politics. Since 1886 the labour members had done nothing to distinguish themselves from their middle-class Radical allies. 'Mabon' was first and foremost a Welsh patriot; W. R. Cremer reserved his passion for the cause of international peace; George Howell and James Rowlands were wholly immersed in London questions. Virtually all that remained was the rump of trade unionists who represented the north-east coalfield. The veteran M.P. for Morpeth, Thomas Burt, maintained in 1889 that it was 'on every ground desirable that the labour member should avoid entangling himself in the meshes of party'. He claimed that the group met frequently to hammer out a common policy. 'On purely labour questions they are actually as they ought to be, a party.'[127] Burt's colleagues had indeed closed their ranks since 1888, introducing a number of useful bills to secure the payment of weekly wages, promote industrial safety, and protect trade union investments. Yet these were minor and non-contentious issues. Instead of accepting the responsibility for formulating an unambiguous labour programme, the group had been content to draft bills relating to electoral registration and the payment of members.

This lack of enterprise reflected a fundamental flaw in the structure of labour representation. Liberal trade unionists were elected to advance the specific requirements of a single industry in a particular

locality; it was no part of their function to voice the nebulous claims
of the labour movement as a whole. Working-class M.P.s were,
therefore, tempted to adopt a narrow trade interest, instinctively
viewing the spokesmen for other occupations as competitors rather
than as partners in a common cause. Such attitudes would not change
so long as the miners enjoyed a comfortable parliamentary advantage
over their rivals. But their notorious conservatism helped to destroy
the credibility of an enduring Lib-Lab partnership. A new breed of
labour politicians merely added the names of Burt and his com-
panions to an already formidable list of Liberal enemies.

4. *London and the Eight Hours Controversy*

At the general election of 1885 Liberals fared worse in London than
in any other part of the country. But their cup of humiliation was
not yet full; the magnitude of the electoral defeat of 1886 eclipsed
even this shattering experience. Within the space of a single year
Liberals saw their representation dwindle from 14 to 11, while the
complement of metropolitan members rocketed from 22 to 62. By
1890 precious by-election gains had raised the total to 13, but the
strength of the survivors was sapped by the unwillingness of one
M.P. to associate with his fellows. The late Attorney-General, Sir
Charles Russell, remained aloof on the frontbench, basking in the
glory which surrounded his dramatic exposure of Richard Pigott.
In the absence of Dilke, narrowly beaten at Chelsea, the minute
faction struggled to maintain any sort of cohesion. Although each
member was anxious to press forward with London questions, the
group lacked the necessary political machinery, and so could not
instantaneously brandish a clear-cut programme.

Three developments rescued the demoralized London Liberals
from oblivion: the formation of the London Liberal and Radical
Union in 1887; the delivery by Morley and Gladstone in December
1888 of the so-called 'Clerkenwell-cum-Limehouse programme';
and, finally, the creation of the London County Council in 1888–9.
The L.C.C. acted as a powerful catalyst of Radical aspirations. Its
very existence generated an awareness that the metropolis was a
self-contained unit worthy of special consideration – not a mere
conglomeration of unrelated interests. Moreover, the proximity of
the first elections to County Hall necessitated the construction of a
Progressive platform at extremely short notice. Fortunately, the
debates on the local government bill had welded the London members into a 'firm and unbroken body'.[128] Under the chairmanship of
James Stuart, a former professor of mathematics, the reanimated
group had methodically dissected those clauses of the bill which

were relevant to London. Sins of omission and commission on the part of the government had excited the Radicals rather more than the question of how vigorously the L.C.C.'s statutory powers would actually be implemented. Londoners took exception to the nomination of aldermen, and resented the independent status granted to the City (which retained its own corporation). They also wished to manage various public utilities, and claimed the right to deprive the Home Office of control over the metropolitan police force. These burning issues formed the nucleus of the programme which London members thrust before a startled House when Parliament reassembled in 1889.

Stuart immediately launched a diatribe against the government for neglecting London interests. Armed with the report of a London Union commission on housing (adopted at a meeting on 14 February), Stuart told a harrowing tale of gross over-crowding, excessive rents, inadequate sanitation, and poor supplies of water. He demanded that the standing orders be revised, so that urban developers who required the sanction of Parliament would not be allowed to pass private bills unless provision had been made to resettle the persons whose houses they proposed to pull down. Stuart was clearly out of order. But when he at last sat down his colleagues resumed the assault by ranging over the whole gamut of London questions from district councils to markets. 'There is a growing indignation in London at the succession of slurs put upon us,' claimed H. L. W. Lawson, the group's secretary. James Rowlands predicted that 'more will be heard of London in this House than has been heard in the past'. The days of silence and indifference had vanished overnight. 'Now London will have to be listened to, and the reforms it requires will have to be dealt with.'[129]

This promise could be redeemed immediately, since the group had already decided to imitate the Welshmen by taking concerted action during the session. They placed their names jointly upon the backs of a procession of bills, covering the main items of the Progressive manifesto which had been adopted by the London Union in August 1888.[130] These measures were drafted with the aid of the twelve-man executive committee, though the services rendered by the London Union do not imply that the metropolitan M.P.s had feebly surrendered the initiative. Half their number (including J. F. B. Firth, member for Dundee) held executive posts in the organization, and three had appropriated the most important offices. Stuart was honorary secretary, Lawson was treasurer, and R. K. Causton was chairman of the general committee. The pretence of prior consultation could be maintained by circularizing every bill in the constituencies for consideration and amendment, but, in reality, form and content were decided in secret by the parliamentary caucus alone.

Once the London programme had been pieced together, fresh difficulties arose. As a matter of convenience each topic was charged to a particular member. Causton, for instance, was an experienced party organizer (and subsequently the author of several manuals on electoral law), so he naturally took control of the infinitely complex subject of voter registration. George Howell attended to the extension of polling hours, while Samuel Montagu utilized his financial acumen to study local taxation. However, this division of labour did not work as smoothly as the outward appearance suggests. Only one of the 14 bills dutifully introduced in 1889 obtained a day for discussion. On 29 May E. H. Pickersgill moved the second reading of his bill to levy a uniform poor rate throughout the metropolis. But although the occasion was unique (the next session drew a complete blank), Pickersgill bungled the affair. Conservatives were not alone in complaining that the text of the bill had only reached them two days beforehand. Sydney Buxton felt that Pickersgill had treated his colleagues 'very badly', since he had wilfully delayed drawing up a scheme until it was 'too late for us to discuss and alter it before it had to be issued'.[131]

By 1890 there were signs that the fragile unity of the London members was in danger of cracking. Serious differences of opinion began to surface in connection with a subject which had been conspicuously absent from the original sheaf of London bills. The precise relationship that ought to exist between the L.C.C. and smaller authorities within the county was a constant source of friction, at least until the creation of metropolitan borough councils in 1899. The London Union discreetly declined to examine the issue until 1890, and its report – though 'carefully considered, settled, and circulated' – failed to produce any flurry of parliamentary activity.[132] Stuart strongly maintained that a measure of such importance should emanate from the government rather than from private members. But his explanation did not carry conviction. Any delay in the overhaul of municipal administration really stemmed from the controversy sparked off by Chamberlain and Dilke in the early 1880s. Chamberlain had always considered that authorities the size of Birmingham were the most perfect units of local government. Dilke, on the other hand, knew from personal experience that the multiplicity of authorities in London had produced hopeless administrative confusion, a situation which had gravely retarded its proper development.[133] These cross-currents could be held in check so long as Firth, the chief advocate of centralization, continued to dominate the London Municipal Reform League. But deep fissures soon emerged after his death in the summer of 1889. During the debate on the Address in February 1890, Rowlands coolly repudiated Stuart's belief that the district councils in contemplation should enjoy 'real powers and real responsibilities'. He protested that it would be a far more satisfactory arrangement if they made the L.C.C. 'strong enough to act as the Central Authority'.[134]

It also became evident that the group was not devoting sufficient attention to those bills which had already been prepared. Grandiose plans for municipal reconstruction would inevitably be paid for by spreading the burden of local taxation. Yet the precise details of this massive proposal had not adequately been thought out. Montagu contemplated a special rate on ground values, and tabled an appropriate bill in February 1890. But the project was 'very crude'. Buxton now began to regret that members of the group were sometimes required to support bills 'with which we may not, individually, altogether agree'. He was determined to alter the defective parts of existing bills 'before they are again issued to the public'.[135] However, little progress seems to have been made with regard to Montagu's scheme. In a debate on land taxation 12 months later (27 February 1891), Stuart announced that after careful consideration his colleagues had framed a resolution on the subject as it affected London.[136] Yet when the London motion on the taxing of ground rents came before the House on 13 March, total confusion reigned in the metropolitan household. Winding up the debate, H. H. Fowler manfully tried to camouflage the disagreeable scene. But no one derived much comfort from his bland assertion that there existed a broad and general concurrence with the principle that those who benefited directly from permanent metropolitan improvements should bear the burden of paying for them.[137]

Stuart discovered to his cost that it was perilous for the layman to tackle the intricate subject of public finance. He lightly suggested that land and buildings ought to be valued separately. But this deceptively simple idea was quite impracticable, and so had to be dropped. The uncertainty concerning what precisely constituted a fair level of taxation paled into insignificance beside more fundamental sources of conflict. Acute problems were caused by the emergence of two divergent schools of fiscal thought. Some Radicals wished to levy a regular annual rate on property, while others preferred to impose a special death duty upon each new generation. Further complications arose when it transpired that the devotees of both methods could not agree as to means. Those who advocated an annual rate assessment were unsure whether by this they meant the taxation of ground rents or the taxation of land values. If ground rents alone were to be mulcted, the appropriate legislation would discriminate against the intermediate rather than the ultimate reversionist. Owners who did not let or lease land would escape the net entirely. On the other hand, if land values were subjected to a special rate (as under the terms of Montagu's bill), it would be the occupying and ultimate owner who would suffer – not the intermediate reversionist. This was because the freeholder would be required to redeem the capital outlay on permanent improvements, while the temporary holder of the land enjoyed all the immediate advantages.

Technicalities of this nature drove those who lacked legal and financial genius to seek refuge in a death duty. Stuart was attracted by the prospect of equalization, increasing the succession duty (which affected realty) until it matched the rate which was at present levied on personalty through the legacy duty. Should the scheme also be graduated, and distributed by the Treasury to each municipality on the familiar principle of local grants-in-aid, then it would closely resemble the plan which officially found favour with Gladstone. However, many Londoners still clung to the tradition of local independence, distrusting the capricious whims of the Treasury. H. L. W. Lawson and T. H. Bolton wanted the L.C.C. to introduce its own death duty rather than accept a share of a common national fund. This alternative scheme would enable the municipality to reduce the annual rate for current expenditure (which was levied on occupiers alone). In addition, it would allow the L.C.C. to set aside part of its revenue to extinguish the debt which had been incurred on behalf of permanent improvements. As the debate on the taxation of ground rents drew to a close, it became obvious that several metropolitan M.P.s preferred this notion of a municipal death duty. Montagu was forced to abandon the bill to tax land values, even though the details of an alternative scheme had not yet been worked out. Thus Londoners were obliged to rest content with Stuart's disingenuous assurance that 'the fact that none of these proposals are complete is no argument against some portion of them or some combination of them being adopted'.[138]

With opinion clearly in a state of flux, Sidney Webb astutely stepped forward with a bold plan to appropriate the unearned increment which accrued to private owners. His remedy was the gradual municipalization of all urban land. This proposal was compatible with more limited schemes to tax land values, but it infuriated the London-based Leasehold Enfranchisement Association, an organization dedicated to the widest possible extension of private ownership. Webb believed that encouraging leaseholders to buy out the interest of the lessor was in principle unjust, since this would merely multiply the number of persons who enjoyed a 'social value' in land which

they had done absolutely nothing to create. Any further fragmentation of estates would also make the application of a land tax exces-
sively complicated. These views brought Webb into conflict with two
London Liberal M.P.s, Lawson and Rowlands, the President and
secretary of the Leasehold Enfranchisement Association. Although
they had failed to incorporate leasehold enfranchisement into the
original London programme, the subject had quickly assumed the
guise of a London question. When piloting a bill on 1 May 1889,
Lawson had carefully stressed the connection between slum housing
in the metropolis and the prevalence of short leases. This strategy
had ensured that every one of his London colleagues would automatically support the bill.[139] Two years later (29 April 1891) the
issue was again raised in Parliament, but on this occasion it was
significant that little emphasis was placed upon metropolitan grievances. Lawson and Rowlands realized that the solid phalanx of
London members had been split asunder in 1890 by the publication
of the Fabian indictment of leasehold enfranchisement. Every M.P.
received a copy of this pamphlet immediately prior to the present
debate. This did not dissuade each member of the London caucus
from voting loyally in favour of Rowlands' bill when put as the
substantive motion. Nevertheless, Buxton, Cremer, and Stuart also
voted for a hostile amendment moved by Haldane. These three dissentients made it abundantly clear that they now regarded leasehold
enfranchisement as an inadequate substitute for a scheme of
municipal ownership based on Webb's ideas.[140]

Lawson could not forgive Webb for sabotaging his cherished
project. Seven Liberals had obeyed Webb's injunction to vote with
Haldane in both divisions, a total sufficiently numerous to topple a
bill which was beaten by just 13 votes. During the Committee stage
of the government's small agricultural holdings bill in April 1892,
Lawson exchanged sharp words with Haldane on the merits of
restricted freeholds and leasehold tenure. 'No landlord is so bad as a
Corporation', he rather sweepingly protested.[141] This preliminary
skirmish led to a full-scale attack on 4 May in connection with the
bill to extend municipal ownership in land which Webb had
entrusted to Haldane. Lawson roundly abused the underhand tactics
adopted by the Fabian Society during the preceding 12 months. He
sneered at their clumsy efforts to touch the unearned increment,
alleging that Webb's bill amounted in reality to a grotesque onslaught upon the very principle of private ownership. 'This Bill will
make it impossible for any person to occupy his home, to carry on
his business, or to earn his livelihood without the leave or licence of
the Local Authority.' Lawson at last revenged himself upon Webb
by acting as teller in favour of a hostile Conservative amendment.

This extreme and unusual course of action appealed only to T. H. Bolton. Eight London Liberals voted against Lawson, while his partner Rowlands deemed it prudent to abstain.[142]

The vendetta waged between Lawson and Webb finally destroyed the unity of the London parliamentary caucus. It was also indicative of the fact that a highly critical stage had been reached in the diseased relationship between Radicals and Socialists in the metropolis at large. Webb had quickly risen to prominence in the London Union, riding on the crest of a socialist wave generated by the popular *Star* newspaper and by a sudden boom in trade union membership. This left-wing surge had threatened to engulf the relatively orthodox policies being advocated by puny London parliamentarians, thus encouraging Webb to appeal over their heads to a more powerful tribunal. Bernard Shaw alleged that the Newcastle programme was a brilliant victory for socialism and a vindication of the Fabian tactic of permeation. He propagated the belief that it had originated in a pamphlet written by Webb in 1888, was subsequently taken up by constituency associations under Fabian direction, and was eventually foisted upon a bemused N.L.F. in October 1891. Recent scholarship has effectively demolished such extravagant contentions.[143] On two vital topics the Newcastle programme ran counter to the Fabian-inspired manifestos issued periodically by the London Union. The N.L.F. not only endorsed the oft-belittled policy of leasehold enfranchisement, but also omitted all reference to the burning question of the statutory eight hour day.

In fact the N.L.F. had long grown accustomed to the tiresome duty of differentiating between the purely Radical and the blatantly socialist proposals which emanated from the metropolis. Such expertise had first been acquired in the autumn of 1888, when Webb maladroitly tried to convince the N.L.F. that only the Fabian Society really comprehended the needs of the masses. 'All his statements are greatly exaggerated,' Schnadhorst wrote on receipt of *Wanted a Programme*. 'The only Association which has passed resolutions reflecting on the Nottingham Resolutions [of 1887] is the one he belongs to – "Holborn", one of the feeblest in London.' Schnadhorst had no intention of listening to a 'few noisy impracticables ... whom no programme can ever satisfy'.[144] However, he was prepared to consider reasonable suggestions, such as those submitted in the following year by James Stuart. The council of the London Union had been summoned to the National Liberal Club on 14 November 1889 to tabulate various resolutions which were deemed worthy of adoption by the N.L.F. at its annual meeting three weeks later. Schnadhorst readily agreed to frame a special resolution on metropolitan local government, and conferred upon Stuart the honour of introducing the first full-blown debate on the subject. At Stuart's request the 'free breakfast table', the taxation of ground rents and land values, and the payment of members, were also added to a lengthy agenda paper. But Schnadhorst rejected those points in the London charter which he knew the traditionalists would not tolerate. The plea for clarity in regard to Liberal intentions concerning the extension of factory legislation and the better housing of the working classes went unheeded. Above all the N.L.F. refused to accept one unofficial addition to the list prepared by the executive of the London Union. At the special conference of 14 November, George Lansbury had openly defied Stuart by proposing an extra motion, seeking to commit the organization to an eight hours policy for public employees. 'Sheer vehemence and persistence' on his part completely overwhelmed the 'good, old-fashioned Liberals and individualistic Radicals' who took umbrage at his presumption.[145]

Lansbury's totally unexpected success demonstrated how completely the context of political debate had been altered by the progress of the recent London dock strike. The strike had helped to bring the eight hours question to the fore because it focused public attention upon the arduous conditions of employment and excessive hours of work endured by the least fortunate among the labouring poor. Webb's intemperate outburst in 1888 had been safely disregarded, but the publication of his draft eight hours bill in November 1889 could not be ignored. Eight hours had suddenly emerged as a test question, a development which emboldened Lansbury to remain on the field of battle. The annual congress of the N.L.F. at Manchester in December was chosen as the site for a decisive engagement. The Bow and Bromley association instructed their intrepid secretary to propose a resolution couched in terms which were identical to those carried by the London Union. Lansbury's sympathetic parliamentary candidate, J. Murray Macdonald, warned him that adoption by the Union was no guarantee that the subject would be aired at Manchester.[146] Webb and Massingham on one side, and Lefevre and Stuart on the other, all advanced pressing reasons why it would be inexpedient to proceed with the resolution. But Lansbury was by his own admission 'pigheaded and obstinate'. He promptly brought his controversial resolution to the notice of J. Renwick Seager and Robert Hudson (who were deputizing in Parliament Street for an absent Schnadhorst), and made no secret of his intention to move it irrespective of whether official recognition was granted or withheld. Lansbury and Macdonald therefore journeyed north fixed in their determination to 'yield to nothing but an absolute denial on the part of the managers of the meeting to let us speak'.[147] The official account of the proceedings at Manchester merely states that

Macdonald was refused permission to move an amendment to the
'omnibus' resolution.[148] But Lansbury's recollection was more
traumatic. He had evidently pushed past Macdonald in his anxiety
to be heard, reaching the speakers' rostrum to the accompaniment of
a bell imperiously rung by Kitson. 'I took no notice. One half of the
audience supported me, the other half tried to howl me down. After
a few minutes I was gently but firmly pushed down the steps, and
thus ended my connection with Liberalism.'[149]

Such unruly scenes did not recur at subsequent congresses. The
mantle of Lansbury now fell upon Webb, whose suave and dignified
manner contrasted strongly with his predecessor's 'fiery honest rough
eloquence'. However, these gentlemanly tactics proved to be no
more effective. Webb's preoccupation with London politics imbued
him with a false sense of optimism concerning the progress which
the eight hours cause was making elsewhere. In his view, the Liberal
party crossed the Rubicon when Roby won a magnificent victory at
the Eccles by-election on an eight hours platform. The conciliatory
tone adopted by Gladstone at West Calder on the following day
(23 October 1890) convinced Webb that all doubts and difficulties in
the path of statutory limitation had been resolved.[150] He rejoiced
when Schnadhorst intimated a desire to allay the dissatisfaction
which existed in London, failing to realize that the executive of the
London Union was brought into consultations on labour issues only
because Hudson thought that he could thereby 'bring them rather
more into line' with the official policy of 'avoiding further discussion of our action on the Eight Hours question'.[151] Consequently,
Webb was caught totally unprepared by the discovery that Schnadhorst intended to omit from the agenda at Sheffield any mention of
the eight hours dispute. For the first time federated organizations
had been invited to submit resolutions which they desired to see
incorporated into the national programme in November. But as the
associations were only allowed eight days grace, Webb was deprived
of the opportunity to circularize the constituencies. Hence a mere
trickle of replies reached party headquarters. Webb correctly guessed
that Federation officials would capitalize upon this weak response
by asserting that there existed no genuine demand for an eight hours
resolution. Several paragraphs to this effect were inserted in the
Federation's annual report, and Schnadhorst instructed the President-
elect (Robert Spence Watson) to quote extracts in his inaugural
address at Sheffield on 20 November. Thus thwarted by the chicanery
of Parliament Street, Webb was forced to confess that owing to his
negligence there could be no advance that year.[152]

This mistake was not repeated at the next annual meeting,
scheduled for Newcastle in October 1891. A cold reception from

Hudson did not deter Webb from promptly imposing the 'mildest of mild' resolutions upon his own constituency of Holborn. The amenable local committee readily agreed to forward the motion to Parliament Street together with an 'express request' that it be included in the agenda paper. Webb now exerted pressure upon leading members of the N.L.F.'s general purposes committee, a select body of 20 persons elected by the unwieldy general committee.[153] Their task was to sit in private with the permanent officials, sift the policy resolutions submitted by local associations, and then select those which were deemed worthy of public recognition. Some members of the general purposes committee were evidently in favour of accepting Webb's eight hours resolution. Spence Watson, for example, had acquired a considerable reputation in connection with the settlement of trade disputes in the Newcastle area, thereby gleaning much practical information on labour questions. However, the weight of his experience was not sufficient to overcome the prejudices of colleagues like Stuart, who had recently ousted Massingham from the editorship of the *Star* because the latter had dared advocate the compulsory eight hour day in its columns.[154] Had Roby and Sir Walter Foster retained their places on the committee – instead of resigning in 1890 – the verdict of the majority might well have been reversed. As matters stood Webb's request was vetoed, and Schnadhorst informed Gladstone that the N.L.F. intended to 'avoid altogether discussing the legal hours question' because opinion within the committee (and in the country) was 'much divided'. Gladstone was reminded that the lack of any clear policy made it 'the more necessary that sympathy should be expressed with all efforts to raise the worker'.[155] But pious sentiments were a wholly inadequate substitute for concrete commitments. By this stage Webb had become thoroughly disillusioned with the Liberal party. As he had anticipated, Spence Watson concocted some 'specious excuse' at Newcastle in order to refuse him a hearing. Webb's patience was finally exhausted. In spite of his persistent efforts to save the party from 'shrinking up into a middle-class group', Webb acknowledged the dismal truth that he personally could do nothing further to help Liberals escape this fate.[156]

A few days after Webb had suffered defeat at Newcastle, the Scottish Liberal Association assembled in Glasgow (7 October) to ratify previous declarations in support of an eight hours bill for miners. Scottish working men had hitherto experienced considerable difficulty in finding a Liberal platform from which to advocate this special cause. In the month preceding Lansbury's triumph at the London Union in 1889, a regional conference in north-east Scotland had 'treated with scorn' an identical motion suggested by representatives of the Aberdeen Trades Council. The chairman had instant-aneously stifled discussion of the eight hours issue by moving and carrying the 'previous question'.[157] A strange situation had then emerged. The Scottish Liberal Association recovered from this momentary aberration and became progressively more daring. Yet its English counterpart resolutely continued to tread with extreme caution after Lansbury's Pyrrhic victory.

This glaring contrast in attitudes seems to indicate that part of the blame for the failure of Webb's missionary enterprise must rest with the evangelist himself. The N.L.F. consistently and jealously guarded its essentially provincial basis and outlook, demonstrating this prepossession as early as 1883. In that year an enormous delegate conference at Leeds had dismissed out of hand a London request to delay pressing for the extension of the county franchise until the reform of metropolitan local government had been accomplished. Webb could not understand why the move to Parliament Street in 1886 did not cure the N.L.F. of its paranoic suspicion of London politicians. He despised the cumbersome machinery of the national organization, and could not conceal his contempt for what Morley proudly referred to as the 'greater deliberateness [and] steadfastness of provincial Radicalism'.[158] Webb was suspect precisely for this reason, having been reared in the hothouse atmosphere engendered by the Fabian Society. In the eyes of many Liberals the intellectual pretensions of the Fabian Society caricatured that insufferable arro-gance which was thought to be a distinguishing characteristic of metropolitan Radicalism. Webb was also justly considered to be lukewarm on the Irish question, since the Fabians were notoriously uninterested in this crucial and complex problem.[159] One Fabian historian (R. C. K. Ensor) noted how frequently Webb 'strangely failed to appreciate the bigness of big issues'.[160] Further troubles stemmed from his relish for intrigue, subtle persuasion, and the application of backstairs influence. Webb was accused of manipu-lating the Liberal party for ends incompatible with the paramount duty of securing Home Rule for Ireland. Loyal Gladstonians were unlikely to extend the hand of friendship to a man who ignored Ireland altogether, and instead attempted to foist upon the party such metaphysical socialist notions as the 'ultimate and gradual extinction of rent and interest' and the 'elimination of private capitalists and middlemen' from public enterprises.

The cumulative effect of these interlocking factors cannot however yield a satisfactory explanation for the persistently hostile attitude of the N.L.F. towards Webb. F. A. Channing was a perfectly orthodox Radical M.P., but even he encountered insurmountable obstacles in 1891 while endeavouring to persuade the officials to adopt at Newcastle a 'bold but not socialistic' labour platform. He wrote to Schnadhorst recommending the insertion of a motion in support of the limitation of railwaymen's hours, a policy which had already been approved (in January) by the parliamentary party and endorsed by the frontbench. According to Channing, Schnadhorst thought that such a declaration 'struck a note that would rally the forces of labour, and invited me to draft words to form part of a resolution which he wished me to move and Sydney Buxton to second, identified as he was with the Fair Wage principle in contract labour'. Channing bitterly regretted that the 'frank acceptance of a "Labour Plank"' should be shelved owing to 'timid counsels at Headquarters'.[161] When William Tuckwell, rector of Stockton, demanded a private explanation in the Tyne Theatre itself, Schnadhorst could only keep muttering that their parliamentary overlords 'want courage – and such men are hard to educate'.[162]

The main culprit appears to have been Morley, whose outright opposition to any form of eight hours legislation almost cost him his seat at Newcastle in 1892. No other Liberal statesman meddled so diligently in Federation affairs. Morley exercised considerable authority as President of the London Union. In this capacity he strove to prevent 'the most headstrong and unscrupulous and shallow of those who speak for Labour' from capturing the Liberal party.[163] In 1889 he had denounced Lansbury's eight hours resolution, and, instead of resigning the Presidency forthwith, he had issued a statement couched in such hostile terms as to render compromise at Manchester impossible.[164] At Sheffield in the following year Morley sought to exploit to the full his intimate friendship with the incoming N.L.F. President, a fellow Novocastrian. He appeared on the platform (20 November) and gleefully reiterated the words spoken by Spence Watson, thus thwarting Webb and postponing any discussion of the eight hours controversy.

Many Radicals were, therefore, reluctant to embarrass their leaders by incorporating an eight hours resolution into the Newcastle programme, being 'hopeful of the effect of time'.[165] The influence exerted by selfish employers was regarded as a far more insidious obstacle to progress. Prosperous industrialists who subscribed to central funds had already implanted exaggerated fears in the minds of the Liberal whips. Augustine Birrell, a barrister, was numbed by the nature of these delusions. Before leaving London in 1889 to contest a by-election at West Fife, certain unnamed whips had gravely assured him that legislation compelling employers to compensate those who suffered industrial injuries would 'cripple, if not destroy' the staple industries of the country.[166] The idea that the N.L.F. was 'wedded to a capitalist or employers' point of view' inevitably gained widespread currency. On the eve of the Newcastle meeting, R. T. Reid (later Lord Loreburn) candidly informed Schnadhorst that although many Federation notables were 'very good men', he had 'heard from some of them sentiments upon the relation of capital and labour analogous to the sentiments of Tory squires on the relation of squire and labourer'.[167] He specifically mentioned the obduracy of industrialists in the West Riding, a thinly disguised reference to Illingworth (a textile manufacturer in Bradford) and Kitson (the Leeds iron and steel magnate). The latter had been President of the N.L.F. since 1883, and his views on labour questions continued to colour the organization's judgement until his retirement in 1890. Kitson, Illingworth, and John Ellis (a colliery proprietor in Nottinghamshire) constituted a triumvirate which could not conceal its contempt for the political and economic demands of labour. Many votes were sacrificed in Leeds at the general election of 1886 merely because Kitson had disdained to go cap in hand to canvass working-class voters. In public life he continued to manifest 'that proud spirit and dignified aloofness which marked much of his relationships with his workmen'.[168] On one memorable occasion in 1890 he opened a meeting at the National Liberal Club by abusing the eight hours policy, going (in Webb's words) 'much too far, was dead against all regulation'.[169]

Atherley-Jones, son of Ernest Jones the Chartist, believed that Kitson spoke on behalf of a 'central body of leading magnates of the middle-class' within the Federation who were 'entirely out of touch with the Labour movement'.[170] Lansbury also thought in this fashion. Personal experience had led him to the conclusion that should he delay action until the iron- and coal-masters of the north had been converted, he might be required to wait till eternity. If such allegations can be substantiated, it would seem that Kitson was personally responsible for crushing every effort to incorporate the eight hours policy into the N.L.F. programme. Even after his retirement from the Presidency, he remained a principal adviser to the committee which secretly scrutinized each suggestion sent in by the local associations. As a member of the general purposes committee, Kitson could, if he wished, erect a barrier through which an eight hours resolution could not penetrate.

The heavy-handed suppression of an advanced labour programme was directly connected with the controversy on the eight hours issue which simultaneously racked the Trades Union Congress. In the late 1880s important ideological divisions had emerged between those who favoured a statutory eight hour day and those who contended that legislation would not be desirable. Between 1887 and 1889 the vital principle at stake was obscured by the vindictive campaign being waged by Keir Hardie against the T.U.C.'s parliamentary secretary, Henry Broadhurst. The issue was further confused by the lack of unity amongst those who mustered on each side. Broadhurst disliked the very idea of State interference, whereas the Northumberland miners – led in Parliament by Burt and Charles Fenwick – opposed legislation on the grounds that this would curtail the bargaining power of trade unionists who already enjoyed a seven hour day. Hence, Cunninghame-Graham discovered that only one labour M.P. (Cremer) was prepared to support his demand that a day be set aside in 1891 to discuss his universal eight hours measure.[171] The sweeping nature of this particular proposal was considered foolhardy by those who saw the necessity of first dividing the opposition by confining their legislative endeavours to certain vulnerable trades. Substantial progress could not be made until the advocates of statutory limitation had decided which strategy would be the most fruitful. The difficulties lessened with the departure of Broadhurst from the T.U.C. leadership in 1890. Shortly before N.L.F. delegates invaded Newcastle in 1891, the T.U.C. assembled in the same city in order to clarify its intentions regarding eight hours legislation. The doctrine of universality was firmly jettisoned. After one of the most protracted debates ever held, the T.U.C. rejected the Fabian concept of 'trade option' and endorsed the more comprehensive alternative of 'trade exception'. However, the old guard did not accept their defeat with quiet resignation. When the miners' eight hours bill was debated in Parliament on 23 March 1892, the labour group was torn asunder, with 'Mabon' and Burt acting as tellers on opposite sides. Fenwick, Broadhurst's successor as the T.U.C.'s parliamentary secretary, actually defied a specific directive from Congress in voting against the bill.[172]

In view of the hesitancy of the T.U.C., Harcourt was perfectly entitled to presume that it would be 'madness for anyone to commit themselves on the subject in the face of such disunion'.[173] It was also unrealistic to have supposed that the N.L.F. would willingly transform meetings of the council into duplicates of the T.U.C. for the sole purpose of reaching definite conclusions on the eight hours question. On the other hand, the deliberate obstruction of debate was an equally unsatisfactory means of resolving the deadlock. Many Liberals considered that simply to eliminate controversy amounted to a cynical breach of the N.L.F.'s original purpose, which was to act as a genuine Liberal 'parliament'. It was felt that the refusal to allow Lansbury and Webb to propose amendments was inconsistent with the general aim of encouraging the 'direct participation of all members of the party in the direction of its policy'.

These misgivings concerning the arbitrary behaviour of the executive were intensified on account of the fact that the constitutional precedents were both erratic and contradictory. In retrospect Kitson alleged that during his tenure of the Presidency the Federation possessed 'no rules, and no laws for the government of the meetings'. Instead, he himself was obliged to 'make the laws and the rules to suit the occasion'.[174] This arrangement obviously invested the President *pro tem.* with considerable discretionary powers. Discussion at council meetings had been restricted in 1883 to topics already mentioned in the agenda. But the regulations which governed simple amendments to existing resolutions were far from precise. When Alderman Kenrick of Birmingham had taken the chair during the absence of Kitson in 1885, a string of amendments had been permitted – even though a seconder for one of these could not be found. Kitson would not tolerate such frivolity, but he exerted his authority mainly to discriminate against particular classes of subject matter. In 1887 a delegation from the Scottish Liberal Association was refused leave to move an amendment containing a declaration in favour of Scottish disestablishment. Twelve months later an attempt to insert a clause relating to the payment of members was decisively crushed. At Manchester in 1889 Kitson authorized an important amendment to a resolution on Welsh disestablishment, a decision taken immediately after Lansbury's eight hours protest had been howled down. Such blatant partiality (or 'apparent rigidity') naturally required a prompt explanation. Kitson therefore enunciated the doctrine that amendments were permissible if the proposer and seconder of the original motion consented, and if the delegates then signified their unanimous approval.

When Spence Watson became President in 1890, the procedures of the Federation were reconsidered. He found it necessary to justify the convoluted behaviour of the executive in more precise terms than Kitson and others had offered in previous years. By 1891 Spence Watson had firmly established the general principle that Federation officials would be acting improperly if they sought to commit local associations to controversial issues which were still in a state of flux. In a lengthy address to the council on 1 October, he also maintained that the purpose of the assembled delegates was not to enter into a wide-ranging political discussion, but to transact formal business and to ratify pre-arranged declarations. Hence, resolutions framed by the executive could either be accepted or rejected – but under no circumstances could they be altered or amended. Spence Watson was clearly perturbed by the probable consequences of any relaxation in the rules. Open debate might destroy the authoritative character of council decisions, an eventuality which would surely undermine the confidence currently felt by leading parliamentarians in the N.L.F. as a responsible organization. 'It is absolutely impossible', he explained, 'to discuss questions in which great numbers of men take a great interest and hold different views in a gathering of this character.' Spence Watson attempted to silence his critics by pointing out that the place for discussion was not the council but the general committee, where a more relaxed atmosphere prevailed. Controversial subjects like the eight hour day could be threshed out at its quarterly meetings, and, when agreement had been reached, the council would be in a position to pronounce a favourable judgement.[175]

A decisive test of the N.L.F.'s good faith with respect to labour questions was whether or not the officials put this admirable theory into practice. In its annual report for 1890 the Federation promised to summon the general committee as soon as the officers were satisfied that there existed a general desire to examine the eight hours issue. A deputation was received by the general committee at its next meeting (19 March 1891), but not one of the delegates present, who represented nearly 100 associations, was prepared even to second a motion dealing with the eight hour day. Although Spence Watson categorically assured the chastened delegation that he personally would see that the committee was recalled 'for the special purpose of discussing this question', no record of such a meeting can be traced.[176] Conferences on specific issues were convened from time to time, one of the most notable being the Rural Reform Conference of December 1891. This particular gathering attracted much attention because the N.L.F. took extensive precautions to ensure that all classes – including agricultural labourers – were adequately represented. Set speeches and formal resolutions were not permitted, and as a result the conference was highly successful. This experiment was the prototype for larger informal conventions, of which the most important were held in 1894 in connection with the parish councils bill and the House of Lords controversy. However, these special facilities were conspicuously denied to the protagonists of an eight hour day, possibly because party tacticians were willing to discuss subjects which were conducive to unity, but were understandably reluctant to exacerbate potential divisions on industrial issues.

Not until 1895 did the N.L.F. seriously attempt to refute the charge that its machinery was both cumbersome and undemocratic. Meetings of the council in 1896–7 were engrossed with the formidable task of revising the constitution. Many delegates genuinely wished to transform the council into a Liberal parliament, though there was some disagreement as to how this object could be achieved. It was popularly felt that the council ought to split up into committees for the simultaneous discussion of various groups of topics. But this refreshing idea was not implemented, and delegates were compelled to accept less drastic procedural changes. By 1898 the rules controversy had lapsed, and fundamental structural alterations in Liberal organization were delayed for nearly forty years. Unfortunately, those modifications which had been successfully accomplished were considered by labour leaders to be either irrelevant or futile. Continual obstruction from the Liberal machine had obliged many to turn in frustration towards the weak and divided bodies which eventually coalesced in the Labour Representation Committee.

5. *The Origins of the Newcastle Programme*

The annual meeting of the N.L.F. at Leeds in November 1886 constituted the first crucial test of the organization's growing prestige, influence, and importance. Morley recognized as much by impressing upon Gladstone his belief that here lay a golden opportunity 'for rallying the stout fellows ... I don't know whether you will be inclined to speak at Leeds, giving us our new points of departure. It would obviously be of immense advantage if you would.'[177] However, Gladstone was alive to certain difficulties which might arise should he comply with Morley's request. He wished if possible 'to wash my hands of general politics' and confine his limited energies 'to winding up things already begun', whereas Leeds was 'in the nature of a *commencement* for the party generally'.[178] The citation of these personal factors alone would have enabled Gladstone to decline Schnadhorst's invitation to be present. But he may also have felt that Morley was over-anxious to merge the collective identity of the frontbench in that of the N.L.F. Some confusion seems to have existed in connection with Morley's precise intentions. Stuart Rendel, for instance, imagined that Morley had arranged to *preside* over the Leeds convention. This alarming notion was probably derived from inaccurate newspaper reports (e.g. *The Times* of 20 October). Gladstone heartily concurred with Spencer in the opinion that it would be 'wiser for ex-Cabinet Ministers not to be too tied by their Resolutions, but to let them work through unofficial members of the party'.[179] He had always drawn a clear distinction between the expediency of allowing the N.L.F. to overhaul electoral organization, and the problems which would surely arise if he permitted 'the reorganization of Liberal *policy* from that centre'.[180] Gladstone firmly believed that this second proposition was absolutely inadmissible, since final decisions on party policy were regarded as the exclusive prerogative of the parliamentary leadership.

Yet so rigid a line of demarcation was extremely difficult to preserve in the fluid situation created by the Home Rule controversy. Gladstone had originally foisted a daring Irish policy upon the party, but once the N.L.F. had been requested to shoulder this heavy burden it could not logically be denied the right to inspect the contents of other measures in the Liberal package. The Federation now chose to masquerade as the custodian of Liberal principles simply because the frontbench had in desperation admitted the representative organization into partnership upon a single issue. This advantage was first exploited at Leeds. A resolution pledging the party to establish 'an Irish legislative body for the management of what Parliament shall decide to be distinctively Irish affairs' was carried by John Ellis amidst tremendous enthusiasm. Since the hero of the Westminster Palace Hotel confrontation had only recently returned from a fact-finding mission in Ireland, it seems unlikely that the actual text of the resolution was the product of collaboration with Harcourt and Morley – the two statesmen in attendance. Indeed, Kitson saw fit to rebuke Rosebery publicly for contemplating a diluted Irish policy. This indisposition to 'show any excess of eagerness to meet the Paper Unionists' served to emphasize the independence of the meeting.[181] But evidence of temerity on Kitson's part did nothing to still the acclamation with which news of events at Leeds was received by every Liberal leader, including Rosebery.[182] The principle embodied in the famous 'Leeds resolution' was gladly accepted as the basis of official policy, a decision pregnant with consequences. The uncompromising stance adopted by the N.L.F. towards the idea of Liberal reunion stiffened the resolve of the principal Gladstonian negotiators at the Round Table Conference. 'The Leeds resolution is an indispensable element in an irreducible minimum,' Morley proclaimed. 'We can, I think – certainly Harcourt and I, who were at Leeds – have no other starting-point.'[183] Reunion therefore ceased to be a practical proposition when it became apparent that the Federation had been granted the freedom to mould the entire party in its own image.

This dramatic accretion of N.L.F. privileges proved to be a mixed political blessing. Although the consolidation of a harmonious relationship between the national leaders and the rank and file produced obvious benefits, such an understanding also placed the Federation in an anomalous situation. The fortunes of the party at large could only be restored if Gladstone took the Federation under his auspices, thus transforming that proud and fiercely independent body into a quasi-official institution. Consequently, a grave risk of contamination arose when Schnadhorst assumed a dual rôle in Parliament Street. Morley clearly foresaw the paralysis which might ensue from this sudden migration to London. He feared that the lively outlook fostered by Birmingham would be subdued by constant contact with officialdom, and that confidence would be sapped by the growth of an unhealthy attitude of servility towards Gladstone. Such pessimistic thoughts were based on the N.L.F.'s cowardly refusal in April 1885 to censure the tortuous Egyptian policy of the then Liberal government. 'The more the affiliated associations', Morley had ruefully concluded, 'the greater the difficulty of getting honest and uncompromising expressions of opinion.'[184] He therefore warned the delegates at Leeds that 'the importance and value of the Federation consist in its being a free and spontaneous exponent of the opinions of Liberals at large throughout the country, uninterfered with, unmodified by, Ministers, ex-Ministers, Whips, or any of that class'.[185] But the audience was more impressed by the unprecedented and glittering array of parliamentarians congregated upon the platform than it was responsive to the candour of Morley's language. In the following year the assembly hall was graced (for the first time since 1877) with the figure of the illustrious commander himself. Gladstone's benediction greatly enhanced the importance of the N.L.F. council as the annual showpiece of party activities. The number of accredited delegates began to rise rapidly, a peak of 3,500 being reached in 1889 after three consecutive visits by Gladstone. But this impressive total was almost halved when Gladstone decided to absent himself from the next congress. Little imagination was required to draw the appropriate conclusion. Expansion had not been due to the inherent quality of rather stereotyped debates, but had stemmed from the attractions of personal contact with the leadership. Schnadhorst was horrified by the bleak prospect of not securing the presence of a single frontbench statesman at Sheffield in 1890. The normally sedate Spence Watson swore that 'so sudden and total an eclipse, after the blaze of the last three years, will mean the collapse of the organization'.[186]

This cringing response naturally gave rise to a feeling that the N.L.F. had been captured by the whips, and was now being manipulated to serve the interests of the party leaders. Such damaging allegations were frequently and zealously repudiated by the N.L.F. Spence Watson was proud of its integrity and independence, but the lengthy explanation which he at last offered at the Huddersfield council on 26 March 1896 contained several flaws. He accepted the self-evident fact that circumstances compelled the Federation to co-operate with the L.C.A., while skilfully brushing aside the pertinent charge that his organization was dependent on the Whips' office for financial support. However, George Leveson-Gower, sometime treasurer of the Home Counties Division, revealed in his memoirs that the Chief Whip interviewed him annually in order to ascertain the amount of financial aid required by each constituency association in the running of its internal affairs.[187] In the absence of any record of accounts, it would be rash to infer that this practice was extensive. The sums involved may have been as derisory as the £100 awarded by Arnold Morley in 1890 to the impoverished North Wales Federation.[188] Nevertheless, Leveson-Gower was suspect at this time on account of his being a junior whip, and the Home Counties Division was further incriminated by the fact that it was actually housed in the same rooms as the Central Association. This seems to indicate that the two rival national organizations worked in unison upon sensitive matters which were not strictly within the competence of the L.C.A.

Financial control in one sphere inevitably suggests that some form of official supervision was also exercised over the policy-making functions of the N.L.F. However, the ubiquitous Whips' office did not assume a critical rôle in this process. Arnold Morley divulged that he possessed only a hazy idea of the correct procedure, maintaining that he personally acted as a mere intermediary between the frontbench and Schnadhorst. The inconsequence of the Chief Whip can be gauged by his inability to suppress in 1889 an N.L.F. resolution censuring the Nationalists for having condoned Balfour's Irish University scheme. Arnold Morley weakly reported that it 'might not be out of place' if Gladstone were to utter a word of warning against such attempts to add 'undigested and ill-considered subjects' to the party programme. Gladstone therefore induced Schnadhorst to make certain (unspecified) textual alterations to the agenda of the Manchester congress.[189]

Spence Watson categorically denied the notion that such bargaining took place. His language in 1896 was precise and carefully chosen. He asserted that 'not a single resolution has ever, at all events since 1886, been suggested, hinted at, drawn, altered, or manipulated by any Whip or leader whatsoever'.[190] Yet the evidence which is available, though fragmentary and incomplete, inexorably points towards an opposite conclusion. In fact, Kitson himself contradicted Spence Watson at Huddersfield by revealing that he had been persuaded to repudiate the Chamberlainite motion at the Westminster Palace Hotel by John Morley, who was then a leading member of Gladstone's third administration. Fortunately, Kitson did not proceed to destroy Spence Watson's credibility by revealing that as chairman of Herbert Gladstone's constituency association, he had been privy to the real motives for flying the Hawarden 'kite'. In the winter of 1885–6 Herbert Gladstone had painstakingly explained that this device was necessary in order to procure from the

N.L.F. a prompt and unequivocal declaration in favour of Gladstonian Home Rule.[191] Spence Watson probably knew nothing of these clandestine negotiations. However, it is difficult to explain why the moralistic Quaker should have suppressed the inconvenient fact that during the intervening decade it had become customary to consult the frontbench with respect to the arrangements for the annual N.L.F. council. Courtesy alone demanded a degree of perfectly innocuous discussion of railway timetables and seating plans with leaders who were preoccupied with parliamentary duties. But the agenda was certainly raised at these interviews, and the provisional text of each resolution was also submitted for scrutiny. By 1888 the party leaders had assumed an important rôle in the framing of these various motions. In that year Morley drew up the three principal resolutions on Irish policy which were designed to occupy a full day's debate. Schnadhorst was loath to countenance the one which covered the subject of Irish land purchase, knowing that any mention of this awkward question would outrage many Radical delegates. Gladstone was therefore asked to pronounce judgement, and he presumably sanctioned Morley's resolution since it subsequently appeared upon the agenda paper.[192]

Spence Watson may have been ignorant of this procedure. Schnadhorst's complex personality had gravely impaired the development of a proper working relationship with his fellow N.L.F. officials. He rarely consulted the President – or even his associates on the general purposes committee – but made himself solely responsible for the conduct of business and the construction of policy resolutions.[193] Schnadhorst's discretionary powers were enormous. Yet he sadly lacked Chamberlain's vision and iron will, and consequently he was incapable of imposing his own wishes upon the frontbench. Chamberlain could barely conceal his contempt for Schnadhorst, and in the years prior to 1886 he had carefully ensured that the responsibility for all important decisions rested firmly in his own hands.[194] When the despised minion eventually ousted his autocratic patron from the N.L.F., it soon became obvious that Schnadhorst was unequal to the task allotted to him. The obscure proprietor of a small drapery shop in Birmingham dared not launch any fresh 'unauthorized' programmes. Schnadhorst was simply too 'unassuming, quiet, and gentlemanlike' to risk offending Gladstone. Whigs like Granville were astounded to learn that, contrary to expectations, the bane of the Conservative party was 'not at all violent in his politics'.[195] In reality, the twin electoral misfortunes of 1885 and 1886 had broken his spirit, plunging him into gloom and despondency. By 1887 Schnadhorst's health was visibly declining, leaving him a mere 'shadow of the formidable figure which had inspired terror in the previous years'. The nature and extent of this physical drawback was painful to the memory of the London journalist J. A. Spender, who recalled that Schnadhorst was 'prematurely old and very deaf, and though he used an ear-trumpet, it was with difficulty that one could carry on a consecutive conversation with him'.[196] In the summer of 1889 Schnadhorst suffered a mental breakdown. Although he resumed his duties in 1890, he became an embarrassment to his employers. Schnadhorst occasionally displayed various distressing symptoms of the incurable insanity which eventually forced his family to commit him (in September 1894) to a private nursing home. Long before this tragic stage had been reached, Schnadhorst's mantle had fallen upon his youthful assistant Robert Hudson. But the new N.L.F. secretary readily bowed to Gladstone's superior wisdom, being in no way equipped to withstand the dictates of the frontbench.

The turning-point in the uneasy relationship between the N.L.F. and the parliamentary leaders came in the summer of 1890, shortly after Schnadhorst's return from a convalescent voyage to South Africa. Schnadhorst's mishandling of the notorious Rhyl resolution on Welsh disestablishment brought into the open a longstanding fear lest an 'active and fussy (and not by any means always *wise*) tail should insist on wagging the head'.[197] Although Schnadhorst had consciously striven to neutralize the Welsh threat and preserve intact the sovereignty of the frontbench, the intended beneficiaries were 'considerably disgusted' by what they regarded as an act of 'consummate impertinence'. Harcourt saw in Schnadhorst's behaviour only a transparent plot to restrict his political discretion and executive authority. He exploded into rage with Schnadhorst for having transgressed the guidelines clearly laid down in preceding years. Frank letters flew from Harcourt and Morley to Schnadhorst, while young Lewis Harcourt toiled at the unrewarding task of restraining the combatants. His unyielding father sternly reminded Schnadhorst that 'if we are to act effectively with the Federation there must be some reciprocity.... We ought to have some communication *beforehand* as to what is intended, and not simply be informed of arrangements already made and policies already settled, in which we have no voice or consultation but which we are expected to carry out at short notice.'[198] However, this measured tone by no means conveyed the intensity of Harcourt's real feelings against the '*subs* who arrange everything according to their own second-rate ideas'. In private he could not repress his 'most profound dislike and contempt' for those wretched 'caucus-mongers' who blithely issued 'unauthorized pronunciamentos'.[199] Harcourt realized full well that Schnadhorst's N.L.F. commitments could no longer be allowed to impinge upon the prerogatives of leadership. Yet he magnanimously avoided a pitched battle because the bewildered Schnadhorst had already been reduced to tears and near-hysteria by the brutality of Morley's remarks, and was clearly in no fit state to bear the lash of Harcourt's ferocious tongue.[200]

Gladstone did not join the hue and cry against the hapless Schnadhorst, and, indeed, seemed completely unaware of the fact that a vital principle was at stake. On no occasion since 1886 had he felt the slightest twinge of anxiety concerning the implications of his close involvement in N.L.F. affairs, remaining quite unmoved by Harcourt's vociferous protests that their attendance at council meetings was both 'a bore and a mistake'. Harcourt openly detested the carnival atmosphere which prevailed at such gatherings, especially since he was always cast as an 'ornamental figure', and obliged to make 'short ornamental speeches' which could produce little permanent benefit to the party. Neither he nor Morley saw any legitimate reason why they should be forced to desert their posts in the House of Commons 'in deference to a provincial caucus'.[201] 'As to Newcastle – damn Newcastle,' Harcourt wrote in more playful vein in 1891. 'I propose that we leave things to Providence, who I believe occupies Himself with the Federation. I suppose that we shall be called before the footlights as understudies to the prima donna.'[202] In contrast, the 'great Panjamdrum' (Gladstone) was content to obey Schnadhorst's instructions, even allowing the experienced stage-manager to list the topics upon which he was required to speak (or was expected to avoid). However, Gladstone rarely followed such advice to the letter, though he tried to conform with traditional requirements. In previous years (1887 and 1888) he had been urged to mention only briefly issues other than that of the Irish. But on both occasions Schnadhorst could not deter Gladstone from speaking at length upon his own version of 'prospective legislation' – items which included electoral reform and the payment of members.[203] During these congresses Gladstone was not so obsessed with Ireland as many hostile critics have imagined. In fact, it was he among the leaders who most strenuously sought to change the whole emphasis of N.L.F. politics *before* the Parnell catastrophe of November 1890 abruptly switched interest from Ireland to domestic problems.

Despite the existence of these disturbing precedents, most historians have tenaciously adhered to the doctrine that Gladstone was a reluctant hostage to Radical demands at Newcastle in October 1891. Yet such a widespread interpretation of Gladstone's behaviour cannot lightly be disregarded, since it is founded upon the testimony of some of Gladstone's closest associates. In the aftermath of the Parnell divorce scandal, Harcourt and Morley considered that the Grand

Old Man would only tarnish his reputation if he succumbed in despair to the temptation to touch 'any of the *fads* which infest the air like midges'. Morley candidly admitted that his revered leader did not understand such questions, 'nor the sentiment that makes them important with our people'.[204] One of the younger Radical nonconformists, H. H. Asquith, later alleged that Gladstone was 'indifferent to, not to say critical of' some of the policies which he had endorsed in a 'somewhat perfunctory fashion' at Newcastle.[205] Rosebery also considered that Gladstone had impulsively accepted a programme which he personally would not be required to implement. All these harsh judgements deserve to be treated with some caution, since they were made at times of acute crisis – and (in the case of Rosebery at least) clearly bore the hallmark of retrospective special pleading. It is also necessary to recall that neither Asquith nor Rosebery had actually witnessed Gladstone's performance in the Tyne Theatre. The former had lost his wife shortly before the N.L.F. meeting, while the latter had suffered a similar bereavement twelve months earlier, prompting him to withdraw altogether from public life. However, the corroboratory evidence proffered by so distinctly qualified an observer as Herbert Gladstone cannot easily be overlooked. He maintained with considerable bitterness that for many years Schnadhorst had unscrupulously exploited Gladstone's old age by systematically weakening his resistance to Radical policy. A weary veteran could easily be induced 'to give this, that, and the other the party imprimatur', and Gladstone had therefore capitulated to Schnadhorst 'against his own feelings and in deference ... to the Federation as a representative body'.[206] Yet even Herbert Gladstone's verdict cannot be accepted as conclusive. When the son of the ex-premier penned this complaint to Robert Hudson, in March 1898, his judgement was clouded by an unbearable emotional predicament. He was shaken by the news that the N.L.F. was about to disparage his father's rôle at Newcastle at a moment when the old man himself was enduring acute suffering upon his death bed.

A fragmentary glimpse of what actually occurred at Newcastle puts another complexion on the matter. Morley claimed in conversation that prior to his own late arrival in the city Gladstone had made no apparent preparation for the fateful speech. 'He had not a single note ready,' Edward Hamilton reported Morley as saying. 'On Friday morning [2 October] he said he must try and put his thoughts together. He ran over the main points of the programme with J.M., and by luncheon he professed to have got his speech in his head with just a note or two jotted down on paper.'[207] Schnadhorst does not appear to have been consulted at this crucial stage. On the contrary, only Gladstone's immediate colleagues were cognizant of the outlines of the proposed address, and were thus capable of deploring beforehand his guarded allusions to the evacuation of Egypt, and of rejecting as invidious the distinction which he drew between different social classes in connection with the payment of members. It is also significant that neither Harcourt nor Morley raised any objection to Gladstone's decision to express his formal approval of the N.L.F. programme. Indeed, at the previous congress Harcourt had specifically stated (21 November 1890) that the construction of party policy was in the Federation's charge. Although Morley took care to distinguish between official policy and elaborate Federation programmes when he spoke at Newcastle (1 October), he, like Harcourt, considered that Gladstone's performance had been a 'great success' in nearly every way.[208] In 1891 there existed no trace of the hostility towards the N.L.F. which they had felt up to 1890, and which they were to make explicit after Gladstone's retirement.[209] Harcourt and Morley certainly did not consider at the time that Gladstone had abdicated his responsibilities by injudiciously committing the leadership to the entire Federation programme.

In his opening remarks at the next meeting of the N.L.F. council, Spence Watson affirmed that Gladstone had endorsed the Newcastle resolutions 'almost *seriatim*'.[210] Close scrutiny of Gladstone's lengthy speech suggests otherwise. He did not obediently and slavishly ratify the Newcastle programme, but, instead, selected for emphasis items which he felt were important and neglected those about which he was not enthusiastic. Thus, he dwelt at length upon the future status and composition of the House of Lords, a subject that did not figure prominently on the Newcastle agenda; and he omitted from his speech the crucial principle of public control over elementary schools, a matter so vital to nonconformists that it had been placed in a special resolution. Moreover, Gladstone's opening references to the evacuation of Egypt and to the need for stringent economy in public expenditure amounted to an admonition to the N.L.F. for adhering to what he regarded as an unwholesome and lop-sided conception of its obligations. He believed that even in opposition Liberals ought to devote much more attention to foreign affairs, and seemed quite prepared to promote further dissensions within the party in order to achieve this feat. Consequently, Gladstone caused disquiet by rejecting the complacent view that the N.L.F. was entitled to limit the scope of its activities to 'parish pump' reforms, and to the search for additional sources of taxation for purely local purposes. Most important of all, Gladstone refused to endorse the policy concerning Welsh disestablishment which had been passed at a mass meeting of delegates on the evening prior to his speech. Although he conceded the point that Welshmen would be foolish to suspend their agitation until a Liberal government had disposed of Irish Home Rule, he was not willing to give Welsh disestablishment priority over all other subjects. Gladstone felt so strongly on the matter that he deliberately chose to remain on the Continent when a motion on Welsh disestablishment was debated in Parliament on 23 February 1892. He continued to savour Rendel's hospitality at Valescure, secure in the knowledge that his absence made it much 'easier to avoid giving any pledge as to the order in which the various measures are to be taken'.[211]

Thus, Gladstone demonstrated that he was by no means anxious to pander to every whim of the N.L.F. However, he also realized that the democratic forces which had recently transformed the party made it impossible for the parliamentary leaders to ignore the wishes of the popular organization. These leaders were unable to reverse the increased power enjoyed by the Federation, nor could they refuse the summons to travel to Newcastle. Undoubtedly, the situation in which they found themselves was potentially dangerous. Even if the frontbench maintained a degree of control over at least some Federation activities, their presence at the annual meetings was certainly compromising. To some extent the leadership was associated with – and therefore bound by – the decisions and policy resolutions of the Federation. For this reason it would soon have been necessary to clarify the rôles of the respective parties, even if the controversial legacy of the Newcastle programme itself had not brought the issue into the open.

Rosebery's brief but unhappy experience as Prime Minister (1894–1895) provoked much unrest concerning the factional pressures which had brought the Newcastle programme into being. He himself was troubled by a series of fierce personal quarrels with Harcourt, and his preoccupation with the problems of Empire later brought him into conflict with Morley. Since he was also anxious to embark upon the hazardous enterprise of a 'clean slate', Rosebery was bound to regard the largely anti-imperialist N.L.F. as a further obstacle to his ambitions. When he addressed the Federation council for the first time in his capacity as premier (18 January 1895), Rosebery sternly rebuked his undiscerning followers for having imposed upon a ministry with only a fragile majority at its command 'a vast programme of measures of first-rate importance'. In a pointed reference to the host nation, he reminded the chastened delegates at Cardiff that they had naïvely failed to appreciate that each of these eminently desirable policies could not be dealt with simultaneously.[212] Rosebery's predictions were fully vindicated by the electoral catastrophe of 1895. After this humiliating rebuff Rosebery plucked up courage to launch a vitriolic attack upon the Federation. At the next annual meeting (27 March 1896) he charged the organization with having thrust a programme upon his predecessor in the leadership, 'with all its consequences, good and evil'. Spence Watson was personally censured for the collapse of an administration which 'with a chivalrous sense of honour [and] with inadequate means . . . had taken a burden too heavy for its back, or the back of any Government or any Parliament to bear'.[213]

Rosebery's tone indicated that the specific question of Gladstone's responsibility for transforming the Newcastle policy into an official party programme had become entangled in the much broader issue of whether the Newcastle programme – or any supplementary programme – was either desirable or electorally advantageous. In the stormy political climate of the late 1890s the controversy over what exactly had occurred at Newcastle was coloured by a strong desire to rid the party of a document which had become a political liability. 'The party needs to make a new start and to shed much of this,' Rosebery privately noted in 1896. 'Its bulk and multifarious aggressiveness constitutes an encumbrance – not an inspiration or assistance'.[214] The N.L.F., severely shaken by the progress of events, was disposed to reach the same conclusion. Federation officials now began to display a less vehement urge to compose programmes and a greater willingness to respect the prerogatives of leadership. Hence, the tradition of cataloguing the various items in the Liberal creed abruptly ceased, never to be revived. In March 1898 Hudson and Spence Watson vigorously denied the charge that the N.L.F. had constructed a programme at Newcastle. They suggested that the term 'programme' was convenient, though grossly misleading. They enunciated with remarkable aplomb the novel theory that N.L.F. resolutions had never been regarded as authoritative declarations, and therefore bound neither delegates nor leaders to any precise policy.[215] This abject surrender of the Federation's precious right to proclaim Liberal intentions meant that the next party leader (Campbell-Bannerman) suffered none of the anguish which had distressed his two illustrious predecessors.

[v]

The Polarities of Radicalism

1. *The Parliamentary Ascendancy of Labouchere*

The jubilant army of Radicals which was elected in 1885 contained an unusually high proportion of raw recruits. These novices arrived at Westminster in January 1886 only to discover to their chagrin that the nucleus of a separate Radical parliamentary organization did not exist. They then turned hopefully towards the renowned triumvirate which had constantly spoken out on their behalf in the late Parliament. But the chief apostles of Radicalism had ceased to collaborate with each other, and so could not provide the distinctive leadership and sound guidance which was urgently required. Dilke was paralysed by the matrimonial scandal which had already begun to wreck his career, and consequently rarely appeared in the House. Chamberlain and Morley were at loggerheads on the Irish question. Both were on the point of entering Gladstone's third cabinet, the former to thwart the premier's Home Rule plans, and the latter to seek an entente with the Irish Nationalists. Clearly, neither they nor Trevelyan (who emerged as a Unionist during his brief period as Secretary for Scotland) had sufficient time and energy at their disposal to heed the strangled pleas of forlorn backbenchers. By a strange irony of fate the sole remaining member of the Radical 'Cabal', Lefevre, was rendered ineffective by the (temporary) loss of his parliamentary seat.

Thus, the situation which existed at the beginning of 1886 was both unprecedented and entirely unforeseen. The party was more Radical in composition than ever before, yet it had never been more uniformly lacking in cohesion, discipline, and clarity of purpose. The new members were urged to rely upon the experience of an 'old parliamentary hand' to steer them through a choppy and uncharted political sea. But Gladstone was naturally preoccupied with the massive task of drafting fresh Irish legislation, and he therefore

left the backbenchers almost entirely to their own devices. Edward
Hamilton noted that the House went 'completely out of hand' in
Gladstone's absence. 'It votes wildly and has no scruples about
supporting individual crotchets in the lobby.'[1] The latitude allowed
to backbenchers became evident as early as 18 February, when the
leaders on both sides were powerless to avoid (by securing the
adjournment) a highly inconvenient discussion of the women's
suffrage bill. Further embarrassments followed in rapid succession,
and during the course of March the government suffered a series of
humiliating rebuffs. Labouchere ominously appeared on the scene on
the fifth, and moved a resolution condemning the hereditary basis
of the House of Lords. Resolutions concerning National engagements and Welsh and Scottish disestablishment were introduced
shortly afterwards. On each occasion Gladstone or Harcourt rose
from the treasury bench in order to urge restraint upon an unruly
band of impatient Liberals. But this advice was constantly ignored,
and in some cases ministers obtained only narrow majorities in the
divisions which ensued. The rebels surpassed these notable performances on the 11th, when Labouchere beat the government in Committee of Supply by 131 votes to 114. Many Radicals resented paying
for the upkeep of royal parks (especially the Duke of Cambridge's
'game preserve' at Richmond). Hence Labouchere adroitly pleaded
that it was unjust to maintain the parks of London out of national
revenues while those in the provinces were dependent on the local
rates.[2] H. H. Fowler made no attempt to disprove this contention
when he calmly and effortlessly restored the original vote on the 18th.
Nevertheless, this tardy clamp-down by the whips could not disguise
the fact that the reduction of an important vote of Supply by so large
a sum as £50,000 was an extraordinary – perhaps unique – occurrence. The process of fragmentation within the party now commenced in earnest. The reckless spirit of independence which
radiated from Labouchere's corner seat below the gangway was a
phenomenon that could not easily be suppressed.

Fortunately, discontented and restless M.P.s were unable to
demand satisfaction in the brief period between the production of
the Irish measures in April and the dissolution in July. A direct
confrontation with the ministry was averted through lack of opportunity. But the incipient challenge could not long be warded off in
the new Parliament, especially now that Liberal statesmen had been
stripped of authority and propelled towards the unglamorous
benches opposite. When the Liberal government and the Conservative opposition had changed places, Bryce alleged that his own frontbench was 'not an Opposition at all in the sense of former days, but
a number of skirmishers, occasionally . . . uniting for a raid upon

the enemy when the old chief appears'.[3] Much of the responsibility for this deplorable state of affairs rested with Gladstone. He alone was capable of restraining those turbulent elements who sat alongside or behind him. Yet because of his anomalous position, Gladstone was singularly unfitted to perform this precarious duty. After his resignation from the premiership, Gladstone had agreed to retain the leadership only on condition that stringent terms were met. The party was left in no doubt that Gladstone remained '*in situ* for the Irish question only', leaving Harcourt to carry all responsibility upon matters for which Gladstone had neither time nor inclination.[4]

At his age Gladstone could not be expected to promise more. But during the winter recess he decided to curtail his public activities still further. Gladstone felt it politic 'to maintain, at any rate for a time, great reserve; to leave the business of general criticism of the Government to others, and rarely to interfere (which involves restricted appearances) except on special cases, or when there may be a change of circumstances'.[5] He proffered Granville the excuse that it was necessary to refute allegations that a despicable 'old man in a hurry' was avid for a return to office. However, Gladstone was chiefly concerned about the marked deterioration in his health. Old age was beginning to take its toll upon even his remarkable and seemingly inexhaustible reserves of energy. The 'wall of deafness' grew 'higher and higher',[6] and each year the onset of fatigue compelled him to spend the winter months recuperating in southern Europe. Under these circumstances, he found it quite impossible to take an active and continuous part in public affairs. He was frequently absent from the House for long periods. As his entrances became less predictable, the anxieties of his lieutenants became correspondingly more intense. No one wished Gladstone to live in the House, but Harcourt had reason to complain that 'nothing can be more perplexing than the fitful appearance and disappearance of a supreme personage'.[7]

Gladstone's conduct created difficulties of a more serious and practical character. He had long betrayed an aversion to formal planning, and during recent premierships he had even been disinclined to summon the cabinet at all. Once he had secured his release from office he certainly showed no disposition to reverse these alarming attitudes. On the contrary, the problems were magnified by the mere fact of his almost continuous unavailability. The first major clash with the Unionist government revealed how this lack of communication and collaboration with colleagues led inevitably to ineffectiveness in the House of Commons. During the bitter and protracted wrangles on the coercion bill of 1887 it became glaringly apparent that Gladstone had not troubled to prepare a coherent strategy upon a subject which interested him deeply. Morley protested that the crucial debates in Committee were 'badly managed' because an errant leader did not exercise sufficient care to ensure that the frontbench took a 'systematic and connected line'. In view of the remorseless operation of the closure, Gladstone ought not to have tolerated a rambling and sprawling discussion on a series of haphazard amendments. An alert tactician would surely have concentrated the attack in a single amendment directed at the government's novel interpretation of conspiracy. 'In plain truth the sin is not obstruction, but drift and muddle,' Morley wryly explained. 'The worst of it is that Mr G. (who is only there a fifth of the time) thinks it is all as it should be.'[8]

Several members of the late cabinet now began to search diligently for an excuse to confront Gladstone on the matter. Rosebery was the first to invent a convenient pretext. In February 1888 he argued with compelling force that the principal Liberal peers met their counterparts in the Commons 'but seldom and as it were by accident'. Taking his courage in both hands, Rosebery complained that there had arisen in consequence 'some want of consistency and congruity in our course as an opposition'. But Gladstone was incorrigible, and tried hard to ignore Rosebery's suggestion that regular briefings could be held at Carlton House Terrace (Gladstone's London home).[9] However, when Gladstone stubbornly declined to reveal his intentions concerning Sir Charles Russell's motion on public meetings in Trafalgar Square (2 March), Morley could no longer tolerate this decision in silence. After hasty consultations with others on the frontbench, he wrote to Gladstone recommending that they should all muster on the Monday of each week during the session 'to decide on the line to be taken on questions likely to arise'.[10] Gladstone still did not favour the idea, though he agreed to discuss the pending local government bill with his colleagues.

The result of this exploratory conference was not entirely satisfactory. According to Spencer their 'Great Chairman revelled in the Budget' for over an hour and a quarter. 'When we got to Local Government [he] hurried discussion, and relegated it, in fact, to a Committee.'[11] This committee on local government petered out in the summer of 1888, and there is no evidence to suggest that Gladstone persevered with weekly meetings during the session. None can be traced – apart from a single conference in March 1889 to consider the increase in naval expenditure.[12] Gladstone characteristically did not attend, preferring either to confide in favoured individuals or else to remain remote and inaccessible. Seclusion on the continent throughout most of the winter recess also enabled him to resist appeals concerning the arrangement of pre-sessional dinners, the traditional prelude to the Queen's Speech. 'No party but ours fasts on the eve of Parliament,' Rosebery gloomily remarked.[13] He personally was obliged to supervise the entertainments in 1889, since Gladstone was clearly determined not to perform this normally agreeable and useful function.

Rosebery's gracious gesture indicated how invidious and even ludicrous was the task allotted to Harcourt as deputy leader. Although Harcourt bore the brunt of the parliamentary burden upon his own shoulders, he was debarred from taking action without prior reference to Gladstone, and was therefore inhibited from summoning colleagues in his own right. Labouring under such insufferable conditions, Harcourt found it impossible to maintain discipline within the parliamentary party. Gladstone had been warned as early as 1887 that this situation might arise. Spencer felt certain that the heir apparent would be quite unable to repress 'a tendency to take independent action on a good many subjects'. In his view Harcourt suffered the disadvantage, 'which was clearly felt by the party', of not having won 'the Confidence of our men in the House, still less of the bulk of the party outside'.[14] The unsuitability of Arnold Morley for the post of Chief Whip was an additional and fatal handicap. He was reputed to be 'business-like, stiff and steady', whereas possession of a genial good humour was the quality really needed in party management.[15] Hence Harcourt, who was remarkably sensitive to any criticism of his parliamentary performances, was liable to lash out in response to admonishment from such a pedestrian source. He deeply resented his growing isolation on the frontbench, and took the strongest exception to Arnold Morley's accounts of discontent below the gangway. Harcourt dismissed these complaints as the grumbles of men who wasted no opportunity for making mischief, and roundly accused the Chief Whip of 'flogging the horse which is dragging the whole load'.[16]

Nevertheless, Harcourt could not fairly blame others for his own inadequacies. Gladstone's reluctance to summon frequent meetings of the parliamentary party to explain his policies had needlessly aggravated an already tense relationship between leaders and followers. Unfortunately, Harcourt was temperamentally unfitted to re-establish a feeling of rapport with humble M.P.s who felt neglected and despised. In the eyes of one seasoned observer (the lobby correspondent H. W. Lucy), the elephantine Harcourt was apt to adopt a 'swaggering, bullying mood' in the chamber, an offence compounded by 'a certain ponderosity of humour and invective'.[17] Harcourt's temper was even more formidable than his physical proportions – and was not to be trifled with, either by friends or subordinates. This notorious susceptibility to sudden and violent fluctuations in mood meant that 'Jumbo' was never easily approached. His lack of sympathy with those who agitated for more decisive leadership was a still more serious deficiency. Harcourt did not seem to be conscious of requests to investigate pressing social questions, or aware of demands for more aggressive tactics in the House. Such powerful cross-currents within the party could be consistently ignored only because long term visions were foreign to Harcourt's nature. He preferred to immerse himself in events as they developed from day to day, being content to 'mark time' in the blissful expectation that 'something will turn up before long'.[18]

Harcourt's serene optimism could, however, be mistaken for wilful neglect, ignorance, or even chronic fatalism. The notion that this was indeed the case became so prevalent that it produced a direct challenge to Harcourt's (and Gladstone's) authority. The revolt was discreetly fomented by Labouchere, who emerged after 1886 as the unofficial spokesman for a core of extreme Radicals. The principal bone of contention was the ambivalent behaviour of a party hierarchy which, in the country, continually denigrated the machinations of a coercionist régime, yet shrank from matching such bold language with resolute action in Parliament itself. On several occasions the official opposition had been content to act as the handmaid to the Unionist government, instead of fulfilling its proper function of assailing ministers. Labouchere could not believe that it was appropriate for dedicated Home Rulers to extricate the foe from embarrassing situations by accepting potentially contentious and awkward legislation in a bi-partisan spirit. He was a vigilant critic of anything which savoured of a private arrangement between the two front-benches, since this doctrine of mutual convenience was hardly consistent with the opposition's paramount duty of thwarting the administration in its Irish policy. Hence, when the government proposed to allow the Duke of Connaught to leave his Indian command in order to attend the jubilee celebrations of 1887, Labouchere poured scorn upon Childers' conciliatory speech. He avowed that backbenchers 'ought invariably to upset' bargains of this nature.[19] In the following year he was dismayed by Gladstone's reluctance to press for drastic revisions in the local government bill. 'If the "party" really believes that a ministry is so good that it ought not to be opposed', Labouchere complained, 'it can hardly expect electors to bestir themselves to change what is so excellent.'[20]

During the winter recess of 1888-9 Labouchere finally decided that prompt and drastic action alone could dam the stream of Conservative success. C. T. Ritchie had been permitted to appropriate all the credit for passing the local government bill; Goschen continued to produce Budget surpluses; and Lord Salisbury persevered with a foreign policy which deservedly won the approval of all parties. The electoral consequences of these achievements preyed heavily upon Labouchere's mind. He planned to pursue an active alternative policy which depended for its success upon the constant harassment of the government. At first he hoped that Gladstone would adopt the strategy as his own, and associate it with a formal declaration on Irish Home Rule. But Gladstone refused to take the initiative, because (unlike Labouchere) he was not prepared to batter down with brute force 'the wall built of 100 bricks' with which the government protected itself in the division lobby.[21] After this rebuff Labouchere set out alone upon the path of devastation and destruction. On 19 March 1889 Goschen accused him of wantonly wasting time during the early votes in Committee of Supply. With his customary frankness and studied insolence Labouchere explained exactly what his new concept of guerilla warfare entailed:

> Guerilla wars before now have proved successful; they waste the forces of the enemy. We are not going to engage in pitched battles against the master of many legions on the other side of the House ... We will throw every obstacle we can in the way of the trans- action of public business. I say what I mean. I believe it is our business to do everything we can to provoke a dissolution.[22]

Labouchere was as good as his word. He had long grown accus- tomed to the rôle of delaying votes in Committee of Supply, but he now placed this irregular activity upon a methodical footing through the creation of a highly successful 'Fourth' party. The appointment of Philip Stanhope and Alfred Jacoby as its authorized whips consti- tuted a visible manifestation of Labouchere's formal separation from official Liberalism. This new group (appropriately dubbed the 'Jacobyns') was capable of mustering approximately 70 votes, not counting the Irish – past masters of the obstructive art. In May 1889 the machine became fully operational, with Stanhope and Jacoby acting as tellers in a series of divisions. Battle was joined on the 6th, when the Jacobyns saw fit to protest against the imprisonment in Ireland of one of their comrades, C. A. V. Conybeare – the disreput- able and universally disliked M.P. for Camborne.

Labouchere immediately received massive support from the rank and file. This enabled him not only to repudiate Gladstone's authority, but also to separate the aged chief from many of those who sat uncomfortably on the frontbench. The cause of a further remarkable upheaval was the controversy in July surrounding the forthcoming marriage of Princess Louise, the question at stake being whether Parliament or the Queen ought to make financial provision for the children of the Prince of Wales. Labouchere naturally

adhered to the latter proposition. As an anti-monarchist he wished
to prove that the Crown possessed sufficient funds for the purpose,
and therefore he insisted on being nominated to the Select Committee which was due to consider the subject. However, it was not
the Queen who suffered as a result of this outburst of republican
feeling. Gladstone, and to a lesser extent Harcourt, were dismayed
to find that their principal lieutenants deserted them in the divisions
which followed. On 29 July even the loyal Morley moved a hostile
amendment. The tide of opinion against additional grants was so
strong that Gladstone was forced against his will to summon a meeting of the parliamentary party. He even accepted an invitation to
dine with Labouchere, who hitherto had been ostracized by society
on account of his compromising marital situation.[23] Gladstone
evidently hoped to persuade Labouchere to abandon wrecking
tactics. But the former could not justify an inherently untenable
position, and consequently he failed to convert the latter to his own
point of view. Gladstone was therefore unable to check the rebellion.
The number of Liberals, including pairs, who were prepared to
support the government dwindled into insignificance (from 37 to 15),
whereas the aggregate of those who defied Gladstone increased
proportionately (from 95 to 162). In fact, had Labouchere not
employed his two 'obnoxious' Jacobyn tellers, the disparity in numbers might have been even more pronounced.[24]

The Prince of Wales' children's bill did not leave the Commons
until 5 August. A badly shaken Harcourt was left with only four
weeks in which to invent 'something to retrieve the horrid mess of
the Royal Grants'.[25] Fortunately, Labouchere had delayed essential
public business to such an extent that important and contentious
measures like the tithe rent-charge recovery bill had not yet entered
Committee. Harcourt was conscious that his future hung in the
balance. The Welsh, Jacobyn, and Nonconformist forces were all
preparing for total war. Unless Harcourt now adopted an equally
bellicose attitude, all respect for his leadership would vanish. He
therefore plunged headlong into the fray, compelling the beleaguered
government to amend the tithe bill so substantially that under the
rules of the House it had to be withdrawn. This personal triumph
removed lingering suspicions concerning Harcourt's fitness for
leadership, and enabled him at last to tighten his slender grip upon
the parliamentary party.[26]

Having regained the initiative from the Jacobyns, Harcourt was
in no mood to listen to the 'wild talk of obstruction' which
Labouchere and his 'hot-headed friends' encouraged. As a strict
constitutionalist he shared Gladstone's opinion that it was absurd to
try and force a dissolution upon a ministry which still commanded

an impregnable majority.[27] Nevertheless, Harcourt did not emerge unscathed from his ordeal. For too long he had pestered the rank and file 'about conscience and consistency, without convincing anyone that he possesses either'.[28] Labouchere knew that Harcourt's approach to public life was essentially negative. The mere quest for party advantage mattered more to Harcourt than either political principles or detailed legislative programmes. A revealing insight into the psychology of the man can be gleaned by perusing his private correspondence. Military analogies bulk large in his thought and constantly recur in his rhetoric; he rejoiced at every opportunity to 'smite' the enemy 'hip and thigh in their retreat'. 'I have always held that a Government is destroyed a great deal more by its own faults than by the exertions of its opponents,' Harcourt strenuously maintained. 'It is a good deal easier to attack than to promulgate a programme of our own.'[29]

Labouchere's philosophy was equally shallow and sterile. His obsession with the pecuniary motives of those who advocated a 'forward' policy in Africa constituted a strand of Radical thought which continued to find vocal expression until his death in 1912. But on domestic issues Labouchere lacked imagination, and symbolized a final and defiant flowering of an archaic brand of mid-Victorian Radicalism. After Chamberlain's defection in 1886 his mind became obsessed with the ramifications of hereditary and corporate privilege. Labouchere's knowledge was truly encyclopaedic upon matters pertaining to the composition of the Civil List, the misuse of the royal prerogative, the prevalence of pensions and sinecures, and the anomalous status of the House of Lords. Every session was peppered with satirical comments upon this wide variety of subjects. But although his tone was often amusing, many of Labouchere's strictures were also tiresome and trivial. Patriotic Conservatives were maddened by these constant offences against decorum, yet he withstood such storms of criticism with cynical detachment. The intrepid guerilla leader therefore held court at the Palace of Westminster, surrounded by Radicals who admired his curious knack of being able to ferret out intimate and unsavoury information which could be exploited to the detriment of the government.

Labouchere's prestige depended upon a capacity to expose wrong-doers, especially those who sat in high places. One of the more beneficial services which he rendered to the country was to unmask the Metropolitan Ratepayers Protection Society as a bogus organization. On 1 March 1887 the corrupt activities of the City Corporation were linked with the name of a former Lord Mayor, the prominent Conservative M.P. Sir Robert Fowler. After this humiliation not even a fanatical City could resist the long overdue reorganization of metropolitan local government. However, other researches by the proprietor of *Truth* did not always have such constructive repercussions. One of his more extraordinary statements was to charge the Chancellor of the Exchequer with wielding a malign influence over foreign policy. On 11 August he accused Goschen of possessing a concealed vested interest in Egyptian bond issues through his connection with the banking house which bore his name. There seemed to be no limit to Labouchere's reckless allegations in Parliament, since these enjoyed immunity from prosecution. On 28 February 1890 he even insinuated that the Prime Minister was implicated in a criminal conspiracy to protect the Prince of Wales from the consequences of the Cleveland Street gaming scandal. Perhaps the most thoroughly documented example of Labouchere's peculiar detective work arose in connection with the proceedings of the Parnell Commission. He revelled in intrigue and personal crises, and these were essential ingredients in the drama which unfolded in the early months of 1889. Appropriately, it was he who brought the government to the brink of disaster by extracting a written confession from Richard Pigott only hours before that miserable creature fled to Spain and committed suicide.

The draughts of strong medicine administered by Labouchere provided the demoralized party with a temporary measure of relief. But as the Liberal recovery gathered momentum, it became apparent that Labouchere exuded a poisonous aura of self-confidence. He soon stood exposed as a political lightweight. The persistent advocate of plans to sandwich justice to Ireland between some appetizing morsels for English Radicals made no genuine effort to produce a clear and specific programme of his own. Although he spoke constantly in the House, Labouchere showed no interest in general legislation. In fact whenever vital social questions like land reform, local government, and taxation were debated, Labouchere was conspicuous by his silence. The explanation is not hard to find. In May 1888 he spoke and voted against so innocuous a measure as Sir John Lubbock's bill to provide overworked shop assistants with a half-holiday in each week. His Northampton partner (and principal lieutenant) invoked the extreme and rigid doctrines of the classical economists – which even Morley had discarded. Both Labouchere and Bradlaugh relentlessly opposed 'immoral' social legislation, which they considered 'would strike a blow at the self-reliance of the individual'.[30] Such behaviour not only helped to destroy their reputations as the friends of labour, but also generated (for Bradlaugh) an incongruous wave of Conservative sympathy. The onset of a terminal illness in 1889 saved Bradlaugh from the political fate which awaited the senior member for Northampton. Nevertheless, he lived just long enough to see the spirit of his fellow obstructionists and backbench agitators broken by the Parnell divorce crisis. This was one scandal from which Labouchere could not profit. 'There is absolutely no fight left in us,' wrote the Welsh Jacobyn David Lloyd George. 'The House simply rushes through business. There is practically no opposition. Labouchere's ... most pungent sayings excite no laughter.'[31]

The saga of Labouchere's political decline came to a sorry end in 1892, when Gladstone denied him a place in the new Liberal government. Labouchere now wished to quit politics and resume his degenerate diplomatic career. In the autumn he cast to the winds all previous convictions relating to patronage and privilege, and importuned Rosebery to send him as ambassador to Washington. This unedifying and degrading public spectacle reduced the tormented suitor to a laughing-stock. When he returned in frustration to his attenuated rump, Labouchere discovered that all respect for his leadership had been lost. The minute faction struggled to maintain its identity between 1893 and 1895. But even with the aid of Dilke, Labouchere could never reach the glorious heights which he had scaled in 1889.

2. *The Genesis of a New Liberalism*

Liberal social reformers found it impossible to co-operate with Labouchere. But the alternatives that were available to these other survivors of the 1886 débâcle were by no means self-evident. According to the peevish Atherley-Jones, the rank and file could be neatly separated into two categories – 'a score or two of elderly business men, who had spent all the energy and interest of their physical and mental activity in the factory and the counting house, [and] a scanty remnant of more or less active and ambitious politicians'.[32] The contrast between the former group and the cluster of young enthusiasts who provided the motive power of the new Liberalism could not have been more marked. One significant and redeeming feature of the 1885–6 crisis was the emergence of a synthesis of scions of historic Liberal families and parvenus from the junior professional classes. Arthur Acland, Sydney Buxton, and – above all – Sir Edward Grey, symbolized continuity with the noble social traditions of the past, whereas brash and ambitious barristers like H. H. Asquith, R. B. Haldane, and Frank Lockwood, reflected the changing social structure and outlook of a party recently elected on a democratic basis. To these ingredients were added Tom Ellis, the folk hero of Wales, and R. C. Munro-Ferguson, a Scottish laird. Two by-elections in 1889 helped to augment the strength of the group, Augustine Birrell and Lord William Compton being returned respectively for West Fife and the working-class constituency of Barnsley.

This select circle of friends exerted a degree of political influence out of all proportion to their numbers, comprising, in the eyes of Morley, 'the flower of the Liberal flock of the future'.[33] Their intellectual capacity was such that almost without exception each quickly established himself as a serious candidate for office. Only the unfortunate Haldane had reason to complain that his very considerable talents went unnoticed. In 1892 Buxton, Grey, Lockwood, and Ellis all received junior posts in the administration, with Munro-Ferguson joining their ranks in 1894 when his patron succeeded to the premiership. The accession of Acland and Asquith to the cabinet, as Vice-President of the Council and Home Secretary respectively, vindicated the unorthodox pressures which the self-effacing Haldane in particular had courageously brought to bear upon the party leaders. Gladstone was anxious to exclude from the cabinet anyone who had not spent a probationary period in minor office. Moreover, his regard for Acland's family pedigree was counterbalanced by the fact that the member for Rotherham was an unfrocked clergyman. Gladstone soon yielded with respect to Asquith, but he was startled to find that his chief advisers were equally adamant that Acland too should be given cabinet status. His resistance only crumbled when it was made clear to him that Acland's promotion was demanded by 'strong influences considered to operate through the H. of C'.[34]

The group's activities prior to this momentous date are difficult to disentangle. Intimate though the relationship was, the participants chose to leave only a vague impression of their work to posterity. Asquith recalled that during the long years in opposition 'we sat together, talked together, generally worked together, and as a rule ... voted together'. They met every week, but since formal procedures were dispensed with, it is hard to assess precisely how each 'made his own contribution to the common stock'.[35] Morley shed no light upon the matter when, in a generous tribute, he spoke of them as 'a working alliance, not a school; they had idealisms, but were no Utopians ... They had conscience, character, and took their politics to heart.'[36]

However, their basic purpose was practical and definite, though rather pretentious. The young Radicals did not wish to see socialist doctrines (even moderate ones) make any headway, since, in their view, these were often indistinguishable from revolutionary visions. But they did protest most vehemently against a widespread indifference within the party to pressing social problems. Each was an enthusiastic advocate of Irish Home Rule, and readily accepted Gladstone's guidance on most matters pertaining to Ireland. Yet none of them were prepared to accept the proposition that because Gladstone chose to concentrate upon settling the Irish question, the entire frontbench were thereby entitled to share his apparent lack of concern for the politics of the post-Gladstonian era. It did not require much foresight to predict that such a change would occur in the not so distant future. Hence the younger men naturally became alarmed lest the appearance of drift and uncertainty which was given to the country should bring discredit upon the party and further prejudice its electoral prospects. The great danger was not an advanced domestic programme but an indefinite one. Haldane believed that the stereotyped procedures of the N.L.F. offered at best a 'rough and inadequate machinery', and could provide no substitute for positive and constructive statecraft. 'Nottingham conferences and abstract resolutions are empty forms, entitled to and commanding no influence or respect,' he provocatively declared in the pages of the *Contemporary Review*. 'They are only of value in so far as they express pent up opinions of a tolerably definite character.'[37]

The great task which confronted the idealists was therefore perfectly specific. They needed to investigate each item of the Liberal programme, stimulate discussion, and provide a framework upon which legislation could be based. Acland was the 'corporate conscience', but since he was also a man of 'strong quiet influence' he did not overtly appear to dominate his associates, many of whom overshadowed him in later years.[38] Nevertheless, it was Acland who repeatedly impressed upon his friends the urgent necessity of undertaking a great deal more detailed work on the Radical programme than Chamberlain himself has been able to accomplish, before the various proposals could be transformed into useful legislation. He quickly mapped out the whole field of possible Liberal legislation, and in the autumn of 1886 divided it up amongst his friends for study.[39] Acland personally concentrated on the relationship between educational policies and the rural programme, believing that the diffusion of knowledge on technical subjects and the adoption of co-operative principles in production would do more than anything else to revitalize the countryside. The lawyers were allocated topics appropriate to their calling. Lockwood proposed to amend the Employers' Liability Act of 1880; Asquith attempted to rationalize the labyrinth of electoral registration; and Haldane explored means of rendering the incidence of local taxation more equitable.

The young Liberals ultimately hoped to re-educate the party in social theory, but the manner in which this could best be achieved was not straightforward. Although the House of Commons provided a convenient and influential forum for the dissemination of fresh ideas, less use was made of the chamber than might reasonably have been expected. When the Parliament of 1886 had run half of its allotted course, Harcourt complained that 'our young men like E. Grey who *can* speak, won't. Asquith ... will never do a day's work for us in the House'.[40] Asquith's reticence was puzzling because he had delivered a remarkable and memorable maiden speech early in 1887 on the subject of Coercion. Through this single action he had deservedly acquired a reputation for being an orator of exceptional precision, economy, and clarity, and by common consent he began to act as spokesman for his less gifted associates. Yet even when he did succeed in catching the Speaker's eye (which in itself was an exceedingly infrequent occurrence) it was usually when an Irish issue came under discussion. His absenteeism was due, in part, to long spells of practice at the Bar, which alone could provide him with an income sufficient to maintain his growing family. In the meantime Asquith's friends were busy drafting resolutions and preparing amendments to bills. However, opportunities for initiating debate were extremely limited. On only one occasion during these early and experimental years were the young Liberals able to make a substantial and sustained contribution to the legislative process. In 1888 Acland commissioned his willing workhorse J. A. Spender to devise a series of amendments to the recently introduced local government bill. Spender produced a whole sheaf of suggestions, though Acland and Asquith discarded all but two as soon as the House entered Committee in June.[41] For some inexplicable reason they concentrated upon the abolition of the property qualification for candidates and upon the payment to councillors of all travelling expenses. In this hesitant fashion the group opened their campaign for fundamental reform in the machinery of local government.

Up to this stage Parliament had proved to be a wholly unsatisfactory sounding-board for tentative and only partially completed schemes. The task of proselytizing needed to be carried on elsewhere, and Acland discovered that his friendship with Robert Hudson opened up a new vista of opportunities within both the national party machine and quasi-official organizations. He had been chiefly instrumental in persuading Hudson and Schnadhorst to create a special Liberal Publication Department, and in 1891 he was elected to the key position of honorary secretary. In association with Spender, Acland now became responsible for the production of a great deal of literature which went beyond a bare recital of the Liberal creed. With Acland at the helm, Sidney Webb was guaranteed a sym-

pathetic hearing for his proposal to do 'what Stuart ought to have
done long ago, viz. actually write down what the London Programme is'.[42] In this pioneering work Acland was greatly helped
by the activities of his friends, who, with the exception of Haldane,
loyally participated in N.L.F. ventures. Shortly after the general
election of 1886 Asquith had written a paper on the registration
question to be read at a regional conference in Leicester. A characteristic oratorical coup at Nottingham in the following year earned for
him the benediction of the party leaders. The reputation enjoyed by
the young zealots was such that at Newcastle in 1891 three of the
early N.L.F. resolutions were entrusted to Grey, Ellis, and Buxton.

Nevertheless, the N.L.F. remained too unwieldy and obstinate an
instrument to undertake the delicate task which the group had in
hand. The intimate and select atmosphere of the Eighty Club provided a more congenial setting. Haldane was the Club's first secretary, and within a few years he was joined on the committee by
Asquith and Grey. Although the Club possessed no permanent
office, its social and political functions helped the young Liberals to
strike up an acquaintance with the party leaders. Asquith and
Haldane quickly acquired a taste for the Fabian tactic of informal
and unobtrusive 'permeation' – even before the Fabian Society
had actually developed the idea. Emboldened by their success, the
two relatively unknown barristers established the custom of inviting
prominent statesmen to an annual dinner party held at the 'Blue
Posts' inn. These light-hearted occasions were strictly non-party
affairs, and the real work of gaining the ear of the Liberal leaders
was performed by the XXXIX Articles Club. Founded in 1886, and
deriving its misleading name from the sum total of its original
membership, the Articles Club consisted in the main of young
Radical M.P.s. Yet conservative industrial magnates like Alfred
Pease (Lockwood's political partner in York) were not excluded, and
the membership list was studded with the names of several Whig
aristocrats.[43] In March 1889 the Club expanded and began to hold a
series of weekly dinners at either the Savoy Restaurant or the
National Liberal Club, Haldane recalling that Rosebery and Morley
frequently graced their table.[44]

The constant attendance of these two statesmen was decisive in
the crystallization of the new Liberalism. Morley wrote of 'our
festive reunions' as having 'a fertility, stimulation, and life in them
that was refreshing'.[45] His friendship with Haldane brought him
into close contact with the array of younger men, and he soon began
to assume the rôle of patron and advisor. According to Haldane,
Morley was 'a Radical politician with a highly critical spirit . . . We
young Liberals looked up to him with deep respect . . . and we

turned to him for counsel gladly'.[46] As a result of these flattering
attentions, Morley began to appreciate exactly why the group was
dissatisfied with the narrow path being trodden by the remainder of
the party. At one stage (January 1888) he went so far as to congratulate Haldane for publishing 'The Liberal Party and its Prospects',
an article which reprimanded the frontbench for neglecting those
issues which did not revolve around the eternal Irish question.[47]

Morley took the lesson to heart. He alone of the party leaders
seemed to be aware of the enormity of the urban social crisis, and
was correspondingly perturbed by the potency of the Socialist
menace. The prevalence of slum conditions, aggravated by extortionate rents, lay at the root of the matter. On 4 April 1888 at Newcastle
he commenced a platform campaign in order to draw attention to
the problem, suggesting that the enfranchisement of leaseholders
and ruthless changes in the incidence of local taxation could provide
a solution. At Clerkenwell in December he spoke feelingly of 'great,
powerful, historic, glorious London [having] a tragedy in the background', a twilight world of such horrific dimensions that it
justifiably aroused 'the impatience and anger of our Socialist
friends'.[48] Morley knew that unless prompt remedial action was
taken the conditions which the urban poor were forced to endure
would assuredly deteriorate still further. In his next public appearance (at Sheffield) he avowed that those who thought otherwise were
'living in a fool's paradise'. Politicians of all parties were thus
presented with a clear and inescapable duty. 'It is circumstances and
it is facts, it is what the people of London see before their very eyes,
that is bringing these questions to the front.'[49]

Haldane fervently hoped that a fundamental reappraisal of the
Liberal programme under Morley's auspices was imminent. But
when he rushed to congratulate his patron, he was dismayed to discover that Morley thought otherwise. Haldane was sternly reminded
that the time was not yet ripe. 'Home Rule remains and must remain
the dividing line, until it is – if only temporarily and provisionally –
got out of the way.'[50] Quite apart from a sense of duty towards
Ireland and of personal loyalty to Gladstone, Morley could not
afford to ignore the susceptibilities of his frontbench colleagues.
After the Sheffield speech it was rumoured that he intended to
preside over a special meeting in London, which was billed as a
demonstration in favour of levying a special tax on landowners to
enable the L.C.C. to construct houses and let them out at a reasonable rent. 'Is it true that you have become a "ball-going Socialist"?'
Harcourt genially enquired. Morley took great pains to assure
Harcourt that he was nothing of the kind, and the conference
eventually went ahead (14 February 1889) without his sanction or

presence.[51] This brief episode illuminates the real nature of Morley's commitment to unconventional ideas. In private conversation he would offer encouragement to earnest social reformers, and would then cheerfully publicize their matured schemes in his speeches. Yet at the same time he would carefully present to the electorate the image of a disinterested and responsible observer, who could not be expected to endorse any particular project until he had carried out his own personal investigation. It was this deep-seated trait in his character which Haldane alluded to when he wrote that Morley was 'a wise, if not always a courageous, critic'.[52]

Although Morley was deeply involved in the social question, Beatrice Webb (then Miss Potter) continued to believe that he had not given it much thought, and so 'did not know even the ABC of labour problems'.[53] But, whatever his faults, Morley was the only high-ranking Liberal who took the trouble to examine new developments in this field, or who dared to comment upon the merits of a bewildering variety of panaceas. Beatrice Webb's judgement was coloured by the simple fact that Morley had arrived at conclusions different from her own on the eight hours question. At an interview with the Socialists of Newcastle on 2 February, he refused to concede that a statutory restriction of working hours was either necessary or expedient. This posture was defended on the grounds that the well-meaning advocates of compulsion had not given sufficient thought to the consequences of rigid enforcement. Morley's statement angered the Fabian Society, but it did not affect his relationship with the young Liberals. Haldane himself published a scathing attack on the Fabian view of the eight hours question, contending that Sidney Webb illustrated 'the advantages and disadvantages of the abstract mind in politics'.[54] In 1892 he even voted against the miners' eight hours bill, because he demurred to the view that conscientious objectors were mere doctrinaire metaphysicians. Practical men like Morley and himself had grasped the fact that the real issue at stake was not the number of hours worked but what level of remuneration actually constituted a living wage.

The capacity of an able-bodied man to maintain his family during his active working life, and to support himself during his own old age, was a problem which had already begun to perplex social reformers. This to Morley was 'a most tremendous [and] vital fact' which went 'to the root of all proposals for bettering the condition of the working people'. In this same speech (22 April 1889) he declared:

There is no subject more urgent than this: that a man who has worked hard all his life ... shall, like every other good servant of the State, know that his days shall not end, as they now too often do, in the workhouse or in poverty. It is an awful fact that in this country, with all its wealth, all its vast resources, all its power, forty-five per cent of the persons who reach the age of sixty are or have been paupers.[55]

A rash of contributory and non-contributory schemes for the provision of national insurance against sickness, leading to pensions in old age, now received Morley's earnest attention. The first of these systems was drawn up by Canon William Blackley, who proposed that between the ages of 18 and 21 every employed person should pay £10 into an annuity fund, and thereafter be entitled to 8s. per week sick benefit, receiving at 70 a pension of 4s. The actuarial soundness of the scheme was doubted by a Select Committee appointed in 1887 (upon which Morley served). No satisfactory answer could be made to the obvious objection that very few lowly paid workers could afford to deposit the mandatory £10 within so short a space of time. In 1891 Chamberlain sought to overcome this difficulty by broaching the concept of a State subsidy. Treasury support would have the effect of both reducing the initial contribution and extending the term over which it could be paid. Chamberlain contemplated a (voluntary) levy of £5 upon each participant before he reached the age of 25; the State would supplement this sum with a £15 credit; and the contributor would then continue to make 40 annual payments of £1, receiving at 65 a pension of 5s. Yet even this less demanding plan was still not applicable to the mass of casual labourers and agricultural workers to whom Chamberlain's £5 entrance ticket was as much beyond their means as Blackley's £10. Hence, the only realistic and fully comprehensive project emanated from a statistician who knew from his own meticulous social surveys exactly what hardships abject poverty entailed. Charles Booth's remedy was devastatingly simple – a non-contributory pension should be provided to all who had need of one. This bold project (first aired in 1891) formed the basis of the plan which Asquith eventually implemented in 1908.

Morley's reaction to these conflicting suggestions was somewhat ambivalent. He realized that a compulsory payment by both employer and employee on the German model would tend to depress wages, and so become an intolerably heavy burden for those who stood most in need of provision for social welfare. On the other hand, there was a danger lest a scheme funded entirely by the State should remove the incentive for personal thrift, and hence discriminate in favour of malingerers. Quite apart from ideological considerations of this kind, Morley had to contend with a degree of opposition from interested parties. Objections from the incorporated and profit-making assurance institutions could be discounted because, in the 1880s, these were relatively small, and were in any case politically unsympathetic towards Liberalism. But any project for national insurance also menaced the independence and future solvency of Friendly Societies. The census of 1891 revealed that nearly half of the adult male population belonged to a movement which reflected the highest ideals of Gladstonian Liberalism. For these reasons the historian of the campaign for national insurance has justly described the Friendly Society movement as 'the most powerful single vested interest encountered by the social reformers of the New Liberalism'.[56]

Morley was therefore compelled to proceed with extreme caution. He confessed that he was 'constantly thinking' of a means to involve the State in a general insurance scheme, but in practice his proposals amounted to very little. To pacify the Friendly Societies he dismissed out of hand the notion of a State-sponsored system of national insurance against sickness and unemployment (the traditional spheres of voluntary activity). Instead, he concentrated his vision on the problem of the aged poor in rural parishes, a field which the Friendly Societies had scarcely begun to penetrate. The 'modest operation' which Morley contemplated was that parish committees might draw up lists of aged persons who merited compassionate treatment. Outdoor relief could then be provided for those who, through no fault of their own, were at present forced to seek refuge in the common workhouse and associate with the 'undeserving poor'. Hence, Morley did not envisage any fundamental overhaul of Poor Law administration. He simply wished to find a middle course between those who were ready to offer relief indiscriminately, and those who were determined to frighten future generations into frugality by retaining a residue of the rigours established by the Commissioners of 1834.[57] Yet even this rather feeble compromise did not find favour with either Harcourt or Spencer. They regarded any 'meddling' with the prevailing system of outdoor relief as 'very dangerous', and forced Morley to admit that though the subject was fit for serious enquiry, it had certainly not become a settled article of Liberal policy.[58]

This steady dilution of Morley's noble ideals did not necessarily mean that he had tacitly abandoned the crusade for social reform. In speeches at Portsmouth, London, and Dundee (in 1889) he fearlessly endeavoured to explain that Socialist theory and Radical practice were not incompatible – in so far as Radicals accepted the doctrine that the State possessed a duty to undertake tasks which might prove difficult or impossible for the individual to perform unaided. The most effective and memorable of these speeches was an address to the Eighty Club on 19 November on the subject of 'Liberalism and Social Reforms'. Nothing startling was said on such burning issues as local taxation, housing, and education. But when Morley referred to the provision of meals for schoolchildren he signalled a wholly new departure in Liberal thought. Webb alleged that he was 'evidently in a state of panic', making a series of 'wild concessions' in order to compensate for his immovability on the eight hours question.[59] But Morley was perfectly conscious of the significance of the step he was taking. The speech was carefully researched, and part of the text had been submitted to his colleagues for their approval – an unusual precaution on Morley's part. When confronted with a plain fact and a proved necessity he had no time for abstract theory. He was evidently shocked by the revelations then being broadcast by investigators appointed by the London School Board. They had recently discovered that more than 44,000 children in the metropolis were habitually in want of food, and that charitable organizations could cope with less than half of that colossal number. The School Board had responded immediately by establishing a London Schools Dinner Association to co-ordinate the independent relief projects.[60] Morley abruptly dismissed the notion that public benevolence might have a pauperizing effect, and he whole-heartedly welcomed the initiative taken by the School Board. In his eyes the fusion of private and municipal charity constituted – if 'carefully organized and discreetly administered' – an exciting new approach to social calamities. The London Schools Dinner Association was therefore a great experiment, an innovation which obviated the oppressive threat of supervision from Whitehall. Improvised local agencies following this pattern enjoyed one further advantage – they kept statutory interference to a minimum. Hence, one of the early achievements of the new Liberalism in 1906 was to empower local education authorities to provide free meals for needy children.

The timing and location of this speech were also highly significant. The Eighty Club was so obviously the haven of the young Radicals that Morley's oration was widely interpreted as a sign that the Liberal leadership had begun to doubt the wisdom of confining their active programme to Ireland. The party had obviously not yet recovered from the shock of seeing Gladstone humiliated in the Royal Grants débâcle, and 'malignants' like Atherley-Jones and G. W. E. Russell were already canvassing (in the pages of the *Nineteenth Century*) the outrageous notion that a retrograde change in policy and leadership might prove necessary.[61] Schnadhorst was one of many who implored Gladstone to launch an entirely fresh campaign in order to 'steady the party (not benefited by new Radical section) and to give us a leverage to go forward with new heart and courage'.[62] Rosebery also regretted this disturbing tendency 'to follow any Apollos who announces that he is in possession of the true doctrine'.[63] He and Morley were agreed that many electors could no longer distinguish between the young Liberal reformers and Labouchere, since even the esoteric Articles Club had not been proof against Jacobyn infiltration. In the present emergency it was imperative to create a public image which would finally 'put an end to the assumption that the Jacobyn tail is the only vital part of the party dog'.[64] Morley and Haldane therefore concocted a suitable plan which the latter broached to Rosebery and Fowler at Mentmore on 2 November. Rosebery agreed to participate when he received assurances that Morley's emissary 'aimed – not at a new party – still less at a conspiracy – but simply at the formation of a *group* bound together by a common point of view rather than any organization, which ... while perfectly loyal to our front bench, [should] stimulate it to really lead the party'.[65] Fowler was immediately dispatched to London for further consultations with Asquith, Buxton, Grey, and Haldane, the proposal finally being ratified at a dinner party convened by Morley on the thirteenth. The philosophy of the coterie was succinctly outlined by Asquith:

> There is, so far as I know, no idea of starting a new organization, but there are many of us who feel (1) that the better kind of Radicalism is not articulate enough, and is unduly backward in putting out constructive proposals; (2) that, to remedy this, we need concerted action and distribution of labours; and (3) that in anything that is done it is well to be in touch with the worthier elements on the front bench.[66]

Harcourt suspected that he was not included among these 'worthier elements', being, in fact, the '*bête noire*' of a circle which was intent on ousting him from the leadership when Gladstone eventually retired. In a recent speech in London Harcourt had announced that Liberals should now transfer their thoughts from Ireland to other great issues, and had concluded with the unguarded statement that a bold reforming policy 'will help to carry Home Rule, and Home Rule will help to carry those other things'.[67] His intentions became plain when he requested a copy of the Clerkenwell programme. Morley knew that such blatant opportunism would offend Conservatives and Radicals alike, especially since his genial friend lacked any real comprehension of its purport. On stern economical grounds Harcourt entirely disapproved of both old age pensions schemes and plans to build cheap houses for the poor, and was also inclined to dismiss the proposed revolution in local government as a dismal and boring science created specially for Acland.[68] These characteristics rendered him incapable of making an original contribution to the discussion of social questions. When it became necessary in 1892 for Harcourt to advocate the extension of L.C.C. powers, the man who had once framed a London government bill could only recite (at Whitechapel on 17 February) the opinion of Rosebery on the matter.

It is important to recall that Harcourt could not legitimately complain that the Radical ginger group disregarded him merely because they spurned his Little England approach to international affairs. Although Asquith flaunted his heretical opinions early in 1889 by joining Rosebery's Imperial Federation League, Haldane (the prime conspirator) continued to regard himself as a staunch Morleyite throughout the crucial autumn of that year.[69] At this stage it was still possible to be drawn by Rosebery's power of personal domination and yet maintain a harmonious working relationship with Morley. The seeds of conflict between Morley and the incipient Roseberyites did not then exist; for the moment the glitter of the perplexing peer did not outshine the prosaic quality of solid common sense possessed by the commoner. Haldane's entire anti-Harcourt strategy was founded on the assumption that co-operation with both patrons was feasible. In return for this mark of confidence Morley was openly prepared to commend the labours of his proteges. At the Eighty Club he lavished praise upon their entirely fresh approach to the complicated question of land valuation, congratulating Haldane in particular for framing a bill which would enable municipalities to intercept the whole of the unearned increment which accrued to private owners.

Haldane's discovery of a practical solution to a problem which had confounded Radicals since 1885 contributed enormously to the development of a new Liberalism. On 6 May 1890 a member of the Articles Club (R. T. Reid) moved a resolution in Parliament, contending that local authorities ought to be allowed to acquire land compulsorily. However, Reid did not belong to the inner circle. He therefore made no attempt to cope with the thorny subject of unearned increment, and patently failed to define the mechanism he would employ to ascertain the fair price. Acland, who seconded the motion, suggested that periodic valuations might be used to extinguish the unearned increment, and in so doing anticipated the remedy outlined by Haldane a week later.[70] This bill came on too late in the sitting of the 14th for the author to attempt anything beyond a hasty summary of the ideas which had prompted his colleague Munro-Ferguson to move a battery of amendments to the Scottish local government bill in the previous session (15 July 1889). The two novel features of Haldane's bill related to the valuation and rating of urban land. Every local council would be permitted to value urban land with a view to subsequent purchase within a period of 20 years. The price to be paid was defined as the actual market value at the time of purchase, minus such increment due to extraneous causes as could be determined upon the basis of the original valuation. The second provision attempted to plug the loophole which allowed vacant building sites to be rated for local purposes at their agricultural value. Haldane wished to provide an incentive to put such land to more intensive use, thereby preventing speculative coups. He therefore proposed to rate every site according to its capital value for building purposes, rather than on the basis of its actual – and often negligible – yield. The owner could choose to be rated at the lower level only if he agreed to the proviso that the municipality could subsequently acquire his land at the reduced capital value. In conclusion Haldane assured the House that, whichever option was taken, an annual levy of four per cent was both 'equitable [and] absolutely devoid of anything like confiscation'.[71]

This conciliatory gesture impressed the many members of his own party who demonstrated their interest in the subject by listening to a brief debate on a bill which had no hope of making further progress; 102 Liberals (including Harcourt and Arnold Morley) voted in support of Haldane, while none ventured into the Conservative lobby.[72] Although the motion was defeated by 42 votes, Haldane seemed on the verge of securing full official recognition for his project. But two years elapsed before the debate could again be resumed, and in the meantime two alternative propositions were beginning to make headway within the party. The first of these competing plans concerned the rating of ground values, being raised on 27 February 1891 by Andrew Provand. His scheme distinguished between the value of the site and of buildings erected upon it, and so provided a simple mechanism for making vacant urban land liable for the payment of local rates (from which it largely escaped). The notion of equity appealed strongly to Gladstone, who, along with 69 other Liberals, voted in favour of Provand's resolution.[73] However, Haldane (who abstained) felt that a rate on land values was open to objection because it was no more than a rate, and so could touch only a fraction of the unearned increment. On the other hand, a levy rising gradually to 20s. in the £ constituted more than a rate, and amounted to nothing less than a thinly disguised method of nationalizing the land. This second and conflicting idea of land nationalization appealed to Henry Georgite Single Taxers like the ubiquitous Dr G. B. Clark of the Land Restoration League. On 10 May 1892 Clark moved an amendment to the government's small agricultural holdings bill, in which he maintained that under no circumstances should any individual be permitted to derive a profit from the inherent value of the soil and site. In the division which ensued he was supported by 23 Liberals and 20 Irishmen. But neither Gladstone, nor Haldane, nor the bulk of the party, showed any sign of sympathy for manifestly inequitable proposals to expropriate landowners without the payment of compensation.[74]

When Haldane at last obtained a full day (4 May 1892) for the discussion of his local authorities (purchase of land) bill, he clearly desired to steer a middle course between the shoals of land nationalization and land value taxation. But he did not altogether succeed. The serious fissures which once more emerged within the Liberal ranks indicated that the twin principles elucidated in 1890 had not yet been thoroughly digested. Only eight Liberals took the extreme step of voting against the second reading. However, the fact that a mere 119 Liberals decided to join Haldane in the lobby suggests that several members preferred to follow Harcourt's example and abstain.[75] Conspicuously placed on the list of absentees were the names of Acland and Tom Ellis. Acland's disappearance was truly astonishing, since (unlike Ellis) he had actually attached his name to a bill which was being sponsored by five of his own Radical associates. Both he and Ellis wished to see the powers of municipal authorities extended in the spheres of housing and town planning. But they probably objected to a bill which had been brought in as an alternative to – and not as the complement of – a separate measure to enfranchise leaseholders. Asquith, Grey, and Haldane now explained why they had not voted for the leasehold enfranchisement bill of 1891. In Asquith's words the trio 'saw no advantage in substituting for a small body of large landowners who ... are more or less amenable to public opinion, a large body of small landowners who ... were absolutely unrestrained by any public authority'.[76]

In order to appreciate the gravity of the situation it is necessary to consider the part played by Acland and Ellis in previous debates on leasehold enfranchisement. Since 1886 they had both served alongside James Rowlands and H. L. W. Lawson on the Select Committee on Town Holdings. This Committee had been able to investigate the whole subject of leasehold tenure on account of an Instruction proposed and carried by Lawson himself. Consequently, the Select Committee had concluded in its 1890 Report that the prevalence of short leases in the west country and in Wales constituted a manifold injustice. In North Wales and Cornwall (where the obnoxious 'three lives' system was inflicted on the populace) the demand for security of tenure through enfranchisement had become very strong. The most vigorous branches of the Leasehold Enfranchisement Association were increasingly concentrated in these remote areas.[77] Acland, who lived in North Wales and held a seat on the Caernarvonshire County Council, and Ellis, M.P. for Merioneth, saw at close quarters the hardships endured by the quarrymen living on the Penrhyn estates. They realized that humble workmen – who built their cottages with their own hands – had no choice other than to accept the harsh terms imposed by a monopolistic landlord. Ellis could not understand why the just claims of rural Wales should be prejudiced solely because leaseholders in London were not usually bona fide occupiers, but property speculators who exploited a housing shortage in order to make money. Acland carried this argument one stage further, accusing the Fabian Society of practically abandoning the working man, since they preferred to succour great ground landlords (like the Duke of Westminster) rather than run the risk of allowing a single owner to profit as a result of enfranchisement.[78]

These discordant attitudes towards the question of leaseholds did not simply reflect the degree of emphasis which each member of the ginger group placed upon the relative claims of urban and rural society. In reality the fundamental clash was one of temperament, those whose outlook was inspired by a sense of passion and emotional involvement differing from those whose approach to social problems was scientific, detached, and impersonal. Acland and Ellis belonged to the former school of thought. In the early 1880s they had met briefly at the Oxford University Palmerston Club, and had then come to share a common political experience through their membership of a curious society known as the Inner Ring. Once they had left Oxford for Parliament, Acland became intrigued by the aura of Celtic nostalgia and romanticism which surrounded Ellis and the cultural missionaries of *Cymru Fydd*. Ellis fervently believed that the enfranchisement of leaseholders was synonymous with the enfranchisement of Wales from the ascendancy of Anglo-Norman landlordism. 'Nationalism of tithe is restoring to the working masses their interest in the land,' he once wrote. 'On the peasant yeomen falls now the burden of the conflict. They are the hostages of our cause.'[79] The whole issue was symbolic of the ethos of national reawakening, especially since nonconformists in the Principality grieved at not being able to obtain permanent sites for their chapels. Acland also longed to liberate village society from the bondage of landlordism. In his view leasehold and other forms of restrictive tenure inhibited the English rural labourer from emulating the example set by his urban counterpart – who had established workmen's institutes and co-operative enterprises. Acland distrusted both theoretical socialist panaceas and the benevolent despotism of the village squire, because neither of these alternatives could possibly foster a spirit of independence and responsibility in the down-trodden classes. 'Give them something to manage for themselves,' he frequently argued. 'Let them have halls of their own, libraries of their own, opportunities for acquiring bits of freehold land in good positions for co-operative societies, chapels, and even houses of their own, and then you will bring out the best in them.'[80]

Such petty sentiments were completely foreign to the nature of the Webbs. Fabian thought was inherently insensitive to individual feelings, being characterized instead by a clinical appraisal of social and economic requirements. Hence the intellectual rigour of their philosophy appealed to Haldane, who had been trained in the fundamentals of German metaphysics at Göttingen. He first came into contact with the Fabian Society not later than March 1888, and was soon struck by the emphasis which the London University lecturer Graham Wallas placed upon the doctrine of perfect con-sistency in word and deed. This idea of consistency also, surprisingly, commended itself – not to a Balliol-trained Asquith – but to the rather docile Grey (who had been sent down from the same college for incorrigible idleness). Grey had no pretensions to great intel-lectual capacity; his chief attributes were physical rather than mental, since he possessed a pleasing stature and a commanding tone of voice. Haldane (like Webb) presented a far less attractive personal appearance, and he and Grey provided a perfect foil for one another. Their friendship blossomed in the autumn of 1888, when each plucked up courage to reject the party line in connection with Balfour's proposals for Irish land purchase. Grey now replaced Asquith in Haldane's affections, though Asquith had been Haldane's closest friend since the days when they were both struggling barris-ters. Haldane could not erase from his memory Asquith's betrayal over Irish land purchase. He recalled that Asquith held fewer views of his own than most, and so proved far more amenable to pressure from the party whips. He also regretfully noted that Asquith's liaison after 1891 with the frivolous Margot Tennant gradually diverted him from the 'sterner outlook on life' which he had hither-to shared with Haldane.[81]

Nevertheless, the two comrades had begun to drift apart even before this change in Asquith's domestic circumstances. The latter grew increasingly uneasy at the path being trodden by the Radical coterie, and was especially suspicious of Haldane's habit of fraterniz-ing with the Fabians. The degree of friction was such that in April 1891 Webb was both astounded and delighted to learn that Asquith had agreed to tell with Haldane in the (first) division against lease-hold enfranchisement.[82] However, shortly after this apparent reconciliation, Beatrice Webb complained that Asquith 'spoilt' a meeting at the end of May between the young Radicals and the Fabians by making sure that 'it *should not go*'.[83] When Asquith eventually read *My Apprenticeship*, he confessed that he could not recall the 'sinister and blighting influence' which he was reputed to have exerted. He presumed that he had simply spurned any overtures which involved more than 'a friendly *rapprochement* for the free interchange of views'.[84] These vague insinuations can now be clarified by reference to the Passfield Papers. At the height of the Parnell divorce scandal (30 November 1890) the Fabians arranged a series of conferences with the progressive Radicals at the London home of Alice Green (widow of the historian J. R. Green). The first consisted of a seven-hour interview between Beatrice Webb and Haldane, at which they discussed the details of a Radical–Socialist programme.[85] The next (and best documented) took the form of a dinner party to which Haldane, Sir Edward and Lady Grey, Wallas and Sidney Webb were invited. Wallas's sarcastic and possibly unreliable account of the proceedings makes it clear that the atmosphere was unpleasant, and that the party broke up on the evening of 24 January 1891 amidst mutual recriminations. The Fabians scorned Haldane's view that a benevolent attitude towards the trade union movement and its rôle in industrial disputes would constitute an adequate labour programme. They then indulged in a long wrangle as to whether the Liberal party was pledged to the payment of members. When the gentlemen adjourned upstairs, Haldane changed the nature of the discussion by asking whether it would be possible to inject new life into the Liberal party by creating a fresh political organization. Under cross-examination he pleaded that the Eighty Club could not properly be exploited as a narrowly partisan educational force, and that it would be impossible for his minute following of six to publish tracts without institutional backing. These excuses did not satisfy the sceptical Fabians. According to Wallas 'we said that if this association was to consist simply of another deliberate fraud on the part of the Liberals we would not touch it with the end of a barge-pole – and so the matter stood adjourned'.[86]

The quarrel did not fester for long, since Webb promptly sought out Haldane to restore their amicable relationship. He reported that Haldane 'dropped his dreamy generalities' when they met, and gave up altogether the idea of creating a new society in which the Fabians might participate.[87] Instead, the latter agreed to work through the existing mechanism of the Eighty Club. In March Haldane summoned the Club's executive committee. A special publications subcommittee was appointed, upon which Haldane, Asquith, Grey, and Webb were elected to serve. On the following day they settled 'quite amicably' a list of a dozen pamphlets and their writers.[88] Webb and

Haldane predictably selected London government and unearned increment as their respective topics, while Grey was allocated rural land. These penny tracts were an instantaneous success, 100,000 copies being distributed in the period preceding the general election. However, Asquith and Acland noticeably remained aloof, the latter possibly because he was too busy at the Liberal Publication Department rectifying the 'appalling' ignorance of the party leaders on those rural questions in which he himself was interested.[89] Despite this setback, Haldane continued to labour at the task of drawing the Fabians into the Liberal fold. In the process he won the confidence of Webb, who had hitherto distrusted him. But Haldane made little headway within his own party, particularly since it was widely felt that Fabian intervention at the Lewisham by-election in August 1891 had been responsible for a rude and unexpected break in a string of Liberal victories.[90] As a last resort Haldane turned to Morley for encouragement and support. 'The Fabians', Morley rejoined, 'interest and stimulate and suggest – but they are loose, superficial, crude, and impertinent. Does that satisfy you?'[91] This rebuff finally quashed Haldane's hopes for a reconciliation with the Fabians and an early reconstruction of the Liberal programme.

Although the frontbench rejected the Fabian philosophy out of hand, it would be erroneous to conclude that Haldane's efforts went entirely unrewarded. In 1891 several progressive ideas on labour questions became accepted articles of Liberal policy. The party leaders exhibited an unprecedented degree of interest and involvement in a wide range of practical issues which directly affected the welfare of the industrial population. In fact, labour legislation seemed to dominate the work of Parliament. When the session recommenced after a short winter recess, F. A. Channing immediately drew the attention of the House to the scandalous working conditions which were inflicted upon railway servants. A protracted strike of railwaymen in Scotland highlighted a situation whereby the persistent working of compulsory and excessive overtime threatened the safety of the travelling public. This consideration made a profound impression upon Campbell-Bannerman, who, in a speech in the heart of the affected district (Coatbridge), was the first statesman to bestow a blessing upon the strikers.[92] Even Harcourt's complacency was jolted by the frightening thought that wholly unqualified strike-breakers were currently being employed to drive express trains. Consequently, he elected to wind up the debate on behalf of the opposition, rising to deplore the obstinacy of the railway company. Two features of this unequivocal parliamentary stand were of special significance. Not only were the strikers technically acting in breach of contract, but Liberal endorsement of trade union militancy also amounted to a vote of censure upon a board of directors which contained Lord Elgin and some of their most influential supporters in Scotland. Much of the credit for inducing Liberals to act according to their social conscience, rather than yield to strong political pressures, must lie with Channing himself. He procured the support of a united party by carefully avoiding any mention of a statutory limitation of hours. His speech was confined to an eminently reasonable demand for the restriction of overtime through Board of Trade intervention,[93] and so the motion of 23 January was lost by only 17 votes. But Channing had so conclusively proved the case for an immediate enquiry into the subject that on 3 February the government graciously appointed a Select Committee.

The Commons just had enough time to recover from the additional shock of seeing the Liberal frontbench extend a welcoming hand to Edmund Robertson's bill to safeguard the legal position of trade unions, before Sydney Buxton raised the thorny question of government contracts. Charles Booth and the Webbs had recently completed a detailed investigation into the horrors of life in domestic workshops throughout the East End – and particularly in Tower Hamlets. Buxton (one of that borough's parliamentary representatives) responded by inviting Webb to help him draft a bill to check sweating.[94] While they were engaged in this task an unexpected opportunity arose. Henry Broadhurst suddenly fell ill, and Buxton was entrusted with the task of moving an equivalent resolution which already stood in the labour member's name. Buxton sensibly followed Channing's example by eschewing any provocative statements. 'I am not proposing to fix the hours of labour or the rate of wages,' he assured the House on 13 February. 'All that I ask is that the State, as a capitalist and employer, shall set a good example.' Clauses demanding model conditions of employment were already written into all government contracts, but Buxton pointed out that these were often ignored because no penalty was attached to any breach of the regulations. He was also convinced that the persistent sub-letting of contracts constituted the principal source of labour exploitation. The introduction of an unnecessary middleman encouraged that condition of unregulated domestic work which lay at the root of the whole sweating system. Proper conditions of employment could only be guaranteed if the State took drastic action to compel each contractor to carry out all government work in duly inspected factories and workshops.[95] Conservatives, naturally, listened to this Fabian-inspired explanation with deep misgivings, but they could scarcely afford to ignore parallel conclusions which had been reached in 1890 by a Select Committee of the House of

Lords. Consequently, Buxton's resolution was slightly altered and then carried *nem. con.*

A fortnight later the Home Secretary, Henry Matthews, moved the second reading of an important factories and workshops bill. Buxton automatically took charge of opposition policy, having successfully established himself as the leading authority on working-class issues. When Matthews had resumed his seat, Buxton rose to protest that the government bill was totally inadequate as a means of curbing the sweating system. Domestic workshops stood in desperate need of regulation, but the official plan perversely contemplated stringent sanitary requirements only in factories. Employers were merely required to keep an up-to-date register of all outwork, which would be accessible to no one except factory inspectors and representatives of local sanitary authorities. However, the absence of adequate sanitary authorities in London posed special difficulties for those who identified this region as a hotbed of sweated labour. Buxton argued that the 'giver-out' (or sub-contractor) ought to be registered instead of the principal contractor, and be severely penalized if he allowed work to be carried out on premises which were known to be unsatisfactory. In his opinion this alternative provision could only be administered effectively if trade unions were allowed unrestricted access to the register of outwork.[96]

Although murmurs of disapproval could be heard on the Liberal benches during Buxton's speech, no one openly challenged the call for more State intervention which had been uttered on the party's behalf. However, Buxton did not wish to offend Liberal employers still further, and he wisely abandoned a series of Webb's amendments relating to customary overtime and sanitary regulations in domestic workshops. The opposition's batteries were concentrated instead upon the government's weakest position. Matthews stoutly defended the system whereby a child was permitted to engage in half-time factory work at the age of 10, and discounted the view (which had recently been expressed by the International Labour Conference at Berlin) that such employment ought not to commence until the age of 11 or 12. But the recommendations of an imposing international tribunal could not be thrust aside so lightly. When the bill returned from Committee in June, Buxton inflicted a decisive defeat upon the government. He carried by 202 votes to 186 an amendment which raised the lower age limit for half-timers from 10 to 11, and thus enabled more than 25,000 children to remain at school for an extra year. The fact that only seven Liberal M.P.s voted against this amendment encouraged Buxton to turn on the following day (the 19th) to the more formidable subject of full-time factory employment. However, his bold attempt to raise the school leaving age from 13 to 14 failed – but only by the narrow margin of 25 votes.[97]

In contrast, the controversial eight hours bill for miners could not generate such an extraordinary wave of enthusiasm amongst the industrialists who studded the Liberal benches. Nevertheless, the fate which awaited children in coal mines must have swayed the votes of several conscience-stricken Liberal employers who might otherwise have baulked at legislation of such a sweeping character. The crucial test came on 23 March 1892, when the Lancashire manufacturer Robert Leake moved the second reading of his mines (eight hours) bill. He stressed that virtually 10 per cent of all underground workers in coal mines (or 48,000 persons) were boys under the age of 16, and that in Northumberland and Durham the proportion of boys to men was considerably higher than the national average. Leake accused the privileged trade unionists in the north-east coalfield of sacrificing the interests of the boys, by making them work a ten-hour day, in order that they themselves could enjoy the benefits of a day limited to seven hours. Thomas Burt did not attempt to deny the allegation, and his failure to do so helps to explain why such improbable figures as Harcourt, Labouchere, John Ellis, and Jacob Bright (elderly brother of the illustrious John) voted in favour of the bill. Altogether 97 Liberals supported Leake, but only 35 trooped with Burt into the opposite lobby.[98] Facts such as these gave some substance to the notion that by 1892 the first stage in the conversion of Gladstonians to the new Liberalism had successfully been accomplished.

The great enigma was how Gladstone would react to these portentous developments in Liberal doctrine. Even in 1892 his attitude towards the social questions which had seized the imagination of advanced reformers remained a matter of conjecture. The stony silence which he invariably maintained whenever Parliament debated issues which affected the welfare of the industrial population certainly created a strong and enduring impression that his mind was in a state of suspended animation. Yet one modern scholar has recently pointed out that the neglect by historians of the extent of Gladstone's Radicalism in his old age is a major deficiency in modern British historiography. Kenneth O. Morgan has shown (with reference to Welsh questions at least) that the invidious stereotype of a wild and incomprehensible Home Rule fanatic is a mere figment of the imagination.[99] It is therefore imperative to ascertain whether equally startling conclusions can be reached in connection with rather more controversial aspects of Liberal policy.

Although the documentary sources are scanty, there exists sufficient evidence to suggest that Gladstone was secretly hostile to social legislation. Whenever the subject of an eight hour day was brought to his notice, he always declared a preference for leaving the trade unions to reach a voluntary agreement with their employers. The misuse of executive power in Ireland had finally convinced him that 'the coercive and rigid operation of public authority' was usually 'infinitely inferior' to the free exercise of personal initiative.[100] On more than one occasion Arnold Morley had reason to fear that Gladstone would cause the party grave embarrassment by adopting 'too uncompromising an attitude' in his speeches, especially in reply to labour deputations.[101] However, Gladstone managed to avoid giving offence to the advocates of statutory limitation until the persistence of the lobbyists finally exhausted his reserves of sympathy and patience. On the eve of the 1892 election he peremptorily declined to discuss the eight hours question with an influential delegation from the London Trades Council. Gladstone eventually relented, but he did not emerge with credit from the belated interview of 16 June. According to Lansbury, 'no beginning even of a comprehension of our wishes seemed to penetrate to the great man's mind'.[102]

Nevertheless, even at this unfavourable moment the outlook did not seem entirely bleak. Gladstone still recognized that those who promoted eight hours legislation acted from unselfish motives, and above all he had not taken the fatal step of voting against Leake's recent bill. In fact, he might well have supported the bill had the author only incorporated some provision for local option, since any measure which took no account of conflicting regional preferences offended his sense of justice. Moreover, Gladstone remained adamant in his belief that 'the class opposition of some employers ought not to deter Parliament from action'.[103] Parliament possessed an unimpeachable title to regulate working conditions, especially in companies which existed solely by virtue of privileges conferred on them by statute. Gladstone was obviously thinking of railway companies at this moment. Channing had just sent him a memorandum containing a powerful indictment of these companies. In a covering letter he had boldly suggested that a public expression of sympathy towards the aggrieved railwaymen would 'not be thrown away politically, while it is a *duty* from the humanity point of view'.[104] On receipt of this document Gladstone astounded the electors of London by speaking in favour of legislation to restrict the hours worked by railway employees.

The impact of this declaration was weakened considerably when the speaker inadvertently proceeded to reveal that he had totally misconstrued the rudiments of Buxton's policy concerning sweating. In fact, when pressed by a questioner in Midlothian towards the

close of the election campaign, Gladstone frankly confessed his
ignorance on the subject.[105] He did not seem to realize that 18
months earlier Buxton had persuaded the government to instruct
each branch of the administration to write fair conditions of employment into all official contracts. In his outdated opinion the central
government would be overwhelmed with wage demands from
spendthrift institutions who were 'at most times ready to enter on a
crusade on the Consolidated Fund'. The expenditure of public
money on model contracts ought therefore to be restricted to local
authorities, which alone could be trusted to exercise some degree of
financial caution. Hence Gladstone felt able to praise without reservations the pioneering work of the L.C.C. in this sphere. But the
London Progressives were reminded that he did so because 'the
jealousy of the ratepayers will balance ... the humanity and philan-
thropy of the Council'.[106]

The esoteric explanation for Gladstone's circumspection lay in the
fact that the moral values of the Christian Church were central to
his being. In *Mrs Warren's Profession* Shaw castigated the kind of
mentality which was absorbed with the sin of prostitution at the
expense of the horrors of industrial society. Gladstone certainly did
not appear to combine his preoccupation with individual salvation
with a lively appreciation of the bleak social realities which drove
desperate women to resort to such dehumanizing activities. He was
slow to transfer his thoughts to the new crusade, especially since he
continued to lament how theology was being replaced by 'the vague
something which they call social reform' as the main issue of public
controversy.[107] In his eyes the employment of young girls as semp-
stresses in domestic workshops (under the watchful supervision of a
matronly outworker) was preferable to their subjection to orthodox
factory disciplines. Gladstone secretly feared that if innocent girls
were enticed into factories, they would be forced to succumb to the
dubious conditions of employment imposed by lascivious factory
owners: 'terms which from what I have heard elsewhere would
sometimes include matter independent of labour and wages'.[108]

Despite this idiosyncratic obsession with moral purity, Gladstone
had in reality become deeply interested in certain other social questions. For example, it is not generally realized that he adopted a
positively Morleyite attitude on the subject of old age pensions. At
the Rural Reform Conference in December 1891 Gladstone protested
that 'until society is able to offer to the industrious labourer at the
end of a long and blameless life something better than the workhouse, society will not have discharged its duties to its poorest
members'.[109] Three months later Gladstone announced in the
Commons that the Liberal party had

come generally to the conclusion that ... it is hard even for the industrious and sober man, under ordinary conditions, to secure a provision for his own old age. Very large propositions ... have been submitted to the public, for the purpose of securing such a provision by means independent of the labourer himself. I am not going to criticize these proposals, and I am only referring to them as signs that there is much to be done ... It is eminently our duty to develop, in the first instance, every means that we may possibly devise whereby, if possible, the labourer may be able to make this provision for himself.[110]

The letting of dwellings and plots of land on a secure tenure and at a low rental were the remedies which Gladstone favoured in the 'first instance'. But he clearly anticipated that these boons might prove to be inadequate, and so he would not repudiate the possibility of a system of State pensions and national insurance being implemented as a last resort.

The Gladstone who obliquely favoured old age pensions was a totally different person from the man who, in the summer of 1886, had refused to campaign in the East End because he knew nothing of the special problems which afflicted the London poor.[111] Twelve months after this confession of ignorance, he could be heard in the metropolis complaining that ground rents were 'great unearned increments', and that the leasehold system led to the 'utter neglect and contempt of every other human interest'.[112] This extraordinary declaration on the social needs of London occurred quite spontaneously, preceding the better known Limehouse programme by a full 18 months. At Limehouse on 15 December 1888 Gladstone took the decisive step of coupling urban land reform and local taxation with the explosive issue of artisans' dwellings. He alleged that these related subjects, together with an amendment of the Employers' Liability Act and the provision of free elementary education, were 'urgent in a high degree'. Although he refused to enter into details, the hordes of zealous Radicals who clamoured to make his acquaintance readily accepted Gladstone's assurances that he was by no means 'indifferent to the wants either of the country at large or of the metropolis'.[113] By this stage J. A. Spender could testify that 'merely to sit by Mr Gladstone and hear his voice and look into his wonderful face was rapture'.[114] John Benn, the Progressive whip on the L.C.C., also 'succumbed to the glamour of those wonderful eyes'. Shortly before the 1892 election he was ushered into Gladstone's presence and invited to render an account of his stewardship, whereupon Benn spoke nervously of housing development, municipal ownership, and the taxation of land values. Gladstone listened attentively, and after asking numerous questions, said: 'Well, well, your proposals, Mr Benn, are advanced, but I should be sorry indeed to check your enthusiasm. You are doing a great work on the Council, and you have my blessing.'[115] These friendly words of support and advice filled the younger breed of Radical politician with courage and determination.

[VI]

Crisis and Recovery
1890-2

1. *The Parnell Catastrophe*

The astounding news that Parnell had refrained from defending himself against the charge of having committed adultery with the wife of a prominent Nationalist politician became public property on Monday, 17 November 1890. In the following week Gladstone published a controversial letter to Morley which contained two memorable sentences:

> Notwithstanding the splendid services rendered by Mr Parnell to his country, his continuance at the present moment in the leadership would be productive of consequences disastrous in the highest degree to the cause of Ireland ... The continuance I speak of would not only place many hearty and effective friends of the Irish cause in a position of great embarrassment, but would render my retention of the leadership of the Liberal party, based as it has been mainly upon the prosecution of the Irish cause, almost a nullity.[1]

This document demonstrated that Parnell's inexplicable behaviour in court had provoked overnight a convulsion which the concentrated forces of Unionism had failed to achieve in the space of five years. Total disarray prevailed in the demoralized Irish camp; the Home Rule policy was effectively discredited throughout Great Britain; and Gladstone hovered on the brink of an inglorious retirement.

The moral lapse cannot by itself account for the widespread revulsion from the person of Parnell which became manifest in the weeks subsequent to the divorce decree. For several years Gladstone and his colleagues had been well aware that Parnell was consorting with Katharine O'Shea. But private knowledge of this illicit liaison had never blinded Gladstone to the practical realities of the case.

Parnell was indisputably the leader of the Irish nation, and after the devastating revelation of the Pigott forgeries in 1889, the Liberal party had shrewdly capitalized upon its identification with the man himself. Unfortunately, by placing Parnell upon a pedestal, the Liberals had created an illusion of sanctity and invincibility, which – when dispelled – served to unleash a storm of abuse and public condemnation. At the bar of public opinion Parnell stood convicted of an unpardonable outrage against the moral law. In private life political leaders were obliged to set an exemplary standard of personal conduct in order that they might enjoy public confidence. In the eyes of the Liberal leaders, Parnell's wilful disregard of this basic requirement constituted a crime more heinous than the offence for which he had been formally convicted. The venial sin might have been overlooked had it not been for the existence of a catalogue of his knavish and ridiculous exploits compiled by the counsel for Captain O'Shea. Parnell was indelibly branded as a master of subterfuge and an unscrupulous liar. The impression that deceit was an integral part of his character was further sustained by the transparent insincerity of his protestations of innocence, assurances which were given to Morley at a Brighton hotel less than a week before the case came to court. Parnell exhibited similar traits in his hectoring manifesto to the people of Ireland, the most damning example being the section in which he betrayed secret information previously communicated to him by Gladstone in December 1889.

Unfortunately for the Liberal party, Parnell did not parade ostentatiously in these new colours until after he had caused almost irreparable damage to the 'union of hearts'. Liberal statesmen had been grievously misled as to the probable outcome of the divorce suit. They discovered too late that no effective precautionary measures could now be taken to sever the connection between themselves and Parnell. The unpleasantness of the disclosures was accompanied by a feeling of intense shock amongst the duped Liberals. But a sense of numbness quickly disappeared, and anger rapidly gave way to panic as party members began to appreciate the enormity of the crisis which confronted them. 'The rage and despair of our party is beyond all words,' Lewis Harcourt reported from the precincts of the Palace of Westminster. 'I have fled from the lobby as I can stand it no longer. . . I believe that this must destroy our prospects at the Election whenever it comes.'[2]

Parnell's untimely behaviour shattered a number of comforting myths which had hitherto created a state of euphoria in the Liberal ranks. Foremost amongst these illusions was the expectation that the government would collapse shortly after the return of Parliament from its autumn recess. This extraordinary degree of buoyant

confidence had not been misplaced, since throughout the greater part
of the first session of 1890 the Unionist administration had suffered
serious setbacks. Large sections of the government programme had
displeased its loyal supporters. Conservatives particularly resented
any additional Irish land legislation, the concept of free elementary
education, and a tithe bill which placed the onus for payment solely
upon the landowner. However, insurmountable problems did not
arise until Liberal Unionists (under the guidance of W. S. Caine)
began to demonstrate in the division lobby their opposition to the
licensing clauses of the local taxation bill. The gravity of the situation
was such that the plan to compensate licensees for the extinction of
their interest was jettisoned with scant ceremony. On 10 July the
hapless W. H. Smith had no option but to announce to a jubilant
opposition that his scheme for procedural reform would also be withdrawn and the tithe and Irish land bills postponed. The humiliation
of the government appeared to be complete. Rather than face a
renewed onslaught from the Liberal benches in November, Smith
(who suffered from poor health) was ready to 'throw up the sponge,
bring about a General Election, and the repeal of the Union'.[3] For
their part the Liberal leaders were anxious to hasten the demise of
the government. Early in November Harcourt impressed upon his
colleagues the advisability of taking the offensive 'in a very decisive
form' as soon as Parliament reassembled. Arnold Morley believed
that it would be possible to defeat the government – or at least to
reduce its majorities drastically – on virtually every item of its programme.[4] Hence the reversal of rôles which was accomplished by
the downfall of Parnell was as sudden and dramatic as it was complete. Unionists now looked forward with renewed confidence and
vigour to the meeting of Parliament on the 25th; Home Rulers, who
had previously hounded the administration and bayed for a dissolution, vanished from the chamber and began to tremble at the
thought of an early appeal to the country.

At no time since the spring of 1887 had Liberals seriously contemplated the possibility of electoral defeat. During the intervening
years an impressive total of 14 net gains had been recorded at by-
elections, and the 'flowing tide' still showed no sign of receding.
On the contrary, these earlier triumphs culminated in 1890 in two
spectacular victories at Barrow and Eccles. Despite a strong Conservative challenge, the official Home Rule candidate captured
Barrow from a Liberal Unionist seeking re-election as a Gladstonian.
At Eccles H. J. Roby wrested from the Conservatives a seat which
had been won by that party even in 1885. Facts like these could not
be controverted, and appeared to bear out Gladstone's long standing
conviction that he would obtain a majority of at least 100 seats in

Great Britain alone. However, the effect of Gladstone's periodic excursions into the novel science of political 'meteorology' was impaired by his amateurish and mathematically unsound methods of computation (which were based on the preposterous assumption that seats could be gained from sitting Liberal members). The author of these false statistics should perhaps also be censured for fostering a degree of over-confidence which ultimately proved to be detrimental to party interests. For example, in his comparisons between the sequence of by-elections of 1874–80 and those of 1886–90, Gladstone stressed the pertinent fact that a marked upsurge in favour of Liberal candidates had only occurred after the Bulgarian crisis had reached its climax. Thus, the 12 by-election gains registered from 1876 onwards had been instrumental in securing the great victory of 1880.[5] But this analogy became a source of acute embarrassment in the climate of opinion which prevailed in November 1890. It was now apparent that the Parnell scandal was a 'horror' comparable in magnitude to the Bulgarian atrocities, and, as such, might erase the record of Liberal victories and set in motion a counter-current flowing strongly in favour of the Unionists.

In retrospect Gladstone confessed that the Parnell holocaust had taught him to exercise a greater degree of caution when assessing electoral trends. The 'high probability' of their accuracy, he wrote, 'may be qualified or reversed by circumstances not yet in view'.[6] Such reservations were hardly relevant to the considerations which applied in the bleak weeks towards the close of 1890. As Arnold Morley made frantic preparations for a sudden dissolution, the worst fears of pessimistic Home Rulers were realized. A by-election was in progress at Bassetlaw, and the outcome of the first test of public opinion since the Eccles contest was awaited with considerable trepidation. The declaration of the poll on 15 December came as a shock to Gladstone. He had adopted the unusual course of campaigning in person in the constituency, but it soon became apparent that his irregular intervention (in speeches at Retford and Worksop on the eleventh) had been an 'unpardonable folly', and one which only aggravated the disgrace of total defeat.[7] During the course of a conversation with Morley at Hawarden two days later, Gladstone divulged how drastically the result had undermined his morale. 'Bassetlaw looks as if we were going back to 1886,' he maintained. 'For me that is notice to quit. Another five years' agitation at my age would be impossible – *ludicrous*.'[8] Arnold Morley hastened to reassure him that these conclusions were unduly pessimistic. He pointed out that had the seat been contested in 1886, the party would have been forced to contend with an adverse majority approaching 1,800 votes rather than with the notional figure of 295 votes (which had been the margin in 1885). If this supposition was correct, it meant that the Liberals had recovered almost 1,000 voters since 1886. Nevertheless, such nebulous evidence could not disguise the harsh reality – that over 400 Liberal voters had vanished since the previous contest. At this point the experienced Schnadhorst rushed to Arnold Morley's defence by affirming that the deficiency in numbers could be attributed to a stale electoral register, bad weather, and the transfer of the Foljambe and Savile influence to the Unionist cause. 'It is impossible to trace any loss to the recent events,' he concluded. 'At present I should say we have sustained no loss, but that there is probably a check to the progress we have been making through the year.'[9]

These crumbs of comfort did little to assuage Gladstone's troubled mind. The Bassetlaw result was certainly not an unmitigated disaster, since the Conservatives had retained far less secure seats in previous by-election struggles. But in the present emergency Bassetlaw seemed to indicate that both the repudiation of Parnell and the ostentatious policy of non-involvement with the internal squabbles of the Irish party had failed to impress the British electorate. Hitherto, Harcourt (who had exerted intense pressure upon Gladstone to publish the notorious letter to Morley) had been capable of writing with satisfaction that such stiff measures had 'saved the English Liberal party which was the paramount consideration. My belief is that Mr G. is stronger today in Great Britain than he was before the row.'[10] Bassetlaw effectively exploded this myth, only to replace it with a pessimism that was equally fallacious. In the minds of the party leaders the illusion of a severe setback overshadowed the reality of an indeterminate conclusion. This dichotomy between belief and reality had important and far-reaching consequences for the Liberal party. In a memorandum which he composed shortly after the Bassetlaw declaration, Morley alleged that 'the situation has changed definitely for the worse in several important respects'. These he cited as being the enmity of Parnell combined with faction in Ireland, and the impression (sustained in particular by the North Kilkenny by-election) that the Nationalist party was subject to the dictates of the Catholic clergy. He concluded that there had been, and would continue to be, 'vague, general, presumptive, and indirect discredit – but a most effectual discredit – of Home Rule policy and its English authors, in the mind of a decisive majority in the British constituencies'.[11] This sombre analysis was undoubtedly premature. However, party tactics were determined to such an extent by the assumption that the electioneering progress since 1886 had been completely undermined, that fallacy superseded truth, and eventually became reality itself.

As this was indeed the case, Morley proceeded to pose a question of the utmost significance. 'How are English Liberals to fight the next election,' he asked Gladstone. Harcourt was ready with a convenient answer. During the course of a hectic and heated exchange of letters with Morley, he made it perfectly clear that his solution to the problem was the abandonment for all practical purposes of the crusade for Irish Home Rule. Nevertheless, after the split in the Irish party, such a course was quite unthinkable. Setting aside any considerations of personal honour and public duty, such an abrupt shift in party strategy was fraught with political dangers. Even Harcourt realized that 'this is not the day or the hour to change front in the presence of the [Parnellite] enemy'.[12] Gladstone's instinctive reaction was to assure Morley that he remained 'extremely indisposed' to recant on the fundamental issue.[13] Yet one of the most astonishing features to emerge with stark clarity from the protracted debate on future strategy was the revelation that Gladstone himself was prepared to forsake the cause to which he had devoted the residue of his political life. Morley was plainly appalled by this exhibition of spontaneous flexibility, and this totally unexpected development helped to convince him that the 'many reasons why we should supplement our Irish policy by English reforms' ought to be disregarded.[14] One of Gladstone's early suggestions was to press forward with a scheme of Irish local government reorganization. This could only be construed as meaning that he now contemplated elective county councils as a possible alternative to – and not the complement of – a fully fledged Irish Parliament. At the turn of the year Harcourt sorrowfully reported that 'the iron has entered into the old man's soul'.[15] Shortly afterwards he opened a letter from Hawarden which contained one 'awfully ominous sentence'. 'I think it is time', Gladstone wrote, 'that the relative position of Home Rule will for platforms and candidates undergo some change, but this will best be done by emphasizing other matters.'[16]

Perhaps, as F. S. L. Lyons suggests, the recoil from Irish Home Rule constituted only a momentary weakening.[17] But the dilemma which confronted the party leaders would remain unresolved so long as they maintained the pretence that nothing untoward had occurred since the verdict in the divorce court. The chief question which awaited solution was how to restore public confidence in the Liberal party without at the same time arousing in Ireland suspicions that Home Rule was about to be shunted into an inaccessible siding. Immediately after Bassetlaw Gladstone tackled this delicate problem. On 23 December he informed Morley that 'what my mind leans to in a way still vague is to rally ourselves by some affirmative legislation taken up by and on behalf of the party. Something of this kind would be the best source to look to for reparative strength.'[18] The relevant items of 'affirmative legislation' were finally settled during the Christmas festivities. On the 26th Gladstone recommended in outline a specified course of action to his Chief Whip. Unfortunately, no copy of this crucial letter can be traced. Arnold Morley conferred with John Morley (probably on the 30th) and posted a transcription of Gladstone's letter, together with a draft of John Morley's impressions upon it, to Harcourt on the same day. This latter document has fortunately been preserved (see appendix B), and when examined in conjunction with the reactions of the recipients, it enables the tenor of Gladstone's original letter to be ascertained. An abbreviated version was also composed for the benefit of Lord Ripon. This indicates that Gladstone considered that his primary duty lay in 'keeping the party well together in England'. He also tentatively suggested that 'one man one vote' with registration reform constituted the most promising article in the existing programme for this purpose.[19]

However, Gladstone's colleagues were in universal agreement that this particular subject was hopelessly inadequate as the cornerstone of a new initiative in domestic politics. Ripon thought that it would be most unwise to build the party's current parliamentary tactics and future electoral appeal upon such slender foundations. Registration reform would not 'standing alone, have go enough about it to secure a good majority', he rejoined.[20] Harcourt summed up the situation with a crisp remark: 'the notion of rallying a shattered party round the bugle call of Stansfeld is not inspiriting'.[21]

In order to appreciate what other issues the Liberal leadership could now raise, it is necessary to go back in time and to indicate how in fact a series of Radical demands were gaining more and more support amongst the rank and file. The alternatives suggested by Gladstone were the direct popular veto and Welsh disestablishment – but these created problems of a different nature to those posed by electoral reforms. There were several drawbacks to raising the standard of disestablishment to serve as the fighting colours in a Liberal recovery. Although the question remained in the forefront (owing to prior commitments), Harcourt at least regarded it as 'a cry and nothing more'.[22] Even Morley and Schnadhorst recognized that there could be no 'rally' in disestablishment. In purely electoral terms this issue affected only about 100 seats, and in these only a marginal advantage could be gained. Wales was so solidly and unrepentantly Liberal that the prospect of wresting a mere handful of seats from sitting Unionists was of dubious value if the standard of Welsh disestablishment served only to rouse the Church of England to defend what she regarded as an indissoluble union.

Party strategists were fully cognizant of the fact that a wrathful
Church had severely damaged the prospects of many innocent
Liberal candidates in English constituencies at the 1885 general
election. Since that date fresh complications had arisen. By 1890
vehement Welshmen had begun to demand that Welsh interests be
granted precedence in the official programme. Should their request
be granted, any political benefits which might accrue would immediately be swamped by a wave of resentment in Scotland. Gladstone
sought to pacify the distrustful Scots by voting in support of Dr
Cameron's Scottish disestablishment motion of 2 May. But he only
added to his woes by emerging from the protective armour of
neutrality. Church of Scotland enthusiasts commenced a vigorous
anti-Gladstone campaign, having already given notice of their intentions at the Ayr Burghs by-election in March. The margin at Ayr
had not been substantial, but the loss of a seat which had been
recovered from a Unionist only two years earlier did not augur well
for Liberal expectations of a sweeping victory in the western counties
at a general election. Gladstone proposed to recover his hold upon
Scotland by undertaking an extended speaking tour of his constituency in the autumn. While final preparations were in progress, he
received alarming and contradictory reports concerning the exact
state of Scottish opinion. On the one hand, Gladstone's election
agent (P. W. Campbell) insisted that no constituency existed where
the Liberal candidate could afford to remain unpledged to disestablishment; while on the other, Rosebery asserted that a plebiscite
on the question would probably fail to produce a national verdict
favourable to disestablishment. Rosebery therefore arrived at a conclusion which the electors of Midlothian had reached through a test
ballot exactly five years earlier. Even Campbell presumed that no
gains could be anticipated in the south and west, and he avowed
with casual resignation that Scottish disestablishment 'has cost us
and will cost votes and seats'. This most unwelcome observation was
accompanied by the information that in Midlothian itself a further
500–600 votes had been irrecoverably lost since 1886 on account of the
Church question.[23] Gladstone had reason to show concern at the
prospect of even a slight diminution of his own considerable
majority, but he did not then realize precisely how lax his professional advisers in the constituency had become in the face of intense
clerical pressure. Consequently, the scale of the erosion which
eventually occurred in 1892 came as an unpleasant surprise to the
distinguished candidate.

The slender majority of only 690 votes which he obtained at the
general election may or may not testify to Gladstone's wisdom in
declining to launch a crusade on behalf of Scottish disestablishment

during the winter of 1890–1. However, one point is absolutely certain. At the moment when the negative decision was taken, the harassment and embarrassment which the ecclesiastically-minded Gladstone had endured at Midlothian in the autumn was still painfully fresh in his memory. Parnell had since created a complex and uncertain situation. This additional factor served to strengthen Gladstone's inclination to avoid inviting any further controversy. Yet some initiative was required of the party leader, a duty which could best be accomplished through a direct appeal to the basic instincts and interests of his followers. In this connection disestablishment amounted to more than a mere legislative goal; it constituted an integral strand in the social and political fabric of Liberalism. Liberationists were primarily nonconformists, and for more than a generation nonconformity had comprised the backbone of the Liberal party. This inescapable truth was amply demonstrated at the annual meeting of the N.L.F. at Sheffield. Fortuitously, the convention was sandwiched between the delivery of the divorce court verdict on 17 November and the opening of the parliamentary session on the 25th. Morley and Harcourt (who were present at Sheffield) reported that the response of the assembled nonconformists – laymen as well as ministers – to the news that Parnell had broken the Seventh Commandment, was unhesitating and decisive.[24] The outcry of righteous indignation perturbed Gladstone and his confidential advisers. They realized that it was imperative to reassure their most ardent supporters that the leadership was alive to their personal requirements – if only because elections were invariably won or lost according to the degree of enthusiasm manifested by the local politicians who controlled every constituency organization. Gladstone, Harcourt, and Morley were not themselves nonconformists, and they might well have exaggerated the consequences in relation to Irish policy of the moral bluster which deafened their ears at Sheffield. Nevertheless, the idea that nonconformist sensibilities could be soothed and party unity restored by concentrating attention on some of the quasi-religious articles in the Liberal creed embedded itself in the minds of the parliamentary strategists.

The selection of an appropriate item was not an unduly difficult task. Liberal audiences were constantly being reminded by Morley that they, as temperance enthusiasts, were engaged in the 'greatest and the deepest moral movement in this country since the anti-slavery agitation'. In private he confessed that it would be a 'blessing' if the party could only 'get heartily to work at questions of this kind, and escape from the tangled business of Ireland'.[25] The prevalence of drunkenness in the late-nineteenth century was clearly detrimental to the moral, social, and physical well-being of the community, and the demand for the regulation – and indeed suppression – of an obnoxious traffic was deeply rooted in nonconformist ideology. Harcourt wrote that 'Temperance is the backbone of the Liberal party *vice* Nonconformity retired.'[26] He also realized that the allegiance of brewers and publicans to the Conservative party was a factor in political life which could be turned to the Liberals' advantage. Home Rulers had recorded their first by-election gain at Burnley in February 1887, a morale-boosting success which was widely attributed to the exertions of the temperance party. Further resounding triumphs at Southampton (1888) and Barrow (1890) had reflected the depth of popular passions on the licensing question. Temperance organizations were active in virtually every constituency, and in order to have the slightest prospect of success Liberal candidates were obliged to defer to their views. This latent advantage had been consolidated by the predisposition of the Unionist government to protect, through generous legislation, the rights of an influential class of political supporters. Although it would be improper to conclude that all Conservatives were antipathetic to the cause of temperance, the machinery which the government contemplated as a means towards reducing the number of licences had provoked fierce resistance from the temperance lobby. The transference of all licensing powers from magistrates to elective county councils (under the terms of the local government bill) was in itself an innocuous enough proposal. But nonconformists had rejected the imputation, enshrined in clause eighteen, that licensees possessed a legal title to compensation in return for the extinction of their interest. Harcourt had sensed that the public mood was hostile to the compensation clauses, and had launched a strenuous campaign against them, culminating in an address to the United Kingdom Alliance in October 1888.[27]

As a result of his identification with the temperance crusade, Harcourt fully appreciated the value of reviving the licensing controversy in 1891 in order to stiffen the political resolve of wayward nonconformists. He believed that aggressive leadership could once again bring the government to its knees. But before any material benefits could be derived from another sustained agitation against abuses in the liquor traffic, it would be necessary for Harcourt to abandon the entirely negative approach of 1888 and 1890. A positive declaration of intent was now required. Yet a constructive policy was not immediately forthcoming, since the Liberal party had grossly neglected the task of working out the details of a satisfactory legislative settlement. Although private members had introduced local veto bills for England, Scotland, and Wales in previous sessions, no thorough discussion actually took place until John Ellis moved a resolution on the licensing question on 28 April 1891. The true explanation for an extraordinary degree of Liberal dilatoriness quickly became apparent as the debate proceeded. Extreme temperance agitators were anxious to repudiate the mere suggestion that the State ought to condone (by regulation) the existence of a wicked and odious traffic. They would not under any circumstances tolerate a remedy which did not entail total prohibition on a local basis. However, their more realistic brethren acknowledged the fact that the direct veto would rarely be used because it was too unrelenting and unwieldy an instrument. Moderates therefore preferred Morley's selection of an option provision, whereby a community could choose whether it wished to scale down the number of licences issued to any given point, or simply refuse to grant new ones. This compromise was acceptable to most schools of temperance opinion, but the machinery contemplated by Morley created additional hazards. His apparently authoritative commitment to the doctrine that local option referenda ought to be conducted by *ad hoc* authorities (similar to the School Boards) antagonized those who – like Samuel Storey – preferred to place their trust in the county and municipal councils.[28]

The development of this unexpected complication was aggravated by the idiosyncratic stance adopted by Gladstone. He regarded total abstention as unnecessary, and saw no legitimate reason why he personally should refrain from consuming alcoholic beverages. He had been extremely reluctant to oppose the compensation clauses in 1888, and although he now expressed a readiness to give temperance 'a forward shove', the movement never claimed his whole-hearted sympathy and support.[29] Harcourt exploded with frustration at such a display of ambivalence:

> Mr G's views upon the Temperance Question are hopelessly impossible. He has never really sympathized with it and does not in the smallest degree appreciate its importance in the sentiments of the party. This is sufficiently proved by his notion that he can satisfy the requirements by 'giving time' to [Sir Wilfrid] Lawson and by admitting the claim to compensation. If he can't mend his hand about this he had better leave it alone altogether.[30]

Gladstone demonstrated the justice of Harcourt's contention in an ingenuous speech at Chester on the eve of the general election. When he referred to the problem of drunkenness, he drew an invidious and unwarranted distinction between various social classes. No vice, he declared, was more 'outrageous' in members of the upper class than over-indulgence in strong drink, whereas in those who led a more precarious existence the sin was 'excusable [and] not unnatural'.[31] This indiscretion was regarded with indignation by all sections of nonconformist opinion, particularly by the multitudes of working men who earnestly avoided temptation and were stalwart advocates of temperance legislation.

The difficulties inherent in the questions of disestablishment and temperance eventually compelled the Liberal leaders to submit regretfully and with a poor grace to Gladstone's original proposition. Their lack of enthusiasm was due to the fact that electoral registration did not affect the material welfare of any important class, nor did the consideration of this arid and technical subject inspire an intense feeling of rapport amongst party members. Nevertheless, the serious deficiencies and anomalies which riddled the entire registration system could not be ignored. In spite of the considerable alteration in franchise requirements which had occurred since the first Reform Act, no corresponding codification of the registration laws had been undertaken since 1843. Gladstone had been unable to rectify this omission during the short Parliament of 1886, and he subsequently viewed with dismay the steady multiplication of abuses arising from the incomplete legislation of 1884–5. One recent authority on the subject has estimated that at least half of those who were not qualified to vote (approximately one-fifth of all adult males) in fact met the franchise requirements, but were eliminated from the voting lists on account of the registration mechanism.[32]

Liberal concern at this defective state of affairs was naturally influenced by considerations of narrow party interest. Three items placed the party at a severe electoral disadvantage, and it was upon these that attention was focused. Firstly, the compilation of the register was both cumbersome and capricious owing to the absence of responsible officials. Overseers lacked the uniform expertise which was required to interpret a mass of complex technical enactments, and the accuracy of the register consequently depended upon the vigilance of party agents in the registration courts. The competent performance of this vital function varied according to the amount of cash placed at the disposal of each local agent – and herein lies the explanation for the Liberals' persistent neglect of the state of the register. The situation remained unaltered even after the creation of a central Elections and Registration Department at Parliament Street in 1889. Failure to compete on equal terms with the Unionists soon convinced the party managers that the political balance could be redressed only through the introduction of a national network of non-partisan registration superintendents supported from public funds.

The second deficiency in the registration system related to the length of the residence qualification and the conditions under which it operated. In the case of the lodger franchise, the obligation to make an annual application for placement on the electoral roll, together with the regulations applicable to successive occupation, clearly discriminated against a large section of the working-class community. As the law stood, even householders were required to submit to a qualifying period of 12 months. Since the preparation of a fresh register involved additional delays, this entailed a minimum wait of at least 18 months. For the unfortunate lodger who changed his residence according to the dictates of his employment, this period could be as long as two and a half years. Such devious acts of discrimination against the lodger was presumed to be an electoral handicap to the Liberal party, especially in London. The idea was therefore conceived that a qualifying period reduced to only three months, plus bi-annual registration, would restore to the lists a substantial proportion of potential Liberal voters.

This insistence upon the retention of a residence qualification – however minimal – suggests that the Liberal party did not contemplate universal male suffrage as the ultimate and logical solution to the franchise question. Had the latter been envisaged, Liberals would surely have laid much more emphasis upon the need to create equal electoral districts. Hence, the widespread use of the popular catchword 'one man one vote' was highly misleading. The expression (which properly pertains to the franchise rather than registration) was confined to a third and final Liberal proposition: that no elector should possess more than a single vote. The division of counties into single member constituencies under the terms of the Redistribution Act of 1885 had greatly increased the number of electors who were entitled to duplicate votes. Sir John Lambert, who had recently retired as permanent secretary to the Local Government Board, calculated in 1888 that in England and Wales alone there were approximately 515,000 duplicate votes out of a total electorate of over five and a half millions. Liberals could no longer afford to ignore the implications of an expanding property vote. James Stansfeld's abortive registration bill of 1886 had contained no provision to curtail plural voting, except in the special case of the metropolitan boroughs.[33] But this apparent lack of concern did not long survive the general election which followed in July. The margin between the British parties in terms of votes cast amounted to a slender 80,000. Gladstone was convinced that the contest represented a victory for the prejudices of the 'classes' over the good sense of the 'masses', and he was quick to point out that the plural vote was exclusively a class vote. In a speech at Birmingham (5 November 1888) he indulged in labyrinthine calculations in an endeavour to prove that the Home Rule policy had been defeated by a majority – not of voters – but of votes. These conclusions did not take sufficient account of the enormous preponderance which the Unionists enjoyed in uncontested constituencies. Nevertheless, Gladstone's assumption that the property franchise had become the Conservative party's secret weapon cannot be disputed. Schnadhorst believed that three-quarters of this privileged vote was currently being cast in favour of Unionist candidates. This rather high estimate did not tally with Lambert's own computations, and a comparison with the dispersal of the plural vote over a longer period suggests that the more balanced observations of the former Civil Servant were probably closer to the truth.[34]

Despite this reservation, it was patently obvious that a thorough revision of electoral and registration law would serve the long term interests of the Liberal party. Parnell had effectively destroyed all expectations of a comfortable majority at the next general election, and without a decisive superiority in the House of Commons a Liberal government could not hope to cope with the obstructive tactics threatened by the Lords. The inevitability of such an outcome constituted a persuasive argument in favour of altering the registration system at the earliest opportunity. Unless the doctored and adulterated electorate had been purified before a subsequent general election, the voters would be unable to compensate a Liberal government adequately if each item in its programme had just been sabotaged by the upper chamber. During the winter of 1890–1 there were therefore two compelling reasons why registration reform could be commended as a temporary solution to Liberal woes. Firstly, it was axiomatic that any sudden revision of the Liberal programme must be acceptable to the Irish party; friendly Nationalists could ill-afford to allow any other purely British question to assume precedence over Home Rule. Secondly, since 1885, Gladstone had repeatedly affirmed that amendment of the registration laws and one man one vote stood in the forefront of his domestic programme. So an additional statement that the issue should now have priority over every other matter would not provoke hostility and suspicion in either Great Britain or Ireland. This manoeuvre would therefore prevent an unseemly scramble for preference on the part of numerous contending factions within the party, and at the same time would nullify any imputation that Home Rule had been dropped from the Liberal programme.

Gladstone's predisposition to convene a meeting of the parliamentary party to explore the shape of future policy indicates that he did not fully appreciate these ulterior designs – still less the sensitivity of political nerves. Harcourt predicted that unless Gladstone could be persuaded to withdraw the summons, all would be 'bedlam and chaos' at the meeting. He and Morley promptly forewarned Glad-

stone that 'if you offer a *tabula rasa*, every other man in the room
would hurry to scribble his own notions thereon ... The present
position [is] too critical for exposure to the wayward blasts that
would be likely to spring up in a party meeting.'[35] Although Gladstone deferred to the judgement of his frantic colleagues, his own
outlook remained unchanged. He was determined to continue the
search for a Radical shibboleth which would distract attention from
the decaying Home Rule policy. A vacancy had arisen at Hartlepool,
and (not wishing to repeat the fiasco of Bassetlaw) Gladstone seized
this opportunity to ascertain which sections of the Liberal programme
were most favoured in the constituency. He proposed that these
issues should then be recommended in an open letter to the Liberal
candidate. In defence of the new stratagem he argued that it had
become obligatory for him to bestow his personal benediction on
candidates at by-elections, and emphasized that he could not remain
'wholly silent' on the situation created by Parnell's folly.[36] Morley
and Harcourt again became extremely agitated, and voiced their
strong objections to Gladstone's clandestine behaviour. Harcourt
rejoined:

> I sincerely hope you will not be forced into a *Hartlepool Mani-
> festo* . . . I doubt very much whether this sort of action much
> affects an election and it always aggravates defeat. At this moment
> it would almost inevitably drive you to define your position as to
> Home Rule more than is at present expedient. If you gave special
> prominence to any other question it would be regarded as putting
> Home Rule in the background, and the selection of any particular
> subject for the first place would cause discontent in the camp of
> those whose hearts, like the Temperance people and the Welsh
> Noncons., are mainly set on other topics.[37]

Gladstone prudently allowed Harcourt four days in which to calm
down before replying. He knew that it would not be possible to
restrict the text of the Hartlepool letter to the usual commendatory
formula, and he was bent on including a direct reference to the
Liberal programme. Once he had completed the final draft, this
unwelcome news was broken to his subordinates. Gladstone explained that after 'reviewing carefully' all the ideas which had been
submitted for his consideration, he had decided to confine his
observations to the single issue of one man one vote. He hastily
added that the Liberal agent at Hartlepool had received instructions
to publish the communication 'only if he was advised (and with
confidence) that it would act beneficially on the election'.[38] In a
postscript Gladstone disarmingly requested Harcourt to draft a bill
to outlaw the semi-military expeditions which were currently being

sent to Africa. But this feeble and transparently obvious attempt to
curry favour with the renowned anti-imperialist did not improve
Harcourt's frame of mind. He complained bitterly to Morley that
Gladstone had refrained from concerting tactics with his colleagues,
and was unduly swayed by the uninformed prejudices of the rank
and file. Morley was equally vexed by Gladstone's secret manoeuvres.
'What a truly extraordinary thing', he wrote, 'to leave an unfledged
candidate to decide at his discretion on the publication of a document of this kind.'[39]

It soon transpired that these misgivings were entirely lacking in
foundation. When the manifesto was at last published on 12 January,
the substance seemed so innocuous that Harcourt briskly dismissed
it as 'hardly worth writing or suppressing'.[40] Gladstone merely
ventured to utter the opinion that the production of a registration
bill would 'supply a sample of our practical intentions'. Harcourt
derived some comfort from a sentence which committed Gladstone
to the task of continuing to denounce coercion in Ireland. Yet this
carefully balanced document failed to restore Liberal equanimity.
Within a week of publication Morley reluctantly informed Harcourt
that he had been authorized by Gladstone to reopen negotiations
with the Irish party. Harcourt was thunderstruck. Since the divorce
court verdict he had constantly sniped at Morley's entrenched ideas
on Irish policy, but the prospect of being thrust into an indirect
relationship with Parnell on the eve of a crucial by-election transformed mutual distrust into open warfare.[41] However, on 22
January news came of the Hartlepool result, an event which restored
to the estranged colleagues a sense of proportion. Contrary to
expectations, a Unionist majority of 912 was converted into a Liberal
surplus of 298. One neighbouring M.P. (Storey) informed Gladstone
that the contest had not been affected by Parnell's escapades, and
that the estimated 800 Irish electors in the constituency had voted
solidly for Christopher Furness, the Liberal candidate.[42] Furness
himself attributed the victory to his constant advocacy of Home
Rule. But this brave assertion should be viewed with caution. The
candidature of two rival ship-builders in a town dominated by ship-
yards inevitably meant that local loyalties and respective employment
policies would play a prominent rôle in determining the outcome.
Unlike his Liberal Unionist opponent, Furness had chosen to culti-
vate the labour vote by pledging himself to eight hours legislation
and old age pensions. Moreover, the promise to engage only members of trade unions in his own yards had secured for Furness the
block vote of the influential sailors' and firemen's union.[43]

It is therefore doubtful whether Gladstone's manifesto had any
discernible effect upon the poll. But Gladstone evidently thought

otherwise, because the result at Hartlepool encouraged him to implement the policy of registration reform at an early date. Despite considerable opposition from Harcourt and Morley, he had already taken preliminary steps in this direction. Through the agency of the Chief Whip, Gladstone had communicated on New Year's Eve with two authorities on the subject, Stansfeld and Trevelyan. Stansfeld replied that he had recently given notice of a bill which fortunately incorporated the vital principle of one man one vote. However, success depended on his being able to secure a favourable place in the ballot for private members' nights, and at present there seemed little likelihood that he would obtain a hearing on the day allotted to him (11 February). In these circumstances Arnold Morley deemed it expedient to withdraw the bill and substitute a resolution. Gladstone, who was kept informed of these manoeuvres, decided that the resolution ought to be made as comprehensive as possible.[44] Stansfeld was detailed to cover the registration proposals, while Trevelyan took charge of the section relating to one man one vote. This arrangement did not prove to be very satisfactory, owing to the delivery of an obscure and rambling speech by Stansfeld on 3 March in an empty House. Yet although the resolution was defeated by the cruelly convincing margin of 102 votes, the impression of anti-climax was not total. The debate was rescued from oblivion by Gladstone's personal intervention in the form of an unusually forth-right and incisive condemnation of plural voting.[45]

Gladstone's initiative enabled him to avoid the unpredictable cross-currents and eddies which the enumeration of a comprehensive programme would inevitably set in motion. In October he reminded N.L.F. delegates at Newcastle that only one subject among the host of issues included on the agenda paper was entitled to precedence. Using the analogy whereby 'a man spends a little time in sharpening his razor before he shaves himself', Gladstone declared that any sittings devoted to the question of improving the machinery of registration would be of immense value.[46] This observation indicates that the Liberal leaders had no intention of handling Stansfeld's resolution so clumsily in the next and final session of the 1886 Parliament. A more methodical strategy was adopted at an important conference held at Althorp in December. Those in attendance agreed to separate registration from one man one vote, and arranged to join in the hectic balloting procedure.[47] Arnold Morley and Stansfeld set the appropriate wheels in motion as soon as Gladstone's instructions from the French Riviera were received. In view of the proximity of a dissolution, Gladstone urged his colleagues 'at once to set agoing the Registration and one man one vote scheme in one shape or other, so that we may be able either to get practical advantage with an improved Registration allowed by the Tories, or to commit them to what will be emphatically an anti-labour vote'.[48]

Unfortunately for Gladstone, Conservatives were not disposed to impale themselves upon either horn of this dilemma. Extrication did not prove to be a particularly difficult exercise. When Lefevre moved the second reading of a plural voting (abolition) bill on 18 May 1892, he was immediately confronted with an amendment demanding the implementation of 'one vote one value' before the principle of one man one vote could be entertained. In other words, Conservatives exploited the occasion by comparing the respective populations of Nationalist Ireland and Unionist England, a numerical exercise which led to the predictable conclusion that the parliamentary over-representation of the former was the grosser abuse of the electoral system. On the 25th the electioneering implications engrained in Stansfeld's electors' qualification and registration bill were confounded by the simple expedient of allowing the measure an unopposed second reading. Secure in the knowledge that the bill would founder in Committee, government spokesmen refused to countenance a hostile amendment moved from their own benches, and were thus able to sustain the impression that the subject was primarily non-contentious. Yet in spite of the disappointing conclusion, these endeavours to reform the electoral system gave rise to an important sequel. For the first time since 1886 the Liberal frontbench had collectively taken the responsibility for framing, and expounding in Parliament, the basic details of a measure which would constitute an essential part of the programme adopted by a Liberal government. This unique consideration ultimately provided Gladstone with the means of escaping from the turbulent waters which encompassed him in the summer of 1892.

2. *The Rural Programme Rediscovered*

In the new climate engendered by Parnell, Liberal statesmen were certain that their Irish policy would not suffice to restore the party to power. Consequently, Home Rule no longer merited the status of unconditional supremacy which it had long enjoyed in the electoral programme. Drastic measures were necessary to stabilize the rudderless Liberal ship, and though Parnell (had he remained as leader) would have refused to tolerate any change of course, his successor, Justin McCarthy, was both too weak and pliable to offer any effective resistance. In the absence of any constraints, Morley and most of his colleagues quickly appreciated the value of clinging to home rule in the English village as a 'sheet anchor'. This choice of terminology was highly significant. The Irish land war had given a new dimension to the problems faced by the English agricultural labourer in the static and stratified conditions of rural life. A trinity of parson, squire, and farmer practised a form of coercion which was as real – if less brutal and conspicuous – than coercion by baton, bayonet, and battering-ram. F. A. Channing, who since 1886 had actively participated in the rural crusade, felt that 'sincere and generous sympathy roused for the grievances of the Irish democracy, only helped to make our land movement for England more potent as a new political force'.[49]

The slogan of Home Rule for the village could therefore be regarded as an effective means of restoring equilibrium in the party. At the back of many Liberal minds was the thought that no future general election could be won unless the party took positive steps to recover those county seats which had been forfeited in 1886. The contrast between the elections of 1885 and 1886 was stark and inescapable. The proportion of seats lost in the counties did not differ materially from losses in the boroughs, but the setback was more serious since a much larger number of Liberal seats were at stake in the former category. The extent of this reverse can be elucidated by comparing the aggregate of votes cast at each election. In 1886 borough candidates (outside London) succeeded in retaining three-quarters of the 1885 vote, but the situation in the English and Welsh counties was entirely different. Here the Liberal vote plummeted by more than half, falling from 1,114,000 to only 525,000. The disparity in these figures cannot be entirely explained by reference to the disproportionate number of uncontested Unionist seats (110 to 42), a feature which was particularly noticeable in the south-east counties. Defeat was certainly aggravated by the defection of Chamberlain and Collings, the labourers' champions; and the disinclination of the rural voter to reaffirm his allegiance of 1885 was hardened by the evident failure of Gladstone's third administration to provide any tangible reward for his unstinted loyalty.

Any strategy designed to restore Gladstone to the premiership had of necessity to be compatible with the interests and wishes of the rural electorate. But although the agricultural labourer held the key to victory, as a political being 'Hodge' remained an enigma. Despite their growing concern for his welfare, Liberal politicians continued to regard the agricultural labourer as a pathetic creature, the victim of a tradition of ignorance and docility. Once the first flush of enthusiasm for the franchise had faded, and gratitude to Gladstone for conceding this boon had begun to diminish, the familiar patriarchs of the soil attempted to reassert their sway. At the 1886 election it became abundantly clear that a combination of spiritual and economic intimidation was instrumental in keeping many

Radical voters away from the polling booth. An election in high summer ensured that the labourer would remain in the fields during the restricted hours of polling, whereas in the lean winter months he was more than ever dependent upon the goodwill of his employer. 'The men are in much distress from lowness of wages,' Herbert Gardner subsequently wrote. 'The local Tory ... has so bullied the labourer for voting Liberal that I have great fear he may choose the broad and easy path of remaining indifferent or voting with those who control his wages and his charities.'[50] Intimidation was alleged to be so widespread that a special committee under Ripon's presidency was appointed by the N.L.F. in 1889 to counter this abuse of electoral law. Cases were reported and enquiries were made, but for some inexplicable reason no practical results were achieved.[51]

The fundamental problem confronting the Liberal party was to unearth the secret of restoring to the down-trodden labourer that elusive spirit of political independence which had been wantonly dissipated between 1885 and 1886. Economic strength would foster political solidarity, and this could best be accomplished through the agency of trade unionism. In the towns trade associations provided the artisan with a sound political education, and had been responsible for the production of an indigenous working-class political leadership. The upsurge in trade unionism which followed in the wake of the London dock strike stimulated this process, but made only a limited impression upon the countryside. The rural labourer could not hope to emulate the example set by his industrial counterpart. Not only was his economic state more precarious, but his union also was demoralized and decaying. The National Agricultural Labourers' Union had been founded in 1872, and soon afterwards could boast of a membership exceeding 86,000. Unfortunately, a severe depression in agriculture had then set in, which resulted in labourers being driven off the land and out of the union. Nevertheless, under the inspired leadership of Joseph Arch, the union once more became a powerful and effective organization. Although total membership had dropped to 10,000 by 1886, the union achieved the remarkable feat of levering its outspoken President into Parliament. The election of Arch for N.W. Norfolk (a constituency which contained the Sandringham estate of the Prince of Wales) was widely regarded as a symbol of rural emancipation. This unprecedented victory seemed to foreshadow an era in which the labourer would be able to articulate his wishes through members of his own neglected class. But Arch failed to make a decisive impact upon the House of Commons, and his defeat at the 1886 election was the prelude to further setbacks. Events during the next few years destroyed the optimistic vision of the labourer himself striking-off the chains which bound him to the established social order. Arch's slack book-keeping methods discredited both himself and the union, and by 1889 these financial irregularities had become such a public scandal that membership slumped to barely 4,000. The union slowly ceased to function as a national organization, and though Arch was again elected in 1892, the national leader of an important social class was destined to fade into obscurity.[52]

Bereft of leadership and unity, the agricultural labourer was quite unable to imitate the bold methods which rival social and regional interests adopted in order to draw attention to their special requirements. Since the intellectually impoverished 'Hodge' could not even articulate his wants and desires, the duty of formulating a rural programme devolved upon a group of sympathizers who had never personally experienced the degrading nature of his existence. The organization which effectively represented the labourer in Parliament was the Liberal County Members Committee. This Committee embraced all M.P.s who sat for rural constituencies, and during the short Parliament of 1886 it met weekly under the chairmanship of Jasper More, member for Ludlow. Under the close supervision of its joint secretaries, Channing and Viscount Ebrington, the Committee took an active interest in a variety of subjects – including land, registration, railway rates, and the promised county government bill. At the general election in July total membership fell from at least 74 to between 50 and 70, but these estimates take no account of the confusion which reigned after the split in the party. Liberal Unionists continued to attend meetings of the Committee, and, for the moment, the attenuated group somehow succeeded in remaining intact. In his memoirs Channing rashly suggested that owing to his personal influence unity of action was maintained 'here and there' on 'common and non-controversial objects' throughout the Parliament of 1886–92. He cited the question of allotments as one instance where harmony prevailed.[53] But it is clear from a perusal of the debates on the labourers' allotments bill of 1887 that the Liberal members of the Committee did not see eye to eye with their Unionist counterparts. A special subcommittee had been instructed to prepare a list of amendments to the government scheme, and the most important item (embodying the principle of 'three acres and a cow') was entrusted to Channing's care. However, Chamberlain and Collings took exception to what the former referred to as procedural chicanery on the part of Channing – through attempting to appropriate the credit for an amendment which properly belonged to the affronted Collings. Neither of the two Birmingham members were strictly entitled to consider themselves as direct representatives of the rural population, but Collings at least must have established a liaison with the County Members Committee. Whatever the exact circumstances, the intrusion of this unpleasant altercation into the debate reveals that the Committee had suffered the fate which sooner or later befell every Liberal organization – namely, the severance of the Unionist from the Gladstonian wing. The presence of this fissure is indeed implied in Channing's observation that the Committee had been reconstructed during the session of 1887, and the chairmanship transferred from the Unionist landowner Jasper More to the wealthy ironfounder and Gladstonian Sir Bernhard Samuelson, member for Banbury.[54]

Six months later a similar purge occurred at the annual meeting of the Allotments and Small Holdings Association. On 16 February 1888 Channing and Sir Walter Foster summarily ejected Collings (the Association's founder) from the chair, and instantaneously transformed the allotments movement into the official organ of Gladstonian Home Rule policy in the countryside. The Liberal M.P.s who packed the new executive committee now felt free to make a significant contribution in Parliament to party thinking on rural questions. Apart from Channing and Foster, perhaps the most influential and vocal members were Herbert Gardner (the next President of the Board of Agriculture), H. P. Cobb of Rugby, C. Seale-Hayne of Mid-Devon, and Halley Stewart. The election of the last named for the Spalding division of Lincolnshire in July 1887 had already made a decisive impact, not only upon the policy of his own party, but also upon the government's programme. Halley Stewart had concentrated upon the burning issue of allotments and small holdings in his by-election campaign, and consequently he succeeded in capturing from the Conservatives an unmistakably agricultural seat – and, moreover, one that had not returned a Liberal member even in 1885. The unexpectedly large margin of 747 votes charged Liberals with excitement, since this was the first real indication that the by-election tide was beginning to flow in a Liberal direction. Defeat stung the government into taking prompt countermeasures. The agricultural labourer had risen to protest against both coercion in Ireland and Conservative neglect of rural problems in England. Coercion could obviously not be abandoned, so the President of the Local Government Board (Ritchie) was commanded to produce an allotments bill. This appeared within a fortnight of the Spalding declaration, enabling Gladstone on 29 July to accuse the premier of showing no interest in the labourers until the vote at Spalding had compelled him to heed their wishes.

The indecent haste with which the government acted provided Harcourt with ample scope for exposing the bill's deficiencies during the second reading debate. He noted that the absence of any clause to ensure that the vendor only received a fair price, plus the limitation of all lettings to one acre, would drastically reduce the supply of land available for allotments, and would thus be of no value to labourers who wished to acquire grazing land.[55] However, the principal Liberal objections were concentrated upon the administrative machinery contemplated by the Conservatives. Although the government did accept the fundamental principle that local authorities should be granted compulsory powers of purchase, the concession was virtually unenforceable because it was hedged in by complicated safeguards. Sanitary authorities (which in rural areas were Boards of Guardians) were not permitted to initiate proceedings against uncooperative landowners unless invited to do so by six parliamentary electors. If such a request was forthcoming, the Guardians were obliged to appeal to Quarter Sessions, and, if successful, were then required to entreat the Local Government Board to implement a private Act of Parliament. The expense and delay inherent in this tortuous procedure were clearly sufficient to deter labourers from tackling recalcitrant landlords. Furthermore, the social and economic station of Guardians (elected on a weighted property franchise) and of magistrates (appointed by the Lord Lieutenant) ensured that the labourer would be discouraged from applying for fertile soil close to his cottage. For these reasons the Act proved to be unworkable, and an amended version was produced in 1890. The new county councils replaced Quarter Sessions as a court of appeal; but the real improvement lay in the frank recognition that Boards of Guardians had neglected the performance of a statutory duty. In cases where the pleas of the labourer had been disregarded, county councils were empowered to discharge functions which properly pertained to the sanitary authority. Nevertheless, the basic flaws in the legislation of 1887 were left untouched, and consequently the amended Act was not successful. A parliamentary return of 1892 indicated that only 1,100 acres had been allotted to labourers since 1887.

This ill-advised attempt to dispose of the allotments question without taking full account of the subsequent reorganization of local government prompted Liberals to reexamine their alternative plans. Prior to the passage of the first Allotments Act, the Liberal county members had been inclined to work within the familiar framework of an *ad hoc* elected authority. They had envisaged parish allotments committees, elected in the vestry, and equipped with compulsory powers to rent or purchase land which could then be let to labourers in perpetuity and without restriction.[56] Cobb had tried to implement this scheme in 1887, but he had been forced to withdraw the bill after a brief debate on 16 May. In the light of the experience gained by watching the operation of Conservative legislation, it soon became apparent that a more comprehensive project was needed. In any case, once the Conservatives undertook the reorganization of local government in 1888, an interim measure ceased to be feasible. Apart from matters of detail concerning licensing, aldermen, and control of the police, Liberal objections to the local government bill centred upon the incomplete nature of the projected legislation. Dilke pointed out that the creation of county councils in isolation was tantamount to erecting a superstructure while forgetting to dig the foundations. In collaboration with Cobb he published copious notes condemning the absence of any attempt to revive the parish. 'Mr Ritchie's unit was the county, and the smaller bodies were neglected.'[57]

Dilke had conceived these ideas on the importance of district councils early in 1885, when he too was President of the Local Government Board. It later transpired that he distrusted parish councils, not only for reasons of administrative convenience, but also because he feared that they would be dominated by Conservatives.[58] Hence it is most improbable that he had ever intended to grant any vital powers to the parish. In his 1885 speeches he had not always referred to the parish as constituting an essential part of the official Liberal scheme, and at Chelsea and Halifax in October he had in fact suggested that the parish ought merely to be remodelled in the style of the Anglo-Saxon folk moot. This solution amounted to little more than the democratization of the village vestry – though the overhaul of vestry government was admittedly a highly commendable task. Procedure was antiquated, chaotic, and obscure; and in many instances the vestry was controlled by the parson and a clique of farmers solely because meetings were deliberately convened during working hours, when the labourer could not possibly attend. For these reasons Liberals unanimously declared that meetings ought always to be held in the evening, and that vestry officials should be elected by secret ballot on the one man one vote principle. However, the resurrection of the parish assembly was a wholly inadequate substitute for an elective council, meeting regularly to make and enforce important political decisions. Yet Dilke continued to presume that a reformed vestry was an almost worthless institution, except as a primitive form of political schooling for the newly enfranchised classes. He therefore reflected the patronizing attitude which both Liberal and Conservative statesmen were prone to adopt towards parish affairs and the administrative acumen of the agricultural labourer.

A predisposition to make the district council (rather than either the parish or the county) the most important unit in the local government structure was deeply engrained in the Liberal leaders, and they experienced some considerable difficulty in discarding the blueprint which Dilke had drawn up in 1885. Yet political exigencies soon demanded some modification in outlook. By 1887 Cobb and his Radical friends had reached the conclusion that the parish and not the district should be made the principal unit.[59] Their clamour became more strident during the debates on the local government bill. In 1888 the 'party as a party' clearly did not possess a coherent 'mind' on the bill, because the county members, under the direction of Gardner and Francis Stevenson of N.E. Suffolk, could not be dissuaded from moving amendments which were calculated to make the parish an effective executive authority.[60] Stansfeld (the official opposition spokesman) disapproved of this inconvenient backbench initiative, especially since he personally wished the larger authorities to be as powerful as possible. The controversy hinged on the question of allotments, and in this respect he realized that the concession of the appropriate powers to the parish was open to obvious objections. He therefore carried his case to the highest level, and reminded Gladstone that parishes were 'very numerous, very various in size and population, and many of them too small to be local government units at all'.[61] But Gladstone had already adopted a position more extreme even than Stansfeld's. He did not believe that the district council – let alone the parish – was competent to acquire, manage, and finance allotments for labourers. Gladstone placed his trust solely in the county councils. But he could not ignore completely the groundswell of opinion within both the parliamentary party and the rural constituency organizations on behalf of the sovereignty of the parish. Once the general committee of the N.L.F. had decided in April 1888 to espouse the cause of the parish as the main unit, it became necessary to reconcile the host of conflicting opinions on the subject. An acceptable division of functions among the various councils would also have to be arranged, and then incorporated into a fully comprehensive scheme of local government reorganization.

Gladstone himself cut the Gordian knot in an address to the N.L.F. council at Manchester in December 1889. He was forced to clarify the situation on account of an injudicious speech which he had delivered six weeks earlier at Southport. On this former occasion he roundly condemned the authorities which were currently administering the Allotments Act, but then proceeded to argue that these powers should be handed over to the county councils. In a brief reference to district councils he made it perfectly clear that he regarded the county as the central pillar of an extended local government structure. 'District councils', he declared, 'are absolutely necessary to give to the county councils their full efficiency.'[62] As the statement stood, Gladstone completely ignored the parish, and so gave credence to the notion that he did not approve of the Radical principle of delegating major executive powers to the smallest conceivable institutions. However, he had not exercised sufficient care to differentiate between the parish and the district, and it is possible that this slackness of nomenclature created some confusion. Many Radicals feared that the district council would be as remote from the village as the county council was already, and therefore could not be relied upon to satisfy the labourers' craving for allotments. Channing and Arnold Morley strongly urged Gladstone to give way on that score.[63] Their warnings produced the desired effect. Gladstone prefaced his explanatory statement at Manchester with the claim that the omission of district councils was a 'tremendous blank' in government policy, and hastily moved on to reassure his critics that he was also conscious of a still greater void:

> You have an allotment law at present [but] it is an inefficient allotment law ... It should be short, simple, and above all local. But perhaps not even the county council can know the exact circumstances of every portion of the county. The members of district councils might not be minutely acquainted with them. You must go to the doors of the men who are immediately concerned.[64]

Gladstone's rather abrupt change of front did not provoke recriminations from those of his colleagues who had hitherto derided parish councils as an instrument of rural regeneration. They accepted without demur the new doctrine that the parish ought to become the principal unit, and a formal declaration to this effect was made by Stansfeld as soon as the House reassembled in February 1890.[65] Hence the erratic Harcourt, who in the previous November had insisted that the district was the 'most important' part of local government, could subsequently proclaim (without a trace of embarrassment) that the district council was 'comparatively unimportant'.[66] The ease with which this transition was accomplished played a large part in the Liberal recovery from the malaise of the Parnell divorce scandal. In this revival it should be noted that the 'one man, one vote' cry had special relevance to the political requirements of the countryside. The decay of the vestry, plus the extremely undemocratic method of electing Boards of Guardians, effectively excluded the bulk of the rural population from participating in the affairs of bodies which impinged directly upon their daily lives. The creation of parish councils would not only dispose of this long standing grievance (and solve the allotments question), but would also present the Liberal party with an opportunity to escape from its Irish difficulties. Acland therefore enjoyed the hearty support of the frontbench when on 14 April 1891 he initiated a full scale debate on the unsatisfactory condition of local government in rural districts.

Yet the government still did not take the demand for village councils and reform of the vestry very seriously. It was assumed, instead, that the resolution was 'intended rather for consumption on public platforms than for practical use in this House'.[67] The number of by-elections which were pending in rural constituencies at the time of this debate certainly gives some credence to the suspicions voiced by H. Hobhouse, Liberal Unionist member for East Somerset. It is reasonable to suppose that the Liberal party was anxious to demonstrate its practical regard for the interests of the agricultural labourer as a means of compensating for the setback incurred in a crucial urban contest during the previous month. Schnadhorst had been prepared for a decisive defeat at Aston Manor (a satellite of Unionist Birmingham), but the declaration of the poll on 21 March exceeded his worst fears.[68] The disaster that overwhelmed the unfortunate Liberal candidate was easily the most cataclysmic of any contest throughout the entire period 1886–92. The Liberal poll shrank by nearly 400 compared with 1886, whereas the victorious Conservative increased his share of the vote by 1,800. This rout revived the spectre of imminent electoral doom, and compelled the party managers to intensify their efforts on behalf of those candidates who were contesting the miniature general election of April–May 1891. The five agricultural divisions involved were Woodstock, Stowmarket, South Dorset, Harborough, and Buckingham. These derived a special significance from the fact that each had been wrested by Unionists from incumbent Liberals in 1886. Gladstone issued a lengthy and detailed manifesto on the eve of the first poll (17 April), evidently hoping that the interest which he and the party had recently shown in rural questions would inspire the labourer to reverse the earlier verdict. His faith in the labourer was not misplaced; without exception the result in each constituency was thoroughly satisfactory: 3,800 votes were recovered in the four seats also contested in 1886, and overall this achievement restored the aggregate Liberal vote to within 700 of the total cast in the triumphal year of 1885. However, in terms of seats gained, only Stowmarket, Harborough, and Buckingham returned to their former Liberal allegiance (though Woodstock was narrowly recaptured in 1892). Buckingham had already been recovered at a previous contest. Nevertheless, the small increase in the fragile majority in this seat was especially notable on account of the disgraceful circumstances associated with the name of the late member (who had been expelled from the House for committing acts of gross indecency).

The spirit of dedication to the needs of the labourer which activated the new recruits was as momentous a feature of the by-elections as the resurgence of party feeling in the labourer himself. These ideals were exemplified in the person of J. W. Logan, the victor of Harborough. He quickly acquired a reputation for being one of the most vigorous and uncompromising exponents of a bold rural policy in the ranks of the county members. One of Logan's first acts as an M.P. was to send his Althorp neighbour a thinly disguised ultimatum demanding the introduction of parish councils and an effective allotments law at the earliest opportunity. He threatened to lead a political secession of agricultural labourers unless these terms were met in full.[69] But Spencer did not require shock therapy, since even the most cursory examination of the by-election statistics must have underlined the value of the rural programme as an electioneering device. Harcourt immediately broadcast the news (in Devon on 11 May) that the result of the next general election would depend upon the mind and vote of the agricultural labourer. An additional resounding by-election gain at Wisbech in July finally convinced Arnold Morley that 'the agricultural vote is with us, and that there is an undercurrent of popular feeling on our side'.[70]

These massive inroads upon the Conservative vote wrought a dramatic change in the official Liberal attitude towards rural questions. Hitherto, the frontbench had not realized that the political enthusiasm which pervaded the countryside could only be sustained if positive steps were taken to justify its existence. They had been content to regale rural audiences with brave words and vague promises, and had escaped altogether from their parliamentary responsibilities by allowing every initiative to come from the County Members Committee. No attention had been paid in 1890 to Cobb's first parish councils bill, and when Acland elected in April 1891 to elaborate upon Cobb's suggestions, Morley had added insult to injury by seconding the motion without bothering to deliver a speech. Consequently, no constraints had been placed upon militants like Seale-Hayne who were bringing the party into disrepute by demanding (among other things) that the parish council should be competent to nominate the parish clergyman and to evict those whom they thought were unsuitable.[71]

This deplorable situation would not have arisen had the Liberal leaders known in their own minds exactly what powers they intended to grant to the villager. Even the faithful columnists of *The Speaker* now became vexed and disturbed by such a baffling failure to formulate the comprehensive and detailed programme which alone could satisfy impatient agricultural labourers. Several communications from an infuriated Rev. William Tuckwell (the self-styled labourers' champion) appeared in July, bluntly criticizing the frontbench for remaining silent.[72] These mounting signs of unrest at last stirred Morley into action. Wisbech had so completely swept away his misgivings that his open air address to the agricultural labourers of Warwickshire at Stoneleigh Park on 3 August can fairly be regarded as the rural equivalent to the famous Eighty Club oration on social reform. After a lengthy description of the hardships endured by the labourer and of the problems created by the continuing exodus of the rural population to the large towns, Morley proceeded to itemize the duties which would be allocated to the parish council. The parish would be responsible for the acquisition of land for allotments, and would, in fact, be entitled to purchase land for any other public purposes – functions which presumably included libraries, chapels, parks, and labourers' cottages. In addition, the village council would control parochial charities, regulate liquor licences, and open the schoolroom in the evenings for public meetings. Morley also anticipated that the parish would manage the local school in conjunction with a regional School Board operated by the district council. This preliminary survey met Cobb's specifications with one exception: Morley did not envisage Boards of Guardians being replaced at the outset. Experience alone could determine whether the parish could safely be allowed to discharge indoor paupers and grant outdoor relief.

Morley's speech set the tone of Liberal activities during the autumn recess. The N.L.F. was already co-operating with the County Members Committee in an effort to compile an exhaustive schedule of rural requirements.[73] In August and September the campaign quickly gathered momentum on account of the publication in the *Daily News* of a series of graphic articles entitled 'Life in our Villages'. The value of these investigations was highlighted by Morley, Harcourt, and Spencer in their speeches towards the close of September, and the intense public debate provided the backcloth to the drama enacted at Newcastle on 2 October. The copious findings of the special commission appointed by the general purposes committee of the N.L.F. were compressed into a single resolution, which was moved from the platform by no less a personage than Lord Ripon. Tuckwell mounted the rostrum in a state of high excitement. 'The friends of the labourer will read this Federation programme with lively satisfaction,' he proclaimed. 'In previous years the resolution affecting their clients has been pitch-forked, with countless other measures, into the congested district of an omnibus resolution. This year it has to itself a significant corner of the paper, together with an apparently endless list of speakers.'[74]

The unprecedented degree of attention now being paid to the particular needs of the humble labourer made a profound impact upon the rural population. At the time of the Newcastle convention a by-election was in progress in North Devon, and *The Times* correspondent was upbraiding the Liberal candidate for subordinating the Home Rule issue to topics which bore more relevance to the material interests of the constituency.[75] But George Lambert, a local farmer, continued to advocate every aspect of the recently published rural manifesto until he had completed a round of 200 village meetings. Such herculean labours were rewarded in November with a resounding victory. Lambert increased the Liberal share of the poll by 1,900, and so converted a Unionist advantage of 1,700 votes into a Liberal majority of 1,200. This dramatic reversal of fortunes amply testified to Tuckwell's long standing conviction that the labourer would vote for Home Rule only if it was sandwiched between parish councils and allotments. His advice did not go unheeded, the party managers being perfectly aware that the resolution passed at Newcastle was too meagre to satisfy the labourers' appetite. The N.L.F. council was clearly not representative from the rural point of view. Very few agricultural labourers had been able to travel as unpaid delegates, and only one (George Ball, parliamentary candidate for East Sussex) had been invited to speak on the main resolution. Consequently, Schnadhorst arranged for a unique convention to be held in London on 10 December, and persuaded Gladstone to meet the delegates for breakfast at the Holborn Restaurant on the following day. Attendance was confined to those who were intimately acquainted with rural problems, and special care was taken to ensure that a substantial proportion of labourers was selected. The agenda was restricted to the terms of the resolution carried at Newcastle, and each delegate wishing to speak was allowed five minutes.[76]

To all outward appearances the Rural Reform Conference was a decided success. Harcourt promptly congratulated Schnadhorst upon 'a good conception greatly conceived', and one 'calculated to have an immense effect on the politics of the future'.[77] On the other hand, Tuckwell complained that the idea of a national conference had been stolen from the Allotments Association and 'worked on wrong lines', because Gladstone 'had not been properly coached, and talked wide of the mark'. But this verdict was soured by his subsequent estrangement from the party, and seems as exaggerated as Channing's fulsome praise of Gladstone's 'magnificent' address.[78] It was true that Gladstone discoursed on rural questions at greater length and with more precision than ever before, but, apart from discussing the merits of allowing the parish to acquire land by lease as well as by outright purchase, he failed to offer any stimulating or original views. Nevertheless, through his contact with the delegates, Gladstone did exhibit a genuine interest in the development of the rural programme. He was greatly moved by his enthusiastic reception, and was impressed by reports (from Lord Carrington) of the 'serious and reasonable tone' adopted by the delegates, and of 'a strong religious feeling pervading all the speakers' remarks'.[79]

These factors coalesced to convince Gladstone of the urgent need to press forward with rural questions prior to the dissolution of Parliament. On 26 February 1892 Herbert Gardner persuaded the government to allow village schoolrooms to be made available for public meetings. This unexpected success encouraged Gladstone to participate actively in the opposition to Henry Chaplin's small agricultural holdings bill. He was abroad during the early stages of the controversy, and so could not reply in person to the President of the Board of Agriculture. But he agreed with Harcourt that there were 'three great points of difference' between themselves and the government, citing these as being:

1. The want of local Councils, alone having sufficient cognizance of the facts.
2. Compulsion.
3. Powers of leasing as well as purchase. I am not sure whether this is as strongly felt by others as by me. At the rural conference it appeared to be felt strongly.[80]

This brief memorandum supplied Gladstone with his text for the second reading debate (24 March). He was relieved to find that Channing and Foster were prepared to place the weight of their authority behind his tentative and mildly unpopular ideas on leasehold tenure. However, the chief significance of the debates lay in other directions. Many parishes were too small to function efficiently, and Gladstone reforged the weakest link in the argument in support of village councils by finally recognizing the principle of grouping. On 4 April Cobb suggested (without contradiction) that a minimum population of 200 should become the deciding factor. Secondly, the Liberal party seized this golden parliamentary opportunity to clarify the financial relationship which ought to exist between parish and county. Gladstone fervently believed that the smaller authority would not be competent to manage the rating, borrowing, and financing provisions of a comprehensive allotments scheme. His proposition that the county council should perform this necessary task was conclusively accepted (again on 4 April) by Cobb and Winterbotham on behalf of the county members.[81] Thus, the spectre of inexperienced councillors bankrupting the parish by indulging in reckless expenditure was finally laid to rest.

Despite an intensive cultivation of the rural vote, the Liberal party did not reap a rich harvest at the general election of 1892. Fifty thousand copies of the verbatim report of the Rural Reform

Conference were circulated in agricultural constituencies during January and February. But the agitation reached a peak too soon. Enthusiasm was certain to wane when the territorial masters of the countryside, scenting danger, sought to re-establish their ascendancy over the labourer. It was also unfortunate that few by-election writs were issued in marginal seats in the final session of a dying Parliament. With the single exception of Rossendale (vacated by Hartington) no further gains were registered by Liberal candidates. Whatever benefit might have accrued from this symbolic victory was negated by the unmistakable symptoms of despondency in the party organization elsewhere. After Rossendale three of the five seats defended by Unionists were left uncontested, whereas in the two constituencies vacated by Liberals, government candidates not only materialized but also succeeded in confining the Liberal margin to the level of 1886.

The electoral omens were certainly inauspicious. Morley and Harcourt had inspected the tables produced by the Whips' office and were resigned to the probability of a narrow majority.[82] Sweeping victories in every part of the country did not occur in July, the Liberal party recording only scattered gains and several unexpected losses. Had the Unionist majority of 118 in 1886 not been whittled down to 66 by the date of the dissolution, it is evident that the net Liberal gain of 58 seats would have been insufficient to restore Gladstone to office. As matters stood the Unionists still controlled 263 English seats (excluding Universities), whereas the Liberals possessed a meagre 197. Liberal candidates succeeded in challenging this massive Conservative superiority in only two regions – London and the agricultural belt stretching from East Anglia to the Humber. In the four eastern counties they gained 11 seats, retained 4 captured at by-elections, and relinquished none. In London the Liberals gained 12 seats, both of the divisions won at by-elections were held, and only St Pancras West was ceded to the Conservatives. Perhaps the most remarkable aspect of this recovery was the fact that Liberal candidates won 17 of the 22 working-class divisions of inner London. But the Liberal performance elsewhere was disappointing. The failure to capture any Unionist seats in Liverpool, Manchester, and especially Birmingham, was accompanied by an inability to penetrate the Conservative domain of south-east England. In the eight counties straddled by Hampshire and Essex only six Unionists were dislodged.

Schnadhorst tried to convince Gladstone that the absence of any real movement of opinion was due primarily to extensive treating and bribery on the part of their opponents. He ascribed the loss of at least 20 seats to contraventions of the Corrupt Practices Act. But such a feeble explanation can only be regarded as a desperate attempt to conceal mismanagement and to justify over-confident predictions. Nor could Arnold Morley honestly allege that the disparity between the by-election trends and the final result was 'more than accounted for by this unlimited expenditure by the drink party'.[83] He and Schnadhorst were quite aware that Liberal candidates could not possibly expect to fare as well at a general election as they had done in by-elections. As early as 1887 the Chief Whip had warned Gladstone that Schnadhorst was able 'to throw an enormous amount of power into the constituencies' only at by-elections. When the great trial of strength came, 'we should not be able to concentrate anything like the same amount of power upon the various constituencies, while on the other side the Primrose League and Parson would still be carrying on their work just the same'.[84] The party managers had since worked hard to counteract the discreet – yet permanent, powerful, and above all local – pressures which the Conservatives could bring to bear upon the electorate. The network of constituency associations was extended, registration was vigorously pursued, millions of pamphlets and leaflets were distributed free of charge, and Liberal vans, equipped with celebrities and salaried lecturers, toured the country.

These careful preparations were vital, but much of their value was lost on account of convulsions in the Irish camp. Parnell's uninhibited vilification of his former Liberal associates had major repercussions upon the conduct of by-elections. Prior to November 1890 the Nationalist party had spent £4,000 per annum on electioneering duties in England.[85] The Irish M.P.s had also grown accustomed (since the Ilkeston contest of March 1887) to the practice of descending upon marginal constituencies in groups of four or five, and then discoursing on the plight of their country. Their presence had undoubtedly swayed the votes of many of those who in 1886 had either abstained or defected to the Unionists. But after 1890 Irishmen no longer appeared regularly upon Liberal platforms. Although by-elections continued to be won at a scarcely diminished rate, the tide now flowed strongly for a Radical domestic programme and not, as hitherto, on behalf of Home Rule. The growing introspection of the Irish members therefore taught the Liberal party self-reliance, and in this limited sense might actually have enhanced its long term prospects. Moreover, Schnadhorst knew that the benefits of Irish loquacity could in no circumstances be enjoyed at a general election. As the Irishmen would surely be immersed in their own individual campaigns, it was perhaps as well that hesitant Liberal voters should learn to live without these torrents of eloquence and instruction.

The dangers of support subsiding on a large scale increased enormously after Parnell's deposition from the leadership. In the

months prior to his premature death in October 1891, Parnell deliberately pricked the bubble of Liberal and Irish optimism. The consequences of such irresponsible and divisive conduct can most clearly
be seen in Ireland itself, where it was imperative to maximize
Ulster's support for Home Rule. In more propitious circumstances
three marginal Unionist-held seats in the province could have fallen
to Protestant Nationalists campaigning on a tenants' rights platform.[86] But instead of reclaiming these precious seats, the quarrelling
Irish factions surrendered three themselves, plus two (quite unnecessarily) in Dublin. Their combined strength dropped from 85 to 80,
cutting Gladstone's overall majority from a possible and relatively
secure 56 to a nominal and unstable 40. It is much more difficult to
ascertain how far Parnell – from the grave – could be held personally
responsible for the failure of the Liberal party to convert England to
Home Rule. His behaviour must have confirmed the prejudices of
those 'floating' voters who instinctively presumed that every Irishman was thoroughly untrustworthy, and that the Nationalist party
was therefore unfit to manage the internal affairs of a nation. Nor
did it escape the notice of committed Unionists that the Catholic
hierarchy had been quick to denounce a Protestant Parnell. There
were also strong grounds for supposing that in recent Irish by-
elections the clergy had exercised an unwarranted degree of spiritual
intimidation over the allegedly illiterate members of their flock.
Lord Salisbury joyfully exploited the inflamed passions of both
Ulster Protestants and the Unionist press, speaking to great electoral
advantage of the curse of ecclesiastical domination in Irish politics.[87]
The 'Orange card' was played with such verve and determination
that Gladstone was caught in an unexpected trap. Ulster had not
previously been regarded as a crucial element in the Home Rule
controversy, but during the 1892 campaign Gladstone was forced to
defend clerical intervention in secular affairs. He was unaccustomed
to the rôle of meek apologist, and this was a branch of oratory in
which he had never distinguished himself. The final Midlothian
campaign was, then, a painful experience for both speaker and
audience. Gladstone was compelled both to justify his unrelenting
attitude towards the Ulster problem and to excuse his circumspection
on labour and Scottish issues. This pedestrian approach did not
augur well for Gladstone's capacity to remain for long at the head
of the next Liberal government.

3. The Full 'Bill of Fare'

Gladstone was staying with Rosebery at Dalmeny when the first
election results were announced. Included in the list of early

declarations was the unwelcome information that Morley had been beaten into second place at Newcastle by the single Conservative candidate. There was no pronounced swing to the Liberals in the English provincial boroughs, and this undoubtedly gave rise to the overwhelming sense of despair which the veteran leader experienced at this time. An inglorious and pathetic close to his distinguished political career loomed large on the horizon. His host, who made no effort to conceal an avid desire to escape altogether from public life, was the last person capable of dispelling the atmosphere of gloom and despondency which pervaded the house.[88] Gladstone's high hopes for a commanding majority in the next Parliament were dashed as each new post brought further cruel disappointment. Undoubtedly, the most bitter blow was the news that he had personally narrowly escaped defeat in his Midlothian stronghold. However, though this Pyrrhic victory was a most mortifying experience, Gladstone was not totally disheartened by the setback. On the day of the Midlothian declaration he surmounted the mood of defeatism which had threatened to engulf him, and composed for Spencer's benefit a dispassionate and business-like analysis of the grim situation (see appendix C).

No trace of resentment or dismay can be discerned in this important and lengthy document. On the contrary, it bears out the validity of two contentions which are central to this study. Firstly, Gladstone realized that the upsurge in Radicalism since 1885 could not be condemned on the grounds that the militants had recklessly created divisions in the party, thereby alienating the electorate and causing the present political stalemate. The persistent clamour of sectional interests ought to be regarded instead as a sign of considerable intellectual vitality and clarity of purpose. Secondly, although Gladstone's willingness to float upon this groundswell of enthusiasm superficially suggests that at moments of crisis his behaviour was purely opportunist and unprincipled, close examination reveals that his reactions were, in fact, often perfectly reasonable and consistent. Unruly elements would never have been subdued had Gladstone not been more conversant with, and sympathetic towards, advanced ideas than many historians have imagined.

Gladstone frankly admitted that such a small parliamentary majority as the Liberals now commanded would inevitably result in a decrease in Liberal momentum concerning Home Rule. Little headway could now be made. On the other hand, he was fully aware that even this precarious majority had been gained owing to emphasis on matters quite apart from Ireland. Circumstances clearly demanded 'some degree of shifting of our polarity', so Gladstone discreetly enquired how the Home Rule axis could be displaced by

English, Welsh, and Scottish reforms. The question posed – and the answers received – were reminiscent of the prolonged debate on future strategy which had taken place 18 months earlier. Gladstone firmly believed that his only hope of preserving the cohesion of a party which was 'not homogeneous throughout' was dependent on one factor: the Irishmen must be persuaded to rest content with some simple administrative changes at Dublin Castle during the first full session of a Liberal government. An immediate repeal of the Coercion Act and the return of evicted tenants to their former holdings were cited as two obvious expedients in a strategy designed to reconcile Nationalists to an abrupt and unexpected departure from the Home Rule highway. Gladstone seemed more than ever determined not to waste precious time in his first session as premier on a bill which would swiftly be aborted by the House of Lords, and so he drew up a confidential memorandum on this delicate matter as soon as the elections were completed. He proposed to proceed in the Commons by way of resolution, imagining that its reintroduction in the Lords, and the subsequent laying of a cabinet minute on the table of both chambers, would guard against any criticism that an abstract resolution was a worthless declaration.[89] But Morley, who was present with Gladstone at Dalmeny in mid-July, was shocked by these disclosures. He had no desire to return to his former post of Chief Secretary if the 'great work' was merely to consist of administrative reorganization. 'The more I think of it, the less can I expect that we can put Home Rule in any way behind English and Scottish measures,' Morley wrote. 'I cruise under the green flag – come what will. If we founder, which is only too probable, at least let us go down with honour.'[90]

Up to this stage Gladstone had hoped that the Irish would exercise restraint on the thorny subject of Home Rule, and might conceivably enter into a formal compact with the Liberals. He derived inspiration and encouragement from the example set in 1835 by Melbourne and his enlightened Irish under-secretary, Thomas Drummond. Although Gladstone was aware that the mouldering Lichfield House precedent could not be exhumed in 1892, he found solace in reminding himself that 'the Melbourne government came in with a British minority, swelled into a majority hardly touching thirty by the O'Connell contingent of forty. And they staid in for six years and a half, the longest lived government since Lord Liverpool's.'[91] Unfortunately, the continued division in the Nationalist ranks rendered this proposition unworkable; Irishmen were no longer under the command of a master of O'Connell's – or Parnell's – stature. At the general election the mutinous Parnellites had been reduced from 33 members to nine, but even this insignificant rump could easily endanger the existence of a Liberal ministry should any delay in the introduction of a Home Rule bill occur. The Parnellites were also capable of exerting an unsettling influence over the Anti-Parnellite majority, since those who remained loyal to the Liberal alliance dared not allow a situation to arise in which their Nationalist enemies could brand them as traitors to the great cause. It was, therefore, feared that every Irish member would absent himself from the House unless Gladstone produced the Home Rule bill at once. Without the constant delivery of these 81 vital Irish votes, no Liberal government could survive for a moment.

Consequently, the Nationalists held the Liberal party 'in the hollow of their hand'; they were 'the pivot on which the manoeuvring turns'.[92] Hence, the oft-quoted remark of Gladstone's that he was 'as fast bound to Ireland as Ulysses was to his mast', is highly misleading. The revision of his earlier plans which this conviction entailed did not spring from Morley's impassioned utterances on the subject of personal duty and public honour; rather, revision was born of more pragmatic thoughts. In the very same letter (to Ripon) Gladstone explained that the cords in question were 'the Irish schism and the limited nature of our majority [which] must in a measure tell upon the form of our proceedings'.[93] The heterogeneous nature of the Gladstonian movement rendered party unity fragile in the extreme, thus compelling the leaders to remain aboard the stricken Home Rule vessel. This unpalatable but nevertheless unavoidable truth was obvious to everybody except Harcourt. Aided and abetted by Labouchere (who coolly asserted that 'self-preservation is the first law of nature')[94] Harcourt was so anxious to postpone Home Rule that he hurriedly concocted a mixture of prospective legislation which he imagined would tempt the Irishmen to attend regularly at Westminster. In various ways one man one vote, the payment of members, and (according to T. P. O'Connor) even local option appealed as much to Nationalists as to British Liberals.[95] But any preparations of this nature were speculative and premature, since Irish reactions to Gladstone's fresh proposals were as yet unknown.

In the unlikely event of both Irish parties agreeing to co-operate unconditionally with Gladstone, the new premier could confidently proceed to assuage the mutual jealousies and misgivings in his own party by grappling with some of the more '*concise* and telling' aspects of the Liberal programme. Hence Morley was commissioned to sound out John Dillon, deputy leader of the majority faction. But consultations could not begin while the Nationalists dallied in Ireland, and the first crucial meeting did not take place until 27 July. After a second interview with the Irish delegation on the morning of the 28th, Morley returned at 2.30 p.m. to Gladstone's London headquarters in Carlton Gardens in an 'electric overcharged state'. His expectant colleagues learnt that the Nationalists were 'uneasy and distrustful', Lewis Harcourt recording that:

> Morley says the Irish insist on having Home Rule pushed straight through the Commons with as little delay as may be and . . . to the exclusion of British measures. W.V.H. resisted this strongly and said he would be no party to the Parnellites dictating to us an absolute surrender of our English programme.[96]

This divergence in outlook concerning Irish policy was not a simple difference of opinion which, in due course, could be smoothed over with little difficulty. On the contrary, it served to fan the flames of antagonism between Harcourt and Morley which had fortuitously remained dormant since February 1891. The quarrel now became much fiercer as Harcourt busied himself with the drawing up of alternative Radical programmes. His abrupt dismissal of the timid view that 'we have moved much too fast and too far towards the Extreme Left in every subject at once' rankled with Morley,[97] who stubbornly refused to swim with the prevailing tide. He thought that there would be no need for a Liberal government to tackle in its first session any non-Irish matters apart from registration and one man one vote. This meagre proposal was remote from Harcourt's grandiose conception of a 'firm front', since that doughty warrior simultaneously informed Gladstone that 'all our cards should be played with a view to strengthening our hands for the next Election a year or two hence'.[98] In a previous letter he had impressed upon Gladstone his strong conviction that:

> The only chance of holding together our majority such as it is will consist in giving satisfaction at once to the various sections of which it consists . . . When Parliament meets in February next we must be prepared to produce Bills on the following subjects
> 1. Temperance Reform and Local Option
> 2. Village Councils with control of schools
> 3. Registration Reform and One Man One Vote
> 4. Payment of Members
> 5. Welsh Disestablishment
> This I think is the *very minimum* of what we should bring forward and is only a fraction of what you pledged us to at Newcastle. Of course they cannot all be carried but with the Taxation Reforms of which you spoke they will fairly meet the immediate demands of our people.[99]

Harcourt was anxious to discover whether this list of measures was acceptable to the various groups within the Radical party, and between 22 and 25 July he conducted a series of interviews at his house in Brook Street. He was pleased to report that the views of the most influential backbenchers were 'convergent upon a few points',[100] explaining exactly what these conclusions were when he arrived at Rendel's house in Carlton Gardens for the conclave of the 28th. Although no precise details of these mysterious negotiations have survived, one point is clear. Morley took umbrage at the notion, evidently broached at the Brook Street conferences, that Irish Home Rule should be thrust aside to make room for a host of Radical projects. But his ardent and familiar plea on behalf of Ireland now went unheeded, for Gladstone as well as Harcourt earnestly desired to appease the growing clamour for a programme which incorporated special sectional interests.

However, it would be wrong to suppose that Gladstone succumbed with reluctance to the logic of Harcourt's persuasive arguments. He had already decided quite independently to introduce a collection of domestic reforms in the event of his obtaining only a small parliamentary majority. A list of suitable measures had been perused by Rosebery at Dalmeny as early as 9 July. Gladstone spent a considerable amount of time thereafter 'inwardly hammering out' those legislative items which might 'help the *British* part of the bill of fare'.[101] Yet he was characteristically slow to divulge the details to the remainder of his colleagues. His method was to suggest particular issues to those who had acquired a special knowledge of a subject, and who might eventually be called upon to frame and carry the relevant legislation. Thus, Spencer was informed only of matters pertaining to the office of Irish Viceroy, and Morley probably received similar treatment. This oblique approach caused a misunderstanding with Harcourt. He was afraid lest Gladstone intended to 'nobble' his colleagues one by one, as in 1886, and was perplexed by his leader's reluctance to return to London and 'discuss in full conclave what are the heads which are the most practicable and expedient to announce at once'.[102] As prospective Chancellor of the Exchequer, Harcourt was merely told that the equalization of death duties and the taxation of ground rents would fulfil the twin conditions of 'concise and drastic' legislation. 'Enfranchising leaseholds', Gladstone mused, 'would I suppose be more complex'.[103] Harcourt jumped to the erroneous conclusion that Gladstone wished to confine his new British programme to these particular items of financial reform. A note of reassurance was promptly forthcoming, and Harcourt was delighted to learn that Gladstone believed in reality that 'we must prepare a series of measures which will be challenges to the Lords and which will give us a stronger position with (London and) the country than Ireland could if alone'.[104] On specific points Gladstone was perfectly conciliatory, demonstrating in connection with the awkward subject of payment of members that he had no desire to obstruct the considered wishes of the party by 'getting upon my high horse without cause'. In conclusion he wrote:

It is more important to observe that your ideas and mine as to the general form of action seem to be much the same. I conceive that we have

1. To cast the balance fairly between Irish and British claims.
2. To anticipate mischief as most probable in the House of Lords.
3. To open on that House as many good *bouches à feu* as possible . . .

I see the not unlikelihood of another Dissolution before Session 1894.[105]

The receipt of such encouraging letters enabled Harcourt to overlook the evasive behaviour of a leader who readily conceded that there was 'much which may be done' while rather perversely contriving to 'reserve details'. No further information could be gleaned on account of the circuitous itinerary which Gladstone now pursued. He did not return at once to the metropolis after leaving Dalmeny on 16 July, but travelled north to George Armitstead's Highland retreat at Braemar in a remote corner of Aberdeenshire. Having spent a few days in complete isolation, he returned to Hawarden, and did not reach London until the 27th. The new session was scheduled to begin on 4 August, but, fortunately for the Liberal party, the necessity for haste vanished when it became known that Lord Salisbury was in the process of drafting the Queen's Speech. 'If we come in,' Gladstone gleefully noted, 'as it will be late in August, with the Supply voted, we shall not want our legislative programme for production.'[106] The Conservative premier had made a serious miscalculation. He was evidently hoping that by remaining in office he could force Gladstone to spell out Liberal policy during the debate on the Address. Unionists would then be able to sit back and enjoy the spectacle of a composite Home Rule majority tearing itself to pieces in a furious scramble to devour scraps from the great man's table. But Gladstone did not need to extend preferential treatment to any section in order to muster sufficient votes in the crucial division. Nationalists and Radicals would surely hold their tongues until the Unionist enemy had been safely ousted, giving the new government a well-earned respite. 'You will not be [Prime] Minister when the vote is taken', Gladstone was reminded, 'and will not be bound to pledge yourself to more than you think fit.'[107] Harcourt took care to ensure that the resolution of no-confidence was framed

so as 'to expose as little surface to criticism as possible', thus mini-
mizing all opportunities to 'open up the question of sectional
divisions'.[108] Gladstone was easily persuaded to omit any reference
to the result of the elections 'as a whole', and he agreed instead to
confine the motion to the bare statement that the existing government did not possess the confidence of the Commons.

This cautious strategy proved to be eminently successful. The
Liberal leaders in both Houses refused to commit themselves to any
particular articles of the Newcastle programme and steadfastly
declined numerous invitations to indicate the nature of their projected Home Rule settlement. As private members the aspiring
ministers were fully entitled (on strict constitutional grounds) to keep
their own counsel, but Gladstone could not avoid giving some
general assurances for the sake of Irish votes and Radical silence.
He pointed out that although his primary duty lay with Ireland, a
Liberal government could not disregard its obligation to continue
governing Great Britain after the second Home Rule bill had been
rejected by the Lords. Gladstone was careful not to cite specific
examples of issues which might profitably be taken up, when he
affirmed that it would be his 'absolute duty' in 1893 to make a
'serious and resolute effort' to deal with a 'considerable portion' of
the Radical programme. 'While there has been so long a possession
of the field in a very great degree by the Irish question', he concluded, 'there has also been this remarkable and probably un-
exampled development of British wants and desires.'[109] This imprecise
statement was sufficient to persuade the entire complement of
Nationalist and Liberal members (except for two who were un-
avoidably absent) to follow Gladstone into the division lobby on
11 August and defeat the Unionist government by 350 votes to 310.

Gladstonian Twilight

The new Liberal cabinet met for the first time on 19 August, whereupon Gladstone announced that as a result of consultations with Morley and Spencer, he had devised a method of satisfying each section of the party in a manner which did not also entail a gross overloading of the legislative machine. He read out a provisional outline of work for the coming session, dividing the Liberal programme into four compartments:

I.   Bills to be worked by the Govt. in the House.
II. Bills to be worked through Grand Committee.
III. Bills of Private Members to be supported by the Govt.
IV. Executive Rule.[1]

Gladstone then asked his colleagues 'to contemplate by preference (except Home Rule) subjects capable of the most concise treatment'.[2] They were advised to give pride of place to a local government scheme which would vest additional powers in the L.C.C., equip parish councils with the power to acquire land compulsorily, and transfer to county councils the control of the police and of licensing. In addition the premier urged the cabinet to accept registration, one man one vote, the transfer of election charges to the rates, employers' liability, and amendment of the conspiracy laws, as necessary items in the ministerial programme. In conclusion, it is probable that Gladstone declared that Wales and Scotland must rest content (at least for the immediate future) with the two Royal Commissions on Land which he had promised Rendel and Trevelyan a few days earlier at Carlton Gardens.[3] Church suspensory bills could therefore be relegated to the third category, their introduction remaining the responsibility of dedicated backbenchers.

Ministers filed out of the cabinet room fully aware of the fact that their leader had no intention of cramming the Queen's Speech with pledges which could never be redeemed by a government with a precarious parliamentary majority. Gladstone was now left with the unenviable task of explaining this eminently reasonable decision to followers who felt that they had been unjustly treated. Channing and other leading rural members were informed through Herbert Gardner that the government could not possibly entertain their request for either an amendment of the Agricultural Holdings Act or the creation of a Commission of Enquiry into the subject of agricultural distress.[4] The Scottish church suspensory bill, which had already been drafted by the Lord Advocate (J. B. Balfour), was unceremoniously handed over to Dr Hunter. The member for Aberdeen was understandably 'a little sore' at being asked by the Chief Whip to arrange a joint ballot amongst his compatriots.[5] In all likelihood Gladstone endeavoured to foist the Welsh church suspensory bill upon Rendel. But Welsh patriots refused to suffer this indignity in silence, Tom Ellis threatening to contrive an 'unexpected misfortune' in the House should the government fail to take the initiative.[6] The discovery that a subordinate minister was rudely interfering with his carefully laid plans caused Gladstone to explode with fury. 'Does he think Welsh Disestablishment can be carried at the same time with a Home Rule Bill and other claims?' the irate premier exclaimed concerning Ellis. 'Or does he recommend making promises through the Queen's Speech with a moral certainty that they cannot be fulfilled, or would he like us to tell the Irish members that they are to be kept at Westminster till all the claims of all the interests have been satisfied?'[7]

Ellis possessed powerful allies in the cabinet, but before Acland, Asquith, and Harcourt could enter the fray there arose a crisis which threatened the government's very existence. The wrath of Gladstone and Harcourt descended upon Rosebery when in September they found that the Foreign Secretary was actively pursuing an imperialist policy in Uganda. Harcourt dispatched lengthy memoranda in all directions, denouncing annexation and pleading for the prompt evacuation of British subjects – while Gladstone stiffly reproached Rosebery for his 'total gross misconception of the relative position of the two offices we respectively held'.[8] The quarrel simmered until the autumn, and was then abandoned, owing to the sudden realization by an exhausted Harcourt that the cabinet had not yet reached agreement on the scope of its legislative programme. Consequently, he convened an impromptu meeting of several junior ministers on 27 October to determine which policies required discussion at the long-delayed autumn planning cabinets. Two days later he requested a private interview with Gladstone and suggested that it might be prudent to extend the programme considerably beyond what had originally been contemplated.[9] But Harcourt so much wanted to convert Gladstone to his treasured local veto scheme that the emissary of Wales and Scotland completely forgot to mention disestablishment. 'It will I think be very difficult to satisfy the *genus irritabile* of Wales and the *perfervidum ingenium* of Scotland unless some notice of this burning question is taken this session,' he wrote on the following day. 'It is not easy to classify it in the list of measures possible to be carried but that will not prevent a very urgent demand for a substantial earnest of action on the part of the Government.'[10] However, Gladstone remained unimpressed by an argument which sprang from despair. He still reserved the right to abandon the two Church suspensory measures, a decision which aroused much hostile comment. In Gladstone's opinion Wales and Scotland could have either a Land Commission or an officially-sponsored suspensory bill – but they could not demand both without offending other portions of the country which were equally 'on the alert to get their share' of the legislative spoils. Such considerations of equity largely explain why Gladstone continued to insist on a Select Committee rather than a prestigious Land Commission for Wales, once Scotland had magnanimously given up her claim to a suspensory bill. He only relented when Harcourt suggested that a slight concession to Ellis would help to silence those implacable Welshmen who viewed the suspensory bill as a poor substitute for immediate disestablishment.[11]

On the other hand, Gladstone readily agreed to expand his by no means inconsiderable programme in less sensitive areas. When cabinet meetings recommenced on 30 October he established committees on registration, temperance and local government, drew up several lists of supplementary reforms, and briskly allocated these to the appropriate ministers for immediate drafting. By 21 November the programme had altered beyond all recognition. It now contained a formidable proportion of labour planks, including bills to reduce the magistrates' qualification to £5, curtail the hours worked by railway servants, facilitate the reporting of industrial accidents, and enforce more stringent regulations in factories and workshops. Acland, Fowler and Mundella subsequently added bills to increase the school leaving age, equalize rates in the metropolis, and pioneer boards of conciliation during industrial disputes. By January 1893 the list had become quite unmanageable, especially since two novices (Fowler and Asquith) were each entrusted with five measures of capital importance. Asquith admitted that the task was beyond him when he implied that the complexities of one man one vote had delayed his attending to the subject of factories and workshops. This easily foreseeable situation enabled Gladstone to run through the table of 24 measures on the eve of the Queen's Speech, striking out inconvenient and potentially embarrassing items like the payment of members.[12]

Gladstone did not selfishly thrust the heavy burden of legislative preparation entirely upon younger and less experienced shoulders during these languid months of parliamentary hibernation. Although the weary premier had originally shown an old man's reluctance to grapple with the immensely complex particulars of Home Rule, he did not in reality require much prompting to attend to this onerous duty. While Harcourt was protesting that they had wasted two hours at the stormy cabinet of 11 November discussing whether there should be any examination of disputed points in the next Home Rule bill, Gladstone quietly slipped into Morley's hands a memorandum containing the essential features of this future measure. He now began to work extremely hard upon the 'knottiest points in the whole affair', especially in connection with the status of Irish representatives at Westminster.[13] As soon as Gladstone had resolved this baffling difficulty to his own satisfaction (by limiting voting rights and reducing numbers to 81), he invited a special committee of the cabinet to draft a comprehensive scheme. However, the basic structure which emerged from the committee on 16 December was virtually Gladstone's own creation. Spencer, Campbell-Bannerman, Bryce and Herschell were consulted on matters of detail, and Morley was occasionally summoned from his 'back-kitchen' at Dublin Castle to negotiate with the Nationalists. Yet none of these willing work-horses possessed sufficient financial expertise to follow their chairman through the labyrinth of quotas, fiscal balances, and Exchequer contributions. Unfortunately, Harcourt – the one minister who actually understood these complicated issues – remained aloof, apparently so that he might freely criticize the atmosphere of secrecy which enveloped the committee. Harcourt also regarded certain crucial aspects of Home Rule with a degree of suspicion which verged on fierce animosity. Gladstone therefore delayed presenting the completed scheme to the full cabinet until the last possible moment. All his reserves of patience and guile were now stretched to appease Harcourt, who, during a succession of January cabinets, sat on a distant sofa glowering at the occupants of the main table. Gladstone wrote soothing explanatory letters, offering his deputy a personal interview before the next cabinet. He adroitly blunted Harcourt's favourite weapon of attack by firing out an assurance that their calculating Irish allies ought to be presented at once with 'something near an ultimatum' regarding financial arrangements. 'It is annoying ... that the figures shift as in a kaleidoscope,' Gladstone stated in a markedly conciliatory tone. 'I am *greatly* pleased with Hamilton's new adaptation of your plan which retains, perhaps even increases, all its great advantages, especially that of giving the Chancellor of the Exchequer a *perfectly free hand.*'[14]

But these friendly overtures brought the premier only temporary relief. Gladstone was scheduled to outline the scope of the Home Rule bill before an expectant House of Commons on 13 February, but on that very morning he received from Harcourt a sudden and deafening broadside. The Chancellor of the Exchequer insinuated that the financial plan had since been altered without his prior consent, and emphatically declared that he would not tolerate any change in Ireland's favour of the balance of imperial revenues. Gladstone struggled to control his temper when reading this appalling document. 'It seems to me altogether too late to attempt alteration of the Bill as it now stands and as it was fixed by the Cabinet after repeated and long deliberation,' he curtly retorted. 'I have publicly announced that the Bill is ready and the serious delay in its circulation, which must result from our reopening now, would of itself terribly discredit both the Government and the question of Home Rule.'[15] However, he did agree to amend (slightly) the offending clause, a gesture of reconciliation which Harcourt grudgingly accepted at a hastily convened cabinet on the 16th.

This altercation adds a new dimension to Gladstone's heroic struggle to carry the second Home Rule bill through the House of Commons. However, Morley could not altogether repress the 'impious thought' that progress would have been far more rapid had the resourceful premier been less impetuous, meddlesome and voluble. 'Mr Gladstone would pick up the paper of amendments, put on his glasses, make up his mind in a twinkling of an eye, with little thought of outlying consequences,' he condescendingly recalled. 'It was glorious, but full of hourly hazard.'[16] Yet, even if there were occasions when Gladstone created unnecessary difficulties by speaking too freely and too frequently, a convincing explanation for his abiding presence lay readily to hand. Someone in authority simply had to remain glued to the frontbench between Harcourt and Morley, otherwise these two estranged lieutenants would sooner or later express in public their contempt and dislike for each other. Perhaps the first – and worst – 'fright of a crisis' occurred shortly after the bill entered Committee in May. Gladstone approved Harcourt's plan to insert a declaration of imperial supremacy in clause one, explaining that it would be foolish to engage the Unionists 'too heavily upon slippery ground' at the outset. 'If my view matters', Morley petulantly rejoined, 'it would be much better if Harcourt . . . could take my place in respect of the routine conduct of the Bill. My only utility has been as a messenger to the Irish leaders.'[17] On this occasion Harcourt rather than Morley appears to have been the wronged party, though this unusual reversal of rôles caused Gladstone considerable mental anguish. Characteristically, he resisted a strong impulse to reveal exactly what he thought of colleagues whose apparent contribution to the legislative effort was to regard each other with icy disdain while continually reproaching their leader for taking unplanned initiatives in the House. In contrast, the premier found it relatively easy to weather a rapid succession of storms unleashed from the benches opposite (where the Nationalists perversely continued to sit). After careful consideration he decided in July to recast the bill in two important respects. On the 12th full voting rights (in place of a curious 'in and out' arrangement) were granted to the Irish members who would now remain at Westminster. Six days later the troublesome financial dispute was placed in abeyance through the creation of an impartial tribunal to review Ireland's contribution to imperial revenues. These deft concessions to wayward Liberals and querulous Parnellites kept the tenuous parliamentary majority intact through 82 tedious sittings, clear proof of Gladstone's skill, resilience, and extraordinary powers of endurance.

The Home Rule bill finally left the Commons on 1 September, exactly one year after the Liberal government had commenced work in earnest. Gladstone could now sit back and contemplate his Irish record with considerable satisfaction. It was no mean feat to have carried a complex and bitterly controverted measure as far as a third reading. In addition, he could justly proclaim that with his approval Morley had systematically wrought drastic administrative changes at Dublin Castle. The loathsome machinery of the Coercion Act was now completely dismantled, prisoners who had been convicted of minor agrarian crimes were released from gaol, and many Catholics were being appointed over the heads of Unionist lord lieutenants to a bench formerly packed with Protestant magistrates. Furthermore, Morley had established a Royal Commission on Evicted Tenants, the composition of which was firmly tilted in favour of the Nationalist cause. Gladstone could have selected this moment of repose to quit the political stage with honour intact. But he bravely scorned this easy route to an early retirement, feeling that the discharge of all Irish obligations needed to be balanced against outstanding debts to other groups of supporters. A battle-weary and visibly ageing premier realized that the domestic part of the government programme had ground to a halt on account of his reluctance to invoke the closure during the protracted Committee stages of the Home Rule bill. He continued to believe that if 'a well constructed and pretty stout programme for this side of the channel were to fail, I certainly should be far from sanguine as to the [immediate] general issue'.[18] In other words, there existed a very real danger that Liberals would offer no resistance when the peers came to exercise their constitutional right to reject unpalatable Irish legislation, unless the party was given some recompense for so gallantly sacrificing many cherished projects upon the altar of Home Rule. Fortunately, Gladstone's aggressive instincts had been aroused by the spoiling tactics of Unionists in both Houses. Nearly all the measures mentioned in the Queen's Speech had sunk without trace after a formal first reading; only Mundella's hours of labour (railway servants) bill had been allowed to reach the statute book. Gladstone therefore decided to re-engage the enemy in a prolonged autumn session, even before the peers had been granted an opportunity to crush the Home Rule bill. He did not flinch from the prospect of further fierce combat, and on 31 August he issued the cabinet with a summary declaration of war.[19] Bills relating to labour disputes, conspiracy, registration, local veto, and the Welsh Church were abandoned on 18 September, the local government bill and the employers' liability bill alone being salvaged from the wreckage.

Gladstone played only a minor rôle in the drama which now unfolded. He was not only incapacitated by the deteriorating state of his eyesight and hearing, but was also distracted by extremely delicate and time-consuming negotiations with two overwrought personages. Morley insisted on replacing Sir Joseph Ridgeway (an inveterate Unionist) as permanent under-secretary at Dublin Castle, while the Queen absolutely refused to relinquish the Duke of Edinburgh's handsome annuity when her second son became a reigning German prince. These troublesome details of patronage entailed a voluminous correspondence, fully justifying the view that during each of his ministries Gladstone was 'always far more bothered over personal matters like appointments than over any amount of national crises'.[20] In these circumstances, Asquith and Fowler received little support from the premier when the Unionists began to clutter up the order paper with hostile and dilatory amendments. However, Gladstone did not shirk the responsibilities of leadership once the House of Lords had set to work on the employers' liability and local government bills. The upper chamber kept on inserting and re-inserting a 'contracting out' clause in the former, and continually mutilated the latter by depriving the parish council of full powers to impose rates and control allotments, charities, and schoolrooms. Such deliberate emasculations were regarded as fatal to both bills. On 20 February 1894 Gladstone tamely dropped the employers' liability bill, ignoring the strictures of disappointed militants mainly because he realized that a hard core of Liberal M.P.s shared the peers' anxiety to protect the status of company insurance funds. The local government bill was an altogether different proposition, there being no fifth columnists in the Liberal ranks. Nevertheless, the government clearly lacked sufficient strength to abandon this long-awaited measure, and cabinet ministers did not relish the prospect of explaining to the electorate exactly why they thought it necessary to devote an unprecedented total of 226 sittings to such futile ends. Gladstone, therefore, accepted the Lords' amendments under duress on 1 March, covering his retreat with the 'sorrowful declaration' that 'differences of fundamental tendency' between the two Houses had provoked 'a controversy which, when once raised, must go forward to an issue'.[21]

While the bills were passing to and fro between the two Houses, Gladstone suddenly revived a notion which he had briefly entertained in the autumn, namely, that the beleaguered ministry should immediately wind up the session and appeal to the country. He wrote to the Chief Whip from Biarritz in February, arguing that the inconvenience attendant upon dissolution 'would be as nothing in comparison with the vast importance of a prompt and timely submission to the nation upon a group of questions which taken together amounts to this, whether the people of the U.K. are or are not to be a self-governing people'.[22] But this bold suggestion was received in London with utter disbelief. Even if the cup of the Lords was indeed overflowing with their misdeeds, Marjoribanks perceived far more acutely than did Gladstone that the condition of party organization was wretched in terms of both cash and candidates. The cabinet therefore telegraphed a peremptory negative. 'Thus there was let slip', Gladstone later maintained, 'an opportunity in my opinion nothing less than splendid for raising decisively an issue of vital importance to popular government: an opportunity which if rightly used would have given the Liberal party a decisive preponderance for the full term of one or probably two Parliaments.'[23] These heroic words were penned in the aftermath of the electoral catastrophe of 1895, raising the possibility that Rosebery's ill-starred administration might not have tottered to an ignominious end had its members only heeded Gladstone's advice 17 months earlier. Such speculations overlook the crucial fact that in February 1894 the cabinet did not share Gladstone's interpretation of the situation. Ministers considered that the real criminal on trial was not the House of Lords but a premier who strenuously sought to avoid any increase in the naval estimates for the forthcoming year. Gladstone had already employed every artifice and exhausted every argument in an endeavour to persuade his colleagues that inflated expenditure on militaristic objectives constituted a grave threat to

European peace. The idea of dissolving Parliament was, then, universally regarded as the final throw of a desperate gambler, a foolhardy attempt to break the iron determination of an overwhelmingly hostile cabinet.

Gladstone admitted in retrospect that resignation became inevitable once the cabinet had made it abundantly clear that his services were no longer required or desired. Possibly he realized that his reputation had suffered irreparable damage as a result of an unreasoning refusal to compromise over the naval estimates. However, it would be unwise to interpret this confession as a sign that the onset of senile decay had rendered the premier both 'mad and drunk' whenever his statements were flatly contradicted and his wishes denied. If he had really been demented, Gladstone would surely have launched a personal attack on the unassuming First Lord for permitting an over-ambitious Admiralty Board to dictate terms to its civilian masters. Yet Spencer was treated with marked courtesy and consideration throughout the crisis. Instead, Harcourt was cast as the arch-villain, and Gladstone expressed his contempt and displeasure by pointedly ignoring the man's presence whenever they came face to face. Such incidents were open to misrepresentation, but there can be no doubt that they reflected Gladstone's deeply felt sense of betrayal. All the insults and indignities which he had endured with quiet fortitude since taking office now welled up inside him, explaining (though not altogether excusing) the excitability of his manner and the violence of his conduct. He could not help contrasting the apparent readiness of Harcourt to accept the Admiralty plan with the same person's furious denunciation of Spencer's more moderate proposals 12 months earlier. Nor could he forgive the Chancellor of the Exchequer for being 'so charmed' by the thought of penalizing armchair jingoes – through the introduction of graduated death duties – that the Treasury became totally incapable of performing its duty as the custodian of the public purse.[24] Gladstone's hackles rose still further when he remembered how, in February 1893, he had been forced to submit to a similar act of flagrant blackmail. On that occasion Harcourt had categorically refused to implement radical budgetary reforms as long as Irish Home Rule remained in the government's legislative programme.[25]

This aspect of the controversy suggests that the question of naval expenditure may not have been the only political reason why Gladstone hastened to submit his resignation to the Queen on 3 March. At the height of the estimates crisis he had informed Acton that 'the world of today is not the world in which I was bred and trained and have principally lived. It is a world in which I have had much difficulty in keeping on terms with, and those difficulties increase and are not confined to this matter.'[26] Gladstone certainly felt ill at ease in connection with several topics which would inevitably occupy a prominent place in the next Queen's Speech, and he made no preparations for the new session (scheduled to commence on the 12th): indeed, he consciously strove to prevent the cabinet from settling the necessary details. In fact, his removal from office only complicated an already intolerable situation. The old leader stubbornly refused to couple resignation with retirement, and his decision to remain in Parliament naturally gave rise to a suspicion that he intended to be a thorn in the flesh of erstwhile colleagues. 'I am not wholly at peace with present tendencies' in Liberal policy, Gladstone subsequently wrote. 'Never did a human being have such a timely cataract for the avoidance of scandals.'[27] It was indeed fortunate that these same medical factors prevented him from ever again appearing in the House.

Three features of the ministerial programme for 1894-5 gave Gladstone cause for anxiety, namely, Harcourt's fiscal and temperance proposals and Asquith's Welsh disestablishment scheme. He was completely taken aback by the revolutionary content of Harcourt's Budget speech of 16 April, describing the concept of a composite estate duty as 'too violent [and] by far the most Radical measure of my lifetime'. In July he composed a lengthy memorandum on the subject, which bore a remarkable similarity to one which Rosebery had previously circulated amongst his cabinet colleagues:

> It involves a great departure from the methods of political action established in this country, where reforms, and especially fiscal reforms, have always been considerate and even tender . . . For the sudden introduction of such change there is I think no precedent . . . And the severity of the blow is greatly aggravated in moral effect by the fact that it is dealt only to a handful of individuals. . . I do not yet see the ground on which it can be justly held that any one description of *property* should be more heavily burdened than others.[28]

It is important to recall that Gladstone whole-heartedly accepted the principle of graduation, especially in connection with incomes derived from urban ground rents. He had recently congratulated Harcourt on his 'advance to Liberalism' on budgetary matters, regarding excessive accumulations of wealth as 'a monster threatening to swallow up the moral life of man'.[29] But he also drew a clear distinction between the ill-gotten gains of the entrepreneur and the historic purpose of owning large tracts of land, 'for real property has more of presumptive connection with the discharge of duty than that which is ranked as personal'. In his opinion it would be a calamity if great estates were either taxed out of existence or the present proprietors forced to sell their heritage intact to a vulgar class of '*neo-ploutoi*'.[30] Perhaps Gladstone momentarily forgot that he enjoyed the status of a country gentleman chiefly because his father had bought the family social respectability after amassing a fortune. Had this document fallen into Harcourt's hands, it would surely have been denounced (as was Rosebery's) as 'a very fine old Tory doctrine ... which the Liberal party are not likely to accept'.[31]

Gladstone was equally averse to Harcourt's next great social experiment, the destruction of a free and open licensing system. He had always considered that prohibitionist legislation ought to be left to private members, who would soon appreciate the need to placate hostile interests before such a sweeping measure could be carried. But Harcourt had overridden this sensible view in the autumn of 1892, and Gladstone rather resented the fact that a local veto bill had been drawn up without any account being taken of his personal scruples.[32] He favoured the scheme proposed in the Lords on 2 March 1893 by the Bishop of Chester and the Archbishop of Canterbury, whereby municipalities would supply liquor through a limited liability company and devote the profits to useful social ends. This was the renowned Gothenburg system, a solution which Chamberlain had advocated in the 1870s despite fierce nonconformist opposition. However, Harcourt's plan contemplated – not State regulation – but suppression by popular demand. Each ward or parish could requisition a poll to determine whether or not public houses should continue to exist within its boundaries. If two-thirds of those voting supported local prohibition, all licences would be permanently withheld unless subsequent polls at three-yearly intervals determined otherwise (by simple majority). Gladstone probably feared that the exclusion of hotels and restaurants from the provisions of the local veto bill would be interpreted as a positive act of discrimination against the working classes, who obviously could not afford to use dining facilities or hold private house parties. Once all official ties had been severed, he felt at liberty to congratulate the bishop of a neighbouring diocese for acting on 'the only lines either promising or tenable'. During the autumn recess of 1894 he expressed these pent-up emotions in an open letter to Sir Henry (now Lord) Thring:

For many years I have been strongly of opinion that the principle of selling liquors for the public profit only offered the sole chance of escape from the present miserable and contemptible predicament, which is a disgrace to the country. I am friendly to local option, but it can be no more than a partial and occasional remedy. The mere limitation of numbers ... is little better than an impos- ture.[33]

This unwarranted attack upon a fundamental article of government policy took the cabinet completely by surprise. Harcourt, in particu- lar, resented an intrusion which could only embarrass the ministry, especially since the 1895 bill would contain fresh clauses allowing voters to opt for the 'imposture' of licence reduction. 'Mr G has managed to make what seems to me a fatal mess of the temperance question,' he declared. 'Does anybody believe that the real temper- ance people are going to accept a State traffic in drink *à la Gothen- burg?* '[34] But there were at least two members of the cabinet (Spencer and Marjoribanks) who thought that Harcourt was impetu- ously surging far ahead of public opinion in this matter.[35] In reality, Gladstone was merely stating (from a safe distance) a view which even the most foolhardy of ministers would never have dared to broach in the presence of an increasingly irascible Chancellor of the Exchequer.

Gladstone now placed Midlothian entirely at the disposal of the Chief Whip. But the government's stock had fallen so low since the change in leadership that the party managers dared not risk a contest in a constituency endowed with such hallowed connotations; defeat would further undermine a parliamentary majority which was steadily dwindling into single figures. So Gladstone was obliged to 'cumber the ground' indefinitely, though he made no secret of his unwillingness to remain as a 'dummy' M.P.[36] This long delay in moving the by-election writ had fatal consequences for the ministry. Midway through the session of 1895 the dummy suddenly came to life. After a private interview in March with his own bishop (St. Asalph), Gladstone informed Marjoribanks (now Lord Tweed- mouth) that he had become 'seriously uneasy' at the implications of Asquith's Welsh disestablishment bill:

Down to this time I have maintained a rigid reserve. I told the Bishop of St. Asalph that I was for the Bill in principle; that I should look at the details when it got into Committee; and that, if I found any to disapprove, I should then have to consider whether I ought to say anything about them except to the Government. I am therefore clear of all difficulties ... [But] I am bound to disapprove of harsh dealing and to conform to that spirit of mild- ness which has invariably gone with Liberal reforms from the time of Lord Grey onwards, though I am not able to say as yet ... what may or may not be my duty in the painful position which will be created if I remain.[37]

Three aspects of the Welsh disestablishment bill offended against Gladstone's refined sense of justice: the clauses relating to the secularization of cathedrals, the confiscation of graveyards, and the prevention of commutation. In fact there was a fourth bone of contention – the abolition of private patronage – but as Gladstone so clearly possessed a pecuniary interest in Hawarden Parish Church, he thought that it would be improper to contest an act 'of pure and absolute plunder'. On 7 May he cancelled his pair for the remaining Committee stages, thus bringing nearer the black hour when he would reappear at Westminster to blast away the cornerstone of government policy. In more propitious circumstances Asquith could have arranged a compromise between timid Liberal churchmen and the Welsh ultras, led by Lloyd George, but a cabinet riven by bitter and interminable disputes simply lacked the will to survive. As the two groups converged upon the doomed ministry in June, Rosebery and Harcourt tacitly agreed that resignation upon a side issue offered them the most convenient avenue of escape,[38] and so the government gently passed away on the 21st, when the opposition carried by seven votes a trivial motion censuring Campbell-Bannerman for failing to supply the army with sufficient cordite.

The later escapades of an ecclesiastically-minded landowner ought not to detract from Gladstone's achievement in presiding over one of the most successful reforming governments of the nineteenth century. A bevy of unusually talented and hard-working ministers inaugurated a series of momentous administrative changes which, taken collectively, amply compensated for an almost complete blockage in the parliamentary mechanism. Mundella quickly created a Labour Department separate from the Board of Trade, appointing a network of local trade unionist correspondents to collect essential statistical information, and arranging for the publication of an official *Labour Gazette*. At the Home Office, Asquith dramatically strengthened the factory inspectorate and initiated numerous enquiries into the conditions which prevailed in dangerous and unhealthy trades. His often overlooked departmental innovations received statutory recognition in the Factories and Workshops Act of 1895, a measure which Asquith skilfully guided through its final stages after the Rosebery ministry had fallen. A stringent code of sanitary and safety precautions now became operative; the existing regulations were extended to various classes of sweated labour – like laundries and building sites – which had consistently been ignored by previous legislators; and the Home Office was at last given sweeping powers to investigate the causes of industrial accidents.

Such bold ventures apparently owed little to a premier who tended to exercise close supervision only over Treasury and Foreign Office affairs. At the very beginning of the government's life, Acland and Rosebery could be heard complaining that Gladstone refrained from laying down any strategic guidelines and virtually left each department to fend for itself. But although Acland acquitted himself nobly by making free education a reality, he also confessed that he never spoke at cabinet meetings and was too afraid of his exalted leader to seek a personal interview.[39] Asquith felt none of these inhibitions, and so could regard Gladstone in a quite different light. Whenever he approached the busy premier with a difficult departmental problem, he was invariably given a sympathetic hearing and usually received some constructive advice. For example, when Asquith proposed in the autumn of 1892 to open Trafalgar Square to public meetings, Gladstone expedited this by dispensing with a formal cabinet and by offering judicious verbal amendments to the draft announcement. Twelve months later he whole-heartedly agreed with the Home Secretary that the government ought to procure a settlement of a protracted and catastrophic national coal strike.[40] The cabinet was summoned immediately, and Gladstone speedily commissioned Rosebery to confer at once with both masters and men. The Foreign Secretary brought peace to the coalfields within a week, vindicating the premier's decision to resort to a novel and potentially hazardous form of State intervention. In fact, Gladstone's readiness to experiment in this fashion indicates that he could claim part of the credit for fostering a climate in the government conducive to administrative and social change.

The acid test of Gladstone's continuing good faith occurred in connection with the question of excessive working hours, an issue which was intimately bound up with prevailing wage rates. It is not generally realized that Gladstone clung to the notion of local option so tenaciously that in August 1892 he had expressed a desire to frame an eight hours bill for miners and include it in the *government* programme for 1893. More cautious colleagues had promptly cancelled an enterprise which, if launched, would surely have alienated a small but vociferous section of the party. Their parliamentary majority was such that ministers dared not offend the score of Liberal M.P.s (consisting of coalowners and representatives from Northumberland and Durham) who joined deputations to Downing Street in the weeks preceding the debate on a private members' bill introduced by Sam Woods. However, Gladstone refused to be blackmailed into submission, courageously expressing the view that much fuller public discussion would soon reveal a means of overcoming regional difficulties. He therefore not only offered Woods the precious commodity of government time (a privilege not extended to other equally deserving causes), but on 3 May he also spoke – and

voted – in support of the second reading. 'The present epoch is one
a little too late ... for us to say we will adhere rigidly to the principle
of non-interference with adult labour,' he declared. 'The main
consideration is ... that a very considerable majority of the miners
in this country are in favour of this Bill.'[41]

This indiscreet juxtaposition of statements naturally invited much
hostile criticism. 'Mr Gladstone has no real sympathy with the
working classes, and a perfect hatred for all forms of Socialism,'
Chamberlain had written while the lobbyists were still active. 'His
concessions are extorted from him, and are the price paid for votes.'[42]
The Fabian Society concocted an even more cynical theory. In
November 1893 Webb and Shaw published a scathing criticism of
the ministry, calling upon the working classes to repudiate Liberalism and organize a separate trade unionist party. 'To Your Tents,
Oh Israel!' created an immediate sensation, especially those passages
which savaged each departmental chief in turn for failing to set an
example as a model employer. However, such strictures were
premature, since Gladstone's crowning moment of glory had not
yet arrived. In the previous December Harcourt and other leading
ministers had urged him to ascertain whether they should increase
the wages of government employees to the standard trade union
rate. The premier immediately complied, instructing Mundella to
conduct a searching enquiry at the infant Labour Department.[43]
When the preliminary investigation had been completed, Campbell-
Bannerman announced to the House on 6 March that ministers had
'ceased to believe in what are known as competition or starvation
wages. . . [We] should be in the first flight of employers'. After
further deliberation he and the Civil Lord of the Admiralty
(Edmund Robertson) rose from the frontbench to report that minimum weekly wages would shortly be raised from 17s. to 19s.[44]
These signal advances were not accurately and fairly reported by the
Fabians; nor did they know of Campbell-Bannerman's earnest
desire to shorten the working day without tampering with the new
wage rates. Philanthropic Liberal employers had already demonstrated that shorter hours did not necessarily curtail output or reduce
profits, a lesson in economic management which Campbell-Bannerman soon learnt when he introduced an experimental eight hour
day into the cartridge factory at Woolwich. In December he propounded a scheme to reduce the working week permanently to 48
hours.[45] Gladstone was pleasantly surprised to hear that a policy of
such tremendous import had reached so advanced a stage. In a
commendatory letter (no longer extant) he advised the Secretary for
War to act in concert with the Admiralty, and to be absolutely
certain that the elimination of seven hours per week could be

continued indefinitely. Campbell-Bannerman promptly forwarded the necessary assurances. He had, indeed, co-operated closely with Spencer, who was equally keen to implement the change as soon as circumstances permitted. 'I am most anxious that *seeing that this has to be done* it should be done in such a way and at such a time as to get for your Government the full credit,' Campbell-Bannerman wrote on 2 January 1894.[46] Having secured Gladstone's formal consent, he informed the Commons on the fifth that a 48-hour week would soon be introduced into all War Office factories. The Admiralty followed suit on 19 March.[47] Thus, the Gladstonian epoch drew to a close upon a note of high expectancy; the retiring premier had indeed helped to sow the seeds of a new Liberalism which Campbell-Bannerman and Asquith ultimately harvested after the great electoral triumph of 1906.

Appendices

APPENDIX A: *The 1885 Election and the effects of Redistribution (in England)*

The impression of sweeping Liberal victories in the counties and of serious setbacks in the boroughs is generally accurate, but requires some amplification.

(1) Although the representation of the six most populous cities (London, Birmingham, Leeds, Liverpool, Manchester and Sheffield) was increased from 36 to 91, the total number of borough seats was *reduced* from 280 to 226 (Table A).

TABLE A

	1880 Lib.	1880 Con.	1880 Total	1885 Lib.	1885 Con.	1885 Total
London	14	8	22	23	36	59
Large cities	9	5	14	12	19	32*
Other boroughs	166	78	244	74	61	135
TOTAL	189	91	280	109	116	226

* Includes 1 Irish Nationalist.

Table A demonstrates that Redistribution appreciably favoured the Conservatives, who won 54 of the 87 new seats. On the other hand, a score more Liberal than Conservative seats were extinguished in the 36 constituencies where representation was reduced. The Liberals were clearly more successful in medium sized and undivided boroughs returning two members than they were in the single member divisions of large cities.

(2) County representation increased from 170 to 231, and the Liberal share rose from 50 members (30 per cent) to 132 members (57 per cent). However, this significant advance can be attributed to the incorporation into the counties of 74 small boroughs, which in 1880 had returned 50 Liberals out of a total of 87 members.

(3) Traditional distinctions between borough and shire were becoming increasingly anachronistic; rural society was no longer based exclusively upon agriculture. The overwhelming majority of dispossessed boroughs were merged into southern county constituencies, and this transfer masked the decline in the real political importance of agriculture. New county divisions were created, not for southern agriculturalists, but for the benefit of the recently enfranchised miners, textile workers, and potters, who resided in the industrial villages and unincorporated townships of northern England. This basic geographical division can be marked by a line drawn from the Humber to the Bristol Channel, and extended northwards to exclude counties on the Welsh border (Table B).

TABLE B

| | 1880 | | 1885 | |
	Lib.	*Con.*	*Lib.*	*Con.*
27 southern counties	21	87	63	66
12 northern counties	29	33	69	33
TOTAL	50	120	132	99

Table B shows that the Liberals owed their success in the counties to the votes of the industrial working class in Yorkshire and Durham as much as to the support of agricultural labourers in East Anglia, Wiltshire and Devon. The most dramatic changes in county representation merely confirmed a trend which had been established in 1880. In that year 58 per cent of Liberal victories in the counties had been registered in the north, whereas in 1885 53 per cent of Liberal successes were still recorded in this region, notwithstanding the 'revolt' of the agricultural labourer.

APPENDIX B: *Morley's Memorandum of 30 Dec. 1890*

(copy enclosed with A. Morley to Harcourt, 30 Dec. 1890, H P). *Rough notes on Mr Gladstone's letter to Arnold Morley of 26 December 1890.*

Direct Popular Veto
Good as far as it goes. It would undoubtedly put heart into the Temperance people. They are no doubt on our side as it is. But the Irish

business will chill them, and they need to be stirred up by warm and active interest in their own question. On the other hand, S. Buxton and other London members assure me that Temperance is very ill-fitted to rouse or please *London*, and I quite believe it.

Irish Local Government
Not much use.
1. The Government profess to have it in hand.
2. Everybody would know that it is not our real policy.
3. If you cannot rally the British Liberals by Home Rule, no Irish cry at all will rally them.

Welsh Disestablishment
As Mr Gladstone says, this would provoke the Scotch Disestablishers. Also it is a complex question which would rouse in its course all the strength of the English Church. On the other hand, it must be kept well to the front. But there is no rally in it.

One Man One Vote
Excellent, of course, and indispensable, but not by itself adequate.

A Labourers' Programme
After much consideration and consultation with men like [the Oxford historian C. A.] Fyffe, A. Acland, etc., I incline to this as a sheet anchor. The Boroughs (other than Metropolitan) *want nothing* except Free Schools. Of course, they have views about the House of Lords, religious equality, etc. But there is no fight in these things, until some practical collision occurs.
　What is a programme. Labourers'?
　A. Parish Councils.
　B. Abolition of Plural Vote for Guardians.
　c. Some relaxation of restrictions on outdoor relief in the case of aged poor. (Spencer however doubted this when I made my Eighty Club speech.)
　D. *Land.* Acquisition of land by local authorities – on the lines of Chamberlain's report on Small Holdings Committee (1890). The measure promised by the Government is supposed to follow the principle of these recommendations. But Chamberlain omits *compulsion*, and he committed the curious indiscretion of voting *for* the maintenance of settlements. Therefore we can go much further than J.C. in two vital particulars.

London
Clerkenwell Programme, or portion thereof.

Free Schools
There is reason to believe that the Government Bill contains at present

no shadow of popular or parental control. Of course, I presume that we shall strongly assent the principle of popular control. But I am earnestly warned by rural experts that we must beware of tooth and nail resistance to Free Schools or we lose the labourers. He wants relief from the pence; and he is not yet educated up to the level of political maxims about popular control over public money.

APPENDIX C: *Gladstone's view of the Political Situation (July 1892)*

(Gladstone to Spencer, 13 July 1892, copy, GP. Add.MSS.44314 ff.32–4). The argument from the by-elections and the computations of our skilled and sober-minded friends at head-quarters appeared to justify the expectation of a minimum majority of 80 or 90, probably rising into three figures. With such a majority we should have been very strong and could have carried Home Rule into the House of Lords with a voice and impetus somewhat imperative. Our majority is now placed by Marjoribanks at 30, and though I do not abandon the hope of its coming near 40, yet it is not homogeneous throughout and much reduces the scale of our immediate powers, as compared with our hopes ten days ago.

I have meditated much on the proper line of policy to adopt, in the event of our coming in, which I suppose the party hardly can avoid.

One consideration to be borne in mind which I think is true, and if true I am sure is vital, is this. That if we had thrown British questions into the shade we should have had no majority at all. And supposing now we were on coming in so to arrange matters as to *appuyer* on Home Rule alone for the Session, we should run a most serious risk with the constituencies which might I think consent to a great deal of temporary sacrifice if they saw us conducting a Parliamentary movement for Home Rule so strong as to have a chance of overawing the House of Lords, but who if they saw immediate Home Rule to be out of the question would feel with some justice that we ought not to postpone all their wants with no hope of an equivalent.

All this looks like some degree of shifting of our polarity and the whole Irish department of our case will require anxious consideration. Postponement of the whole subject of Home Rule over the next Session does not seem to be possible. But if we are not strong enough to carry it at once we shall have to consider our subject mainly under two aspects.

1. What we can do for Ireland, in a situation which forbids simple postponement of the main Irish issue, and also forbids carrying it.

2. What satisfaction we can give to other wants, English, Welsh, and Scotch.

In this view I think we should study the husbanding of our strength for a decisive movement; and I do not despair of its being so husbanded if we address ourselves to those subjects of Liberal legislation which would be both *concise* and telling, in the various divisions of Great Britain.

In Ireland we might repeal Coercion: we might (this is Morley's) make some provision in favour of the evicted tenants: but a main portion of our plan must we both suppose evidently be to *Drummondize* (so to speak) the administration of Ireland. The operation of this method under the Melbourne government was wonderful ... This would require a strong hand. One of the principal subjects of thought in the coming weeks or months is how far it can be done.

Notes

ABBREVIATIONS

CBP	Campbell-Bannerman Papers
DP	Dilke Papers
EHP	Edward Hamilton Papers
GP	Gladstone Papers
GrP	Granville Papers
HP	Harcourt Papers
HGP	Herbert Gladstone Papers
JC	Chamberlain Papers
RyP	Rosebery Papers
SP	Spencer Papers
Ramm	A. Ramm (ed.), *The Political Correspondence of Mr Gladstone and Lord Granville 1876–86*, 2 vols. (Oxford, 1962).

The place of publication of books cited is London, unless otherwise stated.

I *The Radical Dilemma 1880–5*

1. Chamberlain to Dilke, 4 April 1880, J. L. Garvin, *The Life of Joseph Chamberlain*, vol. I (1932) pp. 291–2.
2. Ibid., p. 298, Chamberlain to Collings, 27 April 1880.
3. Chamberlain to Harcourt, 10 April 1880, copy, JC5/38/119.
4. Gladstone to Argyll, 12 April 1880, Duke of Argyll, *Autobiography and Memoirs*, vol. II (1906) p. 347.
5. C. H. D. Howard (ed.), *A Political Memoir 1880–92 by Joseph Chamberlain* (1953) pp. 3–4.
6. Gladstone to Spencer, 19 April 1884, copy, GP, Add. MSS. 44547 f. 58.
7. Dilke to Chamberlain, 29 June 1885, JC5/24/113. S. Gwynn and

G. M. Tuckwell, *The Life of the Rt. Hon. Sir Charles W. Dilke, Bart., M.P.*, vol. II (1917) pp. 149–50. Ramm, I pp. xxxviii–xlviii.

8. Ramm, II p. 19. Gwynn and Tuckwell, *Dilke*, I pp. 517–18. D. W. R. Bahlman (ed.), *The Diary of Sir Edward Walter Hamilton 1880–1885*, vol. II (Oxford, 1972) p. 545. Chamberlain to Dilke, 20 Jan 1883, copy, JC5/24/338.

9. Chamberlain to Gladstone, 3 Feb 1885, Howard (ed.), *A Political Memoir*, p. 112.

10. Viscount Gladstone, *After Thirty Years* (1928) pp. 177–8.

11. Gwynn and Tuckwell, *Dilke*, I p. 356.

12. John Morley, *The Life of William Ewart Gladstone*, vol. III (1903) pp. 5–6.

13. Gwynn and Tuckwell, *Dilke*, I p. 364. D. A. Hamer, *Liberal Politics in the Age of Gladstone and Rosebery* (Oxford, 1972) chap. iv. 1881 Division Lists, nos. 8 and 29.

14. Chamberlain to Morley, 24 Dec 1885, Garvin, *Chamberlain*, vol. II (1933) pp. 147–8. See also D. A. Hamer, *John Morley, Liberal Intellectual in Politics* (Oxford, 1968) chap. ix.

15. F. W. Hirst, *Early Life and Letters of John Morley*, vol. II (1927) p. 167.

16. Chamberlain to Dilke, 2 Feb 1883, Garvin, *Chamberlain*, I p. 389. Chamberlain to J. T. Bunce, 20 March 1884, copy, JC5/8/71.

17. Gwynn and Tuckwell, *Dilke*, II pp. 97–8, 110.

18. Chamberlain to Morley, 2 Feb 1885, copy, JC5/54/602. Morley to Chamberlain, 3 Feb 1885, JC5/54/605.

19. Hamer, *John Morley*, pp. 142, 179.

20. Hirst, *Early Life and Letters of John Morley*, II p. 220.

21. Labouchere to Chamberlain, 18 Sep 1883, JC5/50/14.

22. Gwynn and Tuckwell, *Dilke*, I pp. 361–2. D. A. Hamer (ed.), *The Radical Programme* [*1885*], 2nd edn. (Brighton, 1971) pp. xxxi–xxxiii.

23. Chamberlain to Dilke, 20 Jan 1883, Gwynn and Tuckwell, *Dilke*, I p. 516.

24. Morley to Chamberlain, 24 Dec 1882, JC5/54/466. E. P. Lawrence, *Henry George in the British Isles* (Michigan, 1957) pp. 31–4.

25. Chamberlain to Dilke, 31 Dec 1882, copy, JC5/24/332. Chamberlain to Morley, 26 Dec 1882, copy, JC5/54/468. Chamberlain to E. R. Russell, 22 Jan 1883, copy, JC5/62/4. Hamer (ed.), *Radical Programme*, pp. xi–xii.

26. Morley to Chamberlain, 11 Nov 1883, JC5/54/520.

27. Hirst, *Early Life and Letters of John Morley*, II pp. 176–7.

28. Gwynn and Tuckwell, *Dilke*, I pp. 509–11.

29. Chamberlain to Gladstone, 7 Feb 1885, Howard (ed.), *A Political Memoir*, p. 117.

30. Chamberlain to E. R. Russell, 6 Feb 1885, copy, JC5/62/14.
31. Chamberlain to Dilke, 6 Jan 1885, DP, Add. MSS. 43887 ff. 7–9.
32. Ramm, II pp. 326, 330–1.
33. Chamberlain to Dilke, 3 Jan, 1 and 4 Feb 1885, DP, Add. MSS. 43887 ff. 2, 36–7, 46. Dilke to Chamberlain, 31 Jan 1885, JC5/24/98. Garvin, *Chamberlain*, I p. 560.
34. Trevelyan to Chamberlain, 6 May 1885, JC5/74/10. Trevelyan to Dilke, 23 May 1885, DP, Add. MSS. 43895 f. 83. Gwynn and Tuckwell, *Dilke*, II pp. 135, 143–4.
35. Dilke to Gladstone, 24 April 1885, GP, Add. MSS. 44149 f. 343. Gwynn and Tuckwell, *Dilke*, II p. 119. A. G. Gardiner, *The Life of Sir William Harcourt*, vol. I (1923) p. 526.
36. Chamberlain to Dilke, 26 June 1885, DP, Add. MSS. 43887 f. 154. Gwynn and Tuckwell, *Dilke*, II pp. 154–7.

II *The Radical Programme 1885–6*

1. J. L. Hammond, *Gladstone and the Irish Nation* (1938) p. 702; see also chaps. xxvii, xxxiv.
2. Ibid., p. 371 n.i. Chamberlain to Dilke 27/28 June 1885, Gwynn and Tuckwell, *Dilke*, II pp. 151–2.
3. Argyll to Gladstone, 19 April 1886, GP, Add. MSS. 44106 ff. 85–6.
4. Granville to Argyll, 11 July 1885, Lord E. Fitzmaurice, *The Life of Granville George Leveson Gower, Second Earl Granville K.G. 1815–1891*, vol. II (1905) p. 450.
5. Ramm, II p. 393.
6. Bahlman, *The Diary of Sir Edward Walter Hamilton*, I p. 108. Hammond, *Gladstone and the Irish Nation*, chap. xii, pp. 353–4.
7. Gladstone to Harcourt, 19 Jan 1885, copy, GP, Add. MSS. 44547 ff. 165–6.
8. Gladstone to Dilke, 24 April 1885, Gwynn and Tuckwell, *Dilke*, II p. 120.
9. Ibid., pp. 10–11. Ramm, II pp. 14–15. Gardiner, *Harcourt*, I pp. 482–5.
10. Chamberlain to E. R. Russell, 6 Feb 1885, copy, JC5/62/14.
11. Gladstone to W. H. Gladstone, 3 Oct 1885, Morley, *Gladstone*, I p. 348.
12. Gladstone to Argyll, 12 April 1880, Argyll, *Autobiography and Memoirs*, II p. 347. Gladstone to Granville, 23 Dec 1879, Ramm, I p. 107.
13. Gwynn and Tuckwell, *Dilke*, II pp. 2, 4–5, 71. B. Holland, *The Life of Spencer Compton, Eighth Duke of Devonshire*, vol. I (1911) pp. 403–4.

14. Gladstone to J. A. Godley, 9 Feb 1884, copy, GP, Add. MSS. 44547 f. 38.
15. Gladstone to Granville, 15 Sep 1884, Ramm, II pp. 256–7.
16. Ibid., pp. 227–8, Gladstone to Granville, 16 Aug 1884.
17. Gladstone to Lord Acton, 11 Feb 1885, Morley, *Gladstone*, III pp. 172–3.
18. e.g. Gladstone at West Calder, *The Times*, 24 Oct 1890.
19. Gladstone to Granville, 19 May 1877, Ramm, I p. 40.
20. Ibid., II p. 330, Gladstone to Granville, 31 Jan 1885.
21. Ibid., I p. 40.
22. Gladstone to Hartington, 3 Sep 1885, Hartington to Gladstone, 6 Sep 1885, Holland, *Devonshire*, II pp. 78, 81.
23. Dilke to Sir H. James, [3] Sep 1885, copy, DP, Add. MSS. 43892 ff. 60–1. Chamberlain to Mundella, 25 Jan 1885, Mundella Papers. Howard (ed.), *A Political Memoir*, pp. 111–12. A. L. Thorold, *The Life of Henry Labouchere*, p. 246.
24. Garvin, *Chamberlain*, II p. 8. Chamberlain to Mundella, 9 Nov 1885, Mundella Papers. *The Times*, 6 and 7 Aug 1885.
25. Chamberlain to Dilke, 13 and 31 Oct 1885, DP, Add. MSS. 43887 ff. 186, 197–8.
26. Gladstone to Chamberlain, 8 Nov 1885, JC5/34/45. Gladstone to Hartington, 1 Dec 1885, copy, GP, Add. MSS. 44148 ff. 156–7.
27. Hannah Rosebery to Hamilton, 30 Oct 1885, EHP, Add. MSS. 48611. Chamberlain to Dilke, 24 Oct 1885, DP, Add. MSS. 43887 f. 193.
28. James to Dilke, [2] Sep 1885, DP, Add. MSS. 43892 ff. 56–9.
29. Chamberlain to Dilke, 9 Oct 1885, Garvin, *Chamberlain*, II p. 108.
30. Gladstone to Grosvenor and Grosvenor to Chamberlain, 3 Nov 1885, copies, DP, Add. MSS. 43940 ff. 71–3. Chamberlain to Morley, 5 Nov 1885, copy, JC5/54/652.
31. Ramm, II pp. 405–6.
32. Holland, *Devonshire*, II pp. 78–80.
33. Ibid., p. 73, Hartington to Goschen, 20 Sep 1885.
34. Chamberlain to Dilke, 20 Sep 1885, Garvin, *Chamberlain*, II pp. 95–6.
35. Hammond, *Gladstone and the Irish Nation*, p. 393. Holland, *Devonshire*, II p. 87.
36. Gladstone to Granville, 8 Oct 1885, Ramm, II p. 405.
37. See C. H. D. Howard, 'Joseph Chamberlain and the "Unauthorized Programme" ', *E.H.R.*, vol. LXV (1950).
38. Chamberlain to Collings, 20 Sep 1885, copy, JC5/16/107. Chamberlain to Dilke, 20 Sep 1885, DP, Add. MSS. 43887 ff. 167–8.

39. Gladstone to Hartington, 30 May 1885, Morley, *Gladstone*, III pp. 197–8.
40. Chamberlain to Harcourt, 25 Sep 1885, copy, JC5/38/142.
41. Chamberlain to Collings, 20 Sep 1885, copy, JC5/16/107.
42. Granville to Gladstone, 9 Sep 1885, Ramm, II p. 394.
43. Gladstone to Lord Lorne, 17 Sep 1885, copy, GP, Add. MSS. 44492 ff. 94–5.
44. Gladstone to Granville, 11 Sep 1885, Ramm, II p. 394. Howard (ed.), *A Political Memoir*, pp. 124–5. Holland, *Devonshire*, II p. 87.
45. Chamberlain to Dilke, 20 Sep 1885, DP, Add. MSS. 43887 ff. 167–8.
46. My italics. Gladstone to Chamberlain, 11 Sep 1885, Howard (ed.), *A Political Memoir*, p. 124.
47. Ibid., pp. 95, 127, Gladstone to Chamberlain, 22 Dec 1883, 14 Sep 1885.
48. K. O. Morgan, *Wales in British Politics 1868–1922* (Cardiff, 1963) pp. 63–4.
49. Gladstone to Hartington, 8 Sep 1885, Holland, *Devonshire*, II p. 82. Spencer to Granville, 8 Aug 1885, GrP, P.R.O. 30/29/22A. P. W. Campbell to Gladstone, 24 and 26 Sep 1885, GP, Add. MSS. 44116 ff. 23–5.
50. Gladstone to John Cowan, 22 Sep 1885, copy, GP, Add. MSS. 44548 f. 43.
51. Earl of Selborne, *Memorials, Personal and Political 1865–1895* (1898) vol. II pp. 177–87.
52. Chamberlain to Gladstone, 24 Oct 1885, GP, Add. MSS. 44126 ff. 112–13. Chamberlain to Labouchere, 20 Oct 1885, Thorold, *Labouchere*, pp. 239–40.
53. Hammond, *Gladstone and the Irish Nation*, p. 399.
54. W. S. Crawshay and F. W. Read, *The Politics of the Commons. Compiled from the election addresses, speeches, etc., of the present members*, (1886).
55. Garvin, *Chamberlain*, II p. 37. B. McGill, 'Francis Schnadhorst and Liberal Party Organization', *Journal of Modern History*, vol. XXXIV (1962) p. 26. Dilke to Chamberlain, 15 Nov 1885, JC5/24/143.
56. Gladstone to Grosvenor, 27 Nov 1885, Hammond, *Gladstone and the Irish Nation*, p. 398.
57. Hartington to Gladstone, 3 Dec 1885, GP, Add. MSS. 44148 ff. 158–60. Holland, *Devonshire*, II p. 94. Thorold, *Labouchere*, pp. 239–40.
58. A. Briggs, *History of Birmingham*, vol. II (Oxford, 1952) p. 34. Thorold, *Labouchere*, p. 243.
59. Chamberlain to Mundella, 30 Nov 1885, Mundella Papers.

60. Speeches in Lancashire, *The Times*, 12 Oct and 2 Nov 1885.
61. Rosebery to Dilke, 3 Sep 1885, DP, Add. MSS. 43876 ff. 154-5. Morley to Chamberlain, 3 Sep 1885, JC5/54/622.
62. Speech in Somerset, *The Times*, 13 Oct 1885. Bright to Gladstone, 23 Oct 1885, GP, Add. MSS. 44113 ff. 219-20.
63. Goschen to Granville, 9 and 17 Aug 1885, GrP, P.R.O. 30/29/22A.
64. Hartington to Granville, 3 Oct 1885, Holland, *Devonshire*, II pp. 73-4.
65. Ibid., p. 74, Granville to Hartington, [n.d.].
66. Chamberlain to Harcourt, 30 Sep 1885, copy, JC5/38/143.
67. Chamberlain to Morley, 3 Dec 1885, copy, JC5/54/662.
68. Chamberlain to Dilke, 21 Sep 1885, DP, Add. MSS. 43887 ff. 169-70. Gwynn and Tuckwell, *Dilke*, II p. 185.
69. John Morley, *Recollections*, vol. I (1917) p. 209.
70. Morley to Chamberlain, 13 and 16 Dec 1885, JC5/54/666, Garvin, *Chamberlain*, II p. 133.
71. Chamberlain to Morley, 29 Dec 1885, Garvin, *Chamberlain*, II pp. 149-50. Morley, *Recollections*, I pp. 205-8.
72. Mundella to Gladstone, 15 Dec 1885, GP, Add. MSS. 44258 ff. 211-14.
73. Brett to Chamberlain, 9 Dec 1885, JC5/6/3.
74. Manning to Gladstone, 25 Sep 1887, GP, Add. MSS. 44250 ff. 251-4. Dilke 'memoir', [1885], DP, Add. MSS. 43896 f. 83. Gwynn and Tuckwell, *Dilke*, II p. 191. Hamer, *John Morley*, p. 97.
75. e.g. Sep 1873 p. 285, Oct 1874 pp. 420-8, Jan 1877 p. 56.
76. Hamer (ed.), *Radical Programme*, pp. xxvi-xxvii.
77. See C. H. D. Howard, 'The Parnell Manifesto of 21 November 1885 and the Schools Question', *E.H.R.*, vol. CCXLII, (1947) pp. 44-6.
78. Dilke to Chamberlain, 30 Nov 1885, JC5/24/147. Chamberlain to Mundella, 30 Nov 1885, Mundella Papers. Gwynn and Tuckwell, *Dilke*, II p. 193.
79. *The Times*, 12 and 18 Nov 1885. Gladstone to Chamberlain, 6 Nov 1885, copy, GP, Add. MSS. 44126 ff. 118-19.
80. Selborne, *Memorials*, I pp. 357-8.
81. Gladstone to Granville, 23 May 1877 and 21 Dec 1879, Ramm, I pp. 42, 105. D. C. Lathbury (ed.), *Correspondence on Church and Religion* [by W. E. Gladstone] vol. I (1910) pp. 182-3.
82. Diary, 16 Oct 1885, EHP, Add. MSS. 48641 f. 112. Morgan, *Wales in British Politics*, p. 147.
83. Gladstone to Archdeacon B. Harrison, 24 April 1886, copy, GP, Add. MSS. 44548 f. 76. Selborne, *Memorials*, I p. 360. Lathbury (ed.), *Correspondence on Church and Religion*, I pp. 184-5, 187.

84. Lathbury (ed.), *Correspondence on Church and Religion*, I pp. 182–3, II pp. 75–125. Morley, *Gladstone*, III p. 421.
85. Diary, 20 Oct 1885, EHP, Add. MSS. 48641 f. 116.
86. G. W. E. Russell, 'Joseph Chamberlain: A Phase', *Cornhill Magazine*, Vol. XXXVII (Sep 1914) p. 315.
87. Gladstone to Chamberlain, 6 Nov 1885, Howard (ed.), *A Political Memoir*, p. 134.
88. Speech in Midlothian, *The Times*, 12 Nov 1885.
89. Speeches at Glasgow and Inverness, *The Times*, 16 and 19 Sep 1885. D. C. Savage, 'Scottish Politics, 1885–6', *Scottish Historical Review*, vol. XL, (1961) p. 124.
90. At Warrington, *The Times*, 9 Sep 1885.
91. Chamberlain to Dilke, 20 Jan 1883, copy, JC5/24/338.
92. W. H. G. Armytage, *A. J. Mundella 1825–1897. The Liberal Background to the Labour Movement* (1951) p. 217.
93. Chamberlain to Harcourt, 25 Sep 1885, copy, JC5/38/142.
94. Mundella to Chamberlain, 4 Oct 1885, JC5/55/7. Chamberlain to Collings, 27 Sep 1885, copy, JC5/16/108.
95. Howard, 'Joseph Chamberlain and the "Unauthorized Programme"', p. 487.
96. Illingworth to Bright, 21 Oct 1885, GP, Add. MSS. 44113 ff. 221–222. *The Times*, 2 Oct 1885.
97. Chamberlain to J. T. Bunce, 30 Sep 1885, Bunce to Chamberlain, 3 Oct 1885, JC5/8/79(i) and (ii). Harcourt to Chamberlain, 30 Sep and [Oct?] 1885, JC5/38/34-5. Mundella to Chamberlain, 28 Oct 1885, JC5/55/11. Grosvenor to Gladstone, 6 Oct 1885, GP, Add. MSS. 44316 f. 43.
98. Mundella to Chamberlain, 11 Oct 1885, JC5/55/8.
99. Mundella to Chamberlain, 28 Oct and 8 Nov 1885, JC5/55/11-12.
100. Lefevre to Chamberlain, 5 Nov 1885, JC5/52/6.
101. Dilke to Chamberlain, 21 and 30 Nov 1885, JC5/24/146-7.
102. At Chelsea, *The Times*, 21 Oct, 16 and 19 Nov 1885, and at Worcester, *The Times*, 5 Nov 1885.
103. Dilke to Chamberlain, 19 Nov 1885, JC5/24/145.
104. Mundella to Chamberlain, 11 and 28 Oct 1885, JC5/55/8 and 11. Morley to Chamberlain, 12 Oct 1885, JC5/54/641.
105. Chamberlain to Labouchere, 4 Dec 1885, Thorold, *Labouchere*, p. 246.
106. Chamberlain to Harcourt, 6 Dec 1885, copy, JC5/38/146.
107. Hamer (ed.), *Radical Programme*, pp. xxxv–xxxvii, 5.
108. Labouchere to Chamberlain, 3 Dec 1885, Thorold, *Labouchere*, p. 245.
109. Schnadhorst to Chamberlain, 29 June 1885 and 13 Feb 1886, JC5/63/5 and 9.

110. Chamberlain to Dilke, 9 Sep 1881, Gwynn and Tuckwell, *Dilke*, I pp. 372, 518. c.f. H. J. Hanham, *Elections and Party Management. Politics in the time of Disraeli and Gladstone* (1959) pp. 29–32.
111. At Hull, *The Times*, 6 Aug 1885.
112. James to Dilke [2] Sep 1885, DP, Add. MSS. 43892 ff. 56–9. c.f. Earl Dalhousie to Gladstone, 7 Sep 1885, GP, Add. MSS. 44492 ff. 69–78.
113. *Parl. Deb.*, 3rd Series, 25 Jan 1886, vol. CCCII, pp. 400–3.
114. F. A. Channing, *Memories of Midland Politics 1885–1910* (1918) p. 4.
115. Hamer (ed.), *Radical Programme*, pp. xix–xxii.
116. J. Collings and J. L. Green, *Life of the Right Hon. Jesse Collings* (1920) p. 120. Arnold to Gladstone, 7 Sep 1885, GP, Add. MSS. 44095 ff. 483–4. Chamberlain to Dilke, 7 Sep 1885, DP, Add. MSS. 43887 f. 162.
117. At Ipswich, Hackney and Hull, *The Times*, 15 Jan, 25 July, and 6 Aug 1885.
118. Gwynn and Tuckwell, *Dilke*, II p. 19. c.f. Hamer (ed.), *The Radical Programme*, pp. xxiv–xxv.
119. Morley to Chamberlain, 7 Jan 1883, JC5/54/474.
120. J. A. Spender, *Life, Journalism and Politics*, vol. I (1927) p. 34.
121. *Lectures on the Principles of Political Obligation* (1913) p. 227.
122. *Parl. Deb.*, 3rd Series, 27 Feb 1891, vol. CCCL, pp. 1857–8.
123. Chamberlain to Bunce, 11 June 1885, Garvin, *Chamberlain*, II p. 8.
124. Chamberlain to Dilke, 17 Oct 1885, DP, Add. MSS. 43887 f. 189.
125. Howard (ed.), *A Political Memoir*, pp. 161–3.
126. Gladstone to Hartington, 30 May 1885, Morley, *Gladstone*, III p. 198.
127. Gladstone to Chamberlain, 2 Feb 1886, copy, GP, Add. MSS. 44126 f. 139. Gwynn and Tuckwell, *Dilke*, I p. 527. Dilke 'memoir' [spring 1886], DP, Add. MSS. 43940 ff. 119–20.
128. Gwynn and Tuckwell, *Dilke*, II p. 205.
129. Lord Askwith, *Lord James of Hereford*, (1930) p. 155.
130. *The Times*, 23 Nov 1885.
131. Gladstone to Hartington, 10 Nov 1885, Holland, *Devonshire*, II p. 92. Gladstone to Granville, 5 and 12 Oct 1885, Ramm, II pp. 403, 409.
132. Spencer to Gladstone, 5 Oct 1885, GP, Add. MSS. 44312 ff. 194–5. Kimberley to Gladstone, 13 Sep 1885, GP, Add. MSS. 44228 ff. 205–10. Granville to Gladstone, 12 Oct 1885, Ramm, II p. 410.
133. *The Times*, 23 Nov 1885.
134. Argyll to Gladstone, 29 Jan 1886, Armytage, *Mundella*, p. 237.
135. Goschen to Sir Robert Morier, 10 Feb 1886, A. D. Elliot, *The Life*

of George Joachim Goschen, First Viscount Goschen 1831–1907, vol. II (1911) p. 15. Askwith, *Lord James of Hereford*, pp. 153–4.

136. Herbert Gladstone to W. H. Gladstone, 29 Jan 1886, Hawarden MSS.

137. A. Arnold to Gladstone, 23 Jan 1886, GP, Add. MSS. 44095 ff. 489–90.

138. *A Political Memoir*, p. 193.

139. *Gladstone and the Irish Nation*, p. 478.

140. Harcourt to Gladstone, 9 May 1890, GP, Add. MSS. 44202 ff. 7–8.

141. Chamberlain to Harcourt, 9 Oct 1885, copy, JC5/38/145.

142. Collings to Gladstone, 5 and 7 Feb 1886, GP, Add. MSS. 44494 ff. 185–6.

143. Gladstone to Mundella, 8 Feb 1886, Mundella Papers. C. T. D. Acland to Gladstone, 10 Feb 1886, GP, Add. MSS. 44494 ff. 204–205.

144. Gwynn and Tuckwell, *Dilke*, II p. 211.

145. Gladstone to Granville, 25 March 1886, Ramm, II p. 438.

146. Stansfeld to Gladstone, 26 March 1886, J. L. and B. Hammond, *James Stansfeld, A Victorian Champion of Sex Equality* (1932) pp. 280–1.

147. Gladstone to W. C. Borlase, 10 April 1886, copy, GP, Add. MSS. 44548 f. 68. Borlase to Gladstone, 11 April 1886, GP, Add. MSS. 44496 ff. 220–1.

148. Stansfeld to Gladstone, 17 May 1886, GP, Add. MSS. 44497 ff. 241–2.

149. Cabinet minute, 14 April 1886, GP, Add. MSS. 44647 f. 85. Stansfeld to Gladstone, 29 July 1886, GP, Add. MSS. 44498 ff. 292–3.

150. Rev W. Tuckwell, *Reminiscences of a Radical Parson* (1905) p. 64.

151. *Parl. Deb.*, 3rd Series, vol. CCCIV, pp. 415–16.

152. Howard (ed.), *A Political Memoir*, p. 167.

153. *Parl. Deb.*, 3rd Series, 23 Feb 1886, vol. CCCII, p. 1031.

154. Ibid., 23 March 1886, vol. CCCIII, p. 1724. R. W. Dale to H. Richard, 1 April 1886, Richard Papers, MSS. 5503B. Manning to Gladstone, 5 March 1886, GP, Add. MSS. 44250 ff. 238–9.

155. *Gladstone*, III p. 298.

156. 1886 Division Lists, no. 90. D. W. Crowley, 'The "Crofters' Party", 1885–1892', *Scottish Historical Review*, vol. XXXV (1956) pp. 119–20.

157. Gladstone to Harcourt, 6 Feb 1886, HP. Trevelyan to Gladstone, 11 March 1886, GP, Add. MSS. 44335 ff. 197–8. Gladstone to Trevelyan, 12 March 1886, copy, GP, Add. MSS. 44548 f. 60.

158. Gladstone to Rosebery, 28 April 1886, copy, GP, Add. MSS. 44289 ff. 32–3.

159. Gladstone to Childers, 9 March 1886, copy, GP, Add. MSS. 44548 f. 59.
160. Howard (ed.), *A Political Memoir*, pp. 190–6.
161. Gladstone to Harcourt, 12 Feb 1886, copy, GP, Add. MSS. 44200 ff. 44–5.
162. Cabinet minute, 20 March 1886, GP, Add. MSS. 44647 ff. 46–7. Gladstone to Harcourt, 16 Feb 1886, HP.
163. Chamberlain to Morley, 2 Feb 1885, copy, JC5/54/602.
164. Harcourt to Chamberlain, 30 Sep 1885, JC5/38/34. Chamberlain to Harcourt, 5 Oct 1885, copy, JC5/38/144. Holland, *Devonshire*, II p. 72.
165. Harcourt to Gladstone, 5 June 1886, GP, Add. MSS. 44200 ff. 133–5.
166. *Annual Register*, 1886, p. 147.
167. Chamberlain to Morley, 4 Sep 1885, copy, JC5/54/624.
168. Gwynn and Tuckwell, *Dilke*, II pp. 216–22.
169. Howard (ed.), *A Political Memoir*, p. 179.
170. *The Times*, 10 Nov 1885.
171. Gladstone to Chamberlain, 26 Sep 1885, Howard (ed.), *A Political Memoir*, p. 161. Gwynn and Tuckwell, *Dilke*, II p. 192.
172. Granville to Gladstone, 6 Oct 1885, Ramm, II p. 403.
173. Labouchere to Chamberlain, 31 March 1886, Thorold, *Labouchere*, pp. 289–90.

III *The Liberal Party and Irish Home Rule*

1. Hammond, *Gladstone and the Irish Nation*, p. 487.
2. Spencer to Gladstone, 21 April 1886, GP, Add. MSS. 44313 ff. 68–70.
3. Hammond, *Gladstone and the Irish Nation*, pp. 506–14, 525–30.
4. Labouchere to Chamberlain, 1 May 1886, Thorold, *Labouchere*, p. 301.
5. C. C. O'Brien, *Parnell and his Party 1880–90* (Oxford, 1957) pp. 185–6.
6. Spencer to Gladstone, 11 and 12 June 1886, GP, Add. MSS. 44313 ff. 75–81.
7. Gladstone to Spencer, 12 and 14 June 1886, copies, GP, Add. MSS. 44548 ff. 98–9.
8. *The Times*, 19 and 22 June 1886.
9. Spencer to Gladstone, 20 Aug 1886, GP, Add. MSS. 44313 ff. 92–93.
10. *Annual Register* (1886) p. 274.
11. Hamer, *John Morley*, chap. xiv. *Liberal Politics in the Age of Gladstone and Rosebery*, chaps. vi and vii.

12. Gladstone to A. Illingworth, 19 Nov 1886, copy, GP, Add. MSS. 44499 ff. 180–1.
13. Cabinet minute, *c.* 1 July 1886, GP, Add. MSS. 44647 ff. 125–6. Wolverton to Gladstone, 10 July 1886, GP, Add. MSS. 44349 ff. 210–13. Morley to Gladstone, 19 July 1886, GP, Add. MSS. 44255 ff. 101–2.
14. Harcourt to Morley, 31 Aug 1886, Gardiner, *Harcourt*, II pp. 7–9.
15. Morley to Spencer, 28 Aug 1886, SP. Morley to Harcourt, 29 Aug 1886, HP.
16. Harcourt to Gladstone, 13 Jan 1887, Gardiner, *Harcourt*, II p. 27.
17. Gladstone to Harcourt, 1 Jan 1887, M. Hurst, *Joseph Chamberlain and Liberal Reunion, The Round Table Conference of 1887* (1967) p. 158.
18. Ibid., pp. 284–5, Gladstone to Harcourt, 24 Jan 1887.
19. Diary, 25 Feb 1887, EHP, Add. MSS. 48645 f. 117.
20. Spencer to Gladstone, 27 Feb 1887, GP, Add. MSS. 44313 ff. 114–15. Morley to Spencer, 20 March, 30 July, 5 Aug 1887, SP. Morley to Harcourt, 28 July 1887, HP.
21. Gladstone to Spencer, 25 Feb 1887, SP.
22. Morley to Spencer, 29 and 30 Oct 1888, SP.
23. Gardiner, *Harcourt*, II pp. 65–6.
24. Ibid., pp. 116–18. Harcourt to Gladstone, 13 Oct 1890, GP, Add. MSS 44202 ff. 27–8.
25. Morley to Spencer, 17 Jan, 20 Feb, 8 April 1890, SP.
26. *Parl. Deb.*, 3rd Series, 19 and 20 Nov 1888, vol. CCCXXX, pp. 1570–4, 1669–74. Ibid., 2 Dec 1890, vol. CCCXLIX, pp. 404–409, 439–41. Grey to Haldane, 8 Nov 1890, Haldane Papers, MSS. 5903 ff. 173–4.
27. Gardiner, *Harcourt*, II pp. 4–5.
28. Hurst, *Joseph Chamberlain and Liberal Reunion*, pp. 209, 219.
29. Morley to Spencer, 28 May 1887, SP. Morley to Rosebery, 28 May 1887, RyP, MSS. 10045.
30. Morley to Spencer, 2 June 1887, SP. Morley to Rendel, 6 June 1887, Rendel Papers, MSS. 20570D f. 160. Gladstone to Harcourt, 5 July 1887, HP.
31. Morley to Spencer, 13 Oct 1887, SP. Morley to Harcourt, 13 Oct 1887, HP. Harcourt to Morley, 8 Oct 1887, copy, HP. Harcourt to Gladstone, 10 Oct 1887, GP, Add. MSS. 44201 ff. 181–2.
32. Morley, *Gladstone*, III p. 386.
33. Morley to Harcourt, 18 Nov 1886 and 12 Oct 1889, HP. Harcourt to Morley, 9 Jan 1889, copy, HP. Spencer to Rosebery, 24 Nov 1889, RyP, MSS. 10062. See also Morley's speeches at Edinburgh, Newtown, and Bristol, *The Times*, 3 Dec 1886, 9 Oct 1888, 30 Oct 1889.

34. Campbell-Bannerman to Bryce, 16 Dec 1886, copy, CBP, Add. MSS. 41211 f. 1.
35. *The Times*, 21 Oct 1887.
36. 1889 Division Lists, no. 70.
37. Campbell-Bannerman to Donald Crawford, 16 Nov 1889, copy, CBP, Add. MSS. 41233 ff. 46–9. Bryce to Rosebery, 10 Jan 1890, RyP. J. G. Kellas, 'The Liberal Party in Scotland 1876–1895', *Scottish Historical Review*, vol. XLIV (1965) p. 13.
38. Gladstone to Bryce, 30 Nov and 28 Dec 1886, Bryce Papers, vol. 10.
39. Schnadhorst to Gladstone, 31 May 1887, GP, Add. MSS. 44295 ff. 130–3. Holmes Ivory to Gladstone, 25 Nov 1889, GP, Add. MSS. 44505 ff. 160–2.
40. A. Morley to Gladstone, 6 and 7 Oct 1890, GP, Add. MSS. 44254 ff. 41–2.
41. *Annual Register*, 1890, p. 7. Asquith to Spencer, 12 Jan 1890, SP.
42. Childers to Gladstone, 23 Jan, 10 and 18 Oct 1889, GP, Add. MSS. 44132 ff. 280–1, 294–6, 299–300.
43. Munro-Ferguson to H. Gladstone, 18 Oct 1890, HGP, Add. MSS. 46053 ff. 137–9.
44. Diary, 7 July 1889, EHP, Add. MSS. 48651 f. 36. Marquess of Crewe, *Lord Rosebery*, vol. I (1931) pp. 339–41.
45. Harcourt to Morley, 7 and 20 April 1889, copies, HP. Harcourt to Spencer, 'Easter Sunday' 1889, SP. Morley to Harcourt, 5 April 1889, HP.
46. Gladstone to Rosebery, 7 Aug 1889, copy, GP, Add. MSS. 44289 ff. 90–1.
47. Gladstone to Rosebery, 14 Aug and 3 Oct 1889, RyP, MSS. 10023. Hammond, *Gladstone and the Irish Nation*, pp. 603–5.
48. 'The New Liberalism', *Nineteenth Century*, Vol. XXVI (Aug 1889).
49. Granville to Spencer, 22 Oct 1889, SP. Granville to Rosebery, 22 Oct 1889, RyP.
50. Rosebery to Gladstone, 8 and 11 Nov 1889, GP, Add. MSS. 44289 ff. 105–6. *The Times*, 23 Nov 1889.
51. Gladstone to Spencer, 9 Nov 1889, SP.
52. Gladstone to Rosebery, 21 Oct 1889, RyP, MSS. 10023. Rosebery to Granville, 23 Oct 1889, GrP, P.R.O. 30/29/22A.
53. Harcourt to Spencer, 25 Oct 1889, S.P. Gardiner, *Harcourt*, II p. 149.
54. Morley to Spencer, 28 Oct 1889, SP.
55. Gardiner, *Harcourt*, II p. 150.
56. Harcourt to Morley, 10 Oct 1889, copy, HP.
57. Gladstone to Harcourt, 29 Oct 1889, Gardiner, *Harcourt*, II pp.

149-50. Harcourt to Morley, 27 Oct 1889, ibid., pp. 148-9. Harcourt to Gladstone, 27 Oct 1889, GP, Add. MSS. 44201 ff. 237-8. Harcourt to Granville, 27 Oct 1889, GrP, P.R.O. 30/29/29A.

58. Spencer to Harcourt, 27 Oct 1889, H.P. Spencer to Granville, 27 Oct 1889, GrP, P.R.O. 30/29/22A.
59. Spencer to Gladstone, 8 Nov 1889, GP, Add. MSS. 44314 ff. 5-8.
60. F. S. L. Lyons, *The Fall of Parnell 1890-91* (1960) pp. 320-6. The following paragraphs are largely based on chaps. v, viii and ix.
61. Gardiner, *Harcourt*, II p. 97.
62. Morley to Gladstone, 16 Jan 1891, GP, Add. MSS. 44256 ff. 120-1.
63. Harcourt to Spencer, 29 Nov 1890, SP. Morley to Spencer, 8 Feb 1891, Lyons, *The Fall of Parnell*, p. 248.
64. Morley to Gladstone, 21 Dec 1890, GP, Add. MSS. 44256 ff. 96-8.
65. *Parl. Deb.*, 4th Series, 10, 11, 12 Feb 1892, vol. I, pp. 117, 233-6, 290-3, 328-37. Morley to Gladstone, 16 Feb 1892, GP, Add. MSS. 44256 ff. 192-4.
66. F. E. Hamer (ed.), *The Personal Papers of Lord Rendel* (1931) p. 80.
67. Spencer memorandum, 28 July 1891, SP.
68. Morley to Spencer, 28 July 1891, SP. Morley, *Recollections*, I pp. 278-9.
69. Harcourt to Lewis Harcourt, 29 July 1891, copy, HP. Harcourt to Morley, 3 Jan 1891, copy, HP.
70. Harcourt to Spencer, 24 Nov 1891, SP.
71. Morley, *Recollections*, I pp. 294-5. R. R. James, *Rosebery* (1963) p. 230. Diary, 6 Oct 1891 and 8 Jan 1892, EHP, Add. MSS. 48656 f. 101, 48657 ff. 22-3.
72. Spencer to Gladstone, 1 June 1892, GP, Add. MSS. 44314 ff. 28-30.
73. *The Times*, 20 June 1892.
74. Gladstone to H. Gladstone, n.d. [June 1892] Sir C. Mallet, *Herbert Gladstone, A Memoir* (1932) p. 141. *Annual Register*, 1892, pp. 109-10.
75. *The Times*, 1 July 1892.
76. Harcourt to Gladstone, 3 Jan 1891, GP, Add. MSS. 44202 ff. 47-9. Harcourt to Morley, 2 Nov 1890, copy, HP.
77. Harcourt to Morley, n.d. [Dec 1890] Gardiner, *Harcourt*, II p. 92.
78. *The Times*, 18 March 1891.
79. Spencer to Granville, 30 Sep 1886, GrP, P.R.O. 30/29/29A. Spencer to Gladstone, 30 Sep 1886, GP, Add. MSS. 44313 ff. 98-99. Spencer to Harcourt, 30 Sep 1886, HP.
80. Morley to Spencer, 13 Oct 1886, SP. Harcourt to Spencer, 4 Oct

1886, SP. Gladstone to Spencer, 2 Oct 1886, SP. Spencer to Granville, 11 Oct 1886, GrP, P.R.O. 30/29/29A.

81. Gladstone to Morley, 8 Dec 1886, Morley, *Gladstone*, III p. 371.

82. Harcourt to Spencer, 12 Dec 1886, SP. Harcourt to Morley, 23 Nov 1886, copy, HP.

83. Speech at Edinburgh, *The Times*, 3 Dec 1886.

84. Spencer to Gladstone, 13 Dec 1886, GP, Add. MSS. 44313 ff. 102–5.

85. *Annual Register*, 1887, pp. 40–1.

86. Morley, *Gladstone*, III p. 370. O'Brien, *Parnell and his Party*, pp. 202–6.

87. Morley to Harcourt, 25 Nov 1886, HP. Harcourt to Morley, 20 Nov and 9 Dec 1886, copies, HP.

88. Gladstone to Harcourt, 14 Nov 1890, HP.

89. Morley, *Gladstone*, III p. 379. *Recollections*, I p. 250.

90. *The Times*, 19 Oct 1887.

91. At Hawarden, Wrexham, and Weymouth, *The Times*, 21 Aug and 5 Sep 1888, 10 June 1889.

92. 'The New Liberalism', p. 190.

93. Harcourt to Morley, 8 Oct 1887, copy, HP. Rosebery to Munro-Ferguson, 3 Sep 1888, RyP, MSS. 10017.

94. Morley to Spencer, 22 Oct 1887, SP.

95. Harcourt to Spencer, 3 Nov 1887, SP. Morley to Spencer, 21 Nov 1887, SP. Diary, 10 Nov 1887, EHP, Add. MSS. 48647 f. 64.

96. Morley at Halifax, Spencer at Edinburgh, Harcourt at Portsmouth, *The Times*, 26 and 28 Oct 1887.

97. Morley to Spencer, 28 Oct 1887, SP.

98. Herschell to Spencer, 14 Oct 1888, RyP, MSS. 10062. c.f. Herschell to Spencer, 12 Sep 1888, SP.

99. Herbert Gladstone to H. W. Gladstone, 11 Oct 1888, Hawarden MSS. A. Morley to Gladstone, 31 Oct 1888, GP, Add. MSS. 44253 ff. 200–1.

100. Harcourt to Morley, 19 Oct 1888, copy, HP.

101. Morley to Harcourt, 13 Oct 1887, 26 Oct 1888, HP.

102. Spencer to Granville, 31 Dec 1888, GrP, P.R.O. 30/29/29A.

103. Gladstone to Hamilton, 21 Oct 1887, EHP, Add. MSS. 48608.

104. The following account of Conservative policy is based upon the pioneering work of L. P. Curtis, *Coercion and Conciliation in Ireland 1880–1892, A Study in Conservative Unionism* (Princeton, 1963) chaps. vii–xii, xv.

105. Speech in Midlothian, *The Times*, 22 Oct 1890.

106. *Gladstone*, III p. 412.

107. Speeches at St Helens and Swindon, *The Times*, 30 Sep and 8 Oct 1890.

108. Spencer to Granville, 26 Oct 1890, GrP, P.R.O. 30/29/29A.
109. Diary, 30 Oct 1887, EHP, Add. MSS. 48647 f. 51. H. Gladstone to Catherine Gladstone, 21 Oct 1888, HGP, Add. MSS. 46044 ff. 79–80.
110. Harcourt to Morley, 2 Jan 1891, copy, HP.
111. Dilke to Chamberlain, 5 May 1886, Gwynn and Tuckwell, *Dilke*, II p. 220.
112. Gladstone to Mundella, July 1886, Armytage, *Mundella*, p. 258.
113. Morley to Gladstone, 19 July 1886, GP, Add. MSS. 44255 ff. 101–102.
114. Labouchere to H. Gladstone, 3 Aug 1886, HGP, Add. MSS. 46016 f. 112.
115. Gladstone to Rosebery, 21 Nov 1887, RyP, MSS. 10023.
116. Hamer, *John Morley*, pp. 235–8.
117. *My Life* (1928) p. 69.
118. H. J. Massingham (ed.), *H.W.M. A selection from the writings of H. W. Massingham* (1925) p. 95.
119. S. Maccoby, *English Radicalism 1886–1914* (1953) pp. 40–5.
120. Gladstone to Manning, 22 Nov 1887, GP, Add. MSS. 44250 ff. 265–6.
121. Granville to Argyll, 23 June 1887, Fitzmaurice, *Granville*, II p. 497.
122. Speeches in London, *The Times*, 10 May and 2 July 1888.
123. *The Times*, 5 June 1887.
124. *The Formation of the Liberal Party 1857–1868* (1966) pp. 218–19.
125. *The Times*, 24 Sep 1889. Notes for speech, GP, Add. MSS. 44675 f. 34.
126. Manning to Gladstone, 27 Aug 1890, GP, Add. MSS. 44250 ff. 283–4.
127. Viscount Gladstone, *After Thirty Years*, pp. 89–92.
128. Granville to Spencer, 22 Oct 1889, SP.
129. Spencer to Granville, 25 Sep 1889, GrP, P.R.O. 30/29/29A. Morley to Harcourt, 26 Dec 1889, HP.
130. Speeches at Hawarden and Southport, *The Times*, 24 Sep and 24 Oct 1889.
131. *Parl. Deb.*, 3rd Series, 5 March 1891, vol. CCCLI, p. 269.
132. Manning to Gladstone, 5 Oct 1890, GP, Add. MSS. 44250 ff. 285–286.
133. *The Times*, 24 Oct 1890.
134. Diary, 25 March 1890, EHP, Add. MSS. 48652 ff. 94–5.
135. E. Rogers, 'The History of Trade Unionism in the Coal Mining Industry of North Wales to 1914, chap. ix, Force and Arbitration (1870–1875)', *Denbighshire Historical Society Transactions*, vol. XIX (1970) pp. 200–2.

136. H. A. Clegg, A. Fox and A. F. Thompson, *A History of British Trade Unions since 1889*, vol. I (Oxford, 1964) pp. 72–3, 305–8.
137. *Liberalism* (New York, 1964 edn.) pp. 77–8.
138. *Parl. Deb.*, 3rd Series, 28 Jan 1891, vol. CCCXLIX, pp. 1223–38. Ibid., 4th Series, 22 March 1892, vol. II, pp. 1496–1503.
139. A. Morley to Gladstone, 4 and 6 Dec 1891, GP, Add. MSS. 44254 ff. 161–3, 165–6.
140. *The Times*, 12 Dec 1891.
141. Frederick Rogers, *Labour, Life and Literature, Some Memories of Sixty Years* (1913; ed. David Rubinstein, Harvester Press Society and The Victorians Series) pp. 24–6. M. A. Hamilton, *Arthur Henderson, A Biography* (1938) pp. 15–17. Robert Smillie, *My Life for Labour* (1924) p. 263.
142. *Looking Backwards – and Forwards* (1937) pp. 83–8.
143. Morley, *Gladstone*, III p. 371.
144. Speech at Swansea, *The Times*, 5 June 1887.
145. *Annual Register*, 1890, p. 42.
146. A. Morley to Gladstone, 13 Nov 1890, GP, Add. MSS. 44254 ff. 51–3.
147. 1892 Division Lists, no. 5. Harcourt to Morley, 20 Feb 1892, copy, HP. Harcourt to Gladstone, 24 Feb 1892, GP, Add. MSS. 44202 ff. 131–2.
148. Harcourt to Spencer, 25 Oct 1889, SP.
149. Diary, 7 July 1889, EHP, Add. MSS. 48651 f. 36.
150. *Parl. Deb.*, 3rd Series, 12 May 1887, vol. CCCXIV, pp. 1783–98. 1887 Division Lists, no. 137.
151. Morley to Harcourt, 9 June 1888, HP.
152. Diary, 11 Feb 1890, EHP, Add. MSS. 48652 f. 53.
153. Herschell to Granville, 29 Oct 1889, GrP, P.R.O. 30/29/22A.
154. Harcourt to Lewis Harcourt, 6 Sep 1889, copy, HP.
155. *Parl. Deb.*, 3rd Series, 12 July 1889, vol. CCCXXXVIII, pp. 277–280.
156. Ibid., pp. 488–91.
157. Ibid., 28 Aug 1889, pp. 770–3, 776–7.
158. Gladstone to Parnell, 30 Aug 1889, Hammond, *Gladstone and the Irish Nation*, pp. 645–6.
159. O'Brien, *Parnell and his Party*, pp. 236–7.
160. 'The Irish University Question', *Contemporary Review*, vol. LVI (Oct 1889) pp. 627–8.
161. 'The Middle Class and the New Liberalism', *Nineteenth Century*, Vol. XXVI (Oct 1889) p. 718.
162. *The Times*, 23 Nov and 4 Dec 1889.
163. Morley to Buxton, 25 Nov 1889, Buxton Papers. Buxton memorandum [n.d.] copy, Buxton Papers.

164. S. Leslie, *Henry Edward Manning, His Life and Labours* (1921 edn.) p. 452.
165. Mundella to Leader, 9 Jan 1890, Mundella Papers.
166. *Parl. Deb.*, 3rd Series, 21 Feb 1890, vol. CCCXLI, pp. 910–91.
167. 1890 Division Lists, no. 7.
168. *Parl. Deb.*, 3rd Series, 29 June 1891, vol. CCCLIV, pp. 1758–64.
169. Ibid., 4th Series, 26 Feb 1892, vol. I, pp. 1419–29.
170. 'Free Schools and Public Management', *Contemporary Review*, vol. LVII (March 1890) pp. 443–50. c.f. J. R. Diggle, 'School Fees and Public Management', ibid. (April 1890).
171. *The Times*, 20 March 1890.
172. Harcourt to Morley, 29 July 1890, copy, HP. c.f. Morley to Harcourt, 7 Feb 1890, HP.
173. Morley to Gladstone, 2 June 1891, GP, Add. MSS. 44256 ff. 146–148.
174. N.L.F., *Annual Report* (1891) pp. 22–3.
175. A. W. W. Dale, *The Life of R. W. Dale of Birmingham* (1902) p. 581.
176. *Parl. Deb.*, 3rd Series, 29 June 1891, vol. CCCLIV, pp. 1765–6. 1891 Division Lists, no. 309.
177. N.L.F., *Annual Report* (1896) p. 102.
178. Gladstone to Manning, 9 and 22 Nov 1887, GP, Add. MSS. 44250 ff. 257–8, 265–6. Gladstone, 'Mr Forster and Ireland', *Nineteenth Century*, vol. XXIV (Sep 1888) p. 453.
179. Gladstone to Harcourt, 26 May 1891, HP.

IV *The Anatomy of Caucus Politics*

1. Ellis to his wife, 7 May 1886, A. T. Bassett, *The Life of the Rt. Hon. John Edward Ellis M.P.* (1914) pp. 74–7.
2. Savage, 'Scottish Politics, 1885–6', pp. 130–1. Kellas, 'The Liberal Party in Scotland', pp. 10–11.
3. *Gladstone*, III p. 324.
4. Channing, *Memories of Midland Politics*, p. 52.
5. Gwynn and Tuckwell, *Dilke*, II pp. 222–3.
6. Gladstone to Rosebery, 28 April 1886, copy, GP, Add. MSS. 44289 ff. 32–3.
7. Gladstone to Granville, 17 May, 1 June 1877, Ramm, I pp. 38–9, 43.
8. Gladstone to Morley, 14 May 1886, GP, Add. MSS. 44255 f. 90.
9. Howard (ed.), *A Political Memoir*, p. 228. P. Fraser, *Joseph Chamberlain, Radicalism and Empire, 1868–1914* (1966) pp. 100–101. Diary, 19 May 1886, EHP, Add. MSS. 48643 f. 132.
10. Cabinet minute [n.d.] GP, Add. MSS. 44647 ff. 117–18.

11. Gladstone to Catherine Gladstone, 1 July 1886, Hawarden MSS.
12. Ramm, II p. 459. c.f. P. Magnus, *Gladstone, A Biography* (1963 edn.) pp. 359–61.
13. Herbert Gladstone to Catherine Gladstone [fragment, n.d.] Hawarden MSS.
14. Schnadhorst to Kitson, 11 Aug 1886, Kitson Papers.
15. Chamberlain to Collings, 2 March 1877, Garvin, *Chamberlain*, I p. 259.
16. Mundella to Leader, June 1877, Armytage, *Mundella*, pp. 178–9.
17. Hanham, *Elections and Party Management*, pp. 149–53.
18. Illingworth to Bright, 21 Oct 1885, GP, Add. MSS. 44113 ff. 221–222.
19. Mathers to H. Gladstone, 1 May 1886, HGP, Add. MSS. 46039 ff. 56–7.
20. Kitson to H. Gladstone, 15 May 1886, A. W. Roberts, 'Leeds Liberalism and Late-Victorian Politics', *Northern History*, vol. V (1970) pp. 144–50.
21. Bright to Chamberlain, 5 June 1886, G. M. Trevelyan, *The Life of John Bright* (1913) p. 457.
22. At Nottingham, *The Times*, 19 Oct 1887.
23. Chamberlain to Morley, 6 Feb 1877, Garvin, *Chamberlain*, I p. 258.
24. Armytage, *Mundella*, p. 179. Holland, *Devonshire*, I p. 248.
25. Dilke to Chamberlain, 10 June 1885, JC5/24/110.
26. McGill, 'Francis Schnadhorst and Liberal Party Organization', pp. 24–5. Gwynn and Tuckwell, *Dilke*, II pp. 156–7.
27. Chamberlain to Harcourt, 17 Aug 1885, copy, JC5/38/139.
28. Chamberlain to Dilke, 31 Oct 1885, DP, Add. MSS. 43887 ff. 197–198. Dilke to Chamberlain, 2 Nov 1885, JC5/24/141.
29. Augustine Birrell, *Things Past Redress* (1937) p. 126.
30. A. Morley to Gladstone, 21 April 1892, GP, Add. MSS. 44254 ff. 199–201.
31. Gladstone to G. W. E. Russell, 20 Feb 1892, copy, GP, Add. MSS. 44295 ff. 61–3.
32. Box of cheques, Hawarden MSS.
33. Rosebery to A. Morley, 18 Nov 1889, copy, RyP.
34. Gladstone to Andrew Carnegie, 18 July 1887, copy, GP, Add. MSS. 44500 ff. 193–4.
35. N.L.F., *Annual Report*, (1886) p. 17.
36. Ibid. (1889) p. 12. Schnadhorst to Spencer, 7 Aug 1887, SP.
37. Tuckwell, *Reminiscences of a Radical Parson*, pp. 38–9.
38. Robert Spence Watson, *The National Liberal Federation* (1907) pp. 74–5, 86.
39. Circular, n.d. [Nov 1887] GP, Add. MSS. 44502 f. 151.

40. Wolverton to Gladstone, 5 Jan 1887 [? 1888] GP, Add. MSS. 44349 f. 224.
41. P. Thompson, *Socialists, Liberals and Labour, The Struggle for London, 1885–1914* (1967) pp. 92–3.
42. A. Morley to Gladstone, 2 Nov 1886, GP, Add. MSS. 44253 f. 40.
43. L.C.A., *Specimen Rules for Liberal Associations*, (1886).
44. *The Times*, 12 Jan 1887.
45. Morley to Watson, 14 Dec 1885 and 1 Dec 1887, Hirst, *Early Life and Letters of John Morley*, II p. 271, Spence Watson Papers.
46. Kellas, 'The Liberal Party in Scotland', pp. 2–13.
47. Rendel to A. C. Humphreys-Owen, 24, 26, 27 Nov, 6 (twice), 7, 8, 9, 10, 11, 15, 17 Dec 1886, Glansevern Collection.
48. Rendel to Humphreys-Owen, 18 Dec 1886, Glansevern Collection.
49. Essential background information may be found in Morgan, *Wales in British Politics*, chaps. ii and iii.
50. *Parl. Deb.*, 3rd Series, vol. CCCIII, pp. 351–2. Gladstone to Childers, 9 March 1886, copy, GP, Add. MSS. 44548 f. 59.
51. Richard to Gladstone, 14 June 1886, GP, Add. MSS. 44498 ff. 17–19.
52. *Welsh Members Committee Minute Book* (1886–9) 26 Aug 1886, 28 Jan 1887.
53. *The Personal Papers of Lord Rendel*, pp. 206–7.
54. Morley to Rendel, 6 Nov 1886, Rendel Papers.
55. Morley to Rendel, 30 Oct 1886, Rendel Papers. Rendel to Humphreys-Owen, 31 Oct 1886, Glansevern Collection.
56. Gladstone to Harcourt, 16 Nov 1886, Gardiner, *Harcourt*, II p. 12.
57. Schnadhorst to Spencer, 2 and 19 Nov 1886, SP. Morley to Harcourt, 22 Nov 1886, HP. Spencer to Granville, 23 Nov 1886, GrP, P.R.O. 30/29/22A.
58. Rendel to Humphreys-Owen, 7 Dec 1886, Glansevern Collection.
59. Gladstone to Mundella, 11 Dec 1886, Mundella Papers. Gladstone to Spencer, 12 Dec 1886, SP.
60. Harcourt to Gladstone, 17 Nov 1886, GP, Add. MSS. 44200 f. 183.
61. Harcourt to A. Morley, 1 Sep 1887, copy, HP.
62. Spencer to Campbell-Bannerman, 20 Oct 1887, CBP, Add. MSS. 41228 ff. 313–14.
63. Spencer to Granville, 10 Oct 1887, GrP, P.R.O. 30/29/22A.
64. Morley to Rendel, 3 Dec 1887, *The Personal Papers of Lord Rendel*, pp. 207–8.
65. *The Times*, 20 Oct 1887. Schnadhorst to Rendel, 15 Oct 1887, Rendel Papers.
66. Elgin to Rosebery, 22 July 1888, RyP. Kellas, 'The Liberal Party in Scotland', pp. 13–15.

67. J. G. Kellas, 'The Liberal Party and the Scottish Church Disestablishment Crisis', *E.H.R.*, vol. LXXIX (1964) pp. 39–40.
68. Rev G. Hutton to Gladstone, 5 May 1888, GP, Add. MSS. 44503 ff. 213–15.
69. Schnadhorst to Gladstone, 21 Sep 1891, GP, Add. MSS. 44295 ff. 249–52.
70. *The Times*, 18 Oct 1889. Harcourt to Rendel, 27 and 29 Sep 1889, Rendel Papers.
71. Spencer to Harcourt, 20 Oct 1889, HP.
72. Harcourt to Spencer, 25 Oct 1889, SP.
73. Gladstone to Rosebery, 8 and 10 Nov 1889, RyP, MSS. 10023.
74. *Reminiscences of a Radical Parson*, p. 216. For corrected dating see N.W.L.F. circular, 30 Nov 1889, Rendel Papers, MSS. 19455E f. 526.
75. N.L.F., *Annual Report* (1889) p. 129.
76. Gee to Ellis, 31 May 1890, Ellis Papers.
77. N.L.F., *Annual Report* (1890) pp. 28, 31.
78. Rendel to Humphreys-Owen, 19 June 1890, 28 May 1892, Glansevern Collection.
79. Rendel to Humphreys-Owen, 20 June 1888, Glansevern Collection.
80. Rendel to Richard, 3 Feb 1888, Richard Papers, MSS. 5505B. Richard to Rendel, 4 Feb 1888, Rendel Papers.
81. *Welsh Members Committee Minute Book*, 29 Nov 1888.
82. Ibid., 21 Feb 1889. D. A. Thomas to Ellis, 13 Feb 1889, Ellis Papers.
83. *The Personal Papers of Lord Rendel*, pp. 307–11.
84. *Welsh Members Committee Minute Book*, 7 and 17 July 1889.
85. *Parl. Deb.*, 3rd Series, 13 Aug 1890, vol. CCCXLVIII, pp. 904–6.
86. Ibid., 3 Aug 1891, vol. CCCLVI, p. 1215.
87. Ibid., 4th Series, 28 April 1892, vol. III pp. 1593–1633. 1892 Division Lists, no. 87.
88. N.L.F., *Annual Report* (1879) p. 26.
89. Hanham, *Elections and Party Management*, pp. 132–3.
90. Wolverton to Granville, 1 Oct 1886, 2 and 6 Jan 1887, GrP, P.R.O. 30/29/28A.
91. R. A. Jones to Rendel, 21 and 25 March 1889, Rendel Papers, MSS. 19452D ff. 352–3.
92. E. R. Pease, *The History of the Fabian Society* (1916) p. 112 n.1. Webb, *Wanted a Programme: An Appeal to the Liberal Party* (1888) p. 6.
93. 23 Dec 1891, HGP, Add. MSS. 46022 ff. 181–2.
94. Schnadhorst to Gladstone, 19 Jan 1892, GP, Add. MSS. 44295 f. 266.

95. N.L.F., *Annual Report* (1890) pp. 26-9. Ibid. (1891) pp. 17-18. Harcourt to A. Morley, 10 June 1890, copy, HP.
96. Thompson, *Socialists, Liberals and Labour*, p. 95, quoting Fabian Tract no. 40, (1892).
97. Wilson Papers, MSS. 2499.
98. John Cowan to Gladstone, 24 July 1886, GP, Add. MSS. 44137 ff. 441-2.
99. Fitzmaurice to Gladstone, 28 and 29 Feb, 2, 3 and 6 March 1892, GP, Add. MSS. 44514 ff. 73-8, 81-3, 89-91, 108-13.
100. Trevelyan to Caine, 27 June 1890, J. Newton, *W. S. Caine, A Biography* (1907) pp. 225-6.
101. Schnadhorst to H. Gladstone, 27 June 1892, HGP, Add. MSS. 46053 f. 216.
102. J. G. Kellas, 'The Mid-Lanark By-Election (1888) and the Scottish Labour Party (1888-1894)', *Parliamentary Affairs*, vol. XVIII (1964-5) pp. 325-6.
103. N.L.F., *Annual Report* (1891) p. 21.
104. Schnadhorst to Gladstone, 21 Sep 1891, GP, Add. MSS. 44295 ff. 249-52. Tuckwell, *Reminiscences of a Radical Parson*, p. 221.
105. A. Morley to Gladstone [n.d.] GP, Add. MSS. 44254 f. 21.
106. H. Pelling, *The Origins of the Labour Party 1880-1900*, 2nd edn. (Oxford, 1965) pp. 222-3.
107. N.L.F., *Annual Report* (1891) pp. 18-22.
108. Gladstone to Wolverton, 20 May 1886, copy, GP, Add. MSS. 44548 f. 90.
109. Mappin to Wilson, 27 May 1892, Wilson Papers, MSS. 5947.
110. A. Morley to Gladstone, 21 Dec 1891, GP, Add. MSS. 44254 ff. 167-8. c.f. McGill, 'Francis Schnadhorst and Liberal Party Organization', p. 35.
111. A. Morley to Rosebery, 7 Jan 1892, RyP.
112. W. A. Dalley, *The Life Story of W. J. Davis, J.P.* (Birmingham, 1914) pp. 52-4.
113. S. Webb to B. Potter, 23 Sep 1891, Passfield Papers.
114. *The Times*, 3 Oct 1891.
115. H. Gladstone, 'The Liberal Party and the Labour Question', *Albemarle* (Feb 1892). *After Thirty Years*, pp. 93-4. Bryce to A. Morley, 15 March 1892, HGP, Add. MSS. 46022 ff. 185-6.
116. Kellas, 'The Mid-Lanark By-Election', pp. 324-5.
117. Schnadhorst to Gladstone, 7 July 1892, GP, Add. MSS. 44295 ff. 275-8.
118. Schnadhorst to H. Gladstone, 27 June 1892, HGP, Add. MSS. 46053 f. 216.
119. *Parl. Deb.*, 4th Series, 25 March 1892, vol. II pp. 1927-8.

120. Gladstone to Wolverton, 20 May 1886, copy, GP, Add. MSS. 44548 f. 90. c.f. Mallet, *Herbert Gladstone, A Memoir*, p. 141.
121. Gladstone to Harcourt, 29 May 1886, HP.
122. Gladstone to G. W. E. Russell, 20 Feb 1892, copy, GP, Add. MSS. 44295 ff. 61–3.
123. A. Morley to Gladstone, 4 Oct 1890, 25 Feb 1892, GP, Add. MSS. 44254 ff. 39, 190–1.
124. R. Postgate, *The Life of George Lansbury* (1951) pp. 37–8.
125. My italics. Marjoribanks to Gladstone, 15 Sep 1889, GP, Add. MSS. 44332 ff. 207–8.
126. A. Morley to Gladstone, 1 Nov 1890, GP, Add. MSS. 44254 ff. 45–8.
127. 'Labour in Parliament', *Contemporary Review*, vol. LV (May 1889) p. 686.
128. Stuart, 'The London Progressives', *Contemporary Review*, vol. LXI (April 1892) p. 528.
129. *Parl. Deb.*, 3rd Series, 4 March 1889, vol. CCCXXXIII, pp. 851–885.
130. L.L.R.U., *Annual Report* (1889) pp. 2–7. Ibid. (1890) pp. 5–6.
131. Buxton to Dilke, 24 April 1890, DP, Add. MSS. 43914 ff. 238–41.
132. L.L.R.U., *Annual Report* (1892) p. 2.
133. A. M. McBriar, *Fabian Socialism and English Politics 1884–1918* (Cambridge, 1966) pp. 188–95. Gwynn and Tuckwell, *Dilke*, II p. 190.
134. *Parl. Deb.*, 3rd Series, 20 Feb 1890, vol. CCCXLI, pp. 837–8, 846.
135. Buxton to Dilke, 24 April 1890, DP, Add. MSS. 43914 ff. 238–41.
136. *Parl. Deb.*, 3rd Series, vol. CCCL, pp. 1868–9.
137. Ibid., vol. CCCLI, pp. 933–1013.
138. Ibid., p. 943.
139. Ibid., vol. CCCXXXV, pp. 889–97. 1889 Division Lists, no. 90.
140. Ibid., vol. CCCLII, pp. 1677–1718. 1891 Division Lists, nos. 160, 161.
141. Ibid., 4th Series, 11 April 1892, vol. III, pp. 1217–18.
142. Ibid., vol. IV, pp. 97–102. 1892 Division Lists, no. 104.
143. Thompson, *Socialists, Liberals and Labour*, chaps. v and vii. McBriar, *Fabian Socialism and English Politics*, chap. ix.
144. Schnadhorst to Gladstone, 10 Sep 1888, GP, Add. MSS. 44295 ff. 178–80.
145. Lansbury, *My Life*, p. 72.
146. Macdonald to Lansbury, 16 Nov [1889], Lansbury Papers, vol. I, ff. 89–90.
147. Macdonald to Lansbury, 22 Nov [1889], Lansbury Papers, vol. I, ff. 93–5.
148. N.L.F., *Annual Report* (1889) pp. 126–7.

149. Lansbury, *My Life*, pp. 72–3.
150. Webb to B. Potter, 11 and 17 Oct 1890, Passfield Papers.
151. Hudson to Kitson, 9 June 1890, Kitson Papers.
152. Webb to B. Potter, 22 Oct 1890, Passfield Papers. Morley to Harcourt, 10 Nov 1890, HP. N.L.F., *Annual Report* (1890) pp. 29–30, 49–50.
153. Webb to B. Potter, 10, 17 and 20 Sep 1891, Passfield Papers.
154. H. J. Massingham (ed.), *H.W.M.*, p. 95.
155. Schnadhorst to Gladstone, 25 Sep 1891, GP, Add. MSS. 44295 ff. 258–9.
156. Webb to B. Potter, 17 Sep 1891, Passfield Papers, N.L.F., *Annual Report* (1891) p. 96.
157. K. D. Buckley, *Trade Unionism in Aberdeen 1878 to 1900* (Edinburgh, 1955) p. 132.
158. Webb to B. Potter, 17 Oct 1890, 10 Sep 1891, Passfield Papers. Hamer, *John Morley*, pp. 249–52.
159. McBriar, *Fabian Socialism and English Politics*, p. 119.
160. 'Permeation', in *The Webbs and their Work*, ed. M. Cole (1949) p. 65.
161. Channing, *Memories of Midland Politics*, p. 117.
162. Tuckwell, *Reminiscences of a Radical Parson*, p. 221.
163. Morley to Harcourt, 26 March 1892, Gardiner, *Harcourt*, II p. 171.
164. Postgate, *The Life of George Lansbury*, p. 36.
165. R. T. Reid to Schnadhorst, 16 Sep 1891, GP, Add. MSS. 44295 ff. 253–5.
166. Birrell, *Things Past Redress*, p. 115.
167. Reid to Schnadhorst, 16 Sep 1891.
168. 'C.H.', *In Memory of James Kitson, First Baron Airedale of Gledhow* (Leeds, n.d.) p. 15.
169. Webb to B. Potter, 16 June 1890, Passfield Papers.
170. L. A. Atherley-Jones, *Looking Back, Reminiscences of a Political Career* (1925) p. 82.
171. *Parl. Deb.*, 3rd Series, 15 June 1891, vol. CCCLIV, pp. 433–4. 1891 Division Lists, no. 295.
172. 1892 Division Lists, no. 52.
173. Harcourt to Morley, 12 Sep 1891, copy, HP.
174. N.L.F., *Annual Report* (1896) p. 65.
175. A. L. Lowell, *The Government of England*, vol. I (New York, 1908) chap. xxix.
176. N.L.F., *Annual Report* (1890) p. 30. Ibid. (1891) p. 44. *The Times*, 20 March 1891.
177. Morley to Gladstone, 3 Sep 1886, GP, Add. MSS. 44255 ff. 113–114.

178. Gladstone to Spencer, 2 Oct 1886, SP. Gladstone to Granville, 8 Oct 1886, GrP, P.R.O. 30/29/29A.
179. Spencer to Gladstone, 30 Sep 1886, GP, Add. MSS. 44313 ff. 98–9.
180. Gladstone to Granville, 19 May 1877, Ramm, I p. 40.
181. Morley to Gladstone, 28 Oct 1886, GP, Add. MSS. 44255 ff. 126–127. *The Times*, 4 Nov 1886.
182. Crewe, *Rosebery*, I p. 297. Gladstone to Granville, 4 Nov 1886, GrP, P.R.O. 30/29/29A. Harcourt to A. Morley, 5 Nov 1886, copy, HP. Morley to Spencer, 8 Nov 1886, SP.
183. Morley to Gladstone, 29 Dec 1886, GP, Add. MSS. 44255 f. 163.
184. Morley to Spence Watson, 11 April 1885, Hirst, *Early Life & Letters of John Morley*, II p. 222.
185. *The Times*, 4 Nov 1886.
186. Morley to Harcourt, 5 Sep 1890, HP. Morley to Rosebery, 11 Sep 1890, RyP, MSS. 10045. Schnadhorst to Gladstone, 3 July 1890, GP, Add. MSS. 44295 ff. 229–30.
187. *Years of Endeavour 1886–1907* (1942) p. 44.
188. Humphreys-Owen to Rendel, 8 May 1890, Rendel Papers, MSS. 19464 f. 537.
189. A. Morley to Gladstone, 4 Oct 1887, 3 Nov 1888, 25 and 28 Nov 1889, GP, Add. MSS. 44253 ff. 133–5, 202–3, 277–83.
190. N.L.F., *Annual Report* (1896) p. 58.
191. Ibid., pp. 64–5. *After Thirty Years*, p. 312. H. Gladstone to Kitson, 6 May 1886, Kitson Papers.
192. Schnadhorst to Gladstone, 31 Oct 1888, GP, Add. MSS. 44295 ff. 204–5.
193. Kitson to H. Gladstone, 28 May 1888, HGP, Add. MSS. 46028 ff. 19–20. Mathers to H. Gladstone, 3 June 1888, HGP, Add. MSS. 46039 ff. 88–9.
194. Labouchere to H. Gladstone, 19 May 1888, HGP, Add. MSS. 46016 ff. 131–3. Atherley-Jones, *Looking Back*, p. 83. Beatrice Webb, *My Apprenticeship* (1926) p. 128.
195. Granville to Gladstone, 26 Nov 1886, GP, Add. MSS. 44179 ff. 197–8. Diary, 19 May 1886, EHP, Add. MSS. 48643 f. 132.
196. *Sir Robert Hudson, A Memoir* (1930) pp. 14–15.
197. Herschell to Spencer, 14 Oct 1888, RyP, MSS. 10062.
198. Harcourt to Schnadhorst, 4 Feb 1889, 9 Sep 1890, copies, HP.
199. Harcourt to Morley, 1 Aug and 8 Sep 1890, Harcourt to A. Morley, 1 Aug 1890, Harcourt to Lewis Harcourt, 9 Sep 1890, copies, HP. Morley to Harcourt, 31 July 1890, HP.
200. Lewis Harcourt to Harcourt and Morley, 8 Sep 1890, copies, HP.
201. Harcourt to Morley, 28 Sep 1888, 14 and 15 Nov 1889, copies, HP. Morley to Harcourt, 29 Oct 1888, HP.

202. Harcourt to Morley, 6 Sep 1891, copy, HP. Harcourt to Spencer, 11 Sep 1891, SP.
203. Schnadhorst to Gladstone, 24 Sep 1887, 27 Oct and 3 Nov 1888, 25 Sep 1891, GP, Add. MSS. 44295 ff. 144–7, 199–201, 207–8, 258–9.
204. Morley to Harcourt, 5 Jan 1891, HP. Harcourt to Morley, 8 Sep 1890, 6 Jan 1891, copies, HP.
205. *Fifty Years of Parliament*, vol. I (1926) p. 193.
206. H. Gladstone to Hudson, 9 and 10 March 1898, copies, HGP, Add. MSS. 46020 ff. 10, 15–16.
207. Diary, 6 Oct 1891, EHP, Add. MSS. 48656 f. 96.
208. Morley to Spencer, 7 Oct 1891, SP.
209. Gardiner, *Harcourt*, II pp. 407–8.
210. N.L.F., *Annual Report* (1893) p. 30.
211. A. Morley to Gladstone, 18 Feb 1892, GP, Add. MSS. 44254 ff. 188–9. c.f. *The Personal Papers of Lord Rendel*, pp. 198–9.
212. N.L.F., *Annual Report* (1895) pp. 111–13.
213. Ibid. (1896) pp. 109, 119.
214. Crewe, *Rosebery*, II pp. 522–3.
215. N.L.F., *Annual Report* (1898) pp. 40–2, 53–5. Hudson to H. Gladstone, 9 March 1898, HGP, Add. MSS. 46020 ff. 11–14.

V *The Polarities of Radicalism*

1. Diary, 19 Feb, 12 and 20 March 1886, EHP, Add. MSS. 48643 ff. 19, 39–40, 48.
2. *Parl. Deb.*, 3rd Series, vol. CCCIII, p. 1311.
3. Bryce to Rosebery, 22 May 1890, RyP.
4. Gladstone to Acton, 13 Jan 1887, Morley, *Gladstone*, III p. 355. Morley to Gladstone, 6 Aug 1886, GP, Add. MSS. 44255 ff. 105–6.
5. Gladstone to Granville, 19 Jan 1887, GrP, P.R.O., 30/29/29A.
6. Gladstone to Harcourt, 12 Feb 1889, HP.
7. Harcourt to Morley, 9 Jan 1890, copy, HP.
8. Morley to Rosebery, 28 May 1887, RyP, MSS. 10045.
9. Rosebery to Gladstone, 16 Feb 1888, GP, Add. MSS. 44289 ff. 76–8.
10. Morley to Gladstone, 4 March 1888, GP, Add. MSS. 44255 ff. 240–241. Morley to Harcourt, 5 March 1888, HP.
11. Spencer to Rosebery, 28 March 1888, RyP, MSS. 10062.
12. Kimberley to Ripon, 22 March 1889, Ripon Papers, Add. MSS. 43526 ff. 38–9.
13. Rosebery to Spencer, 16 Feb 1889, SP.
14. Spencer to Granville, 20 Jan 1887, GrP, P.R.O. 30/29/22A.

Spencer to Gladstone, 20 Jan 1887, GP, Add. MSS. 44313 ff. 112–113.

15. Sir Alfred E. Pease, *Elections and Recollections* (1932) p. 216.
16. Harcourt to A. Morley, 16 April 1887, 8 Jan 1889, copies, HP.
17. H. W. Lucy, *A Diary of the Salisbury Parliament 1886–1892* (1892) p. 231.
18. Harcourt to Granville, 10 Jan 1889, GrP, P.R.O. 30/29/29A.
19. *Parl. Deb.*, 3rd Series, 12 May 1887, vol. CCCXIV, pp. 1710–11.
20. DP, Add. MSS. 43941 ff. 79–80.
21. Gladstone to Labouchere, 18 Jan 1889, copy, GP, Add. MSS. 44506 ff. 21–2.
22. *Parl. Deb.*, 3rd Series, vol. CCCXXXIV, pp. 176–9.
23. Diary, 4 July 1889, EHP, Add. MSS. 48651 ff. 31–2. c.f. H. Gladstone to Granville, 19 May 1888, GrP, P.R.O. 30/29/28A.
24. Morley to Rosebery, 7 July 1889, RyP, MSS. 10045. 1889 Division Lists, nos. 174, 261.
25. Morley to Harcourt, 22 Aug 1889, HP.
26. Gardiner, *Harcourt*, II pp. 108–11.
27. Ibid., pp. 166–7. Harcourt to Gladstone, 4 Feb 1892, GP, Add. MSS. 44202 ff. 124–5.
28. Labouchere to Dilke [n.d.], copy, DP, Add. MSS. 43941 ff. 34–5.
29. Harcourt to Morley, 10 June 1888, copy, HP. Harcourt to A. Morley, 20 Sep 1890, copy, HP.
30. *Parl. Deb.*, 3rd Series, 2 May 1888, vol. CCCXXV, pp. 1128–32, 1160.
31. Lloyd George to Ellis, 27 Nov 1890, Ellis Papers. Lucy, *A Diary of the Salisbury Parliament*, pp. 329–31.
32. *Looking Back*, p. 45.
33. Speech at the National Liberal Club, *The Times*, 5 May 1892.
34. Gladstone to Herschell, 15 Aug 1892, copy, GP, Add. MSS. 44515 ff. 156–7. Morley to Harcourt, 13 Aug 1892, HP.
35. *Memories and Reflections 1852–1927*, vol. I (1928) p. 157.
36. *Recollections*, I p. 323.
37. 'The Liberal Creed', *Contemporary Review*, vol. LIV (Oct 1888) pp. 465, 474.
38. Spender, *Life, Journalism and Politics*, I p. 54.
39. Spender, *Sir Robert Hudson*, pp. 19–21, 45.
40. Harcourt to Morley, 9 Jan 1890, Gardiner, *Harcourt*, II p. 152.
41. Spender, *Sir Robert Hudson*, p. 21.
42. Webb to B. Potter, 14 March 1891, Passfield Papers.
43. Pease, *Elections and Recollections*, p. 258 n.1.
44. *An Autobiography* (1929) pp. 104–5.
45. *Recollections*, I p. 323.
46. *An Autobiography*, pp. 94–7.

47. Morley to Haldane, 12 Jan 1888, Haldane Papers, MSS. 5903 f. 71.
48. *The Times*, 13 Dec 1888.
49. Ibid., 23 Jan 1889.
50. Morley to Haldane, 29 Jan 1889, Haldane Papers, MSS. 5903 f. 77.
51. Harcourt to Morley, 27 Jan 1889, copy, HP. Morley to Harcourt, 28 Jan and 2 Feb 1889, HP.
52. *An Autobiography*, p. 97.
53. *My Apprenticeship*, p. 306.
54. 'The Eight Hours Question', *Contemporary Review*, vol. LVII (Feb 1890) p. 245.
55. *The Times*, 23 April 1889.
56. B. B. Gilbert, *The Evolution of National Insurance in Great Britain* (1966) pp. 161–88.
57. Speeches in Newcastle (2), London, and Sheffield, *The Times*, 23 April 1889, 8 Feb 1892, 20 Nov 1889, 21 Nov 1890.
58. Morley to Spencer, 12 and 18 Nov 1889, SP. Harcourt to Morley, 31 Dec 1890, copy, HP.
59. Webb to Dilke, 30 April 1890, DP, Add. MSS. 43914 ff. 244–6.
60. Gilbert, *The Evolution of National Insurance in Great Britain*, pp. 105–6.
61. Gardiner, *Harcourt*, II p. 148.
62. Schnadhorst to Gladstone, 31 July 1889, GP, Add. MSS. 44295 ff. 221–4.
63. Rosebery to Gladstone, 11 Aug 1889, Crewe, *Rosebery*, I p. 339.
64. Asquith to Buxton, 10 Nov 1889, Buxton Papers.
65. Haldane to Munro-Ferguson, 4 Nov 1889, copy, Haldane Papers, MSS. 5903 ff. 139–41. c.f. D. Sommer, *Haldane of Cloan, His Life and Times 1856–1928* (1960) pp. 76–7.
66. Asquith to Buxton, 10 Nov 1889.
67. *The Times*, 24 Oct 1889.
68. Harcourt to Morley, 10 June 1888, 1 Feb and 3 Nov 1889, copies, HP.
69. *An Autobiography*, p. 100. Haldane to Munro-Ferguson, 4 Nov 1889.
70. *Parl. Deb.*, 3rd Series, vol. CCCXLIV, pp. 307–16.
71. Ibid., 14 May 1890, pp. 922–5.
72. 1890 Division Lists, no. 84.
73. *Parl. Deb.*, 3rd Series, vol. CCCL, pp. 1853–64, 1878–85. 1891 Division Lists, no. 70.
74. *Parl. Deb.*, 4th Series, vol. IV, pp. 534–8. 1892 Division Lists, no. 118.
75. 1892 Division Lists, no. 104.
76. *Parl. Deb.*, 4th Series, 4 May 1892, vol. IV, pp. 66–78, 105, 121.
77. D. A. Reeder, 'The Politics of Urban Leaseholds in Late Victorian

England', *International Review of Social History*, vol. VI (1961) pp. 421–2.

78. *Parl. Deb.*, 3rd Series, 1 May 1889, vol. CCCXXXV, pp. 924–31, 952–8.

79. Ellis to Rendel, 6 Oct 1891, Rendel Papers, MSS. 19449D f. 86. Ellis to J. H. Lewis, 31 Oct 1891, copy, Ellis Papers.

80. *Parl. Deb.*, 3rd Series, 6 May 1890, vol. CCCXLIV, pp. 318–21.

81. *An Autobiography*, pp. 101–3.

82. Webb to Haldane, 30 April 1891, Haldane Papers, MSS. 5903 f. 178.

83. *My Apprenticeship*, p. 412.

84. *Memories and Reflections*, I pp. 114–15.

85. Diary of B. Potter, 1 Dec 1890, Passfield Papers.

86. Wallas to B. Potter, 25 Jan [1891], Passfield Papers.

87. Webb to B. Potter, 2 Feb 1891, Passfield Papers.

88. Webb to B. Potter, 3 March 1891, Passfield Papers.

89. Webb to B. Potter, 19 Oct 1891, Passfield Papers.

90. Webb to B. Potter, 31 Oct 1891, Passfield Papers. Munro-Ferguson to Rosebery, 1 Sep 1891, RyP, MSS. 10018.

91. Morley to Haldane, 28 Sep 1891, Haldane Papers, MSS. 5903 f. 190.

92. Elgin to Campbell-Bannerman, 20 Jan 1891, Campbell-Bannerman to Elgin [n.d.] copy, CBP, Add. MSS. 41214 ff. 2–8.

93. *Parl. Deb.*, 3rd Series, vol. CCCXLIX, pp. 904–16, 996–8.

94. Webb to B. Potter, 4 June 1890, 19 and 27 Jan 1891, Passfield Papers.

95. *Parl. Deb.*, 3rd Series, vol. CCCL, pp. 616–25.

96. Ibid., 26 Feb 1891, pp. 1722–30.

97. Ibid., 18 and 19 June 1891, vol. CCCLIV, pp. 803–13, 917. 1891 Division Lists, no. 299.

98. Ibid., 4th Series, vol. II, pp. 1557–67. 1892 Division Lists, no. 52.

99. 'Liberals, Nationalists and Mr Gladstone', *Transactions of the Honourable Society of Cymmrodorion* (1960) p. 46. c.f. *Wales in British Politics*, pp. 133–4.

100. Speech in Midlothian, *The Times*, 24 Oct 1890.

101. A. Morley to Gladstone, 24 Sep 1890, GP, Add. MSS. 44254 ff. 33–6. A. Morley to Harcourt, 23 March 1892, HP.

102. *Looking Backwards – and Forwards*, pp. 87–8.

103. Gladstone to Morley, 22 Aug 1892, copy, GP, Add. MSS. 44256 ff. 233–4.

104. Channing to Gladstone, 28 May 1892, GP, Add. MSS. 44514 ff. 309–10.

105. *The Times*, 12 July 1892.

106. Ibid., 1 June 1892. Buxton to Gladstone, 6 June 1892, GP, Add. MSS. 44515 ff. 16–18.
107. Morley, *Gladstone*, III p. 471.
108. Gladstone to Morley, 22 Aug 1892, copy, GP, Add. MSS. 44256 ff. 233–4.
109. *The Times*, 12 Dec 1891.
110. *Parl. Deb.*, 4th Series, 24 March 1892, vol. II, p. 1711.
111. S. Gwynn (ed.), *The Letters and Friendships of Sir Cecil Spring Rice, A Record* (1929) p. 40.
112. *The Times*, 30 July 1887.
113. Ibid., 17 Dec 1888.
114. *Life, Journalism and Politics*, I p. 43.
115. A. G. Gardiner, *John Benn and the Progressive Movement* (1925) pp. 143–4.

VI *Crisis and Recovery 1890–92*

1. Gladstone to Morley, 24 Nov 1890, Morley, *Gladstone*, III p. 437.
2. Lewis Harcourt to Ripon, 25 Nov 1890, Ripon Papers, Add. MSS. 43636 ff. 171–4.
3. Curtis, *Coercion and Conciliation in Ireland*, pp. 304–8.
4. Harcourt to Morley, 2 Nov 1890, copy, HP. A. Morley to Gladstone, 13 Nov 1890, GP, Add. MSS. 44254 ff. 51–3.
5. 'Electoral Facts of Today', *Nineteenth Century*, vol. XXVI (Dec 1889).
6. Ibid., vol. XXX (Sep 1891) 'Electoral Facts, No. III', p. 239.
7. Morley to Harcourt, 18 Dec 1890, HP.
8. Morley memorandum [17 Dec 1890] Morley, *Gladstone*, III p. 453.
9. Schnadhorst to Gladstone, 21 Dec 1890, GP, Add. MSS. 44295 ff. 233–6. A. Morley to Gladstone, 17 Dec 1890, GP, Add. MSS. 44254 ff. 61–2.
10. Harcourt to Spencer, 1 Dec 1890, SP.
11. Morley memorandum, 21 Dec 1890, GP, Add. MSS. 44256 ff. 96–98.
12. Harcourt to Morley, 30 Dec 1890, copy, HP. Gardiner, *Harcourt*, II pp. 91–3.
13. Gladstone to Morley, 23 Dec 1890, Morley, *Gladstone*, III p. 457.
14. Morley to Harcourt, 26 Dec 1890, Gardiner, *Harcourt*, II p. 92.
15. Harcourt to Morley, 30 Dec 1890, copy, HP.
16. Gladstone to Harcourt, 2 Jan 1891, HP. Morley to Harcourt, 5 Jan 1891, HP.
17. *The Fall of Parnell*, p. 220.
18. Morley, *Gladstone*, III p. 457.

19. Gladstone to Ripon, 29 Dec 1890, L. Wolf, *Life of the First Marquess of Ripon*, vol. II (1921) p. 198.
20. Ibid., pp. 199–200, Ripon to Gladstone, 30 Dec 1890.
21. Harcourt to Morley, 30 Dec 1890, copy, HP.
22. Harcourt to Campbell-Bannerman, 8 April 1890, CBP, Add. MSS. 41219 ff. 13–14.
23. Campbell to Gladstone, 3 Oct 1890, GP, Add. MSS. 44116 ff. 180–181. Rosebery to Gladstone, 16 Oct 1890, GP, Add. MSS. 44289 ff. 127–8. Kellas, 'The Liberal Party and the Scottish Church Disestablishment Crisis', pp. 37, 41–3.
24. Morley to Gladstone, 22 Nov 1890, GP, Add. MSS. 44256 ff. 82–3. Morley, *Recollections*, I pp. 256–7. Gardiner, *Harcourt*, II pp. 83–4.
25. Morley to Spencer, 6 Sep 1891, SP. Hamer, *John Morley*, pp. 244–5, 271–2.
26. Harcourt to Morley [1888] Gardiner, *Harcourt*, II p. 105.
27. Ibid., pp. 103–7.
28. *Parl. Deb.*, 3rd Series, vol. CCCLII, pp. 1657–62, 1664–6.
29. Gladstone to Harcourt, 2 Jan 1891, HP.
30. Harcourt to Morley, 3 Jan 1891, copy, HP.
31. *The Times*, 27 June 1892, c.f. *The Personal Papers of Lord Rendel*, pp. 54, 79.
32. N. Blewett, 'The Franchise in the United Kingdom 1885–1918', *Past and Present*, vol. XXXII (1965). Thompson, *Socialists, Liberals and Labour*, pp. 68–72. P. W. Campbell to Gladstone, 14 Jan 1889, CBP, Add. MSS. 41215 ff. 35–6.
33. Lambert to Gladstone, 27 Oct 1886, 27 Oct 1888, GP, Add. MSS. 44235 ff. 221–2, 227–8.
34. Ibid., Blewett, 'The Franchise in the United Kingdom', pp. 43–50.
35. Harcourt to Morley, 30 Dec 1890, copy, HP. Harcourt to Gladstone, 1 Jan 1891, GP, Add. MSS. 56449. Morley to Gladstone, 31 Dec 1890, GP, Add. MSS. 44256 ff. 103–4.
36. Gladstone to Harcourt, 2 Jan 1891, HP.
37. Harcourt to Gladstone, 3 Jan 1891, GP, Add. MSS. 44202 ff. 47–9. Harcourt to Morley, 1 Jan 1891, copy, HP. Morley to Gladstone, 2 Jan 1891, GP, Add. MSS. 44256 f. 107.
38. Gladstone to Harcourt, 8 Jan 1891, HP.
39. Morley to Harcourt, 9 and 10 Jan 1891, HP. Harcourt to Morley, 8 Jan 1891, copy, HP.
40. Harcourt to Morley, 10 Jan 1891, copy, HP.
41. Gardiner, *Harcourt*, II pp. 94–9.
42. Storey to Gladstone, 22 Jan 1891, GP, Add. MSS. 44512 ff. 52–3.
43. *The Times*, 8, 13, 14, 15 and 20 Jan 1891.
44. Stansfeld to A. Morley, 1 Jan 1891, enclosed with A. Morley to Gladstone, 5 Jan 1891, GP, Add. MSS. 44254 ff. 71–4. Stansfeld

to Gladstone, 8 Jan 1891, GP, Add. MSS. 44512 ff. 20-1. Fowler to Gladstone, 23 Jan 1891, GP, Add. MSS. 44512 ff. 54-5.

45. *Parl. Deb.*, 3rd Series, vol. CCCLI, pp. 65-71.

46. *The Times*, 3 Oct 1891.

47. Morley, *Recollections*, I p. 294.

48. Gladstone and Morley to Harcourt, 2 Feb 1892, HP. A. Morley to Harcourt, 4 Feb 1892, HP.

49. *Memories of Midland Politics*, p. 113.

50. Gardner to Rosebery, 1 March 1888, RyP.

51. Tuckwell, *Reminiscences of a Radical Parson*, p. 202.

52. P. Horn, *Joseph Arch* (Kineton, 1971) chap. xi.

53. *Memories of Midland Politics*, pp. 62-4.

54. *Parl. Deb.*, 3rd Series, 27 Aug 1887, vol. CCCXX, pp. 185-9. Channing to Gladstone, 10 Sep 1887, GP, Add. MSS. 44501 ff. 272-3.

55. *Parl. Deb.*, 3rd Series, 11 Aug 1887, vol. CCCXIX, pp. 138-48.

56. Tuckwell, *Reminiscences of a Radical Parson*, pp. 148-50.

57. 'Memoir' [n.d.], DP, Add. MSS. 43941 ff. 75-7.

58. J. P. D. Dunbabin, 'The Politics of the Establishment of County Councils', *Historical Journal*, vol. VI (1963) pp. 234-5, 238-9.

59. *Parl. Deb.*, 3rd Series, 12 Aug 1887, vol. CCCXIX, pp. 312-13.

60. Fowler to Dilke, 20 Jan 1888, DP, Add. MSS. 43914 ff. 43-4. 'Memoir' [n.d.] DP, Add. MSS. 43941 f. 80.

61. Stansfeld to Gladstone, 26 Oct 1888, GP, Add. MSS. 44505 ff. 57-60.

62. *The Times*, 24 Oct 1889.

63. Ibid., 19 Nov 1889. A. Morley to Gladstone, 25 and 28 Nov 1889, GP, Add. MSS. 44253 ff. 277-83.

64. *The Times*, 3 Dec 1889. c.f. Speech at Lowestoft, ibid., 19 May 1890.

65. *Parl. Deb.*, 3rd Series, 20 Feb 1890, vol. CCCXLI, pp. 770-1.

66. Speeches at Stratford and Derby, *The Times*, 13 Nov 1889 and 14 Aug 1890.

67. *Parl. Deb.*, 3rd Series, vol. CCCLII, pp. 543-4.

68. Schnadhorst to Gladstone, 17 March 1891, GP, Add. MSS. 44295 ff. 239-40.

69. Logan to Spencer, 15 May 1891, SP.

70. A. Morley to Gladstone, 25 July 1891, GP, Add. MSS. 44254 ff. 130-1.

71. *Parl. Deb.*, 3rd Series, vol. CCCLII, pp. 554-6.

72. *Reminiscences of a Radical Parson*, pp. 218-20, 254-7. c.f. *The Speaker*, 6 June 1891, pp. 659-60.

73. N.L.F., *Annual Report* (1891) pp. 23-5.

74. Ibid., pp. 90-2.

75. *The Times*, 27 and 29 Oct, 10 Nov 1891.
76. N.L.F., *The Condition of the Rural Population, A verbatim report of the proceedings of the Rural Reform Conference* (1891) pp. 5–9.
77. Harcourt to Schnadhorst, 13 Dec 1891, copy, HP.
78. *Reminiscences of a Radical Parson*, pp. 221–2. *Memories of Midland Politics*, p. 127.
79. Diary, 10 and 11 Dec 1891, EHP, Add. MSS. 44656 ff. 167, 169.
80. Gladstone to Harcourt, 26 Feb 1892, HP.
81. *Parl. Deb.*, 4th Series, vol. II, pp. 1710–14, 1751. Vol. III, pp. 631–2, 653, 1206.
82. Diary, 18 Oct 1891, EHP, Add. MSS. 48656 ff. 110–11.
83. A. Morley to Gladstone, 15 and 21 July 1892, GP, Add. MSS. 44254 ff. 218, 128–9. Schnadhorst to Gladstone, 7 July 1892, GP, Add. MSS. 44295 ff. 275–8. Schnadhorst to H. Gladstone, 18 July 1892, HGP, Add. MSS. 46053 ff. 220–1.
84. A. Morley to Gladstone, 2 Sep 1887, GP, Add. MSS. 44253 ff. 126–8. Wolverton to Granville, 4 Sep 1887, GrP, P.R.O. 30/29/28A.
85. Curtis, *Coercion and Conciliation in Ireland*, p. 302.
86. Morley to Gladstone, 18 Nov 1891, GP, Add. MSS. 44256 ff. 176–177.
87. Curtis, *Coercion and Conciliation in Ireland*, pp. 324–7, 395–6. Lyons, *The Fall of Parnell*, pp. 171–4, 263.
88. James, *Rosebery*, pp. 237–40.
89. H. G. Hutchinson (ed.), *Private Diaries of the Rt. Hon. Sir Algernon West, G.C.B.* (1922) p. 40. Spencer to Gladstone, 25 July 1892, GP, Add. MSS. 44314 ff. 38–40.
90. Morley to Harcourt, 17 July 1892, HP. Morley to Spencer, 19 July 1892, SP.
91. Morley, *Gladstone*, III pp. 493–4.
92. Morley to Harcourt, 14 July 1892, HP. Kimberley to Ripon, 19 July 1892, Wolf, *Ripon*, II p. 200.
93. Gladstone to Ripon, 23 July 1892, Ripon Papers, Add. MSS. 43515 ff. 68–9.
94. Labouchere to Harcourt, 18 July 1892, HP. Labouchere to H. Gladstone, 27 Aug 1892, HGP, Add. MSS. 46016 ff. 156–9.
95. Harcourt to Gladstone, 19 July 1892, GP, Add. MSS. 44202 ff. 168–73. *Parl. Deb.*, 4th Series, 9 Aug 1892, vol. VII, pp. 238–245.
96. Lewis Harcourt journal, 28 July 1892, HP. F. S. L. Lyons, *John Dillon, A Biography* (1968) pp. 155–6.
97. Morley to Harcourt, 14 July 1892, HP. Harcourt to Morley, 15 July 1892, copy, HP.
98. Harcourt to Gladstone, 19 July 1892, GP, Add. MSS. 44202

ff. 168–73. Morley to Gladstone, 19 July 1892, GP, Add. MSS. 44256 ff. 217–18.

99. Harcourt to Gladstone, 16 July 1892, GP, Add. MSS. 44202 ff. 163–5.
100. Harcourt to Gladstone, 25 July 1892, GP, Add. MSS. 44202 f. 178.
101. Gladstone to Harcourt, 14 July 1892, copy, GP, Add. MSS. 44202 ff. 157–8.
102. Harcourt to Gladstone, 15 July 1892, GP, Add. MSS. 44202 ff. 159–62. Harcourt to Spencer, 13 July 1892, SP. Harcourt to Morley, 13 July 1892, copy, HP.
103. Gladstone to Harcourt, 14 July 1892.
104. Gladstone to Harcourt, 18 July 1892, copy, GP, Add. MSS. 44202 ff. 166–7.
105. Gladstone to Harcourt, 22 July 1892, copy, GP, Add. MSS. 44202 ff. 176–7.
106. Gladstone to Harcourt, 18 July 1892.
107. Harcourt to Gladstone, 19 July 1892, GP, Add. MSS. 44202 ff. 168–73.
108. Harcourt to Gladstone, 3 Aug 1892, GP, Add. MSS. 44202 ff. 200–2.
109. *Parl. Deb.*, 4th Series, 9 Aug 1892, vol. VII, pp. 213–14.

VII *Gladstonian Twilight*

1. Gladstone to Spencer, 2 Aug 1892, SP. Spencer memorandum, [2] Aug 1892, SP.
2. Cabinet minute, 19 Aug 1892, GP, Add. MSS. 44648 f. 2.
3. *Personal Papers of Lord Rendel*, pp. 311–12. Trevelyan to Gladstone, 29 Oct 1892, GP, Add. MSS. 44335 f. 240.
4. Gardner to Gladstone, 14 Dec 1892 and 25 Jan 1893, GP, Add. MSS. 44516 ff. 316–17, 44517 ff. 28–9.
5. Marjoribanks to Gladstone, 3 Sep 1892, GP, Add. MSS. 44332 ff. 227–9. Gladstone to Marjoribanks, 6 Sep 1892, copy, GP, Add. MSS. 44332 ff. 234–5. Gladstone to Balfour, 18 July 1892, copy, GP, Add. MSS. 44515 ff. 110–11.
6. Ellis to Rendel, 25 Aug 1892, Rendel Papers, MSS. 19449D. f. 88.
7. Gladstone to Rendel, 3 Sep 1892, copy, GP, Add. MSS. 44549 f. 6.
8. J. Brooke and M. Sorensen (eds.), *The Prime Ministers' Papers: W. E. Gladstone, 1: Autobiographica* (1971) p. 135.
9. P. Stansky, *Ambitions and Strategies, The struggle for the leadership of the Liberal Party in the 1890s* (Oxford, 1964) p. 16.
10. Harcourt to Gladstone, 30 Oct 1892, GP, Add. MSS. 44202 ff. 274–5.

11. Gladstone to Acland, 23 Oct 1892, copy, GP, Add. MSS. 44549 f. 30. Morgan, *Wales in British Politics*, pp. 122-6.

12. Cabinet minutes, GP, Add. MSS. 44648 ff. 12-13, 16-18, 28, 35-6, 76, 83-4. Acland to Gladstone, 25 Jan 1893, GP, Add. MSS. 44517 f. 25. Fowler to Gladstone, 23 Nov 1892, GP, Add. MSS. 44516 f. 275. Asquith to Gladstone, 30 Nov 1892, GP, Add. MSS. 44516 f. 282.

13. Gladstone to Morley, 15 Nov 1892, copy, GP, Add. MSS. 44549 f. 40. Gladstone memorandum, 11 Nov 1892, copy, GP, Add. MSS. 44257 ff. 29-30. *Private Diaries of Sir Algernon West*, pp. 71-86.

14. Gladstone to Harcourt, 16 and 21 Jan 1893, copies, GP, Add. MSS. 44203 ff. 13-14, 44549 f. 58. Harcourt to Gladstone, 18 Jan 1893, GP. Add. MSS. 44203 ff. 15-16.

15. Gladstone to Harcourt, 16 Feb 1893, copy, GP, Add. MSS. 44549 f. 64. Gardiner, *Harcourt*, II pp. 220-2.

16. *Recollections*, I pp. 359-60.

17. Gladstone to Morley, 14 May 1893, copy, GP. Add. MSS. 44549 f. 87. Morley to Gladstone, 17 May 1893, GP, Add. MSS. 44257 ff. 107-8. *Private Diaries of Sir Algernon West*, pp. 158-60, 173, 191.

18. Gladstone to Morley, 17 Oct 1892, copy, GP, Add. MSS. 44549 f. 26.

19. Cabinet minute, GP, Add. MSS. 44648 f. 118.

20. Bahlman, *Diary of Sir Edward Walter Hamilton*, I p. xlvi.

21. Morley, *Gladstone*, III p. 512.

22. Gladstone to Marjoribanks, 4 Feb 1894, *Private Diaries of Sir Algernon West*, pp. 269-70.

23. *Autobiographica*, p. 116.

24. Ibid., pp. 118-19.

25. Harcourt to Gladstone, 15 Feb 1893, GP, Add. MSS. 44203 ff. 49-52.

26. Gladstone to Acton, 9 Feb 1894, copy, GP, Add. MSS. 44549 f. 185.

27. Gladstone to Spencer, 3 May 1895, SP.

28. *Autobiographica*, pp. 165-7.

29. *Private Diaries of Sir Algernon West*, p. 84. Gladstone to A. Carnegie, 19 Sep 1892, copy, GP, Add. MSS. 44549 f. 12.

30. *Autobiographica*, pp. 165-7.

31. Harcourt to Rosebery, 4 April 1894, Gardiner, *Harcourt*, II p. 285.

32. *Private Diaries of Sir Algernon West*, pp. 149-50.

33. *The Times*, 19 Sep 1894.

34. Harcourt to Morley, 24 Sep 1894, Gardiner, *Harcourt*, II p. 307.

35. Marjoribanks to Gladstone, 29 Nov 1894, GP, Add. MSS. 44332

ff. 286–7. Spencer to Gladstone, 4 May 1895, GP, Add. MSS. 44314 f. 122.

36. Gladstone to Marjoribanks, 17 Oct 1894 and 11 Feb 1895, copies, GP, Add. MSS. 44332 ff. 274–5, 297.

37. Gladstone to Marjoribanks, 30 April 1895, copy, GP, Add. MSS. 44332 ff. 311–14.

38. Ibid. Stansky, *Ambitions and Strategies*, pp. 164–8. Morgan, *Wales in British Politics*, pp. 149–56.

39. *Private Diaries of Sir Algernon West*, p. 144. Armytage, *Mundella*, p. 289. Stansky, *Ambitions and Strategies*, p. 15.

40. Gladstone to Asquith, 14 Oct 1892 and 10 Nov 1893, copies, GP, Add. MSS. 44549 ff. 25, 154.

41. *Parl. Deb.*, 4th Series, vol. XI, pp. 1857–65.

42. Gwynn and Tuckwell, *Dilke*, II p. 289.

43. Harcourt to Gladstone, 16 Dec 1892, GP, Add. MSS. 44202 ff. 296–7. Gladstone to Harcourt, 16 Dec 1892, copy, GP, Add. MSS. 44549 f. 52. Cabinet minute, 17 Dec 1892, GP, Add. MSS. 44648 f. 53.

44. *Parl. Deb.*, 4th Series, 6 March, 27 June, 29 Aug 1893, vols. IX, pp. 1127–34. XIV, pp. 202–4, XVI, pp. 1367–75.

45. J. A. Spender, *Life of Sir Henry Campbell-Bannerman*, vol. I (1932) pp. 142–3. Campbell-Bannerman memorandum, 1 Jan 1894, CBP, Add. MSS. 41233 ff. 176–9. J. Harris, *Unemployment and Politics, A Study in English Social Policy 1886–1914* (Oxford, 1972) pp. 67–70.

46. Campbell-Bannerman to Gladstone, 2 Jan 1894, GP, Add. MSS. 44117 ff. 108–9. Gladstone to Spencer, 9 and 12 Dec 1893, SP. Spencer to Gladstone, 11 Dec 1893, GP, Add. MSS. 44314 f. 97. Spencer to Campbell-Bannerman, 4 Jan and 2 March 1894, CBP, Add. MSS. 41229 ff. 2–3, 10.

47. *Parl. Deb.*, 4th Series, vols. XX, pp. 924–5. XXII, pp. 624–7.

Unpublished Sources

James Bryce Papers, Bodleian Library, Oxford.
Sydney Buxton Papers, Newtimber Place, Hassocks, Sussex.
Sir Henry Campbell-Bannerman Papers, British Museum.
Joseph Chamberlain Papers, University of Birmingham Library, Birmingham.
Sir Charles Dilke Papers, British Museum.
Thomas E. Ellis Papers, National Library of Wales, Aberystwyth.
Herbert Gladstone Papers, British Museum.
W. E. Gladstone Papers, British Museum.
Glansevern Collection (papers of A. C. Humphreys-Owen), National Library of Wales, Aberystwyth.
Earl Granville Papers, Public Record Office.
R. B. Haldane Papers, National Library of Scotland, Edinburgh.
Sir Edward Hamilton Papers, British Museum.
Sir William Harcourt Papers, Stanton Harcourt, Oxfordshire.
Hawarden MSS. (Glynne–Gladstone Papers), Flintshire Record Office, Hawarden.
Sir James Kitson Papers, Sheepscar Library, Leeds.
George Lansbury Papers, British Library of Political and Economic Science.
A. J. Mundella Papers, University of Sheffield Library, Sheffield.
Passfield Papers, British Library of Political and Economic Science.
Stuart Rendel Papers, National Library of Wales, Aberystwyth.
Henry Richard Papers, National Library of Wales, Aberystwyth.
Marquess of Ripon Papers, British Museum.
Earl of Rosebery Papers, National Library of Scotland, Edinburgh.
Earl Spencer Papers, Althorp, Northamptonshire.
Robert Spence Watson Papers, House of Lords Record Office.
H. J. Wilson Papers, Central Library, Sheffield.
House of Commons Division Lists, House of Lords Record Office.
Welsh Members Committee Minute Book (1886–9), Central Library, Newport.

Index

Aberdeen Trades Council, 147–8

Abraham, William ('Mabon'), 130, 137, 151

Acland, A. H. D., and progressive Liberal group, 175–9, 188, 189, 192; and Liberal Publication Department, 178–9, 192; and free education, 101–2, 254; and land reform, 186, 188–90, 192, 259; and local government reform, 178, 186, 190, 225; joins 1892 cabinet, 176; ministerial role, 242, 243, 254

Acland, C. T. D., 46

Adam, W. P., 111

Adams, Francis, 29

Agricultural labourers, 36, 104, 218–220, 223, 226–9, 260

Allotments and small holdings, 20, 35–7, 43–5, 47, 220–30 *passim*, 259; 1887 Act, 220, 221–2; 1890 Act, 222; 1892 Act, 143, 187, 230

Allotments and Small Holdings Association (formerly Allotments Extension Association), 38, 44–5, 221, 229

Arbitration and Conciliation, Boards of, 243, 247

Arch, Joseph, 37–8, 219–20

Argyll, Duke of, 13, 44, 91

Arnold, Arthur, 38

Articles Club, 179, 185, 186

Asquith, H. H., and progressive Liberal group, 175–9, 185, 186, 188, 190–2; distrusts Fabians, 190–2; demands Home Rule details, 66; and the Newcastle programme, 161; and land reform, 188, 190; joins 1892 cabinet, 176; ministerial role, 242, 243, 247, 253–4

Atherley-Jones, L. A., 68, 81, 150, 175, 184

Balfour, A. J., 61, 62, 80–6 *passim*, 100–1

Balfour, J. B., 242

Ball, George, 229

Barclay, J. W., 37

Benn, John, 198–9

Billany, N. B., 18

Birmingham Daily Post, 34

Birrell, Augustine, 149, 176

Bitter Cry of Outcast London, The, 7, 8

Blackley, Canon William, 182

Bolton, T. H., 142, 144

Bompas, Judge Henry, 95

Booth, Charles, 182, 193

Borlase, W. C., 46

Bradlaugh, Charles, 127, 174–5

Brett, Reginald, 28

Bright, Jacob, 195

Bright, John, 25–6, 111

Broadhurst, Henry, 45–6, 151, 193

Bryce, James, 115, 166–7, 244

Buchanan, T. R., 87
Budget, of 1885, 10; of 1886, 50; of 1894, 249, 250–1
Burns, John, 135, 136–7
Burt, Thomas, 137, 151, 195
Buxton, Sydney, and progressive Liberal group, 175–6, 179, 185; and the Fabians, 143, 193, 194; and the London programme, 140, 141, 143, 259; and denominational education, 101, 102; and factory legislation, 149, 193–5, 196–7

Caine, W. S., 51, 87, 112, 116, 132, 202
Cameron, Dr Charles, 118, 207
Cameron, R., 133
Campbell, P. W., 207
Campbell-Bannerman, Sir Henry, 65, 100, 118, 192, 244, 253, 255–6
Carrington, Lord, 230
Causton, R. K., 116, 139, 140
Chamberlain, Joseph, joins 1880 cabinet, 1; his programme thwarted 2–3, 4; lacks parliamentary support of Radicals, 3–5, 6, 9–10; awareness of social problem, 6, 7–8, 37–9; campaigns to oust Whigs, 8–9, 15–20 *passim*, 27, 111–12; remains loyal to Gladstone in 1885, 12–13, 17, 19, 20–1, 22–3; and 'unauthorized' election campaign, 20, 23–41, 47, 50, 52, 110–11, 112; Irish policy to Dec 1885, 10, 13, 40–1, 49; breach with Morley, 4, 27, 165; joins 1886 cabinet, 42; his programme again thwarted, 42–52 *passim*; attacks Gladstone's Irish policy, 42, 49, 51–2, 53, 55; breach with Dilke, 51; as creator and victim of N.L.F. power, 107–12 *passim*, 128, 158; at the Round Table Conference, 60, 61, 63–4, 88; and post-1886 Liberal Unionist party, 87–8, 220; questions Gladstone's integrity, 255; on disestablishment and disendowment, 23, 28–30, 31, 32; and free education, 28–9, 32–3, 35, 47, 51, 102, 110–11;

and land reform (rural), 15, 36–8, 43, 44–5, 220, 259; and land reform (urban), 7, 38–9, 40; and local government reform, 3, 15, 40–6 *passim*, 140; and graduated taxation, 50; and old age pensions, 182
Channing, F. A., and the N.L.F., 108, 148–9; and the county members committee, 220–1; and land reform, 218, 220, 221, 225, 229, 230, 242; and railway hours question, 149, 192–3, 196
Chaplin, Henry, 36, 230
Childers, H. C. E., 66, 170
Church of England, 28, 29, 30–1, 34, 102, 251
Clark, Dr G. B., 65, 97, 187–8
Clergy discipline bills (1891–2), 127–8
Cobb, H. P., 47, 221–30 *passim*
Collings, Jesse, and Chamberlain's education policy, 29, 32, 47, 111; and land reform, 37–8, 47, 220; and the Allotments Association, 38, 221; and 1886 salary dispute, 45–6
Compton, Lord William, 176
Conservative party, in constituencies, 25, 34, 101, 133, 231, 232, 257–8; in Parliament, 86, 127, 202, 209, 217; (for Government legislation see under appropriate headings)
Conspiracy law, 94–6, 241, 247
Conybeare, C. A. V., 171
Costelloe, B. F. C., 19
Cowan, John, 130
Cremer, W. R., 137, 143, 151
Crofters, land legislation for, 14, 48, 241, 243; party of, 48
Crosskey, Dr H. W., 29
Curran, Pete, 95

Daily News, 228
Dale, Dr R. W., 105
Dalziel, J. H., 131
Davitt, Michael, 96
Death duties, 14, 50, 141, 142, 238, 249, 250–1
Derby, Lord, 25, 26, 27

Dilke, Sir Charles, as Chamberlain's ally, 1, 3–4, 5, 6, 10; at Local Government Board, 3, 8, 15; and 1885 election, 24, 27, 29, 34–5, 41, 112, 223; and Home Rule crisis, 46, 51, 52, 88, 108, 165; breach with Chamberlain, 51, 88; and Labouchere, 175; and local government reform, 3, 140, 223

Dillon, John, 71, 236

Dillwyn, L. L., 118, 126

Disestablishment and Disendowment, at 1885 election, 23, 28–32, 34–5; *see also* Scottish disestablishment, and Welsh disestablishment

Duke of Connaught leave bill (1887), 98, 170

Ebrington, Viscount, 220

Ecroyd, Farrer, 25

Education, free schools at 1885 election, 20, 28–9, 32–5, 47, 110–11; and 1886 ministry, 47; public management controversy renewed, 99–106; and 1891 free education bill, 102, 104–5, 106, 259–60; and provision of free meals, 184; and school leaving age, 194–5, 243

Edwards, A. G. (Bishop of St Asalph), 252

Eight hour day, 90, 144–53 *passim*, 181, 196; for railwaymen, 149, 192–3, 196, 243, 247; 1892 miners' bill, 151, 181, 195, 196; 1893 miners' bill, 254–5; introduced by government departments, 255–6

Eighty Club, 115, 179, 184, 191–2

Elections, by –, and 'flowing tide', 202–3, 226–7, 231, 232, 233; contests at, Aston Manor, 226; Ayr, 207; Barrow, 132, 202, 209; Bassetlaw, 203–4; Bristol, 132–3; Buckingham, 226; Burnley, 209; N. Devon, 228–9; S. Dorset, 226; Eccles, 136, 146, 202; Harborough, 226–7; Hartlepool, 214–16; N. Kilkenny, 204; Mid-Lanark, 131; Lewisham, 192; Rossendale, 231; Southampton, 209; Spalding, 221;

Stowmarket, 226; Wisbech, 227; Woodstock, 226

Elections, general, of 1880, 1, 2, 36, 257, 258; of 1885, 24–5, 34–5, 138, 218, 257–8; of 1886, 56–8, 109, 138, 218–19; of 1892, 74–5, 135, 231–232, 233–4

Elgin, Earl of, 122, 193

Ellis, John Edward, 107, 111, 150, 155, 195, 209–10

Ellis, Thomas Edward, and progressive Liberal group, 175–6, 179, 188–189; and land tenure reform, 126, 188–9; and Welsh party, 125–6, 128; and Welsh disestablishment, 121, 242, 243

Employers' liability, 149; 1880 Act, 14; 1893–4 bill, 241, 247–8

Ensor, R. C. K., 148

Esslemont, P., 100

Evans, S. T., 128

Fabian Society, 136, 143, 144, 148, 181, 189, 190–2, 255

Factory legislation, 145, 149, 192–195, 196–7, 243, 253, 255; 1891 Act, 194–5; 1895 Act, 253

Fenwick, Charles, 151

Ferguson, R. Munro, 66, 175, 176, 186

Firth, J. F. B., 139, 140–1

Fitzmaurice, Lord Edmond, 131

Foljambe, F. J. S., 18

Foster, Sir B. Walter, 109, 115, 147, 221, 230

Fowler, H. H., 102, 105, 141, 166, 185, 243, 247

Fowler, Sir Robert, 173

Free Land League, 38, 45

Free trade and protection, 25, 35, 99

Furness, Christopher, 215

Fyffe, C. A., 259

Gardner, Herbert, 103, 219, 221, 224, 230, 242

Gee, Rev. Thomas, 117, 124

George, Henry, 7, 39

Gladstone, Herbert, 3, 52, 85, 112, 134, 157–8, 161

Gladstone, W. E., political and social traditions, 11–12; religious principles, 30–1, 197; flaws in style of leadership, 2–3, 167–9, 238, 254; and 1880–5 ministry, 1, 2–3, 5, 12–17; attitude to Whigs, 15, 17, 89, 113, 135–6; on Chamberlain's disruptive behaviour, 9, 17, 19, 20; postpones retirement, 17–18; and 1885 election, 19–33 *passim*, 43–4, 52; and 1886 ministry, 42–50 *passim*, 54, 55–6, 118, 165–6; and the Home Rule crisis, 13, 41–2, 44, 48–58 *passim*, 63, 87, 88, 90, 97, 108–9; and Irish land purchase, 57–63 *passim*, 73, 74; and Irish representation at Westminster, 64–70 *passim*, 73, 75, 244, 246; on Irish crime and coercion, 76–85 *passim*, 89, 91; on 'classes' v 'masses', 16, 89–91, 93, 113, 212; and 1889 Royal Grants controversy, 98, 171–2; and the 'flowing tide', 202–3, 226; and Parnell divorce crisis, 70–1, 72, 99, 200, 203, 204; re-examines Home Rule policy, 73–74, 205, 215, 234–6, 260–1; and 1890–1 discussion of alternative programmes, 205–6, 208, 210, 213–16; patronage of the N.L.F., 108–9, 112, 120, 154, 156, 157, 158, 160, 229–30; and the Newcastle programme, 134, 160–3, 216; and labour candidates, 132, 133, 134, 135; and party funds, 113, 130–1, 133, 135; and 1892 election, 74–5, 196–7, 233–4; admits progressives to cabinet, 176; and construction of ministerial programme, 234–45, 251, 254, 260–1; and second Home Rule bill, 244–7; and autumn session, 247–8; and naval estimates crisis, 248–9; disenchantment with Liberal policy (1894–5), 249–53; on death duties and graduated taxation, 14, 50, 250–1; on disendowment and clerical discipline, 31–2, 128; and disestablishment in Scotland, 30, 123, 207–8, 243; and disestablishment in Wales, 30, 118, 119–20, 123–4, 125, 162–3, 242, 243, 252–3; economy, passion for, 45–6, 49–50, 162, 197, 248–9; and eight hour day, 146, 196, 254–6; on electoral and registration reform, 15–16, 47, 206, 211–17 *passim*; and factory legislation, 196–7; on free education and voluntary schools, 20, 33, 47, 100, 105–6, 127, 162; and House of Lords reform, 16, 162, 248; and imperialism, 5, 162, 214–15, 242; and land law reform, 2, 15; and land reform (rural), 13–14, 43–5, 221, 224–5, 229, 230, 242; and land reform (urban), 187, 198; and land reform (Wales and Scotland), 14, 48, 241, 243; and local government reform, 14–15, 42, 45, 46, 47, 168, 170, 224–5, 230; and old age pensions, 197–8; and payment of members, 134, 135, 162, 239, 243–4; and Scottish Home Rule, 66; and temperance reform, 210–11, 251–2; and trade unionism, 91–4, 96, 254; reputation as social reformer, 91–2, 195–9, 254–6

Gladstone, Rev. Stephen, 30

Goschen, G. J., and 1885 election, 18–19, 26, 27, 37; as Unionist minister, 127, 170, 171, 174

Graham, R. B. Cunninghame, 132, 151

Granville, Lord, 13, 26, 43–4, 52, 68, 91, 93, 158

Green, Alice, 191

Green, T. H., 39

Grey, Sir Edward, and progressive Liberal group, 175–6, 178, 179, 185, 188, 190, 191–2; and Fabians, 190, 191–2; and Irish land purchase, 63

Griffith, Ellis, 124

Grosvenor, Lord Richard, 24, 44, 112–13, 128

Ground rents and land values, taxation of, 38–9, 141–4, 186–8, 198, 238

Haldane, R. B., and progressive

Liberal group, 175–9, 185, 186, 188, 190–2; and Fabians, 181, 190–192; friendship with Morley, 179–181, 185, 186, 192; and Irish land purchase, 63; and labour questions, 181, 191; and land reform (urban), 143, 186–8, 190, 192

Hamer, D. A., 58

Hamilton, Sir Edward, 61, 161, 166, 244–5

Hammond, J. L., 12, 45

Harcourt, Lewis, 159, 201, 237

Harcourt, Sir William, as Home Secretary, 14; as Chancellor of the Exchequer (1886), 47, 50, 118; and Irish land purchase, 59–63; and Irish representation at Westminster (federalism), 63–9 *passim*, 73, 74, 97; and the Round Table Conference, 60, 63, 155; on Irish crime and coercion, 76, 77, 81–2, 86; stature as acting opposition leader, 167, 169–70, 172–3, 178, 185, 186, 202; and 1889 backbench revolts, 98, 100, 172, 185, 186; and Parnell divorce crisis, 71, 72, 86, 204, 208; desires to shelve Home Rule, 74, 76, 205, 215, 236, 237, 238; and 1890–1 discussion of alternative programmes, 205–16 *passim*, 227; attitude towards N.L.F., 112, 121, 129–130, 155, 159–60, 162, 229; and the Newcastle programme, 160–1, 162, 237; constructs 1892–3 ministerial programme, 236–40, 242–3; obstructs second Home Rule bill, 244–6, 249; other ministerial activities, 249–55 *passim*; and disestablishment in Wales, 118, 120, 121, 123, 159, 206, 243; on economy and taxation, 50, 249, 250, 251; and eight hour day, 151, 192, 195; and free education, 104; and land reform, 47, 187, 221–2, 230; and local government reform, 14, 45, 104, 185–6, 225, 230; and social reform, 180, 183, 185–6, 192, 228, 255; and temperance reform, 209, 210, 243, 251, 252

Hardie, James Keir, 131, 135, 151

Hart-Dyke, Sir William, 127

Hartington, Lord, position threatened by Chamberlain, 9, 18–19, 37, 111; and Gladstone's 'retirement', 17–18; and 1885 election, 19, 20, 25, 26

Healy, Timothy, 103

Henderson, Arthur, 96, 131

Herschell, Lord, 82, 99, 244

Hobhouse, H., 226

Hobhouse, L. T., 95

House of Lords, obstructs Liberal policy, 15–16, 73, 239, 247–8, 260; reform of, 16, 27, 166, 248

Housing, 7–8, 38–9, 139, 143, 180, 198

Howell, George, 137, 140

Hudson, Robert, 145, 146–7, 159, 161, 164, 178

Hunter, Dr W. A., 242

Illingworth, Alfred, 33, 110–11, 132, 150

Imperial Federation League, 66, 186

Ireland: crime and coercion in, during 1880–5 ministry, 4, 10; unrest and the Plan of Campaign, 76–8, 91, 93; and 1887 coercion bill, 79, 167–8; coercion exploited by Liberals, 76, 78–87, 89–91, 93, 95; administrative change under Morley, 235, 246, 261

Irish Home Rule, central board scheme of 1885, 10, 13, 40–1, 49; crisis over 1886 bill, 41–2, 44, 47–9, 51–8, 87–9, 107–9, 111; and Irish representation at Westminster, 55, 57, 63–70, 71, 73, 74–5, 244, 246; and Parnell divorce crisis, 70–4, 76, 204–5, 259; and 1892 election, 74–5, 233, 234–7, 238, 260; and 1893 bill, 244–7, 249

Irish Land Act (1881), 13

Irish land purchase, in 1885, 10, 49; and 1886 bill, 49, 50–1, 54–5, 56–8; post-1886 debate on, 56, 58–63, 71, 73, 74, 85; 1888 Act, 61–2; 1890–1 Act, 62–3

Irish Nationalist party, and first Home Rule bill, 56; parliamentary alliance with Radicals, 48, 97–9, 126, 188; supports denominational education, 99–105; and Parnell divorce crisis, 70–3, 104–5, 204–5, 215, 217, 232–3; and 1892 election, 74, 233, 235–7, 240; and second Home Rule bill, 244, 245–6

Jacoby, Alfred, 171
James, Sir Henry, 19, 36, 37, 43
Jones, R. A., 129

Kenrick, W., 152
Kimberley, Lord, 26, 43–4
Kitson, Sir James, and the Home Rule crisis, 107, 109, 111, 155, 157; and N.L.F. procedure, 122, 152; hostility to labour, 146, 150

Labouchere, Henry, restlessness in 1880–5 Parliament, 5, 6; and 1885 election, 35; and the Home Rule crisis, 52–3, 55, 88; perfects guerilla tactics, 127, 166, 170–3; his sterile philosophy, 173–4, 195, 236; decline, 175
Labour, implications of Irish struggle for, 89–91, 93, 95, 96, 217–18; trade unionism, Liberals and, 91–6, 149–151, 192–3, 194, 195–6, 215, 219–20, 253, 254–6; parliamentary candidates, 130–8; *see also* agricultural labourers
Labour programme, *see* conspiracy law, eight hour day, employers' liability, factory legislation
Lambert, George, 229
Lambert, Sir John, 212–13
Land reform, in 1880–5 ministry, 2, 13–14, 15; at 1885 election, 20, 35–40, 43–4; in 1886, 37, 43, 44–5, 47, 48, 188; in 1892–5 ministry, 238, 241, 242; allotments and small holdings, 20, 35–7, 43–5, 47, 220–230 *passim*, 259; entail and primogeniture, 2, 15, 20; ground rents, land values, and 'unearned incre-

ment', 38–9, 141–4, 186–8, 198, 238; leasehold enfranchisement, 142–3, 144, 188–90, 198, 238; nationalization, 7, 39, 187–8; tenant right, 13–14, 36–7; *see also* Welsh land reform
Land Reform Union, 7
Lansbury, George, admires Gladstone, 96; offered Liberal seat, 136; advocates eight hour day, 90, 145–146, 150, 151, 196
Lawson, H. L. W., 139, 142, 143–4, 188
Lawson, Sir Wilfrid, 210
Leake, Robert, 195
Leasehold enfranchisement, 142–3, 144, 188–90, 198, 238
Leasehold Enfranchisement Association, 142–3, 188
Leveson-Gower, George, 156–7
'Lib-Lab' party, 133, 137–8, 151
Liberal Central Association, democratization of, 110, 112–14, 115–16; and party funds, 112, 113, 133, 156–7; and selection of candidates, 132, 133–4, 135
Liberal County Members Committee, 220–1, 227, 228
Liberal Publication Department, 115, 178, 192
Liberal Unionists, 49, 51, 64, 79, 87–9, 108, 202, 220–1
Liberation Society, 31
Lloyd George, David, 127–8, 175, 253
Local government reform, lack of progress to 1886, 2, 3, 14, 20, 40–7 *passim*; 1888 (county councils) Act, 98, 138–9, 168, 170, 178, 209, 223, 224; in London, 2, 14, 45, 138–9, 140–1, 148, 173–4, 194, 241; in parish and district, 217, 222–30, 259; 1894 (parish councils) Act, 241, 243, 247–8
Local option and local veto, *see* Temperance reform
Lockwood, Frank, 175, 176, 177
Logan, J. W., 227
London, Liberal constituency organization in, 34, 115–16, 129, 135, 144,

145, 147, 231; Liberal programme for, 34–5, 138–45, 168, 180, 186, 189, 197, 198, 241, 243, 254, 259; social conditions and unrest in, 7–8, 90, 92–3, 139, 180, 184, 193; *see also* Local government reform

London and Counties Liberal Union, 108, 115–16

London County Council, 133–4, 138, 197, 198–9

London Liberal and Radical Council, 108, 115

London Liberal and Radical Union, 116, 139, 140, 144–5, 146, 149

London parliamentary party, 138–44

London School Board, 34, 184

London Trades Council, 196

Lucy, H. W., 169

Lyons, F. S. L., 205

McCarthy, Justin, 100–1, 217

Macdonald, J. Murray, 145–6

MacDonald, J. Ramsay, 131

Manning, Cardinal, 28, 29, 92, 93, 101, 102, 106

Mappin, Sir F., 133

Marjoribanks, Edward, opposes Scottish Home Rule, 65, 66; places labour candidates, 132, 135, 136; role in 1892–5 ministry, 242, 248, 252, 260

Massingham, H. W., 90, 145, 147

Mathers, J. S., 111

Matthews, Henry, 194

Mearns, Andrew, 7–8

Metropolitan Radical Federation, 133

Molloy, B. C., 100

Montagu, Samuel, 136, 140, 141, 142

More, R. Jasper, 220, 221

Morgan, Sir G. Osborne, 125

Morgan, Kenneth O., 195

Morley, Arnold, appointed chief whip, 112–13; parliamentary activities, 97, 108, 113, 169, 187, 202, 216; and L.C.A. reorganization, 113, 115–16; and party funds, 113, 133–4, 157; and selection of candidates, 132–4, 136; relations with Schnadhorst, 108, 115, 116, 157,

232; mismanages elections, 113–14, 232; and Parnell divorce crisis, 203–4, 206, 216; and labour questions, 96, 196, 225, 227

Morley, John, threatens Chamberlain's ascendancy (1883–5), 4–6; and 1885 election, 10, 27, 31; breach with Chamberlain, 4, 27, 165; and the Home Rule crisis, 47–8, 88, 107, 157; and Irish land purchase, 57–63 *passim*, 73, 158; and Irish representation at Westminster (federalism), 64–9 *passim*, 73; and the Round Table Conference, 64, 155; on Irish crime and coercion, 5, 77–84 *passim*, 90, 168; patronizes progressive Liberal group, 176, 179–186 *passim*, 192; proposes opposition 'cabinets', 168; and 1889 Royal Grants controversy, 98, 172; and Parnell divorce crisis, 200, 201, 203, 204, 208; remains loyal to Home Rule, 71, 73–4, 205, 215, 235, 237, 238, 259; and 1890–1 discussion of alternative programmes, 205, 206, 208, 213–17 *passim*, 258–60; attitude towards N.L.F., 107, 116, 119, 148, 149, 154–62 *passim*, 208; and the Newcastle programme, 160–2; and 1892 election, 74, 231, 234; and construction of ministerial programme, 235, 236–7, 238, 241, 261; and second Home Rule bill, 244, 245–6; and administrative change in Ireland (1892–5), 235, 246, 247, 261; and disendowment, 29, 31; and disestablishment in Wales, 97, 119–120, 125, 206, 259; and eight hour day, 149, 181; on free education and voluntary schools, 101–2, 103–105, 228, 259–60; and free school meals, 184; and imperialism, 5; and land reform (rural), 228, 259; and land reform (urban), 39, 180, 186; and local government reform, 217, 227, 228, 259; on old age pensions and poor law, 181–3, 228, 259; and temperance reform, 208, 210,

258–9; awareness of the social question, 7–8, 180–4, 227–8; dislikes socialists and socialism, 93, 149, 192

Morley, Samuel, 112–13

Mundella, A. J., early distrust of Chamberlain, 110; and 1885 election, 28, 33–5; role in 1886 ministry, 46, 48–9; at the Board of Trade (1892–4), 243, 253, 255; and disestablishment in Wales, 120; and free education, 33–5, 102

National Agricultural Labourers' Union, 219–20

National Education Association, 99

National Education League, 29

National Liberal Federation, foundation of, 108, 110; provincialism of, 148; Birmingham-Chamberlain ascendancy in, 29, 38, 110–11, 158; and the Home Rule crisis, 107, 108–10, 111, 114, 155, 157–8; reorganization and expansion of, 109–18 *passim*, 156, 211; policy disputes with leaders, 105, 124–5, 154–160, 224; and the Newcastle programme, 75, 144, 149, 160–4, 237; and disestablishment in Scotland and Wales, 29, 119, 120–2, 124, 152, 162; and eight hour day, 144–53; and free education, 29, 32, 33–4, 101, 105, 110–11, 157; and rural programme, 153, 219, 224, 228, 229–30; and role of constituency associations, 128–33, 134, 136; constitution and procedure of, 147, 151–4; council meetings, at Leeds (1879), 128; Bradford (1885), 29, 32, 33, 110–11, 119, 152; Leeds (1886), 119, 120, 154, 155, 156; Nottingham (1887), 64, 80–1, 82, 121–2, 152, 160, 177, 179; Birmingham (1888), 82, 144, 152, 158, 160, 212; Manchester (1889), 101, 124, 144–6, 149, 152, 157, 224, 225; Sheffield (1890), 124–5, 146, 149, 162, 208; Newcastle (1891), 134, 146–7, 148–9, 152–3, 160, 161–3,

179, 216, 228, 229; Liverpool (1893), 162; Cardiff (1895), 163; Huddersfield (1896), 105, 156, 157, 164

National Liberal Federation, Home Counties Division, 116, 156–7

National Liberal Federation of Scotland, 32, 107, 116

Newcastle, Duke of, 15

Newcastle programme, *see* National Liberal Federation

Nolan, J. P., 105

Nonconformists, 32, 33–4, 99–106 *passim*, 208, 209

North Wales Liberal Federation, 116–17, 120, 124, 129, 157

Norwood, C. M., 18

O'Brien, William, 71

O'Connor, Arthur, 98

O'Connor, T. P., 98, 236

Old age pensions, 181–3, 197–8

Parnell, Charles Stewart, offends Chamberlain, 5, 25, 41; and first Home Rule bill, 56; disavows Plan of Campaign, 78; and 1889 Royal Grants controversy, 98, 100; attacks Liberal education policy, 99, 100, 104; visits Hawarden, 67; and divorce crisis, 70–2, 200–1; role after party split, 71–2, 104, 204, 215, 233

Payment of members, 134, 135, 152, 162, 191, 239, 244

Pease, Alfred E., 179

Pickersgill, E. H., 140

Picton, James, 34

Playfair, Sir Lyon, 47

Plumptre, Dr E. H., 33

Plural vote, *see* Registration reform

Progress and Poverty, 7

Provand, Andrew, 39–40, 187

Radical Programme, The, 8, 29, 31–32, 35, 38, 41

Rathbone, William, 119, 126

Redmond, John, 72

Redmond, William, 98

Reed, Sir Edward, 125

Reform and Redistribution Acts (1884–5), 15–16, 257–8

Registration reform, in 1885–6, 20, 47, 166, 212; subsequent debate on, 206, 211–13, 215–17, 259; in 1892 ministerial programme, 241, 243, 247

Reid, R. T., 150, 186

Rendel, Stuart, and N.W.L.F., 116–118, 129; and Welsh party, 125–7; and Welsh disestablishment, 119–126 *passim*, 154, 242; and Welsh intermediate education bill, 126–7; and Welsh land question, 241

Richard, Henry, 34, 118, 125–6

Ridgeway, Sir Joseph, 247

Rigg, Dr J. H., 34

Ripon, Lord, 68, 206, 219, 228

Ritchie, C. T., 221, 223

Roberts, J. Bryn, 126

Robertson, Edmund, 95, 255

Roby, H. J., 136, 146, 147

Rogers, Frederick, 96

Rogers, J. Guinness, 101

Roman Catholics, 28, 29, 41, 99, 102–103, 233

Rosebery, Lord, ignored by Chamberlain, 9, 10, 27; and 1885 election, 26, 27; unenthusiastic about Home Rule, 77, 155; urges federal (Scottish) Home Rule, 66–7, 68; and party funds, 113; proposes opposition 'cabinets', 168, 169; and progressive Liberal group, 179, 185, 186; condemns Newcastle programme, 161, 163–4; and 1892 election, 233–4, 238; role in 1892–5 ministry, 242, 250, 251, 253, 254; and disestablishment in Scotland, 118, 207

Rowlands, James, 137, 139, 141, 143, 144, 188

Royal grants, 1889 controversy over, 98, 171–2

Russell, Sir Charles, 138, 168

Russell, G. W. E., 184

Rylands, Peter, 87

Salisbury, Lord, 73, 101, 174, 233, 239

Samuelson, Sir Bernhard, 221

Saunders, William, 39

Schnadhorst, Francis, and 1885 election, 24, 34, 36, 112; and Home Rule crisis, 108–10, 111, 154; reorganizes N.L.F., 109–10, 115–16, 117–18; and London, 115–16, 129, 144–5, 146; and Wales, 117–25 *passim*, 159, 206; and labour candidates, 132, 134, 135; and a labour programme, 144–5, 146, 147, 149; standing with leaders, 108–9, 121, 155–61 *passim*, 184–5, 229; and by-elections, 204, 213, 226, 232; and 1892 election, 231–2; decline, 158–9, 160

Scottish disestablishment, on the Liberal programme, 30, 32, 122, 123, 207; parliamentary progress of, 118, 207; 1893 suspensory bill, 241, 242, 243

Scottish Home Rule, 65–7, 68, 97

Scottish Home Rule Association, 65

Scottish Labour Party, 135

Scottish Liberal Association, 65, 68, 101, 116, 122, 147–8

Scottish local government bill (1889), 100, 186

Scottish parliamentary party, 48, 65, 118, 125

Seager, J. Renwick, 145

Seale-Hayne, C. H., 221, 227

Selborne, Lord, 23, 29, 30

Sexton, Thomas, 72, 102

Seymour, Judge, 95

Shaw, George Bernard, 129, 130, 144, 255

Shaw-Lefevre, George, 9–10, 27, 34, 54–5, 145, 165, 217

Small agricultural holdings bill (1892), 143, 187–8, 230

Smillie, Robert, 96

Smith, W. H., 127, 202

South Wales Liberal Federation, 116, 117

Spencer, Lord, and 1885 election, 26, 44; and Irish land purchase, 55–62 *passim*, 73; and Irish representation at Westminster (federalism), 65,

69–70, 73, 74; on Irish crime and coercion, 10, 77, 78, 82, 84–5; and the N.L.F., 120–1, 154; on Harcourt's leadership, 169; and disestablishment in Wales, 120–1, 123; and social reform, 93, 183, 227, 228, 256, 259; and construction of 1892 ministerial programme, 74, 234, 238, 241, 244, 252; and 1894 naval estimates crisis, 249

Spender, J. A., 159, 178, 198

Stanhope, Philip, 171

Stanley, Lyulph, 34, 99, 103

Stansfeld, James, 46–7, 212, 216–17, 224, 225

Star, The, 144, 147

Stevenson, F. S., 224

Stewart, Halley, 221

Storey, Samuel, 93, 210, 215

Stuart, James, and Irish policy, 82; and London questions, 138–47 *passim*, 179

Sutherland, Angus, 122

Temperance reform, 4, 98, 202, 208–211, 258–9; local veto (and option) bills of 1893–5, 243, 247, 251–2

Thomas, Alfred, 127

Thomas, D. A., 126

Threlfall, T. R., 133

Thring, Sir Henry, 46, 251

Tillett, Ben, 132

Tilston, W. H., 117

Times, The, 84, 228–9

To Your Tents, Oh Israel!, 255

Trade unions, *see* Labour

Trades Union Congress, 150–1

Trevelyan, G. O., as Chamberlain's colleague, 9–10, 27; role in 1886 ministry, 48, 118, 165; and Irish land policy, 10, 49, 61; rejoins Gladstonians, 87; and electoral reform, 135, 216; and 1892 ministerial programme, 241

Tuckwell, Rev. William, 124, 149, 227, 228, 229

Tweedmouth, Lord, *see* Marjoribanks

Ulster Unionists, 97, 233

Victoria, Queen, 49, 247

Vincent, John, 92

Wallas, Graham, 190, 191

Wanted a Programme, 144

Watson, Robert Spence, and eight hour day, 146, 147, 149, 153; and the Newcastle programme, 162, 164; defines role of the N.L.F., 152–3, 156, 157–8, 164

Watson, Mrs Robert Spence, 8

Webb, Beatrice, 181, 190–1

Webb, Sidney, and London Liberalism, 129, 142–4, 178–9, 193; and the N.L.F., 144–8, 150, 151; and labour candidates, 134; and progressive Liberal group, 181, 190–2, 193, 194; and eight hour day, 145, 146–7, 150, 181, 184; and sweated labour, 193, 194, 255; and urban land question, 142–3, 190

Welsh disestablishment, on the Liberal programme, 23, 30, 118, 119–125, 159, 162–3, 206–7, 259; parliamentary progress of, 97, 118, 123, 126, 163; 1893 suspensory bill, 241, 242, 243, 247; 1895 disestablishment bill, 252–3

Welsh Intermediate Education Act (1889), 126–7

Welsh land reform, 117, 120, 126, 188–9, 241, 243

Welsh National Council, 117, 121, 123, 124, 125; *see also* North Wales Liberal Federation

Welsh parliamentary party, 118–19, 124, 125–8

Whigs, in 1880–5 ministry, 3, 17, 42; and 1885 election, 23, 25–6, 36, 43–44, 112; and Home Rule crisis, 37, 44, 87–8

Whitbread, Samuel, 46

Williams, Arthur, 119, 126

Wilson, H. J., 130, 133

Wilson, J. Havelock, 132, 133, 135

Winterbotham, A. B., 87, 230

Wolverton, Lord, 128–9, 134

Woods, Samuel, 137, 254